Metaverse Security Paradigms

Brij Gupta
Asia University, Taichung City, Taiwan

A volume in the Advances in
Information Security, Privacy,
and Ethics (AISPE) Book Series

IGI Global
Publishing Tomorrow's Research Today

Published in the United States of America by
IGI Global
Information Science Reference (an imprint of IGI Global)
701 E. Chocolate Avenue
Hershey PA, USA 17033
Tel: 717-533-8845
Fax: 717-533-8661
E-mail: cust@igi-global.com
Web site: http://www.igi-global.com

Library of Congress Cataloging-in-Publication Data

CIP Data Pending

ISBN: 9798369338247
isbn: 9798369351680
eISBN: 9798369338254

British Cataloguing in Publication Data
A Cataloguing in Publication record for this book is available from the British Library.

All work contributed to this book is new, previously-unpublished material.
The views expressed in this book are those of the authors, but not necessarily of the publisher.

For electronic access to this publication, please contact: eresources@igi-global.com.

Table of Contents

Detailed Table of Contents

A shared and dynamic online environment consisting of networked communities, programs, and technologies will bring new possibilities for social media, the digital economy, and online experiences. For this reason, we need a medium that can unite these communities in a shared and dynamic online environment. Introduced a virtual world concept called the metaverse, which consists of various interconnected digital spaces, allowing users to interact, work, play, and create in a fully immersive environment. The metaverse combines elements from virtual reality (VR), augmented reality (AR), blockchain, and the internet to create more immersive and interactive experiences. Social media, gaming, e-commerce, and other aspects of the metaverse ecosystem enable diverse activities and a robust virtual economy that generates jobs and business opportunities. This chapter contains the meaning of the metaverse, a brief explanation of metaverse elements, metaverse trends, and challenges, making it easier for readers to understand the metaverse.

This chapter discusses the implementation of AI-driven security measures in virtual worlds, which presumes advanced approaches and solutions implemented to protect users' interactions and the environment of the virtual space in general. The topics discussed within the chapter are related to AI applications in security issues, machine solutions for the purpose of intrusion detection, and behavioral biometrics for user authentication. Each of the topics include practical scenarios connected to IDS and behavioral biometrics. Information on content moderation, policy enforcement, and future directions is given as well. The chapter provides solid proof that metaverse security should include AI-driven solutions through effective case studies, while performance expectations are discussed in each case.

This Chapter explores the concept of Metaverse in depth, focussing on its development from the virtual worlds to modern digital environments. In particular, it describes the architecture of Metaverse, emphasising the layers that allow for present-day virtual experiences and the main concepts that inform them. Moreover, the chapter examines several technological advancements, namely, blockchain, VR/AR, and AI, that play significant roles in the functioning and improvement of Metaverse and the interaction of its users. Furthermore, the introduction discusses the ecological perspective of Metaverse, focussing on the people and the developers as well as the way they interact through the platforms.

The rapid advancement of digital technology has brought significant benefits but also introduced a myriad of cybersecurity challenges. In this context, this chapter, addresses the growing need for a robust understanding of the principles, threats, best practices, and legal and ethical considerations essential for safeguarding digital assets. This chapter explores the core principles of confidentiality, integrity, and availability, delves into prevalent cyber threats and vulnerabilities, and outlines best practices for mitigating these risks. Additionally, it addresses the legal and ethical frameworks governing cybersecurity, emphasizing the importance of compliance and responsible conduct. Understanding these fundamentals is crucial for navigating and securing the increasingly complex digital landscape.

This chapter thoroughly investigates safeguarding the Metaverse's complex infrastructure. The chapter, segmented into four distinct yet interconnected sections, meticulously dissects the multifaceted layers of Metaverse security. Initially, it delves into securing the architectural framework, examining everything from user interfaces to backend databases and underscoring the necessity for robust protocols to shield against various vulnerabilities. The chapter then focuses on strategies for mitigating DDoS (Distributed Denial of Service) attacks, highlighting the importance of advanced network security measures and AI-driven predictive models. Subsequently, it addresses the pivotal need for secure networking in real-time interactions within the Metaverse, emphasizing data encryption, secure authentication, and user privacy. The final section provides a comprehensive overview of cloud security considerations essential for the Metaverse, discussing challenges like data breaches and outlining best practices for maintaining a secure cloud infrastructure. By incorporating diverse perspectives from network engineering to digital ethics, this chapter extensively analyzes the current state and evolving challenges in Metaverse security, aiming to empower developers, policymakers, and users in navigating and reinforcing this novel digital realm's security landscape. Novelty: The source of the novelty is a multidisciplinary approach that combines network security measures, AI-driven predictive models, strong encryption protocols, and thorough cloud security practices to empower developers, policymakers, and users in the process of strengthening the security landscape of the Metaverse. By employing this all-complete perspective, data and service availability, confidentiality, and integrity within the dynamic digital space of the Metaverse are effectively protected.

The field of modern cryptography faces significant standardization and regulatory challenges due to the rapid advancement of technology and the increasing importance of secure communication in various sectors. This abstract delves into the complexities surrounding the standardization and regulation of cryptographic algorithms and protocols.Standardization plays a crucial role in ensuring interoperability, security, and trustworthiness in cryptographic systems. However, the process of developing and implementing cryptographic standards is fraught with challenges such as balancing security requirements with usability, addressing evolving threats, and accommodating diverse stakeholder interests. One of the primary challenges in cryptographic standardization is the tension between the need for transparency and the desire to protect sensitive information. Openness and transparency are essential for building trust and verifying the security properties of cryptographic algorithms and protocols. However, excessive transparency can also expose vulnerabilities and aid adversaries in exploiting weaknesses. Regulatory challenges further complicate the landscape of modern cryptography. Governments and regulatory bodies seek to balance the interests of national security, law enforcement, and individual privacy rights. This often leads to debates over encryption backdoors, key escrow mechanisms, and export controls on cryptographic technologies. Navigating these challenges requires collaboration between cryptographic experts, policymakers, industry stakeholders, and civil society organizations. It involves striking a delicate balance between security, privacy, and regulatory compliance while fostering innovation and advancing the state-of-the-art in cryptography.In conclusion, standardization and regulatory challenges in modern cryptography highlight the intricate interplay between security, technology, and policy. By addressing these challenges through multi-stakeholder collaboration, the cryptographic community can promote the development and adoption of robust cryptographic standards that enhance security and privacy in the digital age.

The humans made graphical world which can be accessed and carved for multiple usage and opportunities, with endless possibilities and no limit. One such in this article is farm- ing and agriculture in the virtual world. How can it be commercialized and made scalable. Minecraft metaverse based game has generated a revenue over $161 million in 2022. Users love reality in graphics, rockstar has made open world and to add more reality they have created different looking people, proper California streets, a proper beaches, real race cars in, etc. GTA (Grand Theft Auto).If we can create a world where the characters have access to shops and services, where the avatars can enjoy in the virtual reality and can buy get access to products and services. In this article we can cultivate our own raw materials and trade them via cryptocurrency. The only thing the players have to maintain is a valid crypto wallet. This platform can be sold to other metaverse based games and generate revenue. The main idea behind buying raw product is to add another layer of reality to it. Proper and different crops can be designed .Some avatars can choose to cultivate and breed cattle in the virtual world and generate revenue in form of crypto currencies and sell them to other avatars. This article provide a comprehensive a comprehensive overview of farming in metaverse with all its challenges opportunities and future aspects. The information contained within this article is intended to aid researchers and other practitioners in the field of AI to refine their approach and to the enhancement in this field. By exploring the various aspects in farming in metaverse will help both experts and non experts to develop various techniques to optimize researches and development.

The metaverse, a convergence of digital and physical realities, presents unprecedented opportunities for interaction and commerce, but also introduces unique security vulnerabilities. This chapter explores the nature of these virtual environments, analyzing inherent weaknesses and the impact of user-generated content. It examines prevalent cyber threats, including malware, phishing, identity theft, and DDoS attacks, providing real-world examples of security breaches. By investigating notable incidents, the chapter highlights the impact on users and platforms and offers mitigation strategies to enhance security measures. Understanding the evolving threat landscape is crucial for developing effective security strategies to safeguard the future of the metaverse.

The User Education and Awareness chapter in Metaverse Security Paradigms tackles the essential aspects of user education and awareness in safeguarding against the myriad security risks. Beginning with an in-depth analysis of common security threats such as data breaches, identity theft, and phishing attacks, the chapter catalogues these risks. Then, it explores the influential roles of community leaders and the adoption of innovative approaches like gamification to establish security as a collective responsibility. The practical implementation of these strategies across diverse virtual platforms is also thoroughly examined. Next, the chapter delves into the processes for reporting and responding to security incidents in the Metaverse. It details the establishment of efficient reporting channels, the formation of rapid response teams, and the use of automated systems for early threat detection. Concluding with a guide on best practices, the chapter equips users with strategies for personal protection, from basic digital hygiene to advanced tactics against complex threats.

Preface

The Metaverse represents the next frontier of digital interaction, blending virtual and augmented realities to create immersive, interconnected environments. As we step into this new realm, the importance of robust security paradigms cannot be overstated. This book, “Metaverse Security Paradigms,” aims to explore the multifaceted aspects of security within the Metaverse, addressing the unique challenges and innovative solutions that define this emerging landscape.

The book begins with an essential primer in Chapter 1, “Understanding the Metaverse,” which lays the groundwork for readers by introducing the fundamental concepts and elements that constitute the Metaverse. Building on this foundation, Chapter 2, “AI-Driven Security Measures in Virtual Worlds,” delves into the role of artificial intelligence in enhancing security protocols within these virtual environments.

Chapter 3, “Delving into the Metaverse: Understanding its Foundations, Dynamics, and Future Prospects,” provides a deeper exploration of the Metaverse's structure and potential evolution. It is followed by Chapter 4, “Foundations of Cybersecurity: Core Principles, Practices, and Emerging Trends,” which offers a comprehensive overview of cybersecurity essentials, highlighting both established practices and emerging trends.

Infrastructure and network security are critical components discussed in Chapter 5, while Chapter 6, “Standardization and Regulatory Challenges in Modern Cryptography,” addresses the complexities of standardizing security measures in a rapidly evolving field. Chapter 7 presents “An Extensive Review of Farming in the Metaverse,” illustrating unique economic activities and their security implications.

Chapter 8, “Navigating the Threat Landscape in the Metaverse: Emerging Risks and Security Strategies,” examines the various threats facing Metaverse users and the strategies to mitigate these risks. This leads into Chapter 9, “Metaverse Security Paradigms,” which synthesizes the key security principles relevant to the Metaverse.

Looking forward, Chapter 10, "The Future of Metaverse Security: Anticipating Challenges and Developing Advanced Protective Measures," anticipates future security challenges and the advanced measures needed to address them. Chapter 11, "Exploring Security and Privacy Challenges for Banks in the Evolving Landscape of the Metaverse," focuses on the financial sector's unique challenges within this virtual space.

Privacy concerns are a major focus of the next few chapters. Chapter 12, "Privacy-Preserving Techniques and User Anonymity in the Metaverse," discusses methods to protect user identity and data, while Chapter 13, "Protection and Management of User Privacy: System Data Security with the Metaserve Approach," introduces a specific approach for managing privacy and security.

Finally, Chapter 14, "Advancements in Metaverse Security: Phishing Website Detection through Optimal Feature Selection and Random Forest Classifier," presents cutting-edge research on combating phishing attacks within the Metaverse, utilizing sophisticated machine learning techniques.

This book aims to be an invaluable resource for researchers, practitioners, and enthusiasts interested in the security dimensions of the Metaverse. By addressing a wide array of topics and providing in-depth analysis, we hope to contribute to the development of secure and resilient virtual environments. We express our gratitude to all contributors and reviewers who have made this book possible and look forward to the continued evolution of security in the Metaverse.

Brij Gupta
Asia University, Taiwan

Chapter 1
Understanding the Metaverse

Agung Mulyo Widodo
Universitas Esa Unggul, Indonesia

Andika Wisnujati
https://orcid.org/0000-0001-6261-7936
Muhammadiyah University of Yogyakarta, Indonesia

Andriyanti M. Asianto
Universitas Esa Unggul, Indonesia

Diah M. Aryani
Universitas Esa Unggul, Indonesia

Mosiur Rahaman
https://orcid.org/0000-0003-0521-2080
International Center for AI and Cyber Security Research and Innovations, Asia University, Taiwan

Varsha Arya
Department of Business Administration, Asia University, Taiwan, & Department of Electrical and Computer Engineering, Lebanese American University, Beirut, Lebanon

Princy Pappachan
https://orcid.org/0000-0001-6728-0228
Department of Foreign Languages and Literature, Asia University, Taiwan

ABSTRACT

A shared and dynamic online environment consisting of networked communities, programs, and technologies will bring new possibilities for social media, the digital economy, and online experiences. For this reason, we need a medium that can unite these communities in a shared and dynamic online environment. Introduced a virtual world concept called the metaverse, which consists of various interconnected digital spaces, allowing users to interact, work, play, and create in a fully immersive environment. The metaverse combines elements from virtual reality (VR), augmented reality (AR), blockchain, and the internet to create more immersive and interactive experiences. Social media, gaming, e-commerce, and other aspects of the metaverse

DOI: 10.4018/979-8-3693-3824-7.ch001

ecosystem enable diverse activities and a robust virtual economy that generates jobs and business opportunities. This chapter contains the meaning of the metaverse, a brief explanation of metaverse elements, metaverse trends, and challenges, making it easier for readers to understand the metaverse.

1.1 INTRODUCTION

When virtually improved physical reality and physically persistent virtual reality meet, a collective virtual shared place known as the "metaverse" is generated. To put it another way, it's a vast, networked virtual universe that includes augmented reality settings and other virtual worlds. Science fiction writer Neal Stephenson popularized the idea of the metaverse with his 1992 book "Snow Crash." The metaverse is portrayed in the book as a fully immersive virtual reality environment where users engage in real-time interactions with digital things and one another. The concept of the metaverse has gained popularity in the tech and entertainment industries in recent years due to developments in online multiplayer gaming, virtual reality, augmented reality, and artificial intelligence (Guo et al., 2016; Krishnamurthy & Trivedi, 2023). Businesses like Decentraland, Epic Games, Facebook (now Meta Platforms), and others have revealed plans to build their own metaverse platforms and initiatives.

This motivates the author to introduce what metaverse is to readers about what metaverse actually is, the elements of metaverse, trends and challenges of metaverse in the future. Thus, it is hoped that this chapter will have contributions:

- An explanation of what the metaverse.
- An explanation of the elements of the metaverse.
- An explanation of how the trend of metaverse and its challenges.

This chapter is structured systematically, the first section contains facts about the development of a shared and dynamic online environment consisting of network communities, programs and technology, including the definition of metaverse. Second section contains an explanation of metaverse elements and Third section is about metaverse development trends and future challenges.

1.2 WHAT IS METAVERSE?

The metaverse is a persistent, networked digital environment where people can create, work, play, socialize, and do business. By allowing users to seamlessly integrate many digital experiences and project their virtual presence across several platforms and environments, it transcends conventional virtual worlds. Among the metaverse's salient features are:

- Immersion: by using augmented reality, virtual reality, and other sensory technologies, the metaverse offers immersive experiences that let users feel fully present in the virtual world.
- Persistence: even in situations in which people are not actively participating, the metaverse persists and changes over time.
- Interoperability: since the metaverse is based on open standards and protocols, it allows devices, platforms, and virtual worlds to communicate with one another.
- Social Interaction: Users can connect, collaborate, and create communities in virtual places, making social interaction a fundamental feature of the metaverse.
- Economic Activity: By enabling the exchange of virtual goods and services as well as digital currency, the metaverse promotes employment, entrepreneurship, and trade.

All things considered, the metaverse is an extremely connected digital environment that dissolves the boundaries between the actual and virtual worlds and gives countless opportunities for discovery, ingenuity, and cooperation (Dwivedi et al., 2022).

Figure 1. Security and Privacy Threats in the Metaverse (Krishnamurthy & Trivedi, 2023).

The internet, blockchain, augmented reality, and virtual reality are all combined in the metaverse to offer more engaging and immersive experiences. One of the primary features of metaverses is their utilization of virtual reality (VR) and augmented reality (AR) technologies, which enable users to engage with and experience lifelike and immersive digital settings. Social interactions in the metaverse can take many different forms, including group chat, online meetings, multiplayer games, and social gatherings. In a virtual environment, users can collaborate, communicate, and meet. There is a market within the metaverse where users can purchase, sell, and exchange digital goods such NFTs (non-fungible tokens), virtual real estate, and gaming gear. Digital currency, or crypto, is frequently used in these transactions. In the metaverse, users have the ability to produce, edit, and distribute their own material. Games, avatars, world designs, and other digital assets fall under this category. It is anticipated that the metaverse would enable seamless platform and virtual world transitions for users, all while protecting their digital assets and identities. Users can experience a blend of virtual and physical reality through the metaverse, which is the fusion of the physical and digital worlds. Metaverses nowadays include things like Roblox, Fortnite, Decentraland, and Horizon Worlds by Meta (previously Facebook). Every platform provides a range of activities, including virtual workspaces, learning, and gaming and entertainment.

1.3 THE EVOLUTION OF VIRTUAL WORLDS

The term "Evolution of Virtual Worlds" describes the advancement and creation of virtual worlds that either replicate or generate wholly new real-world experiences. Virtual world evolution can be seen as an ongoing process of innovation and adaptation, propelled by shifts in user expectations and behaviour as well as technological advancements. The level of complexity in these virtual worlds can vary, from straightforward text-based MUDs (Multi-User Dungeons) to fully immersive 3D settings similar to those in contemporary video games or virtual reality platforms (Liu, 2017).

Virtual worlds have developed as a result of advances in software development, technology, and user experience design. It includes advancements in the fields of social dynamics, interactivity, visuals, and the integration of many multimedia elements. Important developments in the evolution of the virtual world include the following:

- Technological Advancements: Virtual worlds are now more realistic and immersive thanks to improvements in processor power, graphics processing, and networking capabilities. Technological innovations that facilitate improved development, experience, and integration within the metaverse are referred to as technological improvements in support of the metaverse. Users can engage with the virtual environment and with each other in the metaverse, a virtual world idea that mixes virtual reality and augmented reality. Among the technologies facilitating the creation of the metaverse are: through the use of virtual reality (VR), users can enter a completely immersive virtual environment and engage in realistic 3D object and user interaction. Augmented reality, or AR, is the integration of virtual aspects into the actual environment. It enables users to view and interact with digital content overlayed on top of surrounding physical things. Mixed reality (MR) is the creation of an experience that blends a virtual world with the real world by fusing components from both virtual reality and augmented reality. Realistic and dynamic 3D environments, characters, and objects can be created for usage in the metaverse because to the advancements in 3D modelling and animation technology. Artificial Intelligence (AI) is used in the metaverse to create intelligent AI characters and develop surroundings that can change based on human behaviour. AI also helps to improve interactions between users and virtual environments. Furthermore, by allowing the exchange of digital assets, payments, and smart contracts between users, blockchain technology can be utilized to establish virtual economies inside the metaverse. Utilizing gesture recognition, sound, and touch to communicate with the virtual world, spatial computing enables users to engage with virtual worlds intuitively. Cloud computing facilitates the data processing, streaming, and storing required to enable intricate, networked user experiences in the metaverse. By enabling users to sense physical sensations through touch or vibration, haptic feedback technology improves metaverse immersion. Through virtual settings, users can control and interact with real-world physical equipment thanks to IoT integration in the metaverse (Bilgihan et al., 2014; Ioannidis & Kontis, 2023; Valinatajbahnamiri & Siahtiri, 2021).

- User Interaction: As virtual worlds have developed, more intricate interactions between users and their surroundings, as well as amongst users themselves, are now possible. Features like player cooperation, real-time communication, and user-generated content are included in this. The advancement and enhancement of user interaction technology in support of the metaverse pertains to the ways in which users engage with progressively intricate and interconnected virtual worlds. User interaction technologies are changing and evolving in tandem with the metaverse to offer increasingly immersive, intuitive, and connected experiences. Augmented reality (AR) and virtual reality (VR) technologies have emerged as crucial elements in the metaverse's growth. Virtual reality headsets and augmented reality gadgets have evolved over time to become more lightweight, ergonomic, and capable of producing immersive and lifelike visual experiences. Next, by using eye tracking and gesture recognition, enable users to recognize the facial expressions, body language, and eye movements, so that they can interact with virtual surroundings. As a result, the metaverse becomes more realistic and immersive. Natural language processing (NLP) and voice recognition technologies allow users to converse with virtual surroundings by using normal language and voices. Real-time comprehension of commands, queries, and instructions is a capability of advanced natural language processing systems. Tactile Sensation and Haptic Feedback technologies can improve immersive metaverse experiences by enabling users to feel tangible feelings through touch or vibration. This could entail donning gloves or using specialized haptic devices, which give users a tactile sense when interacting with virtual items. With the help of social interaction and avatar personalization technology, users can engage in virtual interactions with one another and alter their avatars to suit their own tastes. As a result, the metaverse offers a more intimate and customized social experience. By utilizing artificial intelligence (AI) and machine learning (ML) technologies in the metaverse, users and virtual environments can interact more effectively. For example, clever AI characters or systems that can modify their surroundings based on user behaviour can be created. Immersive interfaces with wearable technology: Wearable technology, like augmented reality contact lenses or smart glasses, can improve user comfort and mobility when interacting with virtual environments (Cruz et al., 2010; Kim, 2021; Mahnke et al., 2015).

Figure 2. Metaverse with the environment, interface, interaction, security, and privacy (Dwivedi et al., 2022).

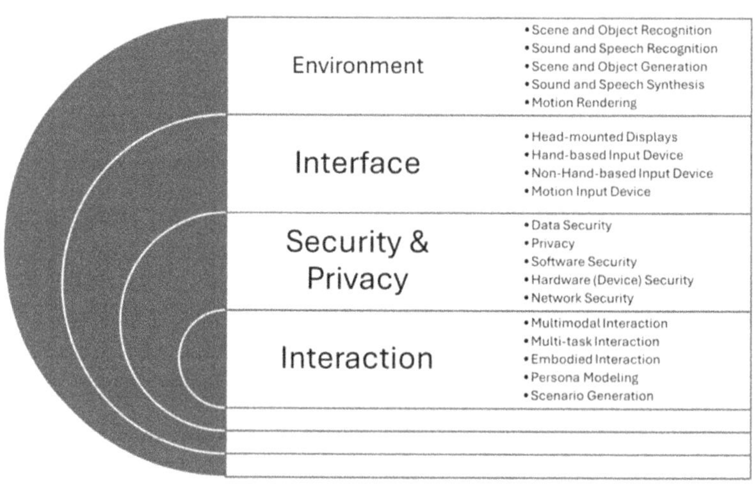

- Social Dynamics: People are creating communities, having social interactions, and forming relationships in virtual worlds, which have grown to be more social places. In the setting of the metaverse, social dynamics are evolving to reflect shifts in how people interact, communicate, and engage with one another in increasingly intricate virtual environments. In tandem with the emergence of metaverse platforms and technology advancements like virtual reality and augmented reality, the metaverse's social dynamics have undergone notable transformations. Enhanced Social Interaction: Users can communicate with others from all around the world in real-time without being limited by geography because to the metaverse. In a virtual setting, users can interact, cooperate, and take part in activities with one another. Online community development is a framework for the emergence and expansion of varied online communities is offered by the metaverse. These communities offer a forum for people to exchange ideas, experiences, and knowledge. They might be founded around common interests, pastimes, occupations, or particular identities. Users are able to design and alter their avatars in the metaverse to suit their own tastes. People may now express themselves artistically and feel more at ease in a virtual setting because to this. Users can collaborate on projects, have meetings or presentations, and share ideas more effectively in the metaverse than they would in the actual world. Furthermore, the metaverse offers a digital marketplace where individuals may purchase and exchange digital products and services, including digital artwork, virtual real estate, and cryptocurrency assets. In a virtual setting, this opens up new avenues for revenue and economic expansion. Concerning user behaviour, privacy, security, and laws in virtual environments, social and ethical contexts are some of the issues that come up in the metaverse. For all users to have a secure and enjoyable experience, metaverse groups and platforms must establish suitable standards and guidelines. Ensuring that everyone can access the metaverse and narrowing the digital divide are difficult tasks. To guarantee that metaverse technology is usable by all societal strata and does not exacerbate current disparities, efforts must be made in this direction (Dong et al., 2023; Hooker et al., 2019; Nah et al., 2010; Park et al., 2010; Zhu et al., 2023).
- Commercialization: Virtual worlds are now major commercial endeavours rather than just experimental or hobbyist endeavours. This covers the creation of in-game purchases, virtual economies, and revenue structures. In the context of the metaverse, commercialization has evolved to reflect shifts in how companies run, engage with clients, and make money in a more virtualized setting. The metaverse has produced a virtual marketplace where people may purchase, sell, and trade digital products and services. This cov-

ers consumer items, game systems, virtual property, and other digital assets. Virtual currencies and cryptocurrencies are frequently used in the metaverse for business purposes. Digital currencies increase the flexibility and speed of transactions by making it easier to purchase, sell, and exchange digital assets in a virtual environment. Companies can use the metaverse as a platform for product and service marketing and promotion. This covers the development of online storefronts, the introduction of new products, marketing efforts, and virtual events. A number of metaverse platforms let users to purchase, construct, and trade virtual real estate, including digital houses, buildings, and commercial spaces. This opens up new metaverse revenue and investment options. Businesses can provide their goods and services to people in the metaverse through virtual stores. This includes a broad spectrum of items, including unique virtual goods and consumer goods. The metaverse offers a venue for creative and engaging sponsorship and advertising. Companies can sponsor events or venues, post adverts in virtual spaces, or work with virtual content creators to promote their products. To give users more varied and integrated experiences, businesses in the metaverse can collaborate and form partnerships with other businesses. This could involve working together on collaborative events, marketing efforts, or product creation. Companies can make money by charging customers for virtual experiences like games, concerts, tours, or business gatherings. Sales of tickets, subscriptions, or virtual products sold throughout the experience can provide this income. A more significant and interconnected virtual environment presents new potential for businesses to grow their reach, boost client engagement, and make money thanks to the metaverse's evolving commercialization. Businesses can develop creative and profitable commercial strategies to suit customer demands and expectations in this digital era by properly employing metaverse technology and platforms (Anne Craig-Lees et al., 2013; Simon, 2010).

- Integration with Other Technologies: New opportunities for immersive experiences and inventive applications have emerged as a result of the convergence of virtual worlds with other technologies like blockchain, augmented reality, and artificial intelligence. The metaverse's integration with other technology has evolved over time, mirroring advancements and enhancements in the relationships and exchanges between the metaverse and other current technologies. As a result, more intricate, integrated, and comprehensive virtual experiences can be created. The following are some facets of how metaverse technology integration has evolved: IoT, or the Internet of Things: Through IoT's virtual environments, users can interact with real-world physical devices thanks to the integration of the metaverse with the Internet of Things. Avatars in the metaverse can be used to control smart home appliances, driverless cars, or environmental sensors. Using ML and AI in the metaverse can enhance user-virtual interactions. Intelligent AI characters, tailored recommendation systems, and the identification of user behaviour patterns to personalize metaverse experiences are all made possible by AI. The creation of a transparent and safe virtual economy is made possible by the combination of blockchain technology and the metaverse. Blockchain is used to make it easier to do business, hold digital assets, and provide people in the metaverse distinct digital identities. Next, the metaverse uses cloud computing to store, process, and stream data in order to support intricately linked user experiences. As part of this, scalable infrastructure for managing a lot of people and content in a virtual setting is provided. By fusing the metaverse with these technologies, users can have a more realistic and immersive experience. Using motion tracking technologies to create interactive experiences, utilizing AR/VR headsets to interact with virtual environments, and producing dynamic 3D material are some examples of this. Sensors and Monitoring Equipment: In the metaverse, sensors and monitoring equipment can be used to track a user's motions, sounds, or emotions and produce relevant reactions in a virtual setting. In the metaverse, this results in a more tailored and responsive experience. Gamification and incentive Systems: Combining gamification technologies and incentive systems with the metaverse can boost user motivation and engagement in virtual environments. The metaverse has the potential to expand into a huge and diversified place that opens up new avenues for virtual world engagement, creativity, and collaboration by fully utilizing the capabilities of current technologies (Bigliani et al., 2016; Gupta & Quamara, 2020; Zeinab & Elmustafa, 2017).

1.3.1. Augmented Reality (AR) and Mixed Reality (MR)

A technology known as augmented reality (AR) blends virtual components into the actual world. During an augmented reality (AR) experience, users utilize gadgets like smartphones, AR glasses, or other devices to view their surroundings as virtual components like text, photos, or 3D objects are superimposed on them. With augmented reality (AR) technology, people may interact with information and digital objects in their real world. Facial filters in social networking apps, GPS navigation that shows routes over actual roads, and visuals from the video game Pokémon GO in actual places are a few examples of applications for augmented reality (Guo et al., 2016; Krishnamurthy & Trivedi, 2023).

Figure 3. The xReality Framework: XR Definitions for the metaverse (Huynh-The et al., 2023).

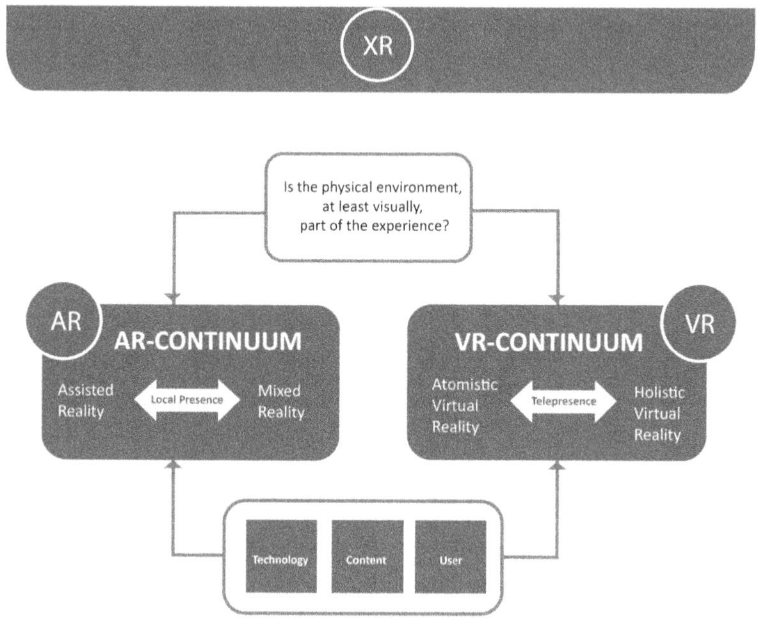

While, a more sophisticated kind of augmented reality, mixed reality (MR) involves fully integrating virtual aspects into the physical world rather than just adding them on top of it. Users can observe and interact with virtual items in MR experiences that seem to exist in their physical surroundings. Compared to AR, this produces a more realistic and immersive experience. In a mixed reality (MR) experience, for instance, users can arrange virtual objects on their desk and engage with them just like they would with actual physical objects. The degree of integration between virtual and physical components is where AR and MR diverge most. In mixed reality (MR), virtual elements appear to be a natural part of the surrounding environment, as opposed to AR where virtual elements just overlap it. Numerous industries, including gaming, education, healthcare, manufacturing, and more, can benefit from the extensive range of applications of these two technologies.

Figure 4. Differences between AR, MR, and VR (Bilgihan et al., 2014).

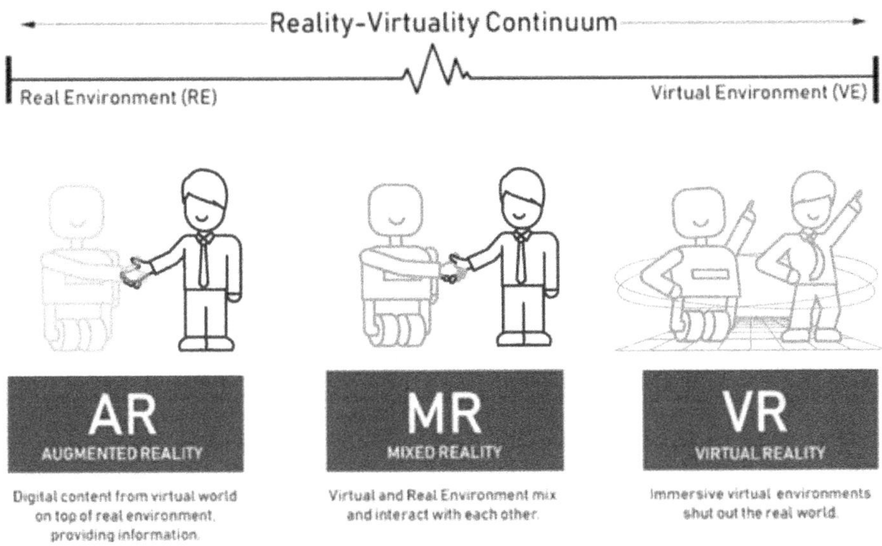

Through the integration of virtual and physical aspects, augmented reality (AR) enables users to perceive and interact with virtual things within their physical surroundings. First and foremost, an augmented reality system needs to be able to identify and comprehend the physical surroundings in which the user is situated. Numerous technologies, including cameras, motion sensors, GPS, and environmental scanning, can be used to do this. Position and Orientation Tracking: The augmented reality system tracks the user's position and orientation in space subsequent to its recognition of the physical world. As a result, virtual components can be precisely positioned inside the real world. The augmented reality technology overlays virtual elements on top of the actual world after determining the user's position and the surrounding surroundings. This could be anything that is shown on the user's device screen, such as text, graphics, animations, or 3D objects. Users are able to engage with virtual items that are presented in the real world. This can be interacting with virtual objects using voice commands, hand gestures, screen touching, or other input methods. Moreover, AR systems are in charge of precisely rendering virtual components inside the real world so that they seem like organic components of it. This covers elements that fit in with the surroundings, like lighting, shadows, and reflections. AR technology needs to adapt to shifts in the user's position and the physical surroundings. This enables, despite changes in the user's location or orientation, virtual elements to stay connected with the surrounding environment (Bilgihan et al., 2014; Ioannidis & Kontis, 2023; Liu, 2017).

AR technology combines position tracking, physical environment identification, virtual element rendering, and user interaction to create experiences that creatively and captivatingly merge the real and virtual worlds.

1.3.2. Internet of Things (IoT)

The idea behind the Internet of Things (IoT) is that different physical objects that are linked to the internet can share data and communicate with one another without requiring direct human-to-human or human-to-computer contact. Put differently, the Internet of Things (IoT) is a network of connected objects that may share data automatically over the internet and speak with one another. The fundamental idea behind the Internet of Things is that these gadgets can gather and share data since they have sensors, software, and internet connectivity built into them. After processing and analysis, this data can be applied to a variety of tasks, such as energy management, automated manufacturing, smart homes, and health monitoring.

Sensors for wind speed, humidity, and temperature in industrial settings are a few examples of Internet of Things devices. Fitness tracker that is linked to a smartphone application. CCTV systems in residences or commercial buildings with internet access. Home appliances or lights that can be managed remotely with a smartphone are known as smart lighting. Ovens or washing machines with online scheduling capabilities [12]. Users have the flexibility and convenience of being able to remotely monitor and operate their gadgets through the internet. By tracking and maximizing the usage of resources like fuel, water, and electricity, IoT can assist in raising operational efficiency. By tracking a user's vital signs, including heart rate or activity level, Internet of Things devices can offer important healthcare data. By keeping an eye out for unusual activity and issuing early warnings of possible risk, IoT can be utilized to increase security at home or in places of business. IoT does, however, come with a number of drawbacks, such as concerns about data security and privacy, standardization, device compatibility, and handling the massive amount of data that IoT devices generate (Carrasco & Chen, 2021; Diène et al., 2020; Valinatajbahnamiri & Siahtiri, 2021).

1.3.3. Artificial intelligence (AI) and machine learning (ML)

Artificial intelligence (AI) and machine learning (ML) play a major role in managing content, enhancing user experience, and building dynamic and responsive virtual environments inside the metaverse (C. Chen et al., 2017; L. Chen et al., 2017).

In order to provide individualized experiences, user behaviour, preferences, and other contextual data are analysed using AI and ML. AI, for instance, is able to recognize patterns of user interaction and modify information, such as avatars or virtual worlds, to suit individual preferences. NLP and speech recognition technologies let users speak naturally in virtual worlds. Artificial intelligence (AI) can comprehend user requests, demands, and instructions and react to them instantly, making the experience more dynamic and natural. In virtual environments, machine learning is utilized to analyse and manage material dynamically. To create a more relevant and engaging experience, ML can, for instance, arrange material according to user preferences, popularity, or the present context. AI is used to generate intelligent and responsive artificial intelligence (AI) characters, or avatars, in virtual worlds. This covers virtual assistants, intelligent agents, and in-game non-player characters (NPCs) that help players explore the metaverse. To improve performance and the user experience in virtual environments, AI and ML are used to analyse system performance statistics, resource utilization, and user behaviour. This enhances metaverse systems' responsiveness, stability, and efficiency (Arnarson et al., 2023; Bouziane et al., 2023).

In virtual environments, artificial intelligence (AI) is used to keep an eye on user activity and enforce security, privacy, and ethics regulations. AI, for instance, is capable of identifying questionable or illegal activity in the metaverse and reacting appropriately. The metaverse can be made more dynamic, interactive, and connected by utilizing AI and machine learning, giving users a more engaging and customized experience. Artificial intelligence, machine learning, and other metaverse technologies create new avenues for virtual creation, invention, and teamwork.

1.3.4. Blockchain Technology

In the context of the metaverse, blockchain technology holds considerable promise, particularly for enabling virtual economics, security, and the development of decentralized ecosystems. Blockchain makes it possible to create digital assets, tokens, and virtual currencies that are used in a metaverse virtual economy. Users no longer need to go through a middleman when purchasing, selling, or exchanging digital assets like virtual real estate, digital art, or game items thanks to blockchain technology. Ownership of Digital Assets: Blockchain makes it possible to record who owns digital assets in the form of decentralized, non-counterfeit able tokens. Users will be able to verify their ownership of digital assets in the metaverse through this clear and safe approach (Hsu et al., 2020; Huynh-The et al., 2023; Li et al., 2023).

In a metaverse virtual economy, smart contracts can automate and enforce agreements. They operate on a blockchain basis. Smart contracts, for instance, can be used to safely and automatically schedule deliveries, exchanges of digital assets between users, and payment. Blockchain technology can be used to safely and encrypted store identity, copyright, and intellectual property information in the metaverse. In virtual environments, this aids in defending the rights of users and content creators.

Blockchain makes it possible to create decentralized marketplaces where people can trade digital assets without depending on centralized authorities or other parties. The metaverse becomes a more equitable, transparent, and welcoming environment as a result. Furthermore, users in the metaverse can establish distinct and safe digital identities through the use of blockchain technology. This identity can be used to engage with services and apps in the virtual world, validate asset ownership, and gain access to the platform. The metaverse may be made more decentralized, safe, and welcoming by utilizing blockchain technology, which will also enable users to benefit from a varied and sustainable virtual economy. In a virtual environment, users can engage in ownership, trade, and other economic activities without fearing for their safety or the security, dependability, or reliability of the system (Li et al., 2023). This section examines the most advanced blockchain-based techniques for the metaverse, focusing on technical aspects such as data acquisition, storage, sharing, interoperability, and privacy preservation. Figure 5 displays the representation of blockchain for the technological aspects discussed before in the metaverse.

Figure 5. Blockchain for technical aspects in the metaverse (Hsu et al., 2020).

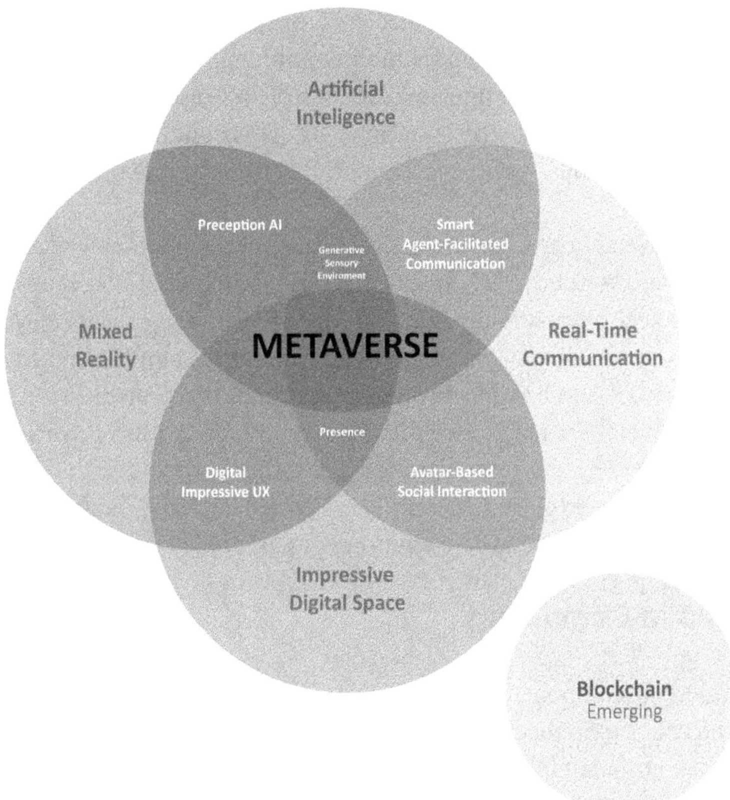

1.3.5. Gamification and Reward Systems

In order to boost user engagement, encourage involvement, and produce more dynamic and interesting experiences, gamification and reward systems can be applied. Users can receive rewards via reward systems for particular tasks completed in a virtual world or for successes. This can involve giving out prizes for finishing tasks, hitting milestones, or taking part in neighbourhood activities. Depending on their performance, activity, or contribution inside the metaverse, users may receive points or scores. These rankings can be used to evaluate user performance against one another, encourage competition, or offer rewards for increased participation in a virtual setting.

Metaverse may include tier and achievement systems that let users advance in the game, accomplish particular objectives, or get respect from other members of the community. It honours users for their commitment and hard work in the virtual setting. As compensation for their involvement or accomplishments in the metaverse, users may be given virtual goods or presents. This could be in the form of virtual money, in-game goods, exclusive content that isn't accessible to other users, or exclusive access.

In the metaverse, participation in events and tournaments can be encouraged by the use of reward systems. Participants that place well in contests could receive gifts, accolades, or access to premium material. In a virtual setting, users may be assigned specific missions or challenges, and upon successfully completing those tasks, they may be rewarded. Users now have a more engaging and difficult metaverse experience as a result. Developers may make the metaverse more dynamic, participatory, and engaging for users by using gamification and reward systems. Users are encouraged to actively interact, explore different features and material, and fortify the online community within the metaverse environment as a result (Abiodun et al., 2021).

1.3.6. Cloud Computing

An essential component of the infrastructure required to enable intricate and networked user experiences is cloud computing. In the metaverse, cloud computing has several significant features. Large-scale, scalable data storage is made possible by cloud computing. This includes the multimedia content, 3D models, textures, and other data required to create and manage virtual worlds in the metaverse. This frees developers from having to restrict the amount of local storage that consumers can access rich and varied material. Cloud computing offers a tonne of computational power for handling large amounts of data, creating visuals, and managing intricate programs in an online setting. This makes it possible for developers to provide users with responsive and realistic experiences even on low-end hardware.

Cloud computing makes it possible for users to access multimedia content—such as images, audio, and video—in a metaverse setting. This lowers latency and boosts user engagement by enabling direct material access for users without the need to download or keep it locally. Metaverse infrastructure can dynamically modify capacity in response to user demand thanks to cloud computing. This makes it possible for virtual environments to support big user bases and maintain high availability without compromising on functionality. In the metaverse, cloud computing enables cooperation and interconnection amongst diverse virtual settings and platforms. It enables users to cooperate in a networked virtual environment, share material, and communicate with users on various platforms (Bibri, 2018).

The imperative for organizations to swiftly embrace and use cloud-based services to address the challenge of managing and processing large volumes of data presents unforeseen risks and implications. Multiple analogous research demonstrate the operational mechanisms of big data utilizing cloud computing technology. The correlation between the extensive utilization of IaaS and PaaS technologies and the exponential expansion of Big Data is to be expected. Platform as a Service (PaaS) enables firms to increase their available resources easily and quickly as needed, resulting in cost savings. Infrastructure as a Service (IaaS) allows for the rapid deployment of substantial computational capabilities. Additional processing and storage resources can be promptly incorporated into this amalgamation. The adaptability of cloud computing allows for the deployment of resources as needed. Consequently, enterprises might avoid the substantial expense of acquiring hardware capacity that they would only utilize intermittently. Figure 6 depicts the utilization of large data cloud computing (Anas et al., 2017).

Figure 6. Cloud computing usage in big data (Li et al., 2023).

Access control, user authentication, and data encryption are just a few of the high security and privacy measures that can be implemented in a metaverse setting thanks to cloud computing. This keeps people safe in virtual environments and safeguards important data. The metaverse may be made more dynamic, responsive, and connected by utilizing cloud computing, giving users a more engaging and cooperative experience. This creates fresh chances for invention, teamwork, and creativity in the virtual environment (Akhtar et al., 2021; Huang et al., 2022).

1.3.7. Sensors and Monitoring Devices

Within the metaverse, sensors and monitoring apparatus play a crucial part in establishing virtual environments that are dynamic, adaptable, and interconnected. The metaverse can make use of a variety of sensors and monitoring devices, including image and camera sensors, biometric sensors, sound sensors, motion and position sensors, environmental sensors, and health sensors. The user's position and movement inside a virtual world are tracked by the use of motion and position sensors. They can be used to change the perspective of the camera, move the user's avatar, or cause actions to be taken in reaction to changes in the user's movement or position. In virtual environments, sound sensors are utilized to pick up on sounds and conversations.

They can be employed for voice-to-voice communication among users, speech command recognition, or sound-related activity detection, like online music performances or chat rooms. In a virtual world, environmental sensors are used to keep an eye on things like air quality, humidity, illumination, and temperature. In virtual worlds, they can be used to produce realistic environmental effects like changing weather and time cycles. Biometric sensors are utilized to quantify and track an individual's physiological or physical activities, including bodily motions, stress levels, and heart rate. They can be applied to develop experiences that are sensitive and adaptable to the user's physical state.

In virtual worlds, objects, motion, and visual changes are detected using cameras and image sensors. They can be applied to virtual environments for security monitoring, object recognition, and user imaging. The virtual environment can be detected with the use of interaction sensors, which pick up on gestures, voice instructions, and screen touches. They enable users to converse with other users in a virtual environment, operate devices, and interact with virtual items.

In virtual worlds, health sensors are utilized to track users' health and well-being. They can be used to monitor and provide feedback or recommendations based on data related to metrics including blood oxygen levels, heart rate, and physical activity levels. Virtual worlds in the metaverse can be made more dynamic, adaptive, and connected to the real world through the employment of sensors and monitoring equipment. They give consumers in a virtual environment a more lifelike, interactive, and customized experience (Kaluarachchi et al., 2021; Putra et al., 2021).

1.4 METAVERSE TRENDS AND CHALLENGES

Future developments in technology, how it is used, and how it affects daily life will be reflected in metaverse trends and problems.

1.4.1. Metaverse Trends

The following are some potential future trends and issues that the metaverse may encounter prospective metaverse patterns that are included: enhanced social contact, development of the virtual economy, improved security and privacy, technological innovation, education and training, and collaboration and partnerships.

Users from all over the world will work together and engage in more social contact within the metaverse. This will make the virtual world friendlier and more inclusive. Trade in virtual products and services will keep growing in scope and complexity as the metaverse's virtual economy continues to grow. This will open up new doors for the digital services, e-commerce, and entertainment sectors. The metaverse will put more of an emphasis on enhancing user security and privacy, which will include safeguarding digital identities, personal information, and online transactions. The primary goal will be to stop fraud, hacks, and improper use of data. Blockchain, quantum computing, artificial intelligence, virtual and augmented reality, and more will all be showcased in the Metaverse. Users will have a more responsive and immersive experience as a result. Users will be able to access online courses, workshops, and certificates from anywhere in the world through Metaverse, which will be the leading platform for remote education and training. More cooperation and partnerships between tech firms, content creators, and other stakeholders will occur in the metaverse (Ioannidis & Kontis, 2023).

1.4.2. Metaverse Challenges

A planned and cooperative approach is needed to address possible drawbacks of relying on technology in the metaverse, such as scalability, interoperability, and integration concerns. Here are a few approaches to resolving this issue:

- Scalability Issues
  - Leveraging cloud technologies from providers such as AWS, Google Cloud, and Microsoft Azure to support large workloads puts users at risk. This technology enables automatic scaling according to demand.
  - The use of edge computing to process data closer to the user's location, reducing latency and improving performance.
  - Implementation of efficient network protocols and data compression to reduce network load and increase access speed.
- Interoperability Issues
  - Develop and adopt open standards for data formats, communications protocols, and APIs that enable multiple platforms and systems to interact seamlessly.

    - Using solutions such as cross-chain bridges and interoperable blockchain frameworks that enable the transfer of data and assets between different blockchains.
    - Encourage collaboration between various stakeholders in the technology industry to align standards and best practices in metaverse development.
- Technology Integration Issues
    - It uses a middleware layer to integrate technologies such as IoT, VR, AR, and AI, so they can work together efficiently. Middleware acts as an intermediary that manages communication and data between different systems.
    - Provides easy-to-use APIs and SDKs for developers, enabling them to integrate metaverse features into their applications more easily.
    - Implement a rigorous testing and validation process to ensure compatibility and optimal performance of various technologies used in the metaverse.

Scalability, interoperability, and technology integration difficulties in the metaverse can be resolved with a planned and coordinated approach, building a more robust and diverse ecosystem.

Overcoming potential limitations related to the digital divide and ensuring inclusivity for users from various socioeconomic backgrounds in the metaverse requires a comprehensive and collaborative approach. Some strategies that can be taken:

- Regarding Network Infrastructure: developing and expanding internet infrastructure to rural and remote areas. This can be done through government investment and public-private partnerships. In addition, it uses satellite technology such as that developed by Starlink and OneWeb to provide internet access in areas that are difficult to reach by traditional cable infrastructure, and encourages the development of locally managed community internet networks to provide more affordable internet access.
- Related to Device Access: providing subsidies or assistance for hardware such as VR headsets, computers and smartphones to low-income communities. Development of VR and AR devices that are more affordable and accessible to more people.
- Education and Training: organizing digital literacy programs to help people understand and use metaverse technology effectively. Technology training for users from various socioeconomic backgrounds to develop the skills needed in the metaverse.
- Relevant and Local Content: develop content that is relevant and appropriate to local needs and culture to attract more users from various backgrounds.

It further provides interfaces and content in multiple languages and ensures accessibility for users with disabilities.

- Inclusive Business Model: uses a freemium business model where basic access to the metaverse is free, with options for premium purchases. Profits from premium users can be used to subsidize access for low-income users. Work with non-profit organizations to provide access and resources to underserved communities.
- Policies and Regulations: encourage the government to implement policies that support digital inclusivity, such as incentives for infrastructure development and support programs for low-income communities. Furthermore, adopt regulations that ensure all metaverse devices and platforms meet accessibility standards.
- Collaboration and Partnerships: develop partnerships between the public and private sectors to share resources and expertise in overcoming the digital divide. Participate in global initiatives aimed at reducing the digital divide and increasing technological inclusivity.

With these steps, it is hoped to reduce the digital divide and ensure that the metaverse can be accessed and enjoyed by everyone, regardless of their socioeconomic background.

While technology integration in the metaverse offers many opportunities, it is important to address security and privacy challenges with a comprehensive approach. This includes the implementation of advanced security technology, strict policies, and ongoing user education. In this way, the risks of data breaches, identity theft, and privacy violations can be minimized, creating a secure and trusted metaverse environment. Potential limitations in the metaverse related to security and privacy can be categorized as follows:

- Data Breaches: metaverses that rely on multiple technologies, such as VR, AR, and blockchain, have many potential points for cyberattacks. Additionally, the use of sophisticated technology can collect large amounts of data, including user behaviour, location, and social interactions, increasing the risk of data breaches.
- Identity Theft: Users' avatars and digital identities can be misused if there are no adequate security mechanisms. The metaverse can be fertile ground for phishing and fraud, where users can be tempted to reveal personal information.
- Protection of Personal Information: Users' personal information can be misused by developers or third parties. Additionally, users may not have sufficient control or awareness of how their data is collected, used, and stored.

To carry out mitigation steps which can be detailed as follows:

- Related to Data Security: implementing end-to-end encryption to protect data during transmission and storage. Uses strong network security protocols, including firewalls, IDS/IPS, and VPN. Next, conduct regular security audits and penetration testing to identify and fix vulnerabilities.
- Related to Identity and Authentication: using Multi-Factor Authentication (MFA) to add an additional layer of security to the login process. Uses blockchain technology to manage digital identities in a decentralized manner, reducing the risk of identity theft. Implementation of a strict identity verification system to ensure that user identities are truly legitimate.
- Regarding Data Privacy: provide a clear and transparent privacy policy that explains how data is collected, used and protected. Gives users full control over their data, including the right to access, update and delete personal data. Collects only the data strictly necessary for the service, reducing the risk of privacy breaches.
- Related to User Education and Awareness: Increasing digital security literacy among users to identify and avoid cyber threats. Provide notifications and warnings to users about suspicious activity or potential threats.
- Regarding Regulations and Compliance: Ensure compliance with privacy and data security regulations such as GDPR, CCPA and others. Obtain security certification from recognized institutions to increase user confidence.

The global and decentralized nature of the metaverse potentially presents significant challenges regarding compliance with different jurisdictions' regulations and law enforcement. However, there are some ways around these potential limitations:

- Encourage collaboration between countries to develop a uniform and harmonized regulatory framework for the metaverse. International organizations such as the UN, OECD, or WTO can play a role in facilitating this discussion. In addition, international standards can be developed that can be accepted by various jurisdictions, especially regarding data security, privacy and digital transactions.
- Monitor regulations in various jurisdictions and adjust internal policies to comply with applicable legal requirements where users are located. Employs an international legal team experienced in various legal systems to ensure regulatory compliance in various countries.
- Using blockchain technology and smart contracts for automation and regulatory enforcement. Smart contracts can regulate compliance with legal pro-

visions automatically. Likewise, utilizing blockchain technology to track and audit transactions in a transparent manner that can be verified by authorities.

- Provide transparency in operational processes and policies, including how data is collected, used and protected. In addition, establishing effective reporting and communication mechanisms with regulators in various jurisdictions to ensure that any violations or problems can be promptly addressed.
- Educate users and developers about the regulations that apply to the metaverse and the importance of complying with them. By conducting awareness campaigns about privacy, security, and legal compliance in the metaverse.
- Collaboration with law enforcement in various countries to deal with emerging issues, including law violations and cyber-crimes. Developing a security platform that can assist in the identification and enforcement of illegal activities in the metaverse.
- Develop and implement a strong data protection policy to protect user privacy and meet global regulatory requirements. Implement monitoring and control systems that ensure activities in the metaverse comply with applicable regulations.
- Advocate and lobby for flexible and adaptive regulations, which can balance technological innovation and legal compliance. Participate in global forums and discussions discussing regulations and laws in the metaverse, to share perspectives and find solutions together.

With this comprehensive approach, regulatory and legal challenges in the metaverse can be addressed, creating an ecosystem that is safe, trustworthy, and compliant with international law.

Addressing potential limitations related to economic inequality, job displacement, and the impact on traditional industries in a metaverse virtual economy requires a multi-faceted approach. Here are some alternative solutions that can be taken:

- Related to Economic Inequality: providing broader access and education about metaverse technologies for underserved groups. This includes digital skills and technology literacy training programs. Additionally, it provides subsidies and incentives for individuals from low economic backgrounds to access the tools and technology needed to participate in the metaverse. Furthermore, encouraging economic development programs that target the development of local businesses and small businesses within the metaverse, ensures that the benefits of the virtual economy are spread widely.
- Related to Job Transfers: provide retraining and upskilling programs for workers impacted by automation and digitalization in the metaverse. This can include training in technology skills, virtual community management,

content design, and software development. Collaborate with industry to create new career paths in the virtual economy, such as jobs in virtual world development, digital asset management, and customer service in digital environments. Governments can play a role by providing financial support and transition programs for workers who lose their jobs due to the shift to a virtual economy.

- Impact on Traditional Industries: encourage traditional industries to adopt and integrate metaverse technology into their operations. For example, the retail sector can adopt virtual stores, while the education industry can use virtual classrooms.
- Collaboration and Partnerships: encourage collaboration between metaverse technology companies and traditional industries to create hybrid solutions that combine the strengths of both sectors. Provide support and incentives for traditional companies to innovate and explore new opportunities emerging from the virtual economy.
- Related to Protection against Exploitation: implement strict regulations to protect workers and users in the metaverse from exploitation. This includes regulations regarding working conditions, fair wages and digital workers' rights. Drive transparency in business and operational practices in the metaverse to ensure that all parties operate in an ethical and fair manner. Conduct awareness-raising campaigns about user and worker rights in the metaverse, as well as ways to report violations or exploitation.
- Equitable Access to the Virtual Economy: develop inclusive business models in the metaverse, such as a freemium model, which allows basic access for free with options for more advanced paid services. Encouraging micro-funding initiatives for individuals and small businesses to start businesses or projects in the metaverse. Building a supportive community and ecosystem that allows individuals from diverse backgrounds to collaborate and thrive in the metaverse.

With a strategic approach that includes education, regulation, collaboration, and innovation support, potential limitations related to economic disparities, job displacement, and the impact on traditional industries can be overcome. This will help create a fair, inclusive and sustainable virtual economy in the metaverse.

Addressing potential limitations regarding ethical use of technology, user behaviour, and social impact of immersive virtual environments in the metaverse requires a comprehensive and layered approach. The following strategies will help create a virtual environment that is safer, fairer, and more rewarding for all users:

- Ethical Use of Technology: develop and adopt a clear code of ethics and guidelines for developers, users, and companies operating in the metaverse. This should include principles such as privacy, security, and fairness. Establish an independent ethics board consisting of technology experts, academics, and community representatives to monitor and assess the ethical implications of metaverse technology. Promote transparency in the use of algorithms and AI in the metaverse, including how data is collected, processed and used.
- User Conduct: establish strict behavioural policies for all users in the metaverse, including rules about harassment, discrimination, and other inappropriate actions. Implement an effective moderation and oversight system to ensure conduct policies are enforced. This can include human moderators and automated detection technology. Furthermore, it provides an easily accessible reporting mechanism for users to report inappropriate behaviour and ensures fair and swift enforcement action.
- Social Impact of Immersive Virtual Environments: provides digital literacy programs that educate users about the healthy and responsible use of immersive technologies. This should include information about balanced screen time and the potential impact on mental health. Conduct studies and research on the social and psychological impacts of immersive virtual environments, and use the results to inform policy and best practices. Encourage positive and inclusive social interactions in the metaverse through platform design that supports collaboration, community support, and meaningful social activities.
- Regulations and Public Policy: Develop regulations that protect users, especially children and teenagers, from the negative impacts of the metaverse. This may include age restrictions, parental controls, and content limitations. Collaborate with governments and non-governmental organizations to develop and enforce regulations aimed at maintaining user safety and welfare.
- User-Centered Design: applies inclusive design principles to ensure that the metaverse is accessible and enjoyable for everyone, including those with disabilities. Giving users more control over their experience in the metaverse, including privacy settings, time management tools, and options for filtering content.
- Community Involvement: Involve the user community in development and decision-making regarding the metaverse to ensure that diverse perspectives and needs are accommodated. Furthermore, establishing discussion forums and working groups that allow users to dialogue about ethical and social issues that arise in the metaverse.

With an approach that includes policy and regulatory development, digital education and literacy, inclusive design, and community engagement, potential limitations regarding the ethical and social implications of the metaverse can be overcome.

Managing user engagement in the metaverse to prevent addiction and ensure a healthy balance between virtual and physical activities requires a proactive and holistic approach as explained below.

- Design that Supports Digital Wellbeing: integrates time management features that allow users to set usage time limits, including reminders to take a break or log off after a certain period of time. Provides a focus mode that minimizes distractions and encourages users to take periodic breaks, similar to the Pomodoro technique. Provide users with usage reports so they can monitor time spent in the metaverse and take action to reduce excessive usage.
- Digital Education and Literacy: running awareness campaigns to educate users about the risks of addiction and the importance of balance between virtual and physical activities. Provide digital literacy programs that teach users, especially children and teenagers, about the healthy and responsible use of technology.
- Parental Involvement and Oversight: provides tools and oversight features for parents to monitor and regulate their children's use of the metaverse, including screen time controls and content restrictions. Educate parents about the impact of immersive technology on children and how to manage their use effectively.
- Balance Virtual and Physical Activities: encourage users to engage in physical activities by integrating gamification elements that combine physical and virtual activities. For example, fitness challenges require real-world activity to earn virtual rewards. Host events or activities that encourage real-world social interaction, such as metaverse user community gatherings in physical locations.
- Regulations and Policies: develop regulations that limit screen time, especially for children and teenagers, to prevent excessive use. Work with health experts to develop official guidelines on the healthy and balanced use of immersive technologies.
- Support and Resources: provides support services for users who may be experiencing technology addiction, including access to counselling and mental health resources. Building a support community within the metaverse that can help users share experiences and strategies for managing their technology use.
- Ethical Design: adopt ethical design principles that consider the long-term impact of user involvement and avoid designs that encourage excessive use.

Provide users with transparency into how certain features are designed to increase engagement, so they can make more conscious decisions about their use.

By combining design that supports digital health, digital education and literacy, parental supervision, physical activity promotion, appropriate regulation, and support services and ethical design, potential limitations related to managing user engagement can be overcome. This will help ensure that users can enjoy the benefits of the metaverse without compromising their health and well-being.

Overcoming potential limitations related to energy consumption and environmental impact in maintaining and expanding metaverse infrastructure requires a sustainable and innovative approach. Some strategies that can be taken are as follows:

- Improved Energy Efficiency: developing and using hardware that is more efficient in energy consumption, such as low-power servers and energy-efficient processors. Design VR headsets, AR, and other devices used in the metaverse with a focus on energy efficiency to reduce power consumption.
- Use of Renewable Energy Sources: build and operate data centres that use renewable energy such as solar, wind and waterpower to reduce the carbon footprint. Collaborate with green energy providers to ensure that network and data centre operations are powered by clean, renewable energy.
- Efficient Energy Management: implement energy monitoring and management systems to ensure efficient energy use in data centre and network infrastructure. Adopt more efficient cooling technologies for data centre, such as liquid cooling or more advanced air cooling.
- Development of Greener Technology: Developing algorithms and software designed to minimize energy use, including optimization of computing and data processing processes. Leverages cloud computing technology for efficient workload distribution and reduces the need for energy-intensive local hardware.
- Environmental Policies and Regulations: Adopt and comply with strict environmental standards for data centre operations and other technology infrastructure. Commit to achieving carbon neutrality through initiatives such as carbon offsets and investment in green projects.
- Education and Awareness: running awareness campaigns about the importance of energy efficiency and environmentally friendly practices among metaverse users and developers. Provides training and certification for data centre developers and operators on best practices in energy management and green technologies.

- Research and Innovation: invest funds in research and development of new, more environmentally friendly and energy efficient technologies to support the metaverse. Collaborate with universities and research institutions to develop innovative solutions that reduce the environmental impact of metaverse technologies.
- Ecosystem Approach: building a sustainable ecosystem in the metaverse that encourages environmentally friendly practices and supports green initiatives. Implement transparency in reporting energy use and environmental impacts, and communicate sustainable efforts to stakeholders.

These steps will help ensure that metaverse development can occur in a sustainable and environmentally friendly manner.

Overcoming potential limitations related to technological obsolescence and the need for continuous updates and innovation requires a proactive and planned approach as follows:

- Modular and Scalable Architecture: develop systems and applications with a modular architecture that allows individual components to be updated or replaced without disrupting the entire system. Design scalable solutions so they can adapt to changing needs and workloads over time.
- Regular Updates and Upgrades: implement a regular update schedule for software and hardware, ensuring all components remain current with the latest technology. Uses an automatic update system to ensure devices and applications always run on the latest version without requiring manual intervention.
- Sustainable Innovation: investing funds continuously in research and development to create new innovations that can be integrated into existing systems. Collaborate with startups, universities and research institutions to encourage innovation and application of the latest technology.
- Backward Compatibility: ensures that newly developed technologies remain compatible with older versions to minimize obsolescence and ensure a smooth transition. Uses open APIs that enable easy integration with new and old technologies, as well as extending the functionality of existing systems.
- Technology Asset Management: create and maintain a complete inventory of all technology assets in use, including hardware and software, to monitor age and need for updates. Perform life cycle analysis for each technology asset to plan updates and replacements before obsolescence occurs.
- Continuous Development (DevOps): adopt DevOps methodology to improve collaboration between development and operations teams, enabling rapid updates and fixes as well as continuous implementation of innovation.

Implement ongoing testing to ensure each update and upgrade does not introduce new problems.

- Community-Based Approach: using and contributing to open-source projects that enable community collaboration and continuous updates from the global developer community. Build user forums and communities that can provide feedback and ideas for further improvement and innovation.
- Training and Skills Development: provide regular training for staff and users to ensure they understand and can utilize new technology effectively. Develop skills development programs to ensure internal teams always have the latest skills in the latest technologies.
- Technology Policy and Strategy: develop a long-term technology strategy that includes plans for continuous renewal and innovation. Carry out regular evaluations and assessments of the technology used to identify the need for updates and innovation.

By adopting these strategies, organizations can overcome potential limitations related to technology obsolescence and ensure that systems and applications remain relevant and can be upgraded as technology advances. This will enable continued innovation and maintain competitiveness in an ever-evolving technological environment.

Managing a dynamic online environment in the metaverse requires a comprehensive strategy for content moderation, user security, and preventing malicious activity. The following are strategies that can be carried out:

- Content Moderation: uses a combination of manual human moderation and AI-based automated technology to effectively monitor and control content. AI can be used to detect harmful behavioural patterns and content that violates policies. Provide comprehensive training for human moderators on policies, moderation tools, and handling sensitive situations. Develop algorithms that can detect and filter dangerous content in real-time, such as hate speech, violence and illegal content. Provide an easily accessible mechanism for users to report inappropriate content or behaviour. This report must be followed up quickly and transparently.
- User Security: implement strong authentication methods such as multi-factor authentication (MFA) to ensure that only authorized users can access their accounts. Maintain user data privacy by implementing end-to-end encryption and a strict privacy policy. Educate users about good cybersecurity practices, such as recognizing phishing and keeping accounts secure. Creates a safe zone within the metaverse where users can interact without fear of harassment or harmful behaviour.

- Malicious Activity Prevention: uses real-time monitoring and analysis technology to detect and prevent malicious activity before it becomes a major problem. Develop an early warning system that can detect and report suspicious or dangerous activity to moderators for follow-up. Collaborate with law enforcement and security agencies to address criminal activities occurring within the metaverse. Implement strict policies and sanctions for violations, including temporary or permanent bans for violators.
- Safety-Enabled Design: designing metaverse environments that are inherently safe and inclusive, reducing opportunities for dangerous behaviour. Provides tools for users to control their interactions, such as blocking or reporting other users, and managing their privacy.
- Policies and Regulations: develop and communicate clear and firm content policies to all users. Ensure compliance with local and international regulations regarding cybersecurity, data privacy and consumer protection.
- Community Collaboration and Participation: work with cybersecurity and privacy experts to continuously improve security measures. Encourage community participation in maintaining security and content moderation through incentive and user reward programs that help maintain a healthy metaverse environment.
- Continuous Evaluation and Improvement: conduct regular evaluations of content moderation and user security policies and practices to ensure their effectiveness. Collect and analyze feedback from users to identify areas requiring improvement.

By adopting this comprehensive and layered approach, potential limitations related to content moderation, user security, and preventing malicious activity in the metaverse can be addressed. This will help create a safe, healthy and inclusive virtual environment for all users.

Overcoming potential limitations related to intellectual property (IP) protection and resolving digital ownership disputes in the metaverse requires a comprehensive and multidimensional approach. Here are some strategies taken:

- Use of Blockchain Technology: uses blockchain technology for registration and verification of digital assets, so that each asset has a clear and unchangeable audit trail. Implement smart contracts to automate transactions and ensure compliance with IP agreements, including royalty payments and usage licenses.
- Digital Identification and Ownership System: uses NFTs to identify and prove unique ownership of digital assets, ensuring that the original creator

and current owner can be verified. Attach verified metadata to digital assets to document information about the creator, creation date, and copyright.

- Strong Policies and Regulations: develop a clear and comprehensive regulatory framework for IP protection in the metaverse, including rules on registration, rights enforcement, and dispute resolution. Promote harmonization of international IP regulations to ensure consistent protection across jurisdictions.
- Platform for Dispute Resolution: establish a special virtual court or arbitration forum to handle IP disputes in the metaverse quickly and efficiently. Develop alternative dispute resolution mechanisms such as online mediation and arbitration that are accessible to all metaverse users.
- User Education and Awareness: launch an awareness campaign to educate users and creators about the importance of protecting IP and their rights in the metaverse. Provides best practices guidance for creators and users on how to protect and respect IP in the metaverse.
- Collaboration with Service Providers: ensure that metaverse platforms have strong IP policies and mechanisms to address IP violations. Implement procedures for removing content that violates IP quickly and efficiently, including notification and takedown processes.
- Enhanced Technology Security: develop and implement anti-counterfeiting technology to protect digital assets from duplication and fraud. Uses encryption and data security technology to protect IP information from unauthorized access and use.
- Legal and Enforcement Support: provides specialized legal services to assist digital asset creators and owners in protecting their IP rights. Cooperate with law enforcement and regulatory agencies to deal effectively with IP violations and provide appropriate sanctions.
- Development of an IP-Supporting Ecosystem: encouraging community initiatives to support IP protection, such as working groups and associations focused on IP issues in the metaverse. Provide incentives for platforms and users who comply with IP policies, such as access to premium features or rewards.

The steps above will create a safe and fair environment for creators and users of digital assets, as well as encourage innovation and creativity in the virtual world.

To maintain sustainable virtual economic growth in the metaverse, there are several strategies that can be considered:

- Regulations and Policies: implementing appropriate regulations to govern economic activities in the metaverse can help prevent exploitation and maintain long-term sustainability. This includes consumer protection, data protection, and fair rules for all business actors.

- Digital Infrastructure: ensure reliable and secure digital infrastructure, including fast internet networks and reliable computing platforms. This is important to support growth and business activities in the metaverse.
- Economic Balance: ensuring that the economy in the metaverse is not only profitable for the big few, but also provides fair opportunities for various parties, including individual users, small business owners, and the creative community.
- Security and Privacy: protects user security and privacy from threats such as identity theft, fraud, and other cyber-attacks that can disrupt economic activities and affect user trust.
- Sustainable Innovation: Driving sustainable innovation in metaverse technologies, including the development of environmentally friendly and energy efficient solutions. This is important considering the environmental impact of large digital infrastructures.
- Education and Awareness: Increase understanding and awareness of the metaverse among users and business owners, including about best practices to ensure long-term economic sustainability.

By combining a thoughtful regulatory approach, innovative technology, and awareness of sustainability challenges, economic growth in the metaverse can be sustained in the long term.

Future Metaverse Difficulties consist of security and privacy, regulation and compliance, inclusivity and accessibility, inclusivity and accessibility, digital inequality, and integration and interoperability. User security and privacy, including the possibility of fraud, identity theft, and cyberattacks, is a significant concern in the metaverse. To ensure metaverse security, a major priority will be the protection of personal information and digital identities. Global regulation of the metaverse will provide difficulties in creating uniform laws and regulations. To safeguard users and encourage creativity in the metaverse, the right restrictions are required. All users, especially those with financial or physical constraints, must have equitable and inclusive access to the metaverse. Obtaining the gadgets, content, and digital infrastructure needed to engage in the metaverse is one of these issues. One major issue is tackling digital inequality globally, which includes things like inadequate infrastructure, restricted internet access, and the inability to pay for the gadgets and services required to access the metaverse. Coordinating and integrating various current platforms, gadgets, and technologies while guaranteeing smooth interoperability will be a difficulty for the metaverse. By doing this, the user experience will be guaranteed to be responsive and uniform throughout the metaverse. Metaverses have the potential to revolutionize human interaction, cooperation, and invention in virtual environments by tackling existing issues and leveraging new trends (Kim, 2021; Krishnamurthy & Trivedi, 2023).

1.4 CONCLUSION

The metaverse's growth is a fascinating adventure with the potential to transform virtual environments and how we work, engage, and enjoy ourselves. In the future, the metaverse offers ever-more immersive, inclusive, and diverse experiences thanks to constantly developing technologies and boundless human innovation. But as things advance, there are obstacles that must be overcome for the metaverse to flourish and offer its users the most advantages possible. Here are some lessons learned about the metaverse's future development, tendencies, and obstacles. The metaverse is still developing, going from a basic virtual world to a dynamic, intricate ecosystem. In order to build experiences that are more responsive and lifelike, cutting-edge technologies like virtual reality, blockchain, artificial intelligence, and quantum computing are used upcoming trends in the metaverse. The growth of virtual economies, more social engagement, technological innovation, and enhanced security and privacy are some of the anticipated trends in the metaverse. Furthermore, industry collaboration, training, and education will find a significant home in the metaverse. Future metaverse concerns include digital inequality, user security and privacy, compliance with regulations, accessibility, and inclusivity, as well as cross-platform integration and interoperability. To build responsive, safe, and equitable virtual environments, governments, businesses, and communities must work together to overcome these obstacles. Metaverses have the potential to play a major role in our lives in the future by leveraging promising trends and overcoming current obstacles. This would allow us to engage in limitless virtual world cooperation, innovation, and connectivity.

1.5 ACKNOWLEDGEMENT

This research work is supported by National Science and Technology Council (NSTC), Taiwan Grant No. NSTC112-2221-E-468-008-MY3 and NSTC 113-2811-E-468-002.

REFERENCES

Abiodun, M. K., Awotunde, J. B., Ogundokun, R. O., Misra, S., Adeniyi, E. A., Arowolo, M. O., & Jaglan, V. (2021). Cloud and big data: a mutual benefit for organization development. Journal of physics: conference series, Akhtar, N., Kerim, B., Perwej, Y., Tiwari, A., & Praveen, S. (2021). A comprehensive overview of privacy and data security for cloud storage. *International Journal of Scientific Research in Science, Engineering and Technology.*

Anas, S., Badhusha, I., Zaheema, O., Faseela, K., & Shelly, M. (2017). Cloud based automated irrigation and plant leaf disease detection system using an android application. 2017 International conference of Electronics, Communication and Aerospace Technology (ICECA), Anne Craig-Lees, M., Harris, J., & Maulana, A. E. (2013). Websites and revisiting behaviour: An investigation of the relative role of predictors. *Marketing Intelligence & Planning*, 31(3), 250–271.

Arnarson, H., Yu, H., Olavsbråten, M. M., Bremdal, B. A., & Solvang, B. (2023). Towards smart layout design for a reconfigurable manufacturing system. *Journal of Manufacturing Systems*, 68, 354–367. 10.1016/j.jmsy.2023.03.012

Bibri, S. E. (2018). The IoT for smart sustainable cities of the future: An analytical framework for sensor-based big data applications for environmental sustainability. *Sustainable Cities and Society*, 38, 230–253. 10.1016/j.scs.2017.12.034

Bigliani, R., Segalotto, J., & Gallotti, G. (2016). Shaping a New Battleground in the IoT Era: Highlights from the 2016 IDC Pan–European Utilities Executive Summit. *IDC Energy Insights, June.*

Bilgihan, A., Okumus, F., Nusair, K., & Bujisic, M. (2014). Online experiences: Flow theory, measuring online customer experience in e-commerce and managerial implications for the lodging industry. *Information Technology & Tourism*, 14(1), 49–71. 10.1007/s40558-013-0003-3

Bouziane, I., Belmokadem, H., & Moussaoui, M. (2023). A Review of Formal Security Verification of Common Internet of Things (IoT) Communication Protocols. 2023 7th IEEE Congress on Information Science and Technology (CiSt), Carrasco, M. D. O., & Chen, P.-H. (2021). Application of mixed reality for improving architectural design comprehension effectiveness. *Automation in Construction*, 126, 103677.

Chen, C., Zhang, K. Z., Gong, X., Zhao, S. J., Lee, M. K., & Liang, L. (2017). Understanding compulsive smartphone use: An empirical test of a flow-based model. *International Journal of Information Management*, 37(5), 438–454. 10.1016/j.ijinfomgt.2017.04.009

Chen, L., Chen, H.-C., Li, Z., & Wu, Y. (2017). A fusion approach based on infrared finger vein transmitting model by using multi-light-intensity imaging. *Human-centric Computing and Information Sciences*, 7(1), 1–17. 10.1186/s13673-017-0110-9

Cruz, P., Salo, J., Muñoz-Gallego, P., & Laukkanen, T. (2010). Heavy users of e-banking and Customer Experience Management: Evidences on intrinsic motivation. *International Journal of Electronic Business*, 8(2), 187–209. 10.1504/IJEB.2010.032093

Diène, B., Rodrigues, J. J., Diallo, O., Ndoye, E. H. M., & Korotaev, V. V. (2020). Data management techniques for Internet of Things. *Mechanical Systems and Signal Processing*, 138, 106564. 10.1016/j.ymssp.2019.106564

Dong, W., Wang, Y., & Qin, J. (2023). An empirical study on impulse consumption intention of livestreaming e-commerce: The mediating effect of flow experience and the moderating effect of time pressure. *Frontiers in Psychology*, 13, 1019024. 10.3389/fpsyg.2022.101902436726500

Dwivedi, Y. K., Hughes, L., Baabdullah, A. M., Ribeiro-Navarrete, S., Giannakis, M., Al-Debei, M. M., Dennehy, D., Metri, B., Buhalis, D., Cheung, C. M., Conboy, K., Doyle, R., Dubey, R., Dutot, V., Felix, R., Goyal, D. P., Gustafsson, A., Hinsch, C., Jebabli, I., & Wamba, S. F. (2022). Metaverse beyond the hype: Multidisciplinary perspectives on emerging challenges, opportunities, and agenda for research, practice and policy. *International Journal of Information Management*, 66, 102542. 10.1016/j.ijinfomgt.2022.102542

Guo, Z., Xiao, L., Van Toorn, C., Lai, Y., & Seo, C. (2016). Promoting online learners' continuance intention: An integrated flow framework. *Information & Management*, 53(2), 279–295. 10.1016/j.im.2015.10.010

Gupta, B. B., & Quamara, M. (2020). An overview of Internet of Things (IoT): Architectural aspects, challenges, and protocols. *Concurrency and Computation*, 32(21), e4946. 10.1002/cpe.4946

Hooker, R., Wasko, M., Paradice, D., Teigland, R., & Hofacker, C. (2019). Beyond gaming: Linking flow, brand attitudes, and purchase intent in realistic and emergent three-dimensional virtual environments. *Information Technology & People*, 32(6), 1397–1422. 10.1108/ITP-11-2017-0407

Hsu, C.-L., Chen, W.-X., & Le, T.-V. (2020). An autonomous log storage management protocol with blockchain mechanism and access control for the Internet of Things. *Sensors (Basel)*, 20(22), 6471. 10.3390/s2022647133198399

Huang, S., Zhang, X., Chen, N., Ma, H., Zeng, J., Fu, P., Nam, W.-H., & Niyogi, D. (2022). Generating high-accuracy and cloud-free surface soil moisture at 1 km resolution by point-surface data fusion over the Southwestern US. *Agricultural and Forest Meteorology*, 321, 108985. 10.1016/j.agrformet.2022.108985

Huynh-The, T., Gadekallu, T. R., Wang, W., Yenduri, G., Ranaweera, P., Pham, Q.-V., da Costa, D. B., & Liyanage, M. (2023). Blockchain for the metaverse: A Review. *Future Generation Computer Systems*, 143, 401–419. 10.1016/j.future.2023.02.008

Ioannidis, S., & Kontis, A.-P. (2023). Metaverse for tourists and tourism destinations. *Information Technology & Tourism*, 25(4), 483–506. 10.1007/s40558-023-00271-y

Kaluarachchi, T., Reis, A., & Nanayakkara, S. (2021). A review of recent deep learning approaches in human-centered machine learning. *Sensors (Basel)*, 21(7), 2514. 10.3390/s2107251433916850

Kim, J. (2021). Advertising in the metaverse: Research agenda. *Journal of Interactive Advertising*, 21(3), 141–144. 10.1080/15252019.2021.2001273

Krishnamurthy, R., & Trivedi, S. (2023). Understanding User Experience in the Metaverse. In *Handbook of Research on Consumer Behavioral Analytics in Metaverse and the Adoption of a Virtual World* (pp. 204–222). IGI Global. 10.4018/978-1-6684-7029-9.ch010

Li, J., Herdem, M. S., Nathwani, J., & Wen, J. Z. (2023). Methods and applications for Artificial Intelligence, Big Data, Internet of Things, and Blockchain in smart energy management. *Energy and AI*, 11, 100208. 10.1016/j.egyai.2022.100208

Liu, C.-C. (2017). A model for exploring players flow experience in online games. *Information Technology & People*, 30(1), 139–162. 10.1108/ITP-06-2015-0139

Mahnke, R., Benlian, A., & Hess, T. (2015). A grounded theory of online shopping flow. *International Journal of Electronic Commerce*, 19(3), 54–89. 10.1080/10864415.2015.1000222

Nah, F. F.-H., Eschenbrenner, B., DeWester, D., & Park, S. R. (2010). Impact of flow and brand equity in 3D virtual worlds. [JDM]. *Journal of Database Management*, 21(3), 69–89. 10.4018/jdm.2010070103

Park, B., Ahn, S., & Kim, H. (2010). Blogging: Mediating impacts of flow on motivational behavior. *Journal of Research in Interactive Marketing*, 4(1), 6–29. 10.1108/17505931011033533

Putra, K. T., Chen, H.-C., Ogiela, M. R., Chou, C.-L., Weng, C.-E., & Shae, Z.-Y. (2021). Federated compressed learning edge computing framework with ensuring data privacy for PM2. 5 prediction in smart city sensing applications. *Sensors (Basel)*, 21(13), 4586. 10.3390/s2113458634283140

Simon, F. (2010). The experiential aspects of online search information for new customers to a website. *Canadian Journal of Administrative Sciences/Revue Canadienne des Sciences de l'Administration, 27*(4), 292-305.

Valinatajbahnamiri, M., & Siahtiri, V. (2021). Flow in computer-mediated environments: A systematic literature review. *International Journal of Consumer Studies*, 45(4), 511–545. 10.1111/ijcs.12640

Zeinab, K. A. M., & Elmustafa, S. A. A. (2017). Internet of things applications, challenges and related future technologies. *World Scientific News*, 67(2), 126–148.

Zhu, P., Liu, Z., Li, X., Jiang, X., & Zhu, M. X. (2023). The influences of livestreaming on online purchase intention: Examining platform characteristics and consumer psychology. *Industrial Management & Data Systems*, 123(3), 862–885. 10.1108/IMDS-07-2022-0430

Chapter 2
AI-Driven Security Measures in Virtual Worlds

Akshat Gaurav
Ronin Institute, USA

Kwok Tai Chui
Hong Kong Metropolitan University, Hong Kong

ABSTRACT

This chapter discusses the implementation of AI-driven security measures in virtual worlds, which presumes advanced approaches and solutions implemented to protect users' interactions and the environment of the virtual space in general. The topics discussed within the chapter are related to AI applications in security issues, machine solutions for the purpose of intrusion detection, and behavioral biometrics for user authentication. Each of the topics include practical scenarios connected to IDS and behavioral biometrics. Information on content moderation, policy enforcement, and future directions is given as well. The chapter provides solid proof that metaverse security should include AI-driven solutions through effective case studies, while performance expectations are discussed in each case.

INTRODUCTION TO AI IN METAVERSE SECURITY

In recent years, the integration AI in metaverse has been a hot topic under research and discussions. As researchers work through the challenges of using AI within metaverse to protect our digital lives, mul- tiple studies bring discussion on deploying AI technologies for security benefits. One of the important dimensions

DOI: 10.4018/979-8-3693-3824-7.ch002

which is recommended in all these studies has been basically AI for trustworthy transac- tions, robust statistics security, and privacy inside through, every other referential metaverse (Ibrahim, 2024). This synergy of AI and blockchain enabled optimization envisions that secure transaction can be carried out by the metaverse while transacting in highly secured manner thus addressing critical security concerns specific to digital realm (Radanliev, 2024).

Furthermore investigated by researchers are the usage of AI-driven solutions to meet metaverse security issues. Studies on AI-based solutions including security of penetration-oriented problems and addressing likely hacking threats (Park et al., 2022) have been under progress. Furthermore underlined as a fundamental component of security solutions is the capacity of real-time AI algorithms to react and control cyber events in the metaverse (Rejeb et al., 2023).

Moreover, blockchain and artificial intelligence technologies improve the security of digital assets within the metaverse. Emphasizing the need of appropriate data management procedures, researchers

Table 1. Key Areas of AI Application in Metaverse Security

Key Area	Description
Trustworthy Transactions	Ensuring secure and transparent transactions within the metaverse using AI and blockchain
Robust Statistics	Using AI to gather and analyze statistical data to identify and mitigate security threats
Privacy Protection	Implementing AI to safeguard user privacy and manage sensitive information securely
Penetration Security	Addressing potential penetration threats using AI solutions
Cyber Situation	Management Utilizing AI algorithms to manage and respond to cyber threats within the metaverse
Asset Security	Enhancing the security of digital assets with ma- chine learning techniques
Intelligent Healthcare	Developing AI-powered healthcare systems in the metaverse for better health management
Semantic Detection	Enabling semantic detection for secure and smooth social interactions within the metaverse

have noted that using machine learning methods may help security of metaverse assets be enhanced (Ghantous, 2022) This integration of blockchain and artificial intelligence not only helps to build intel- ligent healthcare systems within the metaverse but also improves cyber security, where virtual reality and physical world merge to promote interactions between people and humans (G. Wang et al., 2022).

In the metaverse, all kinds of social interaction and AI technologies are present that make it possible for semantic detection, knowledge modeling, avatar coordination. For such a smooth and secure inter- action within the social metaverse, these capabilities would be imperative in order to overcome certain information processing challenges as well coordination amongst users (Y. Wang et al., 2023). In ad- dition, a metaverse is where people can interact using AI and blockchain technology to perform various activities beyond the physical world (Saerang, 2023)

Cybersecurity remains a critical concern in the AI-based metaverse, with researchers highlighting existing security challenges and the need for robust cybersecurity measures. Studies have underscored the importance of addressing cybersecurity risks associated with AI models, distributed systems, and network vulnerabilities to establish a trustworthy metaverse environment (Pooyandeh et al., 2022). Additionally, the future of cybersecurity in the metaverse is intertwined with advancements in AI, machine learning, and quantum computing, necessitating a proactive approach to mitigate evolving cyber threats (Jim, 2023).

As the metaverse continues to evolve, the development of AI-powered applications becomes essen- tial for enhancing user experiences and ensuring security. Researchers have proposed frameworks that

Table 2. Security Challenges in AI-Based Metaverse

Security Challenge	Description
Cybersecurity Risks	Addressing risks associated with AI models, distributed systems, and network vulnerabilities
Data Privacy	Ensuring data privacy through advanced AI techniques
Network Vulnerabilities	Mitigating network vulnerabilities using AI-driven security measures
Ethical AI Implementation	Ensuring ethical use of AI in the metaverse to prevent misuse and ensure user trust
Evolution of Cyber Threats	Proactively addressing evolving cyber threats with advancements in AI and machine learning

leverage AI technologies such as natural language processing, computer vision, and machine learn- ing to support metaverse application development (Zhu, 2022). By fusing blockchain and AI with the metaverse, researchers aim to create a secure environment where users can interact and train AI models without compromising data privacy (Q. Yang et al., 2022).

AI-POWERED INTRUSION DETECTION SYSTEMS

In the area of digital security, the utilization of AI-based Intrusion Detection Systems (IDS) has gar- nered significant attention due to their ability to enhance threat detection and response mechanisms. Various studies have explored the application of intelligent algorithms in IDS to detect and prevent cyber-attacks effectively. The general architecture of AI-based intrusion detection is presented in Fig- ure 1. For instance, khodaie et al. (2014) emphasized the role of intelligent algorithms in detecting attacks within IDS, highlighting the importance of capturing and analyzing inbound and outbound traf- fic to identify unusual patterns. This underscores the significance of leveraging AI to enhance the capabilities of IDS in monitoring network traffic and identifying potential security breaches.

Furthermore, the integration of artificial intelligence technology in IDS has produced creative ideas like SensorWebIDS, which blends web mining methods with anomaly and use detection for online environments. Proposed SensorWebIDs as a complete IDS system encompassing network sensors, log diggers, and audit engines to evaluate web request parameters for intrusion detection. This shows how to use artificial intelligence algorithms to harvest and evaluate data from many sources thereby enhancing the security posture of digital systems. Moreover, multi-stage IDS systems have been investigated to strengthen security in the Internet of Things (IoT) environment.

Figure 1. AI-Based Intrusion Detection System

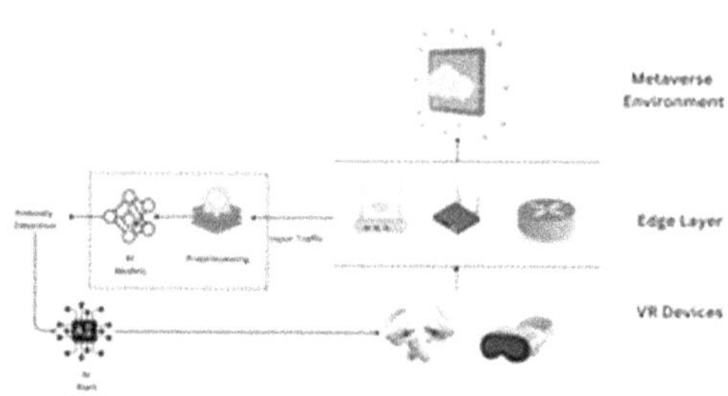

Within the framework of cyber-attack prediction, Jain & Waoo (2023) presented an Artificial Neural Network (ANN) method for using IDS to project cyber-attacks. Their work concentrated on using ANN to monitor network behavior and instantly spot any intrusions. This emphasizes how aggressively artificial intelligence-based IDS identify and reduce cyber risks before they become more serious.

Furthermore suggested to identify and handle different kinds of hostile assaults is the employment of Information Security Protection Systems grounded on real-time intrusion detection. Emphasizing the need of intrusion detection technology in actively spotting and stopping harmful activity within computer networks, Qian & Zhang (2017); Gupta et al. (2022) This emphasizes the critical role artificial intelligence-powered IDS plays in preserving digital infrastructure security and integrity.

Within the industrial IoT space, the creation of intrusion security detection systems grounded on cutting-edge algorithms such Multi-layer Perception Networks and LightGBM has become very im- portant. Deng (2024); Law et al. (2021) examined the creation of Industrial IoT Intrusion Security Detection Systems to use machine learning methods for improving intrusion detection capability in industrial environments. This shows how customized AI technology may be to handle certain security issues in industrial IoT settings.

Moreover, the meeting of blockchain technology with artificial intelligence has opened the path for creative metaverse security solutions. MetaCIDS, a privacy-preserving collaborative IDS for the metaverse that combines blockchain and online federated learning to fight threats like DoS assaults and malware injections, was presented by Truong & Le (2023); Gupta & Narayan (2021). This draws attention to how well artificial intelligence-powered IDS may strengthen virtual environment security systems.

BEHAVIORAL BIOMETRICS FOR USER AUTHENTICATION

An original method to improve security and user verification procedures is behavioral biometrics for metaverse user authentication. A subclass of biometric authentication, behavioral biometrics seeks to authenticate persons by means of distinct patterns in their behavior. This approach belongs to the larger area of biometric authentication, which include face recognition and physiological biometrics like fingerprints. Conversely, behavioral biometrics authenticate users by means of voluntary motions including gait, keyboard dynamics, and other behavioral characteristics (Papaioannou et al., 2023). Figures 2 show many types of behavioral biometrics.

Figure 2. Type of Behavioral Biometrics

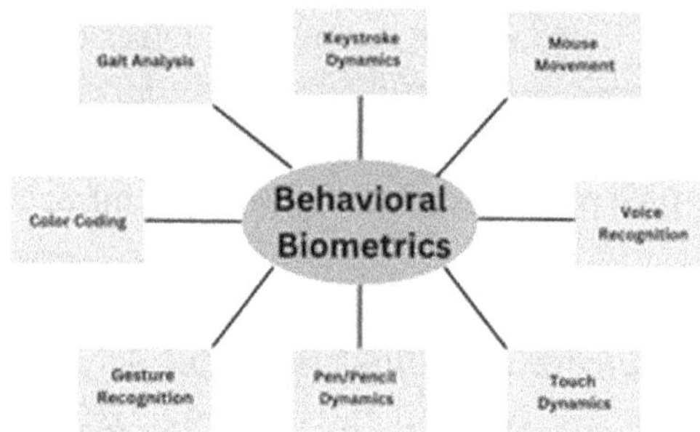

Behavioral biometrics-based authentication's constant character is one of its main benefits as it en- ables continuous user verification all while user engagement with digital systems. Hu et al. (2022) underlined the possibility of smooth and safe user authentication by use of behavioral biometrics cap- tured by built-in sensors in cellphones, therefore guaranteeing ongoing authentication. This constant authentication method fits very well the dynamic and interactive character of the metaverse, in which users interact in real-time across many activities.

K. Yang et al. (2022) suggested a safe authentication framework based on behavioral biometrics to allow dynamic authentication by continually collecting and analyzing user biometrics in order to solve the problems related with static biometrics. By adjusting to consumers' evolving behavioral patterns, this dynamic authentication procedure improves security and reduces the metaverse environment's dan- gers of illegal access and identity fraud.

Furthermore, the seamless and user-friendly login experience provided by behavioral biometrics in user authentication is Emphasizing the ease and adaptability of behavioral biometrics for develop- ing seamless and continuous user authentication systems, Buriro et al. (2021); Gaurav et al. (2021) highlighted their fit for uses needing continuous user verification. This user-centric approach fits the objective of giving the metaverse's seamless and immersive user experience.

Papaioannou et al. (2022); Yadav & Gupta (2021) underlined in the framework of risk-based user authentication the possibilities of risk-based user authentication using behavioral biometrics to raise authentication dependability while maintaining usability, so balancing security and user experience. Using behavioral biometrics, this risk-based method creates a more strong authentication mechanism that changes with metaverse environment danger level.

Moreover, the integration of behavioral biometrics with cutting-edge technologies like blockchain helps to improve metaverse user authentication security even more. Behavioral biometrics combined with blockchain technology can help to create tamper-proof, transparent, and more safe user authenti- cation systems. Truong & Le (2023); Agrawal (2020) presented MetaCIDS, a collaborative IDS for the metaverse integrating blockchain and online federated learning to improve security measures, includ- ing behavioral biometrics-based authentication. This connection guarantees avatars' traceability and boosts the general security system in virtual surroundings.

DEEP LEARNING FOR REAL-TIME THREAT DETECTION

Deep learning has increased skills to instantly recognize and react to security concerns, therefore be- coming a useful tool for real-time threat detection in the metaverse. Table 3 shows the relative perfor- mance of deep learning IDS with conventional ones. By use of deep learning algorithms in threat de- tection systems, companies may enhance their cybersecurity defenses and protect virtual environ- ments from developing hazards. Deep learning networks' scalability and efficiency for real-time threat detec- tion have been underlined by research by Zamri et al. (2023); Gupta et al. (2009), therefore stressing their fit for dynamic settings such as the metaverse. Organizations may rapidly and precisely identify threats using deep learning skills to safeguard digital assets and metaverse user interactions.

Dealing with the difficulties presented by new and unidentified cyber-attacks depends on the real- time threat identification using deep learning. Roshan (2024); Raj et al. (2023) examined the per- formance of machine learning and deep learning-based network intrusion detection systems in seeing security risks but emphasized the continuous difficulties in spotting fresh threats in real-time. Deep learning algorithms enable their adaptation to shifting threat environments and efficient anomaly de- tection by excelling at automatically learning sophisticated patterns from data. In the metaverse, where dangers might arise in many unexpected ways, this flexibility is very vital.

Moreover, integrating deep learning methods into intrusion detection systems (IDS) has great po- tential to improve the identification of sophisticated cyberat- tacks. Kalnawat (2024); Gurjot & Yash (2024) underlined how well deep learning approaches could automatically extract complex character- istics from data, therefore enabling efficient feature extraction and anomaly detection for important infrastruc- ture. Deep learning models may improve the capacity of IDS in spotting complex threats inside the metaverse environment by independently learning patterns and representations from data.

Deep learning models have shown great accuracy and efficiency in the setting of real-time detection of certain cyber threats such malware injections and cross-site scripting assaults. Using deep learning, Ayo et al. (2021); Vajratiya (2024) presented a framework for real-time detection of cross-site scripting

Table 3. Comparison of Traditional IDS and Deep Learning-Enhanced IDS

Feature	Traditional IDS	Deep Learning-Enhanced IDS
Detection Speed	Moderate	High
Accuracy	Varies, often lower	High
Ability to Handle Complex Patterns	Limited	Excellent
Adaptability to New Threats	Low	High
Maintenance Requirements	High	Moderate
Real-Time Processing Capability	Moderate	High
False Positive Rate	Higher	Lower
Learning from Data	Rule-based, manual updates	Automatic, continuous learning

assaults on cloud-based online applications, therefore highlighting the possibilities of this method for exact threat identification. Organizations may proactively find and stop harmful activity in real-time by using deep learning algorithms, therefore protecting important metaverse digital assets.

Furthermore, the combination of deep learning with cutting-edge technologies such as federated learning and blockchain promises to improve metaverse real-time threat detection capacities. Using federated learning, Priyadarshini (2024) presented a deep learning model for anomaly detection of IoT cyber-attacks in smart cities, therefore highlighting the possibilities of creative solutions to immediately address threats. Using federated learning and split learning approaches helps companies improve the accuracy and efficiency of virtual environment threat detection systems.

AI IN CONTENT MODERATION AND POLICY ENFORCEMENT

Representing in Figure 3, AI is a major player in content moderation and policy enforcement within the metaverse as it provides creative methods to control user-generated material and guarantee a secure and inclusive virtual environment. Advanced artificial intelligence technologies are necessary for effective and efficient content moderation as traditional moderation techniques typically fail to keep pace with the enormous amount of material produced in the metaverse (Sanghvi, 2023). Metaverse systems using artificial intelligence algorithms may examine user behavior, preferences, and interactions to provide customized content and experiences specifically for each (Ibrahim, 2024).

Finding hate speech and improper material is one of the main uses for artificial intelligence in content control. Using blockchain technology to augment content moderation efforts, et al. pre- sented "MetaHate," an AI-based hate speech detection system for safe online gaming in the metaverse (Sanghvi, 2023). This AI-powered system shows how well sophisticated technology may be used to enforce rules and preserve a polite and inclusive virtual community.

Figure 3. AI-Based Content Monitoring

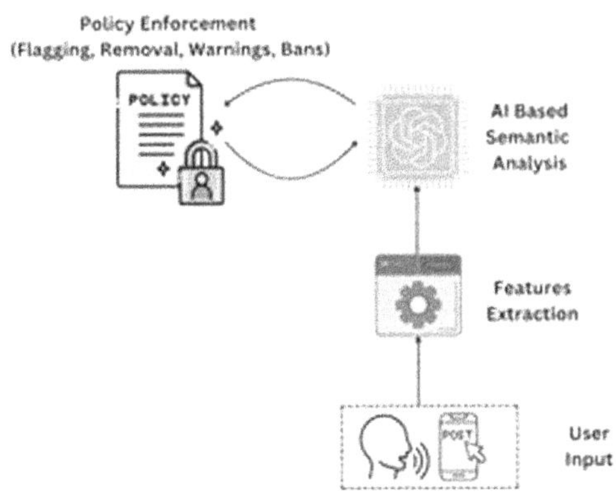

Furthermore, artificial intelligence systems may examine interactions and user behavior to find any policy infractions and apply metaverse community norms. Real-time user activity monitoring by AI systems helps them to identify abnormalities, flag improper material, and take early action to guarantee platform policy compliance (Amzat, 2023). By means of this proactive policy enforcement, a safe and friendly virtual community is promoted as well as a pleasant user experience is preserved.

AI technologies are very important in identifying and fixing destructive activities in the metaverse in the framework of stopping cyberbullying and guaranteeing user safety. With AI-powered technologies enabling content moderation and enforcement operations, Upadhyay et al. (2023) underlined the need of applying clear regulations, educational campaigns, and community-building activities to combat cyberbullying. Using artificial intelligence for real-time monitoring and intervention helps platforms build a safe atmosphere that discourages abusive conduct and supports good relationships.

Moreover, the combination of artificial intelligence with blockchain technology provides improved responsibility and openness in policy execution and content regulation. Platforms may guarantee trans- parent, consistent, and resistant to manipulation moderation judgments by using blockchain for im- mutable record-keeping and AI for content analysis (Sanghvi, 2023). Blockchain and artificial intelligence together improve user confidence in the metaverse ecosystem and help to reinforce the integrity of content moderation systems.

Regarding ethical issues with metaverse development, underlined the need of following rules such the Santa Clara Principles in the United States and the Digital Services Act (DSA) in the European Union for content moderation and policy implementation. (Boni, 2023). By automating content moder- ation procedures and guaranteeing that user-generated material conforms with ethical and legal norms, artificial intelligence technology may help platforms in complying with regulatory obligations.

FUTURE TRENDS IN AI-DRIVEN METAVERSE SECURITY

Future advances in AI-driven metaverse security are expected to change the digital terrain and provide creative ideas to guarantee a secure, improved cybersecurity policies, and immersive virtual environ- ment. Establishing a metaverse that gives user security and safety depends on the deployment of strong and user-centric frameworks(Sharma, 2024). Future metaverse security is predicted to be shaped in great part by the integration of powerful AI technologies into content filtering, threat identification, and policy execution.

Furthermore integration of AI with blockchain technologies showing promise for enhancing the se- curity of digital assets within the metaverse. Ghantous (2022) underlined the advantages of combining blockchain and artificial intelligence to effectively manage data and thereby enhance the security of metaverse digital assets. Organizations may build safe and open systems for controlling digital assets and guaranteeing data integrity in virtual environments or metaverse by using blockchain technology and machine learning techniques.

AI-driven techniques are efficient in spotting the security attacks in the metaverse, thereby address- ing real-time threat detection. Emphasizing the need of artificial intelligence in meeting the compu- tational demands of immersive AI-driven applications and 3D worlds, **?** presented the computational challenges and solutions driven by cloud-edge-end computation frameworks to enable the metaverse on resource-constrained edge devices. AI technologies and edge computing let companies guarantee effective data processing in the metaverse ecosystem and improve real-time threat detection capacity.

Moreover, developments in attack detection, privacy protection, and threat intelligence will define the metaverse security powered by AI going forward. Emphasizing the part AI in improving security measures and user experiences, Ahsani et al. (2023) presented the activation of many AI-driven technologies like gesture recognition, computer vision, and emotional understanding in the metaverse. Using AI skills for anomaly detection and behavior analysis helps companies to proactively find and fix security risks in real-time, therefore guaranteeing a safe and dependable metaverse environment for users.

By allowing intelligent privacy protection, the combination of edge computing technologies with AI-driven IoT solutions can improve metaverse security. Future developments in AI-driven IoT focuses on privacy protection and intelligent data analysis within the AI-driven IoT environment, therefore enabling increased security measures in the metaverse. Organizations may maintain data confidence and secure private data in virtual environments by using AI for intelligent data analysis and privacy protection.

CONCLUSION

This chapter has demonstrated that AI can be useful in intrusion detection, user authentication real-time threat detection, and content moderation for virtual worlds like metaverse. Advances in AI techniques not just help security but also work to solve concerns around privacy as well as ethical issues. With the new developments expected in virtual experiences, it is imperative that forward-looking AI-powered security solutions are deployed to detect threats and build user confidence within the Metaverse. Re- search on this area will continue and it is expected that the next generation of technological advances in the games industry can help to shape safer communities within virtual worlds.

REFERENCES

Agrawal, D. P. (2020). *Recent advances in security, privacy, and trust for internet of things (iot) and cyber-physical systems (cps)*. Chapman and Hall/CRC.

Ahsani, V., Rahimi, A., Letafati, M., & Khalaj, B. (2023). Unlocking metaverse-as-a-service the three pillars to watch: privacy and security, edge computing, and blockchain. doi: /arxiv.2301.0122110.48550

Amzat, O., & Adewojo, A. A. (2023). Metaverse-infused academic libraries: A glimpse into the future. *Library Hi Tech News*, 40(10), 17–19. 10.1108/LHTN-10-2023-0187

Ayo, I., Abasi, W., Adebiyi, M., & Alagbe, O. (2021). An implementation of real-time detection of cross-site scripting attacks on cloud-based web applications using deep learning. *Bulletin of Electrical Engineering and Informatics*, 10(5), 2442–2453. 10.11591/eei.v10i5.3168

Boni, M. (2023). Ethical challenges related to the metaverse development - hypothesis. 10.5772/intechopen.1001112

Buriro, A., Gupta, S., Yautsiukhin, A., & Crispo, B. (2021). Risk-driven behavioral biometric-based one-shot-cum-continuous user authentication scheme. *Journal of Signal Processing Systems for Signal, Image, and Video Technology*, 93(9), 989–1006. 10.1007/s11265-021-01654-2

Deng, Y. (2024). Design of industrial iot intrusion security detection system based on lightgbm feature algorithm and multi-layer perception network. *Journal of Cyber Security and Mobility*, 327-348. 10.13052/jcsm2245-1439.1327

Gaurav, A., Gupta, B. B., Hsu, C.-H., Castiglione, A., & Chui, K. T. (2021). Machine learning technique for fake news detection using text-based word vector representation. In *Computational data and social networks: 10th international conference, csonet 2021, virtual event, november 15– 17, 2021, proceedings 10* (pp. 340–348). 10.1007/978-3-030-91434-9_33

Ghantous, N. (2022). Empowering metaverse through machine learning and blockchain technology: a study on machine learning, blockchain, and their combination to enhance metaverse. 10.14293/S2199-1006.1.SOR-.PP97BSJ.v1

Gupta, B. B., Joshi, R. C., & Misra, M. (2009). Defending against distributed denial of service attacks: issues and challenges. *Information Security Journal: A Global Perspective, 18*(5), 224–247.

Gupta, B. B., Mamta, , Mehla, R., Alhalabi, W., & Alsharif, H. (2022). Blockchain technology with its application in medical and healthcare systems: A survey. *International Journal of Intelligent Systems*, 37(11), 9798–9832. 10.1002/int.23014

Gupta, B. B., & Narayan, S. (2021). A key-based mutual authentication framework for mobile con- tactless payment system using authentication server. [JOEUC]. *Journal of Organizational and End User Computing*, 33(2), 1–16. 10.4018/JOEUC.20210301.oa1

Gurjot, S., & Yash, R. (2024). *Advancements in metaverse gaming technologies.* https://insights2techinfo.com/advancements-in-metaverse-gaming-technologies/. (Accessed: 2024-01-30)

Hu, M., Zhang, K., You, R., & Tu, B. (2022). Relative attention-based one-class adversarial autoen- coder for continuous authentication of smartphone users. doi: /arxiv.2210.1681910.48550

Ibrahim, A. (2024). The role of artificial intelligence in the metaverse. *Arts and Design Studies*. Retrieved from https://api.semanticscholar.org/CorpusID:269580244

Jain, J., & Waoo, A. (2023). An artificial neural network technique for prediction of cyber-attack using intrusion detection system. *Journal of Artificial Intelligence Machine Learning and Neural Network*, 33-42. 10.55529/jaimlnn.32.33.42

Jim, J., Hosain, M. T., Mridha, M. F., Kabir, M. M., & Shin, J. (2023). Toward trustworthy metaverse: Advancements and challenges. *IEEE Access : Practical Innovations, Open Solutions*, 11, 118318–118347. 10.1109/ACCESS.2023.3326258

Kalnawat, A. (2024). Safeguarding critical infrastructures: machine learning in cybersecurity. *E3s Web of Conferences, 491*, 02025. 10.1051/e3sconf/202449102025

Khodaie, F., Jamali, M., & Farazan, A. (2014). The Use of Intelligent Algorithms to Detect Attacks in Intrusion Detection System. International Journal of computer Applications Technology and Research, 9(3), 579-584.

Law, K. M., Ip, A. W., Gupta, B. B., & Geng, S. (2021). *Managing iot and mobile technologies with innovation, trust, and sustainable computing*. CRC Press. 10.1201/9780367822750

Papaioannou, M., Mantas, G., Essop, A., Sucasas, V., Aaraj, N., & Rodriguez, J. (2022). Risk estima- tion for a secure & usable user authentication mechanism for mobile passenger id devices. 10.1109/CAMAD55695.2022.9966915

Papaioannou, M., Pelekoudas-Oikonomou, F., Mantas, G., Serrelis, E., Rodriguez, J., & Fengou, M.-A. (2023). A survey on quantitative risk estimation approaches for secure and usable user authentication on smartphones. *Sensors (Basel)*, 23(6), 2979. 10.3390/s2306297936991690

Park, W., Siddiqui, I., & Qureshi, N. (2022). Ai-enabled grouping bridgehead to secure penetration topics of metaverse. *Computers, Materials & Continua*, 73(3), 5609–5624. 10.32604/cmc.2022.030235

Pooyandeh, M., Han, K., & Sohn, I. (2022). Cybersecurity in the ai-based metaverse: A survey. *Applied Sciences (Basel, Switzerland)*, 12(24), 12993. 10.3390/app122412993

Priyadarshini, I. (2024). Anomaly detection of iot cyberattacks in smart cities using federated learning and split learning. *Big Data and Cognitive Computing*, 8(3), 21. 10.3390/bdcc8030021

Qian, Y., & Zhang, S. (2017). Information security protection system based on intrusion detection from real time angle. 10.2991/mecs-17.2017.93

Radanliev, P. (2024). Integrated cybersecurity for metaverse systems operating with artificial intel- ligence, blockchains, and cloud computing. *Frontiers in Blockchain*, 7, 1359130. Advance online publication. 10.3389/fbloc.2024.1359130

Raj, B., Gupta, B. B., Yamaguchi, S., & Gill, S. S. (2023). *Ai for big data-based engineering applica- tions from security perspectives*. CRC Press. 10.1201/9781003230113

Rejeb, A., Rejeb, K., & Treiblmaier, H. (2023). Mapping metaverse research: Identifying future research areas based on bibliometric and topic modeling techniques. *Information (Basel)*, 14(7), 356. 10.3390/info14070356

Roshan, K., & Zafar, A. (2024). ae-integrated: Real-time network intrusion detection with apache kafka and autoen- coder. *Concurrency and Computation*, 36(11), e8034. Advance online publication. 10.1002/cpe.8034

Saerang, A. (2023). Accounting profession in metaverse era - nft. *E3s Web of Conferences, 426*, 02052. 10.1051/e3sconf/202342602052

Sanghvi, H., Bhavsar, R., Hundlani, V., Gohil, L., Vyas, T., Nair, A., Desai, S., Jadav, N. K., Tanwar, S., Sharma, R., & Yamsani, N. (2023). metahate: Ai-based hate speech detection for secured online gaming in metaverse using blockchain. *Security and Privacy*, 7(2), e343. Advance online publication. 10.1002/spy2.343

Sharma, S., Singh, J., Gupta, A., Ali, F., Khan, F., & Kwak, D. (2024). User safety and security in the metaverse: A critical review. *IEEE Open Journal of the Communications Society*, •••, 1–1. 10.1109/OJCOMS.2024.3397044

Truong, V., & Le, L. (2023). Metacids: privacy-preserving collaborative intrusion detection for meta- verse based on blockchain and online federated learning. 10.36227/techrxiv.23183642.v1

Upadhyay, U., Kumar, A., Sharma, G., Gupta, B., Alhalabi, W., Arya, V., & Chui, K. (2023). Cyberbullying in the metaverse. *Journal of Global Information Management*, 31(1), 1–25. 10.4018/JGIM.325793

Vajratiya, V. (2024). *Metaverse in healthcare domain.*https://insights2techinfo.com/metaverse-in-healthcare-domain/. (Accessed: 2024-01-30)

Wang, G., Badal, A., Jia, X., Maltz, J., Mueller, K., Myers, K., Niu, C., Vannier, M., Yan, P., Yu, Z., & Zeng, R. (2022). Development of metaverse for intelligent healthcare. *Nature Machine Intelligence*, 4(11), 922–929. 10.1038/s42256-022-00549-636935774

Wang, Y., Zhou, S., & Yan, M. (2023). Social metaverse: challenges and solutions. doi: /arxiv.2301.1022110.48550

Yadav, K., & Gupta, B. (2021). *Clustering based rewarding algorithm to detect adversaries in feder- ated machine learning based iot environment. In 2021 ieee international conference on consumer electronics (icce).*

Yang, K., Zhang, Z., Tian, Y., & Ma, J. (2022). A secure authentication framework to guarantee the traceability of avatars in metaverse. doi: /arxiv.2209.0889310.48550

Yang, Q., Zhao, Y., Huang, H., Xiong, Z., Kang, J., & Zheng, Z. (2022). Fusing blockchain and ai with metaverse: A survey. *IEEE Open Journal of the Computer Society*, 3, 122–136. 10.1109/OJCS.2022.3188249

Zamri, N. F. M., Tahir, N. M., Ali, M. S. M., Ashar, N. D. K., & Abd Almisreb, A. (2023). Real time snatch theft detection using deep learning networks. *Journal of Advanced Research in Applied Sciences and Engineering Technology*, 31(1), 79–89.

Zhu, H. (2022). Metaaid: a flexible framework for developing metaverse applications via ai technology and human editing. doi: /arxiv.2204.0161410.48550

Chapter 3
Delving Into the Metaverse:
Understanding Its Foundations, Dynamics, and Future Prospects

Brij B. Gupta
Department of Computer Science and Information Engineering, Asia University, Taichung, Taiwan

Kwok Tai Chui
Hong Kong Metropolitan University, Hong Kong

Akshat Gaurav
Ronin Institute, USA

Konstantinos Psannis
University of Macedonia, Greece

ABSTRACT

This Chapter explores the concept of Metaverse in depth, focussing on its development from the virtual worlds to modern digital environments. In particular, it describes the architecture of Metaverse, emphasising the layers that allow for present-day virtual experiences and the main concepts that inform them. Moreover, the chapter examines several technological advancements, namely, blockchain, VR/AR, and AI, that play significant roles in the functioning and improvement of Metaverse and the interaction of its users. Furthermore, the introduction discusses the ecological perspective of Metaverse, focussing on the people and the developers as well as the way they interact through the platforms.

DOI: 10.4018/979-8-3693-3824-7.ch003

1. INTRODUCTION

Metaverse which was initially considered as the extension of virtual world, now considered as the important part of digital world. With the development of the latest AR/VR and AI technologies metaverse is considered as the network of virtual words (Figure 1)(D´ıaz-Chieng, Auza-Santiv´an˜ez, and Castillo 2022; Gupta et al. 2024a; D´ıaz-Chieng, Auza-Santiv´an˜ez, and Castillo 2022; Gupta et al. 2024b).

Latest technologies like cloud computing, AI, Deep learning, AR/VR, helps to bridge the gap between the real world and virtual world. These technologies plays a important role in the development of complex concepts of metaverse (Feng, Wang, and Su 2022; Deveci et al. 2022; Feng, Wang, and Su 2022; Deveci et al. 2023; Hasan 2023; Xie et al. 2023).

There is a wide application of metaverse in different areas like education sector, metaverse can help the students from different background to learn and understand the new concepts and topics. Currently, metaverse is focusing to improve the learning experience of gen z with the help of AI and AR/VR technologies. This development

Figure 1. Metaverse and Real world

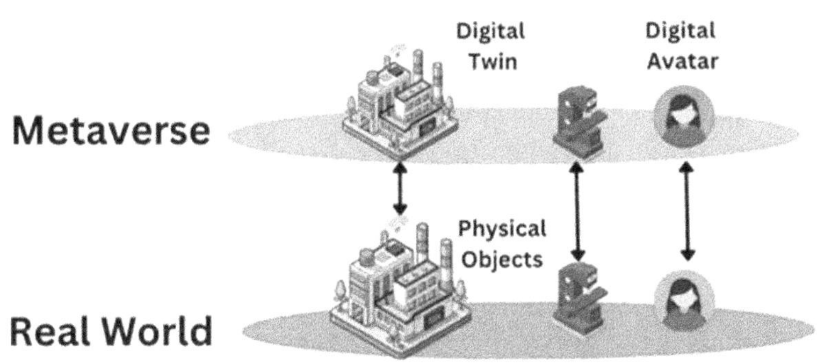

shows the application of metaverse in different area of life(Tlili et al. 2022; Gupta et al. 2023; Tlili et al. 2022; Gokasar et al. 2023; Agrawal 2020).

Moreover, the Metaverse is not the place only for entertainment and education: from a broader perspective, it also touches upon some areas of our lives, which are related to mental health and well-being (Paquin et al. 2023; Gupta, Gaurav, and Chui 2023; Paquin et al. 2023; Sethi 2022). The Metaverse can be defined as persistent virtual worlds in either virtual or augmented reality. The types of the activities it supports are as diverse as social networking and games and shopping and work. In other words, it is the wide variety of applications available in the Metaverse that defines the fact that it is not just a virtual world anymore. From a less profound perspective, the notion of the Metaverse still touches upon a seemingly restricted aspect of people's daily routine, in which education, adult learning, and knowledge of new disciplines exist on the periphery.

Additionally, the integration of Internet of Things (IoT) and blockchain technologies has further enriched the Metaverse experience by enabling decentralized management and ownership within the virtual domain (Din 2023; Singh, Malhotra, and Sharma 2022). This integration allows for real-time reflections of physical world events, weather changes, and architectural landscape evolution within the Metaverse, enhancing its temporal congruity with the real world (Din 2023). The incorporation of IoT and blockchain technologies showcases how the Metaverse has evolved to incorporate elements of real-world dynamics and interactions.

Moreover, human-avatar interaction plays a pivotal role in shaping the Metaverse experience, emphasizing the network of shared virtual environments where individuals can engage and interact through their avatars (Lam et al. 2022; Gupta and Panda 2022). This interaction fosters a sense of presence and connectivity within the Meta- verse, contributing to its evolution as a space for socialization, collaboration, and immersive experiences (Lam et al. 2022; Gaurav 2023). The emphasis on human-avatar interaction underscores the evolution of the Metaverse as a platform for interpersonal engagement and virtual communication.

In essence, the term "Metaverse" has evolved from a concept of a singular virtual world to a complex network of interconnected digital spaces, influenced by advancements in technology, changing educational needs, diverse applications in daily life, and enhanced user interactions. The evolution of the Metaverse reflects a dynamic progression towards a more immersive, interconnected, and multifunctional digital environment that continues to shape how individuals interact, learn, and engage within virtual environment.

Table 1. Key Milestones in the Evolution of Virtual Worlds

Year	Virtual World	Key Features	Impact on Meta-verse Develop ment
1978	MUD1	Text-based, multi-player	Foundation for online multiplayer games
1997	Ultima Online	Graphical inter-face, persistent world	Pioneered MMORPGs
2003	Second Life	User-generated content, virtual economy	Introduced virtual real estate and commerce
2004	World of Warcraft	Immersive, large-scale MMORPG	Popularized online gaming

2. THE EVOLUTION OF VIRTUAL WORLDS

The history of virtual worlds has several milestones. They have shaped the develop- ment and outcomes of many technologies and their incorporation into different fields. Virtual worlds have started as multi-user online computer gaming environments, and the first spaces that have been created were considered to be the 3D spaces (Warbur- ton 2009). Such worlds have been aimed at the creation of a gaming and entertaining place where people would be able to interact and feel in such worlds. Later, various applications related to education, socializing, or commerce were integrated into the concept of virtual worlds.

One significant milestone in the history of virtual worlds is the emergence of com- plex social relationships and virtual communities within these digital spaces (Andrade 2009). Virtual worlds evolved into powerful social platforms that attracted millions of users worldwide, leading to the formation of intricate social networks and economies within these virtual environments. This shift highlighted the transformative potential of virtual worlds in fostering human interaction and collaboration on a global scale.

The exponential growth of virtual worlds in recent years has been accompanied by a surge in user engagement and the development of virtual economies (Patterson et al. 2019). With over a billion people accessing virtual environments and the virtual goods market reaching billions of dollars, virtual worlds have become integral to modern society, offering diverse opportunities for socialization, entertainment, and economic activities. This widespread adoption underscores the increasing relevance and impact of virtual worlds in the digital age.

Technological advancements have played a crucial role in shaping the evolution of virtual worlds, particularly in the realm of augmented reality (AR) and virtual reality (VR) (Billinghurst, Clark, and Lee 2015). From early research in the 1960s to the widespread availability of AR and VR technologies in the 2010s, there has been a continuous progression towards seamlessly integrating real and virtual worlds. These advancements have enhanced the immersive nature of virtual worlds, blurring the boundaries between physical and digital realities and opening up new possibilities for interactive experiences.

Virtual worlds have also gained traction as platforms for delivering simulation-based educational experiences to students (Chodos et al. 2012). Educational institutions have increasingly turned to virtual worlds as tools for enhancing learning outcomes and providing students with immersive and engaging learning environments. The use of virtual worlds in education represents a significant milestone in leveraging technology to transform traditional teaching methods and cater to diverse learning styles.

Moreover, the integration of virtual worlds with Internet of Things (IoT) technologies has further expanded the capabilities and functionalities of these digital envi- ronments (Han et al. 2022). By synchronizing virtual worlds with IoT services and data, users can access a wide range of virtual services, from driver training simulations to online route optimization for smart goods delivery. This integration highlights the potential of virtual worlds to simulate real-world scenarios and provide users with interactive and dynamic experiences.

In the context of mental health and well-being, virtual worlds have emerged as promising tools for clinical psychology and eHealth interventions (Gorini et al. 2008). The use of 3D virtual worlds in clinical psychology offers new avenues for delivering therapeutic interventions and behavioral treatments, leveraging the immersive and in- teractive nature of virtual environments to support individuals with substance-related disorders and other mental health challenges. This application of virtual worlds under- scores their versatility in addressing diverse societal needs and promoting well-being. Overall, the history of virtual worlds is characterized by a series of transformative milestones that have redefined how individuals interact, learn, and engage in digital environments. From their early origins in online gaming to their current role as multi- faceted platforms for socialization, education, and commerce, virtual worlds continue to evolve and shape the way we experience and navigate the digital landscape.

3. ARCHITECTURE OF THE METAVERSE

The architecture of the Metaverse consists of several core components that work to- gether to provide a seamless virtual experience. These components include cloud-based systems for avatar physics emulation and graphics rendering computation, which are fundamental in modern Metaverse architectures dhelim et al. (2022). By utilizing cloud computing, these systems can efficiently manage the complex computational tasks necessary for rendering realistic graphics and simulating avatar physics, crucial for creating immersive virtual environments.

Another vital component of the Metaverse architecture is the integration of various technologies to enable real-time and seamless interaction between the physical world and the virtual world (Kalita and Gurusamy 2022). This integration encompasses technologies such as sensing, communication, and high-computing devices collaborat- ing to synchronize physical and virtual experiences within the Metaverse. By effectively blending these technologies, users can participate in interactive and dynamic virtual environments that replicate real-world interactions.

Moreover, the Metaverse architecture incorporates elements of extended reality (XR) and the Internet of Things (IoT) to enhance connectivity and interoperabil- ity between virtual and physical environments (Guan, Irizawa, and Morris 2022). By integrating XR technologies like virtual reality (VR) and augmented reality (AR) with IoT devices, the Metaverse can establish hyper-connected environments that offer users a seamless and immersive experience. This integration facilitates the smooth interaction of virtual agents and objects between virtual and physical spaces, enriching the overall user experience.

Figure 2. Metaverse Architecture

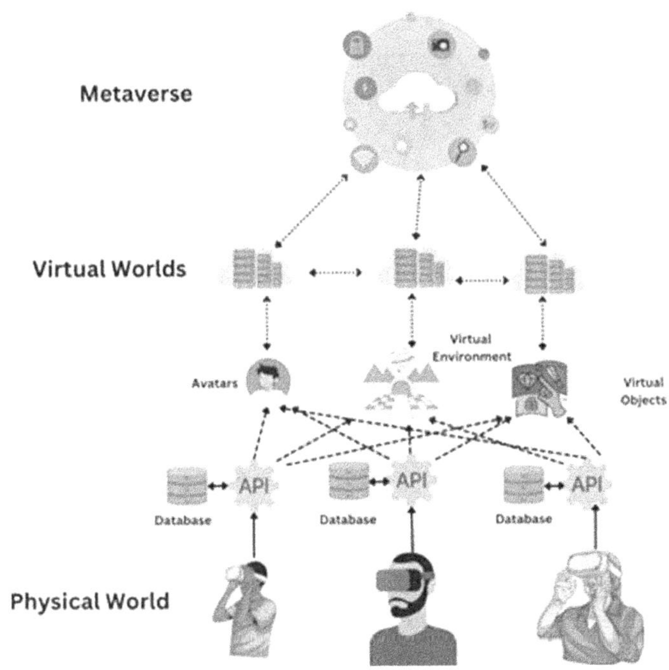

Additionally, the Metaverse architecture includes distributed and dynamic reputation-based resource allocation systems to optimize resource utilization and en- hance user experiences (Kalita and Gurusamy 2022). These systems utilize reputation mechanisms to allocate resources efficiently, ensuring users have access to the necessary computing resources and services in real-time. By dynamically al- locating resources based on reputation scores, the Metaverse can deliver a seamless and responsive vir- tual environment for users.

Furthermore, the Metaverse architecture incorporates digital twin technologies to develop intelligent design solutions for engineering applications within virtual envi- ronments (Stary 2023). Digital twins enable the modeling and simulation of physical entities in the virtual space, allowing for the validation of system behaviors and the optimization of implementation architectures. By leveraging digital twins, the Meta- verse can improve the design and operation of complex systems, providing users with a more immersive and interactive experience.

Moreover, the Metaverse architecture integrates user experience (UX) design princi- ples to ensure that virtual environments are intuitive, engaging, and satisfying for users (Delgado 2022). Through collaboration with developers, designers, and users, Meta- verse architects can create user-centric experiences that cater to the diverse needs and expectations of users. This focus on UX design helps enhance user engagement and satisfaction within the virtual environment, contributing to a seamless and immersive virtual experience.

4. KEY TECHNOLOGIES BEHIND THE METAVERSE

4.1. *Blockchain*

To establish secure and decentralized virtual economies within the Metaverse, blockchain technology is essential. Blockchain technology offers an open and decen- tralized solution for building sustainable virtual economies and constructing value sys- tems within the Metaverse (Wang et al. 2023). By integrating blockchain technology into the Metaverse architecture, virtual economies can benefit from decentralization, transparency, and immutability, enhancing the overall security and trustworthiness of economic transactions (Aloqaily et al. 2023). Blockchain technology ensures the secu- rity and transparency of virtual economies within the Metaverse by securely storing and sharing data through a decentralized system that uses cryptography to safeguard information (Zhong 2023).

Figure 3. User Authentication in Metaverse by Blockchain

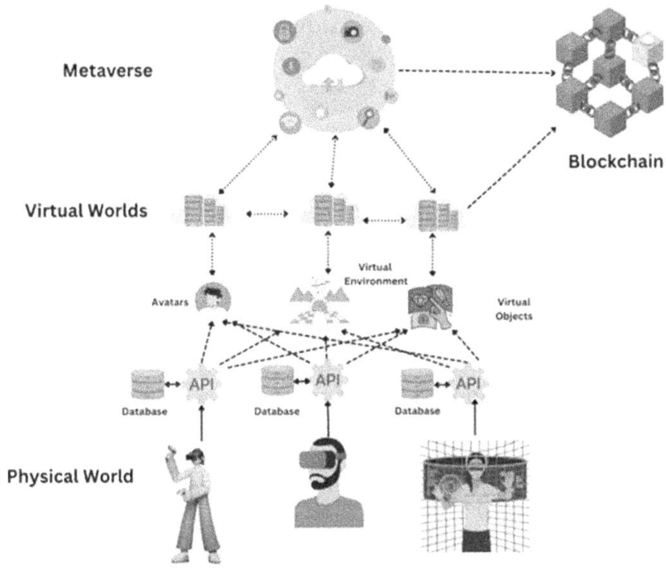

Moreover, blockchain technology enables the creation of decentralized autonomous organizations (DAOs) within the Metaverse, redefining resources, production relations, and organizational structures in a revolutionary manner (Qin et al. 2023). By lever- aging blockchain technology, DAOs can operate autonomously and transparently, fa- cilitating decentralized decision-making processes and governance structures within virtual economies. The integration of blockchain technology into the Metaverse ar- chitecture ensures trustless social and economic interactions through decentralized consensus mechanisms (Momtaz 2022).

Furthermore, blockchain technology supports the creation of non-fungible tokens (NFTs) within the Metaverse, allowing for the validation of digital assets and the es- tablishment of secure asset ownership (Sutikno 2023). NFTs enable the tokenization of virtual assets, such as digital art and collectibles, providing a secure and decentral- ized mechanism for trading and ownership verification within virtual economies. The use of blockchain technology in conjunction with NFTs enhances the authenticity and provenance of digital assets, fostering a vibrant and secure virtual economy.

Additionally, blockchain technology facilitates secure semantic communication for AI-generated content in the Metaverse, enabling decentralized data circulation and economic activities between virtual service providers and edge devices (Lin et al. 2023). By leveraging blockchain-aided semantic communication, the Metaverse can establish secure and efficient data flows, supporting economic transactions and content sharing in a decentralized manner. The integration of blockchain technology into the Metaverse architecture ensures reliable distributed computing, enabling secure and efficient data processing and communication within virtual environments (Jiang et al. 2021).

4.2. *Virtual Reality (VR) and Augmented Reality (AR)*

Virtual Reality (VR) and Augmented Reality (AR) are essential technologies for pro- viding immersive experiences within the Metaverse. These technologies play a crucial role in creating realistic and engaging virtual environments that enable users to in- teract with digital content in a more intuitive and immersive manner (Yang et al. 2022). VR technology allows users to be fully immersed in a computer-generated en- vironment, providing a sense of presence and enabling interaction with virtual objects and spaces as if they were real (Yang et al. 2022). On the other hand, AR overlays digital information onto the physical world, enhancing the user's perception of reality by adding virtual elements to their surroundings (Calabr`o et al. 2022).

The integration of VR and AR technologies in the Metaverse enhances the user experience by creating a seamless blend of virtual and physical worlds, enabling users to engage with digital content in a more natural and intuitive way (Rostami and Maier 2022). These technologies enable multi-sensory interactions with virtual environments, digital objects, and other users, fostering a sense of presence and immersion within the virtual space (Rostami and Maier 2022). By leveraging VR and AR, the Metaverse can offer users a more interactive and engaging experience that transcends traditional forms of digital interaction.

Furthermore, VR and AR technologies are instrumental in enabling users to create and customize their virtual identities, known as avatars, within the Metaverse (Gonzalez-Argote 2022). Avatars serve as digital representations of users in the vir- tual world, allowing them to navigate and interact with the environment and other users (Gonzalez-Argote 2022). VR technology enables users to embody their avatars and engage in immersive experiences, while AR can enhance the user's physical surroundings by overlaying digital information onto the real world, creating a seamless integration of virtual and physical elements (Gonzalez-Argote 2022).

Figure 4. VR/AR Technology and Metaverse

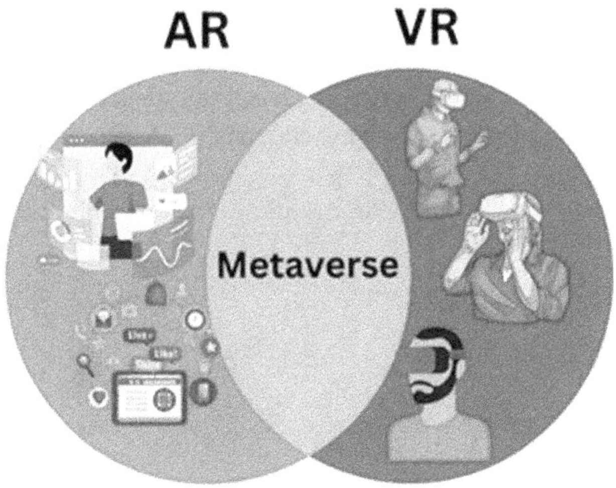

Moreover, VR and AR technologies facilitate real-time communication and collab- oration within the Metaverse, enabling users to interact with each other and share experiences in virtual environments (Samala et al. 2023). These technologies support social interactions, virtual meetings, and collaborative activities, allowing users to connect with others and engage in shared experiences regardless of physical distance (Samala et al. 2023). By leveraging VR and AR for communication and collaboration, the Metaverse fosters a sense of community and connectivity among users, enhancing the overall immersive experience.

Additionally, VR and AR technologies are essential for enhancing the visual- ization and representation of data within the Metaverse, enabling users to explore and in- teract with complex information in a more intuitive and engaging manner (Kabanda, Chipfumbu, and Chingoriwo 2022). These technologies provide users with interactive and immersive data visualization tools, allowing them to analyze and interpret data in a virtual environment (Kabanda, Chipfumbu, and Chingoriwo 2022). By leveraging VR and AR for data visualization, the Metaverse can offer users a more dynamic and interactive way to engage with information and make informed decisions.

4.3. *Artificial Intelligentce*

Artificial Intelligence (AI) is instrumental in the development of intelligent virtual en- vironments and Non-Player Characters (NPCs) within the Metaverse. By utilizing AI technologies, virtual environments can be enriched with intelligent behaviors, adap- tive responses, and lifelike interactions, thereby enhancing the immersive experience for users (Zhang et al. 2022). AI aids in creating intelligent NPCs that can serve as tu- tors, tutees, or peers in educational settings, offering personalized support, simulation, and decision-making services (Zhang et al. 2022). These intelligent NPCs improve the educational experience by providing tailored guidance, facilitating interactive learning scenarios, and fostering engagement within virtual environments.

The incorporation of AI in the Metaverse allows for the establishment of Intelligent

Figure 5. Metaverse System for AR Services

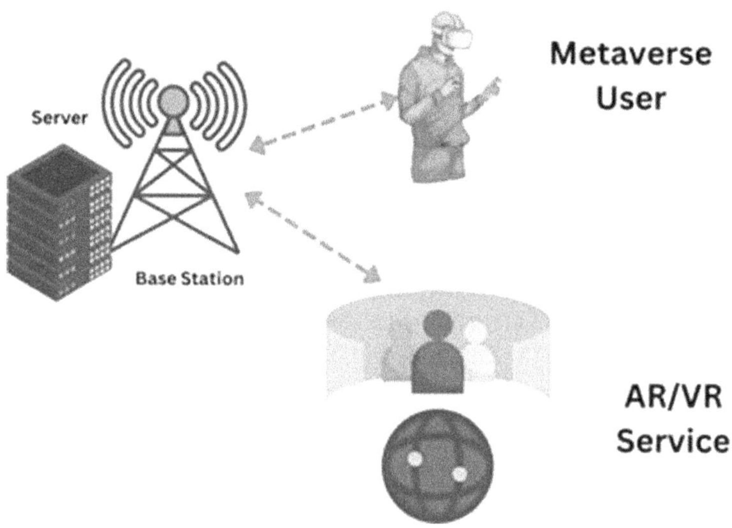

Table 2. AI Applications in the Metaverse

Application	Description	Benefits
Intelligent NPCs	AI-driven characters that interact with users	Increased engagement and realism
Content Generation	AI-created environ- ments and objects	Personalized and scal- able content
User Personalization	Tailored experiences based on user data	Improved user satisfac- tion

Virtual Environments (IVE), where AI-powered agents and creatures engage with users in dynamic and responsive ways (Grech, Mehnen, and Wodehouse 2023). AI technologies empower these virtual environments to simulate realistic interactions, adjust to user preferences, and deliver personalized experiences tailored to individual users or user groups (Grech, Mehnen, and Wodehouse 2023). By integrating AI into the design of virtual environments, developers can enhance interactivity, engagement, and realism, resulting in a more immersive and dynamic user experience.

Furthermore, AI contributes to the creation of automated virtual learning experiences through NPCs, enabling the development of interactive and adaptive educational content within the Metaverse (Mitra 2023). AI-driven NPCs can facilitate virtual learn- ing scenarios, offer feedback, and customize learning materials based on user interac- tions, preferences, and performance (Mitra 2023). These intelligent NPCs enhance the educational value of virtual environments by providing personalized learning experi- ences, encouraging active engagement, and supporting knowledge acquisition across various subject areas.

Moreover, AI technologies facilitate the generation of intelligent agents and avatars within the Metaverse, enhancing the realism and interactivity of virtual environments (Gonzalez-Argote 2022). AI-powered non-player characters can exhibit lifelike behav- iors, respond to user inputs, and engage in dynamic interactions, creating a more immersive and engaging virtual experience (Gonzalez-Argote 2022). By incorporating AI-driven NPCs into virtual environments, developers can enrich the social dynamics, storytelling, and gameplay experiences within the Metaverse, fostering a more interactive and engaging user experience.

Additionally, AI contributes to the development of intelligent virtual assistants and guides within the Metaverse, providing users with personalized support, recommenda- tions, and assistance in navigating virtual environments (Agrati 2023). These AI-driven virtual assistants can offer real-time guidance, address user queries, and facilitate inter- actions within the virtual space, enhancing the user experience and promoting seamless engagement within the Metaverse (Agrati 2023). By leveraging AI technologies for vir- tual assistance, users can access personalized support and information, enhancing their overall interaction and immersion within virtual environments.

5. THE METAVERSE ECOSYSTEM: USERS, DEVELOPERS, AND PLATFORMS

5.1. *User*

In the Metaverse, users exhibit diverse motivations for participating in the virtual environment. These motivations include:

- Entrepreneurial Users: Some users are motivated by financial gain, creative ex- pression, and the opportunity to build virtual businesses Lee (2024).

- Exploration and Enjoyment Seekers: Another group is primarily motivated by exploring the virtual world and enjoying unique experiences (Lee, Lee, and Bae 2023).
- Socializers and Entertainment Seekers: Users seek social connections, entertain- ment, and leisure activities (Sowmya et al. 2023).
- Educational Users: Some users leverage the Metaverse for learning, training, and skill development (Jeon 2023).
- Creative and Artistic Users: Users express themselves, create digital content, and engage in artistic endeavors (Oh 2023).
- Gamers and Interactive Experience Seekers: Users seek immersive game-play, social interactions, and dynamic experiences (Li and Yu 2023).
- Innovators and Early Adopters: Some users explore new technologies and inno- vative digital experiences (Ferrigno 2023).
- Professional and Business Users: Users leverage the Metaverse for network-ing, marketing, and economic opportunities (Adetayo et al. 2023).

5.2. *Developers*

Developers are essential in the creation and maintenance of the Metaverse, contribut- ing to the development of immersive virtual environments and ensuring the smooth operation of digital experiences within this intricate ecosystem. Their responsibilities include designing, developing, and optimizing various aspects of the Metaverse, such as virtual worlds, interactive experiences, applications, and tools. The skills required for developers in the Metaverse encompass a wide range of technical expertise and creative capabilities.

A fundamental aspect of Metaverse development is programming, where develop-ers utilize their skills in computer science, mathematics, and software engineering to create innovative virtual environments and interactive experiences Gonzalez-Argote (2022). Proficiency in programming languages like C++, Python, JavaScript, and Unity is crucial for constructing immersive virtual worlds, designing interactive elements, and

implementing complex functionalities within the Metaverse. Developers also need a strong grasp of algorithms, data structures, and computational logic to enhance per- formance and user experiences in virtual environments.

In addition to programming skills, developers in the Metaverse must have knowl-edge of emerging technologies such as blockchain, artificial intelligence, and virtual reality to improve the functionality and interactivity of virtual environments (Nguyen et al. 2022). Understanding blockchain technology is vital for establishing secure and decen- tralized systems within the Metaverse, ensuring data integrity, transaction security, and digital asset management. Proficiency in artificial intelligence enables developers to create intelligent NPCs, virtual assistants, and interactive elements that enhance user engagement and immersion in virtual environments.

Furthermore, developers working in the Metaverse often utilize development frame- works and tools like Unity, Unreal Engine, and Blender to design and construct virtual worlds, 3D models, animations, and interactive elements (Duan 2021). These tools of- fer developers the necessary resources to create visually appealing and interactive virtual environments, allowing them to bring their creative visions to life within the Metaverse. Proficiency in using these development tools is crucial for streamlining the development process, optimizing performance, and delivering high-quality virtual experiences to users.

Moreover, developers in the Metaverse must stay informed about industry standards, best practices, and emerging trends in Metaverse technology to ensure continuous improvement and innovation of virtual environments (Rawat and Alami 2023). By adhering to Metaverse architecture guidelines, standards, and requirements, devel- opers can design scalable, interoperable, and immersive virtual experiences that meet the evolving needs of users. Continuous learning and professional development are es- sential for developers to adapt to new technologies, tools, and methodologies in the rapidly evolving Metaverse landscape.

5.3. *Platforms*

To compare major Metaverse platforms like Decentraland, Roblox, and Meta's Horizon Worlds in terms of features and strengths, we can draw insights from the available literature.

Table 3. Comparison of Major Metaverse Platforms

Platform	Unique Features	Business Model
Decentraland	Decentralized, user-owned virtual land	Land sales, transaction fees
Roblox	User-generated games and experiences	In-app purchases, subscriptions
Horizon Worlds	VR-based social experiences	Platform fees, advertising

- Decentraland:- Decentraland is a decentralized virtual reality platform that al- lows users to create, trade, and interact with their digital content (S¨aks 2022).
    - It offers users the opportunity to establish virtual businesses, engage in economic activities, and create unique digital experiences (S¨aks 2022).

- Decentraland leverages blockchain technology for secure asset management and decentralized systems within the platform (Weinberger 2023).
- The platform provides users with the ability to create, trade, and interact with digital assets using non-fungible tokens (NFTs) (Agarwal et al. 2022).
- Decentraland is known for its focus on digital real estate, virtual commerce, and immersive experiences (Ante, Wazinski, and Saggu 2023).

- Roblox:- Roblox is an online multiplayer platform and virtual gaming world that has gained popularity for its immersive gameplay experiences (Blackwood 2023).
    - The platform offers a wide range of user-generated content, including games, virtual experiences, and social interactions (Bawa 2022).
    - Roblox features virtual storefronts for brands like Nike and Gucci, virtual tours of museums, and virtual events like concerts and fashion shows (Ante, Wazinski, and Saggu 2023).
    - Users on Roblox can engage in social, cultural, and economic activities within the virtual environment (Bawa 2022).
    - Roblox prioritizes immersive VR experiences and interactive gameplay for users (Blackwood 2023).

Meta's Horizon Worlds:- Meta's Horizon Worlds is a collaboration tool that en- ables virtual collaboration and interaction regardless of physical location (Mohamed, Naqishbandi, and Veronese 2023).

- The platform offers users the ability to create virtual worlds, games, and workspaces for social and professional purposes (Chen et al. 2022).
- Horizon Worlds is part of Meta's vision for the metaverse, focusing on virtual collaboration, social interactions, and immersive experiences (Chen et al. 2022).
- The platform provides users with tools for creating, customizing, and sharing virtual content within the virtual environment (Mandolfo, Baisi, and Lamberti 2022).
- Horizon Worlds aims to facilitate virtual collaboration, remote work, and social interactions through immersive virtual experiences (Mohamed, Naqishbandi, and Veronese 2023).

6. CONCLUSION

This chapter has provided an in-depth exploration of the Metaverse, charting its evo- lution from early virtual worlds to today's sophisticated digital environments. By examining the architecture of the Metaverse and the essential components that en- able its seamless operation, we have highlighted the critical role of technologies like blockchain, VR/AR, and AI. Additionally, the diverse ecosystem comprising users, de- velopers, and platforms was analyzed, showcasing their interconnected roles in shaping the Metaverse. Understanding these elements is crucial as the Metaverse continues to impact various aspects of society, from economy to culture. As we advance, the in- tegration of these technologies and the evolution of virtual worlds will undoubtedly revolutionize how we interact, work, and play in the digital realm.

REFERENCES

Adetayo, A., Adekunmisi, S., Abata-Ebire, B., & Adekunmisi, A. (2023). Metaverse academic library: Would it be patronized? *Digital Library Perspectives*, 39(2), 229–240. 10.1108/DLP-04-2022-0036

Agarwal, U., Tandon, D., Sharma, V. K., & Mishra, P. K. (2022). Metaverse technology: An overview. *International Research Journal of Modernization in Engineering Technology and Science*. Advance online publication. 10.56726/IRJMETS31452

Agrati, L. (2023). Tutoring in the metaverse. study on student-teachers' and tutors' perceptions about npc tutor. *Frontiers in Education*, 8, 1202442. Advance online publication. 10.3389/feduc.2023.1202442

Agrawal, D. P. (2020). *Recent Advances in Security, Privacy, and Trust for Internet of Things (IoT) and Cyber-Physical Systems*. CPS.

Aloqaily, M., Bouachir, O., Karray, F., Ridhawi, I., & Saddik, A. (2023). Integrating digital twin and advanced intelligent technologies to realize the metaverse. *IEEE Consumer Electronics Magazine*, 12(6), 47–55. 10.1109/MCE.2022.3212570

Andrade, N. (2009). Striking a balance between property and personality: The case of the avatars. *Journal of Virtual Worlds Research*, 1(3). Advance online publication. 10.4101/jvwr.v1i3.362

Ante, L., Wazinski, F., & Saggu, A. (2023). Digital real estate in the metaverse: An empirical analysis of retail investor motivations. *Finance Research Letters*, 58, 104299. 10.1016/j.frl.2023.104299

Bawa, S. (2022). Impact of metaverse applications on social anxiety of teenagers. *International Journal of Health Sciences and Research*, 12(7), 185–188. 10.52403/ijhsr.20220727

Billinghurst, M., A. Clark, and G. Lee. 2015. "A survey of augmented reality." .10.1561/9781601989215

Blackwood, G. 2023. "<em>roblox</em> and meta verch." *M/C Journal* 26. .10.5204/mcj.2958

Calabr'o, R., Cerasa, A., Ciancarelli, I., Pignolo, L., Tonin, P., Iosa, M., & Morone, G. (2022). The arrival of the metaverse in neurorehabilitation: Fact, fake or vision? *Biomedicines*, 10(10), 2602. 10.3390/biomedicines1010260236289862

Chen, Y., Wang, M., Liu, Y., & Ruo-yu, L. (2022). The impact of scenarios on the performance of entrepreneurial imaginativeness: Evidence from an experiment. *Frontiers in Psychology*, 13, 813657. Advance online publication. 10.3389/fpsyg.2022.81365735432125

Chodos, D., Stroulia, E., King, S., & Carbonaro, M. (2012). A framework for monitoring instructional environments in a virtual world. *British Journal of Educational Technology*, 45(1), 24–35. 10.1111/j.1467-8535.2012.01370.x

Delgado, C. (2022). User experience (ux) in metaverse: Realities and challenges. *Metaverse Basic and Applied Research*, 1, 9. 10.56294/mr20229

Deveci, Muhammet, Pamucar, Dragan, Gokasar, Ilgin, & K¨oppen, Mario, and Brij B Gupta. (2022). Personal mobility in metaverse with autonomous vehicles using Q-rung orthopair fuzzy sets based OPA-RAFSI model. *IEEE Transactions on Intelligent Transportation Systems*.

Deveci, M., Pamucar, D., Gokasar, I., & K¨oppen, M. Brij B Gupta, and Tugrul Daim. 2023. "Evaluation of Metaverse traffic safety implementations using fuzzy Einstein based logarithmic methodology of additive weights and TOPSIS method." *Technological Forecasting and Social Change* 194: 122681. dhelim, s., T. Kechadi, L. Chen, N. Aung, H. Ning, and L. Atzori. 2022. "Edge- enabled metaverse: the convergence of metaverse and mobile edge computing." 10.36227/techrxiv.19606954

D´ıaz-Chieng, L., J. Auza-Santiv´an˜ez, and J. Castillo. 2022. "El futuro de la salud en el metaverso." *Metaverse Basic and Applied Research* 1: 1. . Feng, X., X. Wang, and Y. Su. 2022. "An analysis of the current status of metaverse research based on bibliometrics." *Library Hi Tech* 42: 284–308. https://doi.org/.10.56294/mr20221

Din, I. (2023). Integration of iot and blockchain for decentralized management and ownership in the metaverse. *International Journal of Communication Systems*, 36(18), e5612. Advance online publication. 10.1002/dac.5612

Duan, H. 2021. "Metaverse for social good: a university campus prototype." /arxiv.2108.08985.10.1145/3474085.3479238

Ferrigno, G., Di Paola, N., Oguntegbe, K. F., & Kraus, S. (2023). Value creation in the metaverse age: A thematic analysis of press releases. *International Journal of Entrepreneurial Behaviour & Research*, 29(11), 337–363. 10.1108/IJEBR-01-2023-0039

Gaurav, A. 2023. "Navigating New Realities: Machine Learn- ing in the Metaverse." https://insights2techinfo.com/ navigating-new-realities-machine-learning-in-the-metaverse/. Accessed: 2024-01-30.

Gokasar, I., Pamucar, D., Deveci, M., Gupta, B. B., Martinez, L., & Castillo, O. (2023). Metaverse integration alternatives of connected autonomous vehicles with self-powered sensors using fuzzy decision making model. *Information Sciences*, 642, 119192.

Gorini, A., Gaggioli, A., Vigna, C., & Riva, G. (2008). A second life for ehealth: Prospects for the use of 3-d virtual worlds in clinical psychology. *Journal of Medical Internet Research*, 10(3), e21. 10.2196/jmir.102918678557

Grech, A., Mehnen, J., & Wodehouse, A. (2023). An extended ai-experience: Industry 5.0 in creative product innovation. *Sensors (Basel)*, 23(6), 3009. 10.3390/s2306300936991718

Guan, J., J. Irizawa, and A. Morris. 2022. "Extended reality and internet of things for hyper- connected metaverse environments." .10.1109/VRW55335.2022.00043

Gupta, B. B., Gaurav, A., Albeshri, A. A., & Alsalman, D. (2023). New paradigms of sustainable entrepreneurship in metaverse: A micro-level perspective. *The International Entrepreneurship and Management Journal*, 19(3), 1449–1465. 10.1007/s11365-023-00875-0

Gupta, B. B., Gaurav, A., Arya, V., & Alhalabi, W. (2024a). The evolution of intellectual property rights in metaverse based Industry 4.0 paradigms. *The International Entrepreneurship and Management Journal*, 20(2), 1–16. 10.1007/s11365-023-00940-8

Gupta, B. B., Gaurav, A., & Chui, K. T. 2023. "Deep CNN Based Anomaly De- tection in Centralized Metaverse Environment." In *2023 IEEE International Conference on Advanced Networks and Telecommunications Systems (ANTS)*, 1–6. IEEE.

Gupta, B. B., Gaurav, A., Chui, K. T., & Arya, V. 2024b. "Deep Learning- Based Facial Emotion Detection in the Metaverse." In *2024 IEEE International Conference on Consumer Electronics (ICCE)*, 1–6. IEEE. 10.1109/ICCE59016.2024.10444217

Gupta, T., & Panda, S. P. (2022). Cloudlet and virtual machine performance enhancement with CLARA and evolutionary paradigm. [IJCAC]. *International Journal of Cloud Applications and Computing*, 12(1), 1–16. 10.4018/IJCAC.298322

Han, Y., Niyato, D., Leung, C., Kim, D., Feng, S., Shen, S., & Chen, M. 2022. "A dynamic hierarchical framework for iot-assisted metaverse synchronization." https://doi.org//arxiv.2203.03969.10.48550

Hasan, A. 2023. "Preventing Metaverse Cyberattacks: Security is- sues and Threat Mitigation." https://insights2techinfo.com/ preventing-metaverse-cyberattacks-security-issues-and-threat-mitigation/. Accessed: 2024-01-30.

Jeon, B., & Heo, C. (2023). An empirical study on influential factors in adopting metaverse technology for educational services. *The Korean Career Entrepreneurship & Business Association*, 7(5), 73–88. 10.48206/kceba.2023.7.5.73

Jiang, Y., Kang, J., Niyato, D., Ge, X., Xiong, Z., & Chen, M. 2021. "Reli- able distributed computing for metaverse: a hierarchical game-theoretic approach." https://doi.org//arxiv.2111.10548.10.48550

Kabanda, G., Chipfumbu, C., & Chingoriwo, T. (2022). A cybersecurity model for a roblox- based metaverse architecture framework. *British Journal of Multidisciplinary and Advanced Studies*, 3(2), 105–141. 10.37745/bjmas.2022.0048

Kalita, A., & Gurusamy, M. 2022. "D2r2: distributed and dynamic reputation based resource allocation in metaverse." 10.36227/techrxiv.21395316

Lam, K., L. Yang, A. Alhilal, L. Lee, G. Tyson, and P. Hui. 2022. "Human-avatar interaction in metaverse." .10.1145/3551626.3564936

Lee, E., Lee, W., & Bae, I. (2023). What is the draw of the metaverse? personality correlates of zepeto use motives and their associations with psychological well-being. *Cyberpsychology, Behavior, and Social Networking*, 26(3), 161–168. 10.1089/cyber.2022.016436827586

Lee, S., Chang, Y., Lee, O.-K. D., Ryu, S., & Yin, Q. (2024). Exploring online social platform affordances for digital creators: A multi-method approach using qualitative and configurational analysis. *Industrial Management & Data Systems*, 124(4), 1501–1530. 10.1108/IMDS-12-2023-0951

Li, M., & Yu, Z. (2023). A systematic review on the metaverse-based blended english learn- ing. *Frontiers in Psychology*, 13, 1087508. Advance online publication. 10.3389/fpsyg.2022.108750836687938

Lin, Y., Du, H., Niyato, D., Nie, J., Zhang, J., Cheng, Y., & Yang, Z. (2023). Blockchain-aided secure semantic communication for ai-generated content in metaverse. *IEEE Open Journal of the Computer Society*, 4, 72–83. 10.1109/OJCS.2023.3260732

Mandolfo, M., Baisi, F., & Lamberti, L. (2022). How did you feel during the nav- igation? influence of emotions on browsing time and interaction frequency in im- mersive virtual environments. *Behaviour & Information Technology*, 42(8), 1216–1229. 10.1080/0144929X.2022.2066570

Mitra, S. (2023). Mctavcrsc! *International Journal of E-Adoption*, 15(2), 1–21. 10.4018/IJEA.316537

Momtaz, P. (2022). Some very simple economics of web3 and the metaverse. *Fintech*, 1(3), 225–234. 10.3390/fintech1030018

Nguyen, C., Hoang, D., Nguyen, D., & Dutkiewicz, E. 2022. "Metachain: a novel blockchain- based framework for metaverse applications." /arxiv.2201.00759.10.1109/VTC2022-Spring54318.2022.9860983

Oh, Y., Yi, J., & Kim, J. (2023). What enhances or worsens the user-generated metaverse experience? an appli- cation of bertopic to roblox user ewom. *Internet Research*. Advance online publication. 10.1108/INTR-03-2022-0178

Paquin, V., Ferrari, M., Sekhon, H., & Rej, S. (2023). Time to think "meta": A critical viewpoint on the risks and benefits of virtual worlds for mental health. *JMIR Serious Games*, 11, e43388. 10.2196/4338836661284

Patterson, N., M. Hobbs, F. Jiang, and L. Pan. 2019. "Cyber security insights into self- proclaimed virtual world hackers." .10.5121/csit.2019.91107

Qin, R., Ding, W., Li, J., Guan, S., Wang, G., Ren, Y., & Qu, Z. (2023). Web3-based de- centralized autonomous organizations and operations: Architectures, models, and mech- anisms. *IEEE Transactions on Systems, Man, and Cybernetics. Systems*, 53(4), 2073–2082. 10.1109/TSMC.2022.3228530

Rawat, D., & Alami, H. (2023). Metaverse: Requirements, architecture, standards, status, challenges, and perspectives. *Ieee Internet of Things Magazine*, 6(1), 14–18. 10.1109/IOTM.001.2200258

Rostami, S., & Maier, M. (2022). The metaverse and beyond: Implementing advanced multiverse realms with smart wearables. *IEEE Access : Practical Innovations, Open Solutions*, 10, 110796–110806. 10.1109/ACCESS.2022.3215736

S¨aks, E. (2022). Using cinematic virtual reality to get acquainted with the metaverse. *Baltic Screen Media Review*, 10(2), 252–271. 10.2478/bsmr-2022-0019

Samala, A., Ambiyar, A., Boji'c, L., Indarta, Y., Ipalakova, M., Denden, M., Ta¸s, N., & Dewi, I. (2023). Metaverse technologies in education: A systematic literature review using prisma. *International Journal of Emerging Technologies in Learning*, 18(5), 231–252. 10.3991/ijet.v18i05.35501

Sethi, A. (2022). *Security and Privacy in Metaverse: Issues, Challenges, and Future Op- portunities*. Cyber Security Insights Magazine.

Singh, G., Malhotra, M., & Sharma, A. (2022). An adaptive mechanism for virtual machine migration in the cloud environment. [IJCAC]. *International Journal of Cloud Applications and Computing*, 12(1), 1–10. 10.4018/IJCAC.311504

Sowmya, G., Chakraborty, D., Polisetty, A., Khorana, S., & Buhalis, D. (2023). Use of metaverse in socializing: Application of the big five personality traits framework. *Psychology and Marketing*, 40(10), 2132–2150. 10.1002/mar.21863

Stary, C. (2023). Digital process twins as intelligent design technology for engineering meta- verse/xr applications. *Sustainability (Basel)*, 15(22), 16062. 10.3390/su152216062

Sutikno, T. 2023. "Non-fungible tokens, decentralized autonomous organizations, web 3.0, and the metaverse in education: from university to metaversity." https://doi.org/10.31219/osf.io/5mjae

Tlili, A., Huang, R., Shehata, B., Liu, D., Zhao, J., Metwally, A., Wang, H., Denden, M., Bozkurt, A., Lee, L.-H., Beyoglu, D., Altinay, F., Sharma, R. C., Altinay, Z., Li, Z., Liu, J., Ahmad, F., Hu, Y., Salha, S., & Burgos, D. (2022). Is metaverse in education a blessing or a curse: A combined content and bibliometric analysis. *Smart Learning Environments*, 9(1), 24. Advance online publication. 10.1186/s40561-022-00205-x

Wang, Y., Su, Z., Zhang, N., Xing, R., Liu, D., Luan, T., & Shen, X. (2023). A survey on metaverse: Fundamentals, security, and privacy. *IEEE Communications Surveys and Tutorials*, 25(1), 319–352. 10.1109/COMST.2022.3202047

Warburton, S. (2009). Second life in higher education: Assessing the potential for and the barriers to deploying virtual worlds in learning and teaching. *British Journal of Educational Technology*, 40(3), 414–426. 10.1111/j.1467-8535.2009.00952.x

Weinberger, M. (2023). A comparison of virtual worlds based on the metaverse maturity model. *ITU Journal : ICT Discoveries*, 4(4), 537–548. 10.52953/REVF5378

Xie, Y., Li, P., Nedjah, N., Gupta, B. B., Taniar, D., & Zhang, J. (2023). Pri- vacy protection framework for face recognition in edge-based Internet of Things. *Cluster Computing*, 26(5), 3017–3035. 10.1007/s10586-022-03808-8

Yang, Y., Siau, K., Xie, W., & Sun, Y. (2022). Smart health. *Journal of Organizational and End User Computing*, 34(1), 1–14. 10.4018/JOEUC.308814

Zhang, X., Chen, Y., Hu, L., & Wang, Y. (2022). The metaverse in education: Definition, framework, features, potential applications, challenges, and future research topics. *Frontiers in Psychology*, 13, 1016300. Advance online publication. 10.3389/fpsyg.2022.101630036304866

Zhong, Y., Wen, J., Zhang, J., Kang, J., Jiang, Y., Zhang, Y., Cheng, Y., & Tong, Y. (2023). Blockchain-assisted twin migration for vehicular metaverses: A game theory approach. *Transactions on Emerging Telecommunications Technologies*, 34(12), e4856. Advance online publication. 10.1002/ett.4856

Chapter 4
Foundations of Cybersecurity:
Core Principles, Practices, and Emerging Trends

Akshat Gaurav
Ronin Institute, USA

Varsha Arya
Asia University, Taiwan

ABSTRACT

The rapid advancement of digital technology has brought significant benefits but also introduced a myriad of cybersecurity challenges. In this context, this chapter, addresses the growing need for a robust understanding of the principles, threats, best practices, and legal and ethical considerations essential for safeguarding digital assets. This chapter explores the core principles of confidentiality, integrity, and availability, delves into prevalent cyber threats and vulnerabilities, and outlines best practices for mitigating these risks. Additionally, it addresses the legal and ethical frameworks governing cybersecurity, emphasizing the importance of compliance and responsible conduct. Understanding these fundamentals is crucial for navigating and securing the increasingly complex digital landscape.

DOI: 10.4018/979-8-3693-3824-7.ch004

1. PRINCIPLES OF CYBERSECURITY

1.1. *Introduction to Cybersecurity*

1.1.1. Definition and Importance of Cybersecurity

Cybersecurity is a crucial aspect of protecting information resources in cyberspace from cyber threats and attacks. The National Institute of Standards and Technology (NIST) defines cybersecurity as the ability to protect the use of cyberspace from cyber attacks (Tran, Beuran, and Hasegawa 2023; Gupta 2021). It involves safeguarding information resources, users, and individuals from falling prey to cyber threats (Veiga 2016; Gupta and Quamara 2018b). Cybersecurity aims to preserve the confidentiality, integrity, and availability of digital technologies through the development of defense strategies (Alexei and Alexei 2023; Sharma and Gupta 2018). It extends beyond tech- nological aspects and encompasses all dimensions of an organization (Neri, Niccolini, and Martino 2023; Tewari and Gupta 2020).The European Union's Cybersecurity Act defines cybersecurity as activities nec- essary to protect network and information systems, users, and other affected per- sons from cyber threats (Soldatos, Pra¸ca, and Jovanovi´c 2021; Gupta and Quamara 2018a). Cybersecurity involves protecting data, systems, and networks from cyberat- tacks (Alqahtani and Kavakli 2020). It is crucial for ensuring the security of critical infrastructures in various sectors such as air transport, healthcare, finance, and in- dustry (Stevens 2018; Tewari and Gupta 2018b). Moreover, cybersecurity readiness is essential for organizations, especially in the ICT sector, to effectively combat cyber threats (Neri, Niccolini, and Martino 2023; Tewari and Gupta 2018a; Gupta et al. 2023).

To enhance cybersecurity, frameworks are developed to protect resources, predict threats, and educate employees at all levels of an organization (Alqudhaibi et al. 2023; Bhardwaj and Kaushik 2022). Cybersecurity certification plays a vital role in increas- ing trust in the digital era and requires collaboration among stakeholders (Matheu et al. 2020; Choudhary and Singh 2022; Xie et al. 2023). Additionally, cybersecurity awareness is crucial for online safety and risk mitigation (Erendor and Yıldırım 2022; Dubey, Kumar, and Chhabra 2022). Developing a common understanding of cyber- security terminology and risks is essential due to its multidisciplinary nature (Cains et al. 2021; Gaurav, Arya, and Santaniello 2022).

1.1.2. Historical Context and Evolution of Cybersecurity

The evolution of cybersecurity has been influenced by historical events and techno- logical advancements. Cybersecurity has transitioned from a reactive approach to a more proactive and strategic discipline. The European Union's cybersecurity policy has evolved since the 1990s, with challenges arising from member states' reluctance to delegate decision-making power Renda (2022). This highlights the complex inter- play between national interests and collective security efforts in shaping cybersecurity policies.

Understanding the timeline of cybercrimes is crucial for comprehending the evolution of cybersecurity practices. As cyberattacks have become more frequent and sophisticated, there is a growing need for preemptive actions to mitigate potential threats (AllahRakha 2024; Sharma 2022). The development of defense strategies in re- sponse to cyber threats has been pivotal in enhancing cybersecurity readiness (Sadik et al. 2020).

Technological advancements, such as the integration of new computing and com- munication technologies, have given rise to cyber-physical systems, impacting the cy- bersecurity landscape (Monteiro, Rodrigues, and Souza 2023). Additionally, the future of cybersecurity is being influenced by quantum computing, which presents new chal- lenges to traditional cryptographic methods (Brijwani, Ajmire, and Thawani 2023;

The historical trajectory of cybersecurity discourse mirrors the evolving nature of cyber threats and defense mechanisms. From early stages of understanding cyber risks to the current emphasis on machine learning and AI in cybersecurity, the field has continuously adapted to address emerging challenges (Ren, Lu, and Xu 2018) (Yan et al. 2022). The convergence of artificial intelligence and blockchain technologies further complicates the cybersecurity landscape, necessitating innovative solutions to ensure data security and privacy (Bhumichai 2024).

In response to the changing cybersecurity landscape, there has been a shift towards enhancing cybersecurity education and accreditation to meet the demands of the digital era (Crick et al. 2019). The significance of global efforts to secure critical infrastructure from cyberattacks underscores the interconnected nature of cybersecu- rity challenges (Wibowo 2022). Moreover, the development of ethical frameworks for cybersecurity research reflects the increasing recognition of ethical considerations in cybersecurity practices (Reidsma, Ham, and Continella 2023).

Figure 1. Core Principles of Cyber Security

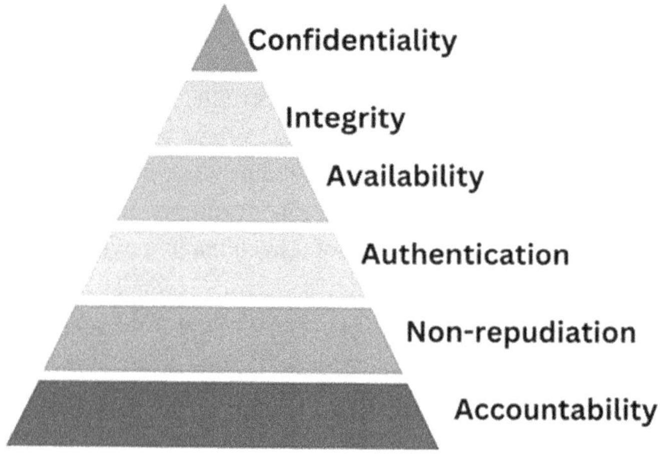

1.2. *Core Principles of Cyber Security*

1.2.1. Confidentiality

Confidentiality in cybersecurity is a fundamental principle that focuses on controlling access to information, operations, and disclosure of system elements. It ensures that sensitive data is only accessible to authorized individuals or systems, thereby prevent- ing unauthorized disclosure or exposure of information (Alexei and Alexei 2023). The protection of confidentiality is essential for maintaining the privacy and security of data, preventing breaches, and upholding trust in digital systems (Costanzo, Shao, and Gu 2016).

The CIA triad, which includes confidentiality, integrity, and availability, forms the cornerstone of cybersecurity practices. Confidentiality ensures that information is kept private and only accessible to authorized users, protecting it from unauthorized access or disclosure (Alexei and Alexei 2023). It is crucial for safeguarding sensitive data, such as personal information, financial records, and intellectual property, from cyber threats and breaches (Costanzo, Shao, and Gu 2016).

In the context of cybersecurity, confidentiality is closely linked to data protection and privacy. Ensuring confidentiality involves implementing encryption, access con- trols, and secure communication protocols to prevent unauthorized access to sensitive information (Fortino et al. 2022). By maintaining confidentiality, orga- nizations can mitigate the risk of data breaches, identity theft, and unauthorized disclosure of pro- prietary information (Sadik et al. 2020).

Moreover, confidentiality plays a vital role in various sectors, including healthcare, finance, and government, where the protection of sensitive data is paramount. For instance, in telemedicine, maintaining patient confidentiality is crucial to comply with privacy regulations and build trust with patients (Sabrina and Defi 2021). Similarly, in the financial sector, confidentiality is essential for protecting customer financial data and preventing fraud (Park 2015).

1.2.2. Integrity

Integrity in cybersecurity ensures that data remains accurate, consistent, and unaltered throughout its lifecycle. It involves protecting information from unauthorized modifications, ensuring data retains its original state, and is free from tampering or corruption (Goebel and Rajamani 2021). Data integrity is crucial for maintaining trust in digital systems, preventing unauthorized changes, and upholding the reliability of information (Song, Skuric, and Ji 2020).

In cybersecurity, integrity is closely linked to data protection and ensuring informa- tion authenticity. Encryption, digital signatures, and checksums are used to verify data integrity and detect unauthorized alterations (Song, Skuric, and Ji 2020). By maintain- ing data integrity, organizations can prevent data manipulation, unauthorized access, and data corruption, safeguarding the accuracy and reliability of information (Goebel and Rajamani 2021).

Data integrity is essential across various sectors such as healthcare, finance, and critical infrastructure. For example, in healthcare systems, ensuring the integrity of patient records is vital for accurate medical care and patient trust (Safkhani et al. 2020). Similarly, in financial institutions, data integrity is crucial for preventing fraud and ensuring transaction accuracy (Zeadally et al. 2020).

Integrity also plays a critical role in industrial control systems, where data integrity manipulation can have severe consequences on operational processes and safety. Pro- tecting communication data integrity in industrial control systems is essential for pre- venting disruptions and ensuring critical infrastructure reliability (Song, Skuric, and Ji 2020).

1.2.3. Availability

Availability in cybersecurity refers to ensuring that information and resources are accessible and usable when needed. It involves maintaining the continuous operation of systems, networks, and services, thereby preventing disruptions and downtime that could impact productivity and functionality Mendoza et al. (2023). Availability is a critical component of the CIA triad, alongside confidentiality and integrity, and is essential for ensuring that data and services are consistently accessible to authorized users (Sarker, Furhad, and Nowrozy 2021).

In cybersecurity, availability is closely linked to resilience and disaster recovery. Organizations implement measures such as redundancy, failover systems, and backups to ensure continuous availability of critical services in the event of cyber incidents or system failures (Sivan-Sevilla 2018). By prioritizing availability, organizations can minimize service disruptions, maintain business continuity, and mitigate the impact of cyberattacks (Macnish, Inguanzo, and 2019).

The importance of availability extends across various sectors, including healthcare, finance, and critical infrastructure. In healthcare, ensuring the availability of electronic health records and medical systems is crucial for delivering timely and effective patient care (Schaaf, Tekinerdo˘gan, and C¸ atal 2021). Similarly, in the financial sector, main- taining the availability of online banking services is essential for customer satisfaction and trust (Shevchenko, Skladannyi, and Spasiteleva 2023).

Moreover, availability plays a significant role in industrial control systems and IoT devices, where uninterrupted operation is essential for maintaining operational effi- ciency and safety. Protecting the availability of these systems is critical for preventing disruptions that could have far-reaching consequences on industrial processes and in- frastructure (Alexei and Alexei 2023).

1.2.4. Authentication

Authentication in cybersecurity is the process of verifying the identity of users or de- vices attempting to access a system or network. It involves confirming the authenticity of individuals or entities through various methods such as passwords, biometrics, se- curity tokens, or multi-factor authentication Uysal and Akgu¨n (2023). Authentication is a critical security measure used to establish trust between users and systems, ensur- ing that only authorized entities can access sensitive information or resources (Elarco et al. 2021).

The importance of authentication in cybersecurity lies in its role as the first line of defense against unauthorized access and cyber threats. By requiring users to au- thenticate their identity before accessing systems or data, organizations can prevent unauthorized users from gaining entry and protect against data breaches or malicious activities (Wiercioch, Teufel, and Teufel 2018). Authentication acts as a gatekeeper, controlling access to critical assets and ensuring that only legitimate users can interact with sensitive information (Papaioannou et al. 2023).

Authentication is essential for safeguarding data integrity, confidentiality, and avail- ability. By implementing robust authentication mechanisms, organizations can prevent unauthorized modifications, ensure data privacy, and maintain the continuous avail- ability of services (H¨oyhty¨a and Martio 2020). Strong authentication practices are crucial for protecting against identity theft, fraud, and unauthorized access to sensi- tive information (Setianingsih et al. 2021).

Moreover, authentication plays a vital role in various sectors, including healthcare, finance, and industrial systems. In healthcare, authentication is crucial for securing electronic health records and ensuring patient privacy (Motohashi et al. 2019). In financial institutions, authentication is essential for protecting customer accounts and preventing fraudulent activities (Alamri, Crowley, and Richardson 2022). In industrial systems, authentication helps secure critical infrastructure and prevent unauthorized access to control systems (Hahn, Sun, and Liu 2016).

1.2.5. Non-repudiation

Non-repudiation in cybersecurity ensures that a party cannot deny the authenticity or origin of a communication, transaction, or action they have performed, providing evidence to prove the validity of a message or transaction and holding individuals accountable Wilson (2021). It is crucial for establishing trust, accountability, and in- tegrity in digital interactions.

Implementing non-repudiation measures helps organizations ensure that parties in- volved in a transaction cannot later deny their participation or the validity of the transaction, thereby preventing disputes, fraud, and unauthorized activities (Montanaro et al. 2018)(Abawajy and Islam 2017).

Non-repudiation is essential in finance, healthcare, and legal industries. In financial transactions, it prevents parties from denying payments or authorizations, enhancing trust and security (Villiers and Calitz 2020). In healthcare, it maintains patient record integrity and ensures healthcare provider accountability (Swanzy 2024).

In legal contexts, non-repudiation is crucial for proving the authenticity and integrity of digital evidence. It helps establish the validity of electronic signatures, con- tracts, and communications, providing reliable evidence in legal disputes (Alqudhaibi et al. 2023).

1.2.6. Accountability

Accountability in cybersecurity refers to the concept of holding individuals, organiza- tions, or entities responsible for their actions, decisions, and compliance with cyber- security policies, regulations, and best practices. It involves establishing clear roles, responsibilities, and ownership of cybersecurity measures to ensure that all stakehold- ers are answerable for their contributions to maintaining a secure and resilient cyber environment Orji (2018).

The importance of accountability in cybersecurity lies in its role in promoting trans- parency, trust, and adherence to cybersecurity protocols. By establishing accountabil- ity mechanisms, organizations can track and monitor cybersecurity activities, iden- tify potential vulnerabilities, and respond promptly to security incidents (Abrahams 2024). Accountability helps create a culture of responsibility and ownership, fostering a proactive approach to cybersecurity risk management (Raposo 2022).

Accountability is crucial for ensuring that cybersecurity measures are effectively implemented and maintained across all levels of an organization. It helps prevent security breaches, data leaks, and unauthorized access by ensuring that individuals are aware of their responsibilities and the consequences of non-compliance (Sawyer 2021). By promoting accountability, organizations can enhance their cybersecurity posture, protect sensitive information, and mitigate cyber threats (Alashi and Badi 2020).

In the context of regulatory compliance and legal frameworks, accountability plays a significant role in demonstrating due diligence and adherence to cyberse- curity stan- dards. Organizations that prioritize accountability are better equipped to address com- pliance requirements, protect customer data, and uphold the trust of stakeholders. Ac- countability also facilitates effective incident response and re- covery efforts, enabling organizations to learn from security incidents and improve their cybersecurity practices

2. COMMON CYBER THREATS AND VULNERABILITIES

2.1. *Types of Cyber Threats*

2.1.1. Malware

Malware, short for malicious software, encompasses various types of software designed to infiltrate, damage, or gain unauthorized access to computer systems or networks. The impact of malware can be significant, ranging from data breaches and financial losses to system disruptions and privacy violations. Here are some common types of malware and their impacts:

- Viruses: Viruses are programs that replicate themselves by attaching to other files or programs. They can corrupt or delete data, slow down system perfor- mance, and spread to other systems, causing widespread damage.

Figure 2. Malware Types

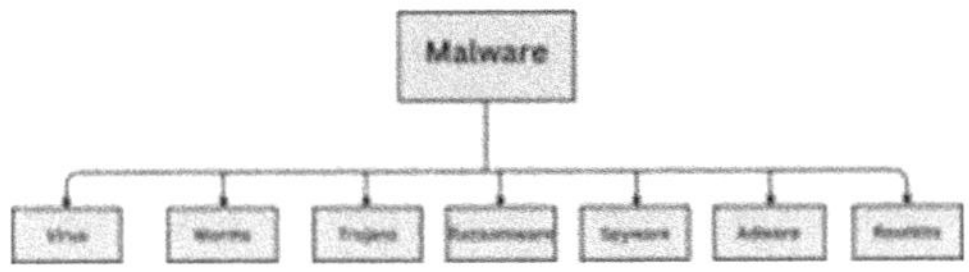

- Worms: Worms are self-replicating malware that spread across networks without user intervention. They can consume network bandwidth, overload servers, and propagate rapidly, leading to network congestion and system crashes.
- Trojans: Trojans disguise themselves as legitimate software to trick users into downloading and executing them. They can steal sensitive information, create backdoors for attackers, and cause system instability.
- Ransomware: Ransomware encrypts files or locks users out of their systems until a ransom is paid. It can lead to data loss, financial extortion, and operational disruptions, impacting businesses and individuals alike.
- Spyware: Spyware secretly monitors user activities, collects personal information, and sends it to third parties without consent. It can compromise privacy, steal sensitive data, and expose users to identity theft.
- Adware: Adware displays unwanted advertisements, redirects web traffic, and collects user data for targeted advertising. It can slow down system performance, disrupt browsing activities, and compromise user privacy.
- Rootkits: Rootkits are stealthy malware that hide their presence on infected systems. They can give attackers full control over compromised devices, evade detection by security tools, and persistently maintain access to systems.

2.1.2. Phishing and Social Engineering Attacks

Phishing is a form of social engineering attack where cybercriminals use deceptive tac- tics to trick individuals into revealing sensitive information, such as login credentials, financial details, or personal data. Phishing attacks typically involve sending fraud- ulent emails or messages that appear to be from legitimate sources, such as banks, government agencies, or reputable organizations, to deceive recipients into clicking on malicious links or providing confidential information (Braun et al. 2014).

Social engineering attacks, like phishing, exploit human vulnerabilities rather than software vulnerabilities, making awareness and education crucial in mitigating the risks associated with these attacks (Salem, Hossain, and Kamala 2010). Phishing attacks can lead to severe consequences, including financial losses, identity theft, data breaches, and reputational damage for individuals and organizations (Bitaab et al. 2021). By impersonating trusted entities and using psychological manipulation, phishers aim to deceive unsuspecting victims and exploit their trust to gain access to sensitive information (Kalio 2022).

Phishing attacks can manifest in various forms, such as email phishing, SMS phish- ing (smishing), voice phishing (vishing), and spear phishing, each tailored to target specific individuals or organizations (Dutta 2021). Attackers often employ sophisti- cated techniques to create convincing and authentic-looking messages that lure recipients into disclosing confidential information or performing actions that compromise security (Lee et al. 2021).

Figure 3. Phishing Attack

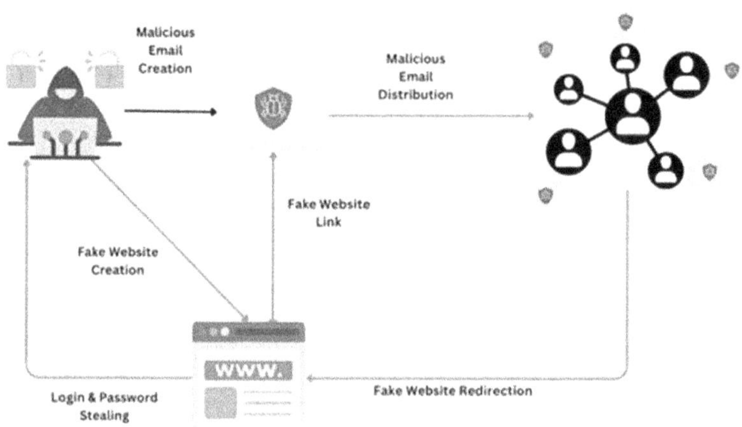

To combat phishing attacks, organizations and individuals can implement security measures like email filters, anti-phishing software, multi-factor authentication, and security awareness training to educate users on recognizing and avoiding phishing attempts (Aburrous et al. 2010). By raising awareness, enhancing cybersecurity prac- tices, and implementing effective detection and prevention strategies, individuals and organizations can reduce the risk of falling victim to phishing attacks and protect themselves against potential threats (Thakur and Pathan 2022).

2.1.3. Denial of Service (DoS) and Distributed Denial of Service (DDoS) Attacks

Denial of Service (DoS) and Distributed Denial of Service (DDoS) attacks are mali- cious activities aimed at disrupting the availability of online services by overwhelming target systems with a high volume of traffic or requests, rendering them inaccessible to legitimate users.

- DoS Attack
    - In a DoS attack, a single source, such as a compromised computer or server, floods a target system with an excessive amount of traffic, causing it to become unresponsive and unable to handle legitimate requests.
    - DoS attacks can lead to service disruptions, downtime, and loss of revenue for organizations, as well as damage to reputation and customer trust.
- DDoS Attack
    - DDoS attacks involve multiple sources, often a network of compromised devices known as botnets, coordinated to launch a massive volume of traffic or requests at a target simultaneously.
    - DDoS attacks are more sophisticated and challenging to mitigate than DoS attacks due to their distributed nature and the use of multiple attack vec- tors.
    - DDoS attacks can overwhelm network bandwidth, exhaust system resources, and disrupt online services, leading to significant financial losses

Figure 4. DDoS Attack Architecture and reputational damage for businesses.

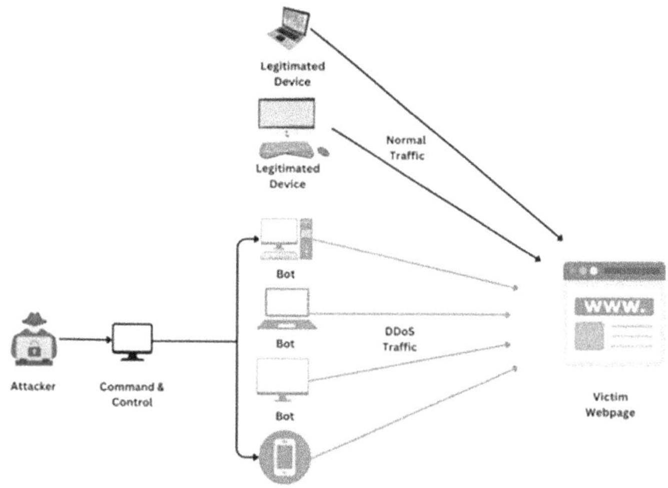

- Impacts of DoS and DDoS Attacks
    - Service Disruption: DoS and DDoS attacks can render online services, web- sites, or networks inaccessible, causing disruptions to operations and ser- vices.
    - Financial Losses: Organizations may suffer financial losses due to downtime, decreased productivity, and potential revenue loss resulting from DoS and DDoS attacks.
    - Reputation Damage: Persistent or high-profile DoS and DDoS attacks can tarnish an organization's reputation, erode customer trust, and impact brand credibility.
    - Data Breaches: In some cases, DoS and DDoS attacks may serve as a distrac- tion or precursor to more damaging cyber incidents, such as data breaches or network intrusions.
    - Mitigation Challenges: Mitigating DoS and DDoS attacks requires robust cybersecurity measures, such as network monitoring, traffic filtering, and the use of specialized DDoS protection services.

2.1.4. Advanced Persistent Threats (APTs)

Advanced Persistent Threats (APTs) are a sophisticated class of cyber threats that pose significant risks to governments, organizations, and individuals worldwide. APTs are characterized by their stealthy, persistent, and targeted nature, often orchestrated by well-resourced adversaries with specific objectives, such as cyber espionage, data theft, or sabotage. These attacks are designed to remain undetected for extended periods, allowing threat actors to maintain control over compromised systems and extract valuable information without raising suspicion Sahabandu et al. (2018).

Figure 5. Advanced Persistent Threats (APTs)

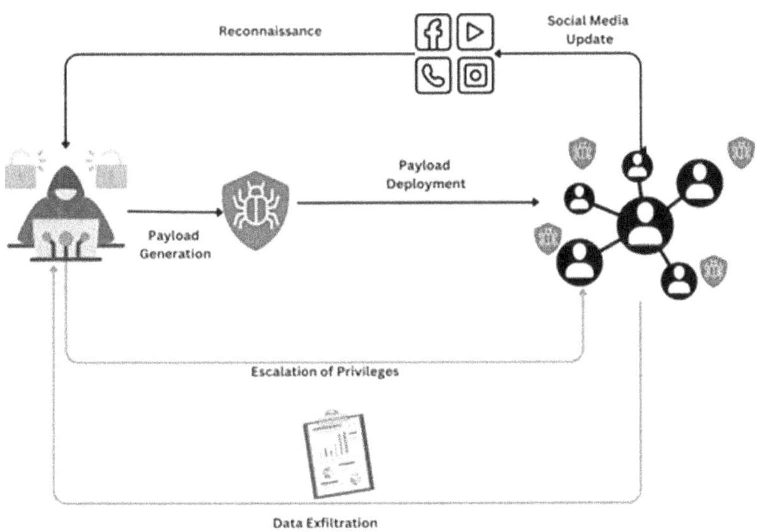

APTs leverage advanced attack techniques, multiple vectors, and zero-day exploits to infiltrate networks, evade detection, and establish long-term access to target sys- tems. By employing social engineering tactics, spear phishing, malware, and other sophisticated methods, APT actors can bypass traditional security measures and ex- ploit vulnerabilities to achieve their malicious goals (Berrada et al. 2020).

The impact of APTs can be severe, leading to data breaches, intellectual property theft, financial losses, reputational damage, and operational disruptions. A successful APT attack can compromise sensitive information, disrupt critical infrastructure, and undermine the security and stability of organizations, governments, and critical systems (Yang et al. 2017).

Detecting and mitigating APTs require advanced cybersecurity strategies, threat intelligence, and proactive defense mechanisms. Organizations must implement robust security controls, network monitoring, anomaly detection, and incident response capa- bilities to detect, contain, and eradicate APTs before significant damage occurs (Moon et al. 2014).

By understanding the characteristics and tactics employed by APTs, organizations can enhance their cybersecurity posture, strengthen their defenses, and protect against the evolving threat landscape. Collaboration, information sharing, and continuous se- curity awareness are essential in combating APTs and safeguarding against sophisti- cated cyber threats in today's digital environment (Chizoba and Kyari 2020).

2.2. *Common Vulnerabilities*

2.2.1. Software Vulnerabilities

Software vulnerabilities refer to weaknesses or flaws in software applications, systems, or networks that can be exploited by threat actors to compromise the security, integrity, or availability of the software. These vulnerabilities can arise from errors in design, implementation, configuration, or maintenance, and they can be exploited to launch cyber attacks, gain unauthorized access, or cause system malfunctions.

Figure 6. Buffer Overflows

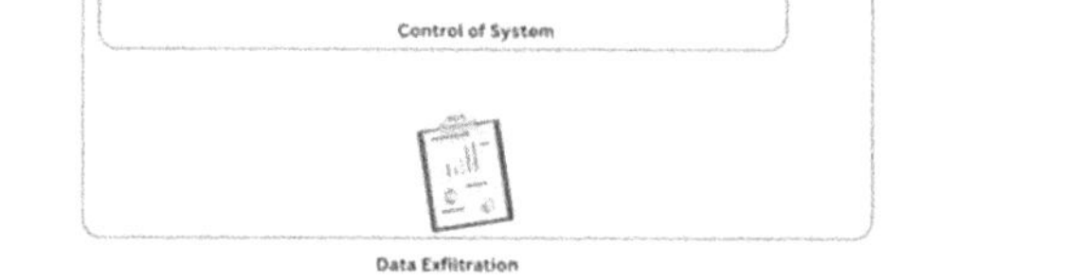

Software vulnerabilities can manifest in various forms, including:

- Buffer Overflow: A common vulnerability where an application writes more data to a buffer than it can hold, potentially leading to memory corruption and unau- thorized code execution.

- SQL Injection: A type of vulnerability in web applications that allows attackers to manipulate SQL queries through user input, potentially leading to data breaches or unauthorized access to databases.
- Cross-Site Scripting (XSS): A vulnerability that allows attackers to inject mali- cious scripts into web pages viewed by other users, leading to session hijacking, data theft, or website defacement.
- Insecure Authentication: Weak or improperly implemented authentication mech- anisms can lead to unauthorized access, account takeover, and data breaches.
- Insecure Deserialization: Vulnerabilities in deserialization processes can be ex- ploited to execute arbitrary code, leading to remote code execution and system compromise.

The impact of software vulnerabilities can be significant and may include:

- Data Breaches: Vulnerabilities that allow unauthorized access to sensitive data, leading to data breaches and privacy violations.
- System Compromise: Exploitation of vulnerabilities can result in system com- promise, unauthorized access, or control by malicious actors.
- Financial Losses: Vulnerabilities can be exploited for financial gain, such as steal- ing payment information, conducting fraudulent transactions, or ransomware attacks.
- Reputation Damage: Publicly disclosed vulnerabilities can damage an organiza- tion's reputation, erode customer trust, and lead to loss of business.

Figure 7. Side Channel Attacks

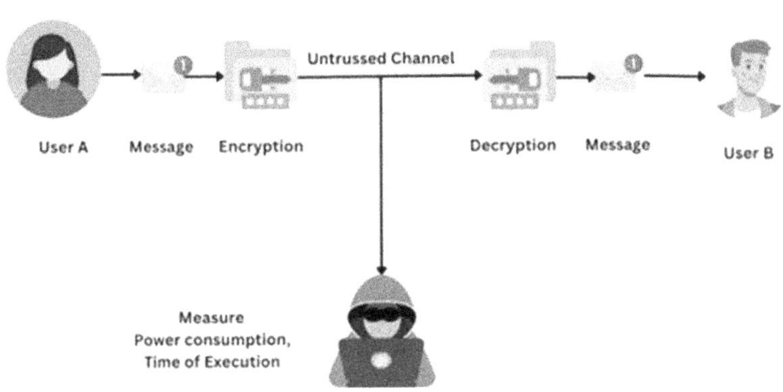

2.2.2. Hardware Vulnerabilities

Hardware vulnerabilities refer to weaknesses or flaws in the physical components of computer systems, devices, or networks that can be exploited by attackers to compro- mise security, gain unauthorized access, or disrupt operations. These vulnerabilities can stem from design flaws, manufacturing defects, configuration errors, or outdated firmware, and they can pose significant risks to the integrity and confidentiality of data stored or processed by hardware components.

Some common types of hardware vulnerabilities include:

- Side-Channel Attacks: These attacks exploit unintended information leakage from hardware components, such as power consumption, electromagnetic emis- sions, or timing variations, to extract sensitive data or cryptographic keys.
- Rowhammer Attacks: Rowhammer attacks target memory modules by repeatedly accessing specific memory rows to induce bit flips in adjacent memory cells, potentially leading to data corruption or privilege escalation.
- Firmware Vulnerabilities: Vulnerabilities in firmware, such as BIOS or device firmware, can be exploited to gain persistent access to hardware components, bypass security controls, or install malicious code that persists across reboots.
- Hardware Trojans: Malicious modifications or backdoors inserted during the manufacturing or supply chain process can create hardware Trojans that compromise the security and functionality of devices.
- Fault Injection Attacks: These attacks involve injecting faults, such as electromagnetic interference or voltage glitches, into hardware

3. CYBERSECURITY BEST PRACTICES

3.1. *Security Frameworks and Standards*

3.1.1. NIST Cybersecurity Framework

The National Institute of Standards and Technology (NIST) Cybersecurity Frame- work provides comprehensive guidelines to help organizations manage and mitigate cybersecurity risks. It includes three main components:

- Core: A set of cybersecurity activities, desired outcomes, and applicable references, organized into five functions: Identify, Protect, Detect, Respond, and Recover.
- Implementation Tiers: Describe the extent to which an organization's cybersecurity risk management practices align with the characteristics defined in the Framework.
- Profiles: Represent the alignment of standards, guidelines, and practices to the Framework Core in a way that meets the business requirements and risk toler- ance.

3.1.2. ISO/IEC 27001

ISO/IEC 27001 is an international standard for information security management systems (ISMS). It helps organizations manage the security of assets such as financial information, intellectual property, employee details, and information entrusted by third parties. Key elements include:

- ISMS: A systematic approach to managing sensitive company information.
- Risk Management: Identifying, assessing, and treating risks to the organization's information assets.
- Continuous Improvement: Regularly updating and improving information secu- rity measures.

3.1.3. CIS Controls

The Center for Internet Security (CIS) Controls are a set of best practices designed to help organizations improve their cybersecurity defenses. These controls are prioritized and categorized to provide a clear roadmap for organizations of all sizes:

- Basic Controls: Fundamental steps like inventory and control of hardware and software assets.
- Foundational Controls: Best practices that form a critical foundation for cyber- security, such as email and web browser protections.
- Organizational Controls: Advanced controls involving policies, procedures, and automation to continuously monitor and defend systems.

3.1.4. COBIT (Control Objectives for Information and Related Technologies)

COBIT is a framework created by ISACA for IT management and governance. It provides a comprehensive framework that helps enterprises achieve their IT governance and management objectives:

- Principles and Enablers: Focuses on aligning IT with business goals and manag- ing IT risks.
- Processes: Defines processes in IT governance and management, helping organi- zations ensure their IT infrastructure supports their business goals.
- Maturity Models: Provides maturity models to assess the capability and perfor- mance of IT processes.

3.1.5. PCI DSS (Payment Card Industry Data Security Standard)

PCI DSS is a set of security standards designed to ensure that all companies that accept, process, store, or transmit credit card information maintain a secure environ- ment. The key requirements include:

- Build and Maintain a Secure Network: Implement firewalls and secure configu- rations.
- Protect Cardholder Data: Encrypt transmission of cardholder data across open, public networks.
- Maintain a Vulnerability Management Program: Use and regularly update anti- virus software or programs.
- Implement Strong Access Control Measures: Restrict access to cardholder data by business need to know.
- Monitor and Test Networks: Track and monitor all access to network resources and cardholder data.
- Maintain an Information Security Policy: Develop and maintain a policy that addresses information security for employees and contractors.

3.2. *Technical Best Practices*

By implementing technical best practices for network security, organizations can strengthen their defenses, mitigate cyber risks, and protect their network infrastructure from a wide range of cyber threats and attacks. It is essential to continuously assess and improve network security measures to adapt to evolving cyber threats and ensure the confidentiality, integrity, and availability of network resources.

- Implement Network Segmentation: Divide the network into separate segments to limit the spread of potential threats and contain breaches.
- Use Strong Authentication: Implement multi-factor authentication to enhance access control and prevent unauthorized access to network resources.
- Regularly Update and Patch Systems: Keep all network devices, software, and firmware up to date with the latest security patches to address known vulnera- bilities.
- Encrypt Network Traffic: Use encryption protocols such as SSL/TLS to secure data in transit and protect sensitive information from eavesdropping.
- Monitor Network Traffic: Deploy intrusion detection and prevention systems to monitor network traffic, detect suspicious activities, and respond to potential threats in real-time.
- Implement Access Controls: Enforce least privilege access controls to restrict user permissions and limit access to sensitive data and critical systems.
- Backup and Disaster Recovery: Regularly backup critical data and systems, and establish a disaster recovery plan to ensure business continuity in the event of a cyber incident.
- Conduct Regular Security Audits: Perform regular security assessments, penetra- tion testing, and vulnerability scans to identify and address security weaknesses in the network.
- Educate Users: Provide security awareness training to employees to educate them about cybersecurity best practices, phishing awareness, and social engineering tactics.

3.3. *Operational Best Practices*

By implementing operational best practices for cybersecurity, organizations can en- hance their security posture, reduce the risk of cyber threats, and protect their assets and data from potential security breaches and attacks. It is essential to continuously review and update cybersecurity practices to adapt to evolving threats and ensure the resilience of the organization's cybersecurity defenses.

- Establish a Cybersecurity Incident Response Plan: Develop a comprehensive in- cident response plan outlining roles, responsibilities, and procedures to effectively respond to and mitigate cybersecurity incidents.
- Regular Security Training and Awareness: Provide ongoing cybersecurity train- ing to employees to raise awareness of security threats, best practices, and the importance of cybersecurity hygiene.

- Implement Access Controls: Enforce strong access controls, least privilege prin- ciples, and user authentication mechanisms to restrict access to sensitive data and critical systems.
- Regular Security Audits and Assessments: Conduct regular security audits, vul- nerability assessments, and penetration testing to identify and address security weaknesses in the network and systems.
- Patch Management: Implement a robust patch management process to ensure that all systems, applications, and devices are up to date with the latest security patches and updates.
- Network Monitoring and Logging: Implement network monitoring tools and log management systems to detect suspicious activities, monitor network traffic, and investigate security incidents.
- Data Encryption: Encrypt sensitive data at rest and in transit to protect it from unauthorized access and ensure data confidentiality.
- Backup and Recovery: Regularly backup critical data and systems, and test backup and recovery procedures to ensure business continuity in the event of a cyber incident.
- Vendor Risk Management: Assess and manage the cybersecurity risks posed by third-party vendors and service providers to ensure the security of outsourced systems and data.
- Incident Reporting and Communication: Establish clear incident reporting pro- cedures and communication channels to ensure timely reporting of security inci- dents and coordination of response efforts.

4. THE LEGAL AND ETHICAL CONSIDERATIONS IN CYBERSECURITY

4.1. *Introduction to Legal and Ethical Considerations*

In the rapidly evolving landscape of cybersecurity, legal and ethical considerations play a crucial role in shaping policies, practices, and decision-making processes to ensure the protection of data, privacy, and digital assets. As organizations and individuals navigate the complexities of cybersecurity threats and challenges, adherence to legal frameworks and ethical standards is essential to mitigate risks, uphold trust, and comply with regulatory requirements.

Legal frameworks, such as data protection laws, cybersecurity regulations, and pri- vacy statutes, establish guidelines and requirements for safeguarding sensitive information, preventing data breaches, and holding entities accountable for cybersecurity incidents. Compliance with these legal mandates is imperative to avoid legal repercus- sions, financial penalties, and reputational damage resulting from non-compliance.

Ethical considerations in cybersecurity encompass principles of integrity, transparency, accountability, and respect for privacy rights. Ethical decision-making in cy- bersecurity involves balancing the need for security measures with the protection of individual rights, ethical data handling practices, and responsible use of technology. Upholding ethical standards in cybersecurity ensures that data is handled ethically, users' privacy is respected, and cybersecurity measures are implemented in a fair and transparent manner.

Navigating the intersection of legal and ethical considerations in cybersecurity re- quires a comprehensive understanding of regulatory requirements, ethical frameworks, and industry best practices. By integrating legal compliance and ethical principles into cybersecurity strategies, organizations can enhance their resilience to cyber threats, build trust with stakeholders, and demonstrate a commitment to protecting data and privacy in the digital age.

As cybersecurity continues to evolve, the integration of legal and ethical considerations will remain essential in shaping cybersecurity policies, fostering a culture of security awareness, and promoting responsible cybersecurity practices to safeguard digital assets and mitigate cyber risks effectively.

4.2. *Cybersecurity Laws and Regulations*

4.2.1. General Data Protection Regulation (GDPR)

- Region: European Union (EU)
- Overview: GDPR is designed to protect the privacy and personal data of EU cit- izens. It imposes strict rules on data handling, requiring organizations to obtain explicit consent before collecting personal data and ensuring data protection by design and by default.
- Key Provisions: Data subject rights, breach notification, data protection officer (DPO) requirements, significant penalties for non-compliance.

4.2.2. California Consumer Privacy Act (CCPA)

- Region: California, USA
- Overview: CCPA enhances privacy rights and consumer protection for residents of California. It grants consumers the right to know what personal data is being collected about them, to whom it is being sold, and to access, delete, and opt out of the sale of their personal data.

- Key Provisions: Right to access information, right to delete information, right to opt-out of data selling, enhanced transparency requirements.

4.2.3. Health Insurance Portability and Accountability Act (HIPAA)

- Region: USA
- Overview: HIPAA establishes national standards for the protection of health information. It mandates secure handling of protected health information (PHI) by healthcare providers, insurers, and their business associates.
- Key Provisions: Privacy Rule, Security Rule, Breach Notification Rule, administrative, physical, and technical safeguards for PHI.

4.2.4. Federal Information Security Management Act (FISMA)

- Region: USA
- Overview: FISMA requires federal agencies and their contractors to implement information security programs to protect government information and opera- tions. It emphasizes risk management and compliance with NIST standards.
- Key Provisions: Information security policies, risk assessments, security controls, continuous monitoring.

4.2.5. Payment Card Industry Data Security Standard (PCI DSS)

- Region: Global
- Overview: PCI DSS is a set of security standards designed to ensure that all companies that accept, process, store, or transmit credit card information main- tain a secure environment. It aims to protect cardholder data and reduce credit card fraud.
- Key Provisions: Secure network, protection of cardholder data, vulnerability management, access control, monitoring and testing, information security policy.

4.2.6. Sarbanes-Oxley Act (SOX)

- Region: USA
- Overview: SOX was enacted to protect investors from fraudulent financial re- porting by corporations. It includes provisions related to the management and reporting of financial data, including IT controls over financial reporting systems.

- Key Provisions: Internal controls and procedures, auditor independence, corpo- rate responsibility, enhanced financial disclosures.

4.2.7. Personal Information Protection and Electronic Documents Act (PIPEDA)

- Region: Canada
- Overview: PIPEDA governs how private sector organizations collect, use, and disclose personal information in the course of commercial business. It aims to balance individuals' right to privacy with the needs of organizations to collect and use personal data.
- Key Provisions: Consent requirements, access to information, data protection principles, complaint procedures.

4.2.8. Cybersecurity Information Sharing Act (CISA)

- Region: USA
- Overview: CISA promotes the sharing of cybersecurity threat information be- tween the federal government and the private sector. It aims to enhance the collective cybersecurity posture by facilitating timely sharing of threat data.
- Key Provisions: Information sharing protocols, liability protection for shar- ing entities, privacy and civil liberties protections.

4.3. *Intellectual Property Protection*

Cybersecurity plays a critical role in protecting intellectual property (IP) from cyber threats and unauthorized access. Intellectual property, which includes patents, trade- marks, copyrights, and trade secrets, represents valuable assets for organi- zations and individuals, and safeguarding this information is essential to maintain competitiveness, innovation, and business success.

Cybersecurity measures are crucial in protecting intellectual property from var- ious cyber threats, such as data breaches, hacking, insider threats, and intellectual prop- erty theft. By implementing robust cybersecurity practices, organizations can mitigate the risks associated with cyber threats and ensure the confidentiality, integrity, and availability of their intellectual property assets.

Some key cybersecurity practices that can help protect intellectual property include:

- Access Control: Implementing strong access controls and user authentication mechanisms to restrict access to sensitive intellectual property and ensure that only authorized individuals can access and modify the information.
- Encryption: Encrypting sensitive intellectual property data at rest and in transit to protect it from unauthorized access and ensure data confidentiality.
- Regular Security Audits: Conducting regular security audits, vulnerability as- sessments, and penetration testing to identify and address security weaknesses that could expose intellectual property to cyber threats.
- Employee Training: Providing cybersecurity awareness training to employees to educate them about the importance of protecting intellectual property, recog- nizing potential threats, and following security best practices.
- Incident Response Plan: Developing and implementing an incident response plan to effectively respond to cybersecurity incidents involving intellectual property, including containment, investigation, and recovery procedures.
- Vendor Risk Management: Assessing and managing the cybersecurity risks posed by third-party vendors and service providers who have access to intellectual property to ensure that they adhere to security standards and practices.

5. CONCLUSION

This chapter has highlighted the critical elements of cybersecurity, from foundational principles to the spectrum of threats and vulnerabilities. Emphasizing best practices and adherence to legal and ethical standards is essential for building a robust cyber- security posture. Understanding these fundamentals empowers individuals and orga- nizations to implement effective security measures, mitigate risks, and navigate the complexities of the digital world with confidence. As cyber threats continue to evolve, maintaining a solid grasp of cybersecurity fundamentals remains paramount in safe- guarding information and systems.

REFERENCES

Abawajy, J., & Islam, R. (2017). Applications and techniques in information and network security. *Concurrency and Computation*, 29(23), e4351. Advance online publication. 10.1002/cpe.4351

Abrahams, T. (2024). Cybersecurity awareness and education programs: A review of em-ployee engagement and accountability. *Computer Science It Research Journal*, 5(1), 100–119. 10.51594/csitrj.v5i1.708

Aburrous, M., Hossain, M., Dahal, K., & Thabtah, F. (2010). Experimental case studies for investigating e-banking phishing techniques and attack strategies. *Cognitive Computation*, 2(3), 242–253. 10.1007/s12559-010-9042-7

Alamri, B., Crowley, K., & Richardson, I. (2022). Cybersecurity risk management frame- work for blockchain identity management systems in health iot. *Sensors (Basel)*, 23(1), 218. 10.3390/s2301021836616816

Alashi, S., & Badi, D. (2020). The role of governance in achieving sustainable cybersecurity for business corporations. *Journal of Information Security and Cybercrimes Research*, 3, 97–112. 10.26735/EINT7997

Alexei, A., & Alexei, A. (2023). The difference between cyber secu- rity vs information security. *Journal of Engineering Science*, 29(4), 72–83. 10.52326/jes.utm.2022.29(4).08

AllahRakha, N. (2024). Transformation of Crimes (Cybercrimes) in Digital Age. *International Journal of Law and Policy*, 2(2).

Alqahtani, H., & Kavakli, M. (2020). Design and evaluation of an aug- mented reality game for cybersecurity awareness (cybar). *Information (Basel)*, 11(2), 121. 10.3390/info11020121

Alqudhaibi, A., Deshpande, S., Jagtap, S., & Salonitis, K. (2023). Towards a sustainable future: Developing a cybersecurity framework for manufacturing. *Technological Sustainability*, 2(4), 372–387. 10.1108/TECHS-05-2023-0022

Berrada, G., Cheney, J., Benabderrahmane, S., Maxwell, W., Mookherjee, H., Theriault, A., & Wright, R. (2020). A baseline for unsupervised advanced persistent threat detec- tion in system-level provenance. *Future Generation Computer Systems*, 108, 401–413. 10.1016/j.future.2020.02.015

Bhardwaj, A., & Kaushik, K. (2022). Predictive analytics-based cybersecurity framework for cloud infrastructure. [IJCAC]. *International Journal of Cloud Applications and Computing*, 12(1), 1–20. 10.4018/IJCAC.297106

Bhumichai, D., Smiliotopoulos, C., Benton, R., Kambourakis, G., & Damopoulos, D. (2024). The convergence of artificial intelligence and blockchain: The state of play and the road ahead. *Information (Basel)*, 15(5), 268. 10.3390/info15050268

Bitaab, M., Cho, H., Oest, A., Zhang, P., Sun, Z., Pourmohamad, R., Kim, D., ... 2021. "Scam pandemic: how attackers exploit public fear through phishing." https://doi.org//arxiv.2103.12843.10.48550

Braun, B., Johns, M., Koestler, J., & Posegga, J.. 2014. "Phishsafe." .10.1145/2557547.2557553

Brijwani, G., P. Ajmire, and P. Thawani. 2023. "Future of quantum computing in cyber secu- rity." 267–298. .10.4018/978-1-6684-6697-1.ch016

Cains, M., Flora, L., Taber, D., King, Z., & Henshel, D. (2021). Defining cyber security and cyber security risk within a multidisciplinary context using expert elicitation. *Risk Analysis*, 42(8), 1643–1669. 10.1111/risa.1368733586204

Chizoba, O. J., & Kyari, B. A. (2020). Ensemble classifiers for detection of advanced persistent threats. Global Journal of Engineering and Technology Advances, 2(2), 001-010.

Choudhary, S., & Singh, N. (2022). Analysis of security-based access control models for cloud computing. [IJCAC]. *International Journal of Cloud Applications and Computing*, 12(1), 1–19.

Costanzo, D., Shao, Z., & Gu, R. (2016). End-to-end verification of information-flow security for c and assembly programs. *SIGPLAN Notices*, 51(6), 648–664. 10.1145/2980983.2908100

Crick, T., Davenport, J. H., Irons, A., & Prickett, T. (2019, October). A UK case study on cybersecurity education and accreditation. In 2019 IEEE Frontiers in Education Conference (FIE) (pp. 1-9). IEEE.

Da Veiga, A. (2016, July). A cybersecurity culture research philosophy and approach to develop a valid and reliable measuring instrument. In 2016 SAI computing conference (SAI) (pp. 1006-1015). IEEE.

De Villiers, J. E., & Calitz, A. P. (2020). A Supplementary Tool for Web-archiving Using Blockchain Technology. *The African Journal of Information and Communication*, 25, 1–14.

Dubey, H. A. R. S. H. I. T., Kumar, S. U. D. H. A. K. A. R., & Chhabra, A. N. U. R. E. E. T. (2022). Cyber Security Model to Secure Data Transmission using Cloud Cryptography. *Cyber Secur. Insights Mag*, 2, 9–12.

Dutta, A. (2021). Detecting phishing websites using machine learning technique. *PLoS One*, 16(10), e0258361. 10.1371/journal.pone.025836134634081

Elarco, D. N., Mamangun, J. X., Lescano, K. N., Lumongsud, A. G., Camacho, R. E., Domingo, A. J., ... & Briones, E. J. (2021). A comparative analysis on the acceptance and use of telemedicine between physicians and patients in selected Metro Manila healthcare institutions. A comparative analysis on the acceptance and use of telemedicine between physicians and patients in selected Metro Manila healthcare institutions, 88(1), 27-27.

Fortino, G., Guerrieri, A., Pace, P., Savaglio, C., & Spezzano, G. (2022). Iot platforms and security: An analysis of the leading industrial/commercial solutions. *Sensors (Basel)*, 22(6), 2196. 10.3390/s2206219635336368

Gaurav, A., Arya, V., & Santaniello, D. (2022). Analysis of machine learning based ddos attack detection techniques in software defined network. [CSIM]. *Cyber Security Insights Magazine*, 1(1), 1–6.

Goebel, K., & Rajamani, R. (2021). Policy, regulations and standards in prognostics and health management. *International Journal of Prognostics and Health Management*, 12(1). Advance online publication. 10.36001/ijphm.2021.v12i1.2908

Gupta, B. B. (Ed.). (2021). *Cloud Security: Concepts, Applications and Perspectives*. CRC Press.

Gupta, B. B., & Quamara, M. (2018a, February). Multi-layered cloud and fog based secure integrated transmission and storage framework for IoT based applications. In 2018 5th International Conference on Signal Processing and Integrated Networks (SPIN) (pp. 462-467). IEEE.

Gupta, B. B., & Quamara, M. (2018b). A dynamic security policies generation model for access control in smart card based applications. In Cyberspace Safety and Security: 10th International Symposium, CSS 2018, Amalfi, Italy, October 29–31, 2018 [Springer International Publishing.]. *Proceedings*, 10, 132–143.

Hahn, A., C. Sun, and C. Liu. (2016). "Cybersecurity ofscadawithin substations." 1–17. .10.1002/9781118755471.sgd055

H¨oyhty¨a, M., & Martio, J. (2020). Integrated satellite–terrestrial connectivity for au- tonomous ships: Survey and future research directions. *Remote Sensing (Basel)*, 12(15), 2507. 10.3390/rs12152507

Kalio, S. (2022). Phishing Attack: Raising Awareness and Protection Techniques.

Lee, J., Lee, Y., Lee, D., Kwon, H., & Shin, D. (2021). Classification of attack types and analysis of attack methods for profiling phishing mail attack groups. *IEEE Access : Practical Innovations, Open Solutions*, 9, 80866–80872. 10.1109/ACCESS.2021.3084897

Macnish, K., & Inguanzo, A. (2019). Smart information systems in cybersecurity. *Orbit Journal*, 2(2), 1–26. 10.29297/orbit.v2i2.105

Matheu, S., Hernandez-Ramos, J., Skarmeta, A., & Baldini, G. (2020). A survey of cy- bersecurity certification for the internet of things. *ACM Computing Surveys*, 53(6), 1–36. 10.1145/3410160

Mendoza, A. L., Hernandez, R. S., Quezada, M. T. P., & Hernandez, R. V. (2023). Cybersecurity among University students from Generation Z: A comparative study of the Undergraduate Programs in Administration and Public Accounting in two Mexican universities. *Tem Journal-Technology Education Management Informatics*, 12(1), 503–511.

Montanaro, U., Dixit, S., Fallah, S., Dianati, M., Stevens, A., Oxtoby, D., & Mouzakitis, A. (2018). Towards connected autonomous driving: Review of use-cases. *Vehicle System Dynamics*, 57(6), 779–814. 10.1080/00423114.2018.1492142

Monteiro, L., Rodrigues, Y., & Souza, A. (2023). Cybersecurity in cyber–physical power sys- tems. *Energies*, 16(12), 4556. 10.3390/en16124556

Moon, D., Im, H., Lee, J. D., & Park, J. H. (2014). MLDS: Multi-layer defense system for preventing advanced persistent threats. *Symmetry*, 6(4), 997–1010.

Neri, M., Niccolini, F., & Martino, L. (2023). Organizational cybersecurity readiness in the ict sector: A quanti-qualitative assessment. *Information and Computer Security*, 32(1), 38–52. 10.1108/ICS-05-2023-0084

Orji, U. (2018). The african union convention on cybersecurity: A regional response to- wards cyber stability? *Masaryk University Journal of Law and Technology*, 12(2), 91–130. 10.5817/MUJLT2018-2-1

Papaioannou, M., Pelekoudas-Oikonomou, F., Mantas, G., Serrelis, E., Rodriguez, J., & Fengou, M.-A. (2023). A survey on quantitative risk estimation approaches for secure and usable user authentication on smartphones. *Sensors (Basel)*, 23(6), 2979. 10.3390/s2306297936991690

Park, D. (2015). Draft of national cybersecurity act. *International Journal of Security and Its Applications*, 9(11), 105–112. 10.14257/ijsia.2015.9.11.11

Raposo, V. (2022). 'i'm right behind you': Digital contact tracing under euro- pean law. *Maastricht Journal of European and Comparative Law*, 29(4), 434–450. 10.1177/1023263X221116227

Reidsma, D., van der Ham, J., & Continella, A. (2023, February). Operationalizing cybersecurity research ethics review: from principles and guidelines to practice. In *2nd International Workshop on Ethics in Computer Security, EthiCS 2023*. Internet Society.

Ren, Z., Lu, W., & Xu, S. (2018). Preventive and reactive cyber defense dynamics is globally stable. *IEEE Transactions on Network Science and Engineering*, 5(2), 156–170. 10.1109/TNSE.2017.2734904

Renda, K. (2022). The development of eu cybersecurity policy: From a coordinating actor to a cyber power? *Ankara Avrupa Calismalari Dergisi*, 21(2), 467–495. 10.32450/aacd.1226890

Sabrina, M., & Defi, I. (2021). Telemedicine guidelines in south east asia—A scoping review. *Frontiers in Neurology*, 11, 581649. Advance online publication. 10.3389/fneur.2020.58164933519669

Sadik, S., Ahmed, M., Sikos, L., & Islam, A. (2020). Toward a sustainable cybersecurity ecosys- tem. *Computers*, 9(3), 74. 10.3390/computers9030074

Safkhani, M., Rostampour, S., Bendavid, Y., & Bagheri, N. (2020). Iot in medical amp; phar- maceutical: Designing lightweight rfid security protocols for ensuring supply chain integrity. *Computer Networks*, 181, 107558. 10.1016/j.comnet.2020.10755835023996

Sahabandu, D., B. Xiao, A. Clark, S. Lee, W. Lee, and R. Poovendran. 2018. "Dift games: dynamic information flow tracking games for advanced persistent threats." .10.1109/CDC.2018.8619416

Salem, O., Hossain, A., & Kamala, M. (2010, June). Awareness program and ai based tool to reduce risk of phishing attacks. In 2010 10th IEEE International Conference on Computer and Information Technology (pp. 1418-1423). IEEE.

Sarker, I., Furhad, H., & Nowrozy, R. (2021). Ai-driven cybersecurity: An overview, security intelligence modeling and research directions. *SN Computer Science*, 2(3), 173. Advance online publication. 10.1007/s42979-021-00557-0

Sawyer, G. (2021). A review of the cybersecurity programs in the united states army. *Journal of Information Technology*, 5(1), 22–30. 10.53819/81018102t2017

Schaaf, K., & Tekinerdo˘gan, B. (2021). A feature-based approach for guiding the selection of internet of things cybersecurity standards using text mining. *Concurrency and Computation*, 33(21), e6385. Advance online publication. 10.1002/cpe.6385

Setianingsih, L., Pulungan, R., Putra, A., Wibowo, M., & Syarip, . (2021). Risk assessment methods for cybersecurity in nuclear facilities: Compliance to regulatory require- ments. *International Journal of Advanced Computer Science and Applications*, 12(9). Advance online publication. 10.14569/IJACSA.2021.0120979

Sharma, K., & Gupta, B. B. (2018). Attack in smartphone Wi-Fi access channel: State of the art, current issues, and challenges. Next-Generation Networks: *Proceedings of CSI-2015*, 555-561.

Sharma, S., & Singh, S. K. (2022). IoT and its uses in Security Surveillance. Insights2Techinfo, pp1.

Shevchenko, S., Skladannyi, P., & Spasiteleva, S. (2023). Mathematical methods in cy- bersecurity: Catastrophe theory. *Cybersecurity Education Science Technique*, 3(19), 165–175. 10.28925/2663-4023.2023.19.165175

Sivan-Sevilla, I. (2018). Complementaries and contradictions: National security and privacy risks in u.s. federal policy, 1968–2018. *Policy and Internet*, 11(2), 172–214. 10.1002/poi3.189

Soldatos, J., Pra¸ca, I., & Jovanovi'c, A. (2021). *Cyber-Physical Threat Intelli- gence for Critical Infrastructures Security: Securing Critical Infrastructures in Air Transport, Water, Gas, Healthcare, Finance and Industry*. Now Publishers.

Song, Z., Skuric, A., & Ji, K. (2020). A recursive watermark method for hard real-time in- dustrial control system cyber-resilience enhancement. *IEEE Transactions on Automation Science and Engineering*, 17(2), 1030–1043. 10.1109/TASE.2019.2963257

Stevens, T. (2018). Global cybersecurity: New directions in theory and methods. *Politics and Governance*, 6(2), 1–4. 10.17645/pag.v6i2.1569

Swanzy, P., Abukari, A. M., & Ansong, E. D. (2024). Data security framework for protecting data in transit and data at rest in the cloud. *Current Journal of Applied Science and Technology*, 43(6), 61–77. 10.9734/cjast/2024/v43i64387

Tewari, A., & Gupta, B. B. (2018a). A lightweight mutual authentication approach for RFID tags in IoT devices. *International Journal of Networking and Virtual Organisations*, 18(2), 97–111.

Tewari, A., & Gupta, B. B. (2018b). A robust anonymity preserving authentication protocol for IoT devices. In *2018 IEEE International Conference on Consumer Electronics (ICCE)* (pp. 1-5). IEEE.

Tewari, A., & Gupta, B. B. (2020). Security, privacy and trust of different layers in Internet-of-Things (IoTs) framework. *Future Generation Computer Systems*, 108, 909–920. 10.1016/j.future.2018.04.027

Thakur, J., & Pathan, A. (2022). Innovations of phishing defense: The mechanism, mea- surement and defense strategies. *International Journal of Communication Networks and Information Security (Ijcnis)*, 10(1). Advance online publication. 10.17762/ijcnis.v10i1.2991

Tran, T., Beuran, R., & Hasegawa, S. (2023). Gamification-based cybersecurity awareness course for self-regulated learning. *International Journal of Information and Education Technology (IJIET)*, 13(4), 724–730. 10.18178/ijiet.2023.13.4.1859

Uysal, E., & Akgu¨n, M. (2023). P/key: Puf based second factor authentication. *PLoS One*, 18(2), e0280181. 10.1371/journal.pone.028018136758004

Wibowo, A. (2022). The importance of global effort to secure space sec- tor from cyberattack. *Intermestic Journal of International Studies*, 7(1), 298. 10.24198/intermestic.v7n1.14

Wiercioch, A., Teufel, S., & Teufel, B. (2018). The authentication dilemma. *Journal of Software*, 13(5), 277–286. 10.17706/jsw.13.5.277-286

Wilson, D. (2021). Cybersecurity. *Cybersecurity*. Advance online publication. 10.7551/mitpress/11656.001.0001

Xie, Y., Li, P., Nedjah, N., Gupta, B. B., Taniar, D., & Zhang, J. (2023). Pri- vacy protection framework for face recognition in edge-based Internet of Things. *Cluster Computing*, 26(5), 3017–3035. 10.1007/s10586-022-03808-8

Yan, F., Wen, S., Nepal, S., Paris, C., & Xiang, Y. (2022). Explainable machine learning in cybersecurity: A survey. *International Journal of Intelligent Systems*, 37(12), 12305–12334. 10.1002/int.23088

Yang, L., Li, P., Yang, X., & Tang, Y. (2017). Security evaluation of the cy- ber networks under advanced persistent threats. *IEEE Access : Practical Innovations, Open Solutions*, 5, 20111–20123. 10.1109/ACCESS.2017.2757944

Zeadally, S., Adi, E., Baig, Z., & Khan, I. (2020). Harnessing artificial intel- ligence capabilities to improve cybersecurity. *IEEE Access : Practical Innovations, Open Solutions*, 8, 23817–23837. 10.1109/ACCESS.2020.2968045

Chapter 5
Infrastructure and Network Security

Mosiur Rahaman
https://orcid.org/0000-0003-0521-2080
International Center for AI and Cyber Security Research and Innovations, Asia University, Taiwan

Sai Sravanthi Bakkireddygari
Department of Computer Science and Information Engineering, Asia University, Taiwan

Sourasis Chattopadhyay
https://orcid.org/0009-0000-7435-6550
Kalinga Institute of Industrial Technology, India

Alven L. Gomez
Northern Bukidnon State College, Philippines

Varsha Arya
Department of Business Administration, Asia University, Taiwan, & Department of Electrical and Computer Engineering, Lebanese American University, Beirut, Lebanon

Shavi Bansal
Insights2Techinfo, India, & UCRD, Chandigarh University, Chandigarh, India

ABSTRACT

This chapter thoroughly investigates safeguarding the Metaverse's complex infrastructure. The chapter, segmented into four distinct yet interconnected sections, meticulously dissects the multifaceted layers of Metaverse security. Initially, it delves into securing the architectural framework, examining everything from user interfaces to backend databases and underscoring the necessity for robust protocols to shield against various vulnerabilities. The chapter then focuses on strategies for mitigating DDoS (Distributed Denial of Service) attacks, highlighting the importance of advanced network security measures and AI-driven predictive models. Subsequently, it addresses the pivotal need for secure networking in real-time inter-

DOI: 10.4018/979-8-3693-3824-7.ch005

actions within the Metaverse, emphasizing data encryption, secure authentication, and user privacy. The final section provides a comprehensive overview of cloud security considerations essential for the Metaverse, discussing challenges like data breaches and outlining best practices for maintaining a secure cloud infrastructure. By incorporating diverse perspectives from network engineering to digital ethics, this chapter extensively analyzes the current state and evolving challenges in Metaverse security, aiming to empower developers, policymakers, and users in navigating and reinforcing this novel digital realm's security landscape. Novelty: The source of the novelty is a multidisciplinary approach that combines network security measures, AI-driven predictive models, strong encryption protocols, and thorough cloud security practices to empower developers, policymakers, and users in the process of strengthening the security landscape of the Metaverse. By employing this all-complete perspective, data and service availability, confidentiality, and integrity within the dynamic digital space of the Metaverse are effectively protected.

INTRODUCTION:

The Metaverse is a huge and interconnected network of virtual environments where users can communicate, socialize, and do business in a fully immersive environment. It is considered the next frontier in digital interaction. The intricate infrastructure of this virtual world is made up of cloud-based services, real-time data processing, backend databases, and user interfaces (Dwivedi et al., 2022). Ensuring a unified and captivating user experience is based upon the flawless execution of these components. The architecture of the Metaverse must constantly change as it develops to meet the needs of users and keep up with technological breakthroughs (Pyae et al., 2023).

Security in this ecosystem is crucial since the Metaverse is increasingly becoming a part of our digital life. Because the Metaverse is so linked, there is an increased risk of data breaches, cyberattacks, and privacy violations (Kaur et al., 2023). Strong security protocols are necessary to preserve users' confidence, safeguard their private data, and guarantee the Metaverse infrastructure's stability. Creating and implementing comprehensive security plans is essential as more and more areas of our lives move into the Metaverse, and the potential implications of security failings get progressively worse (Tukur et al., 2023).

This large digital ecosystem is supported by the Metaverse's architectural framework, which includes backend databases, user interfaces, and several supporting protocols. Maintaining the integrity and dependability of the Metaverse depends critically on ensuring the security of these core components.

The User Interface

Among users in the Metaverse, user interfaces (UIs) serve as the main point of contact. Preventing against typical vulnerabilities like malware, phishing attempts, and unauthorized access is part of securing these interfaces. The best ways to prevent UIs from being compromised are to implement robust authentication procedures, conduct frequent security audits, and educate users (Sharma et al., 2024).

Databases at the Backend

Being the primary target of cyberattacks, backend databases hold enormous volumes of sensitive user and transactional data. Regular vulnerability assessments, access control procedures, and strong encryption techniques are necessary to guarantee the security of these databases. Furthermore, identifying and containing any breaches before they cause major harm can be simplified using advanced threat detection systems (Tariq et al., 2023).

Security Requirements

To enable data sharing and communication amongst its many components, the Metaverse depends on several protocols. To stop data interception, manipulation, and unwanted access, strong security protocols must be established and followed. Data integrity and secure connections are mostly dependent on protocols like advanced encryption standards (AES), SSL/TLS, and HTTPS.

The Metaverse can create a safe and reliable environment for users to conduct a range of activities, from social interactions to business transactions, by strengthening these fundamental components, which include user interfaces, backend databases, and security protocols (Chen et al., 2024).

The Metaverse is vulnerable to assaults known as Distributed Denial of Service (DDoS), which attempt to overwhelm its infrastructure and interfere with services. It is imperative to mitigate these attacks to preserve the Metaverse's availability and stability. The effective defenses against DDoS attacks discussed in this section emphasize the significance of AI-driven predictive models and smart network security mechanisms.

Enhanced Network Security Systems: Effectively detecting and neutralizing DDoS assaults requires the deployment of strong network security measures.

Intrusion Detection Systems: By deploying powerful IDS and firewalls, attackers can be stopped from overwhelming the network by filtering out hostile traffic and unusual operations.

Traffic Analysis: Identifying and filtering suspicious traffic allows for the maintenance of service access for authorized users. This is accomplished by employing traffic analysis tools to track network traffic patterns.

Restricting and Modulating Traffic: By implementing strategies for limiting and throttling traffic, network overload can be avoided, and the effects of DDoS attacks can be lessened.

HOW AI CAN MITIGATE DDOS ATTACKS ?

Anomaly Detection:

Using artificial intelligence (AI) algorithms to examine past traffic data, anomaly detection entails spotting regular trends and highlighting anomalies that might point to a DDoS assault. Statistical analysis, clustering, and classification are examples of machine learning approaches that are often used for this (Alzoubi et al., 2024).

Think of a Metaverse platform that suddenly sees a spike in traffic as an example. Systems that use artificial intelligence (AI) to discover anomalies, such as those that use the k-means clustering algorithm, compare past data with their current traffic patterns. The system issues an alert if it notices an odd increase that isn't consistent with normal user behavior (such as an abrupt surge of requests from a certain IP address or area). Security professionals can investigate and react to the attack before it causes a major disturbance thanks to this proactive detection.

Machine Learning Theory and Mechanism:

To become better at anticipating and averting DDoS attacks, machine learning models especially those that rely on supervised and unsupervised learning constantly learn from fresh data. By using labelled samples of both legitimate and malicious traffic in their training datasets, these models learn over time (Garba et al., 2024).

Example: A supervised learning model, like a neural network, is used by a Metaverse platform. It has been trained on large datasets of traffic patterns. The model adjusts its parameters in real time to improve its forecasting power. For example, the model learns to identify which kinds of traffic spikes are indicators of impending attacks after identifying and thwarting multiple DDoS attempts. As a result, its ability to anticipate future attacks and recommend preventive actions like requiring temporary user authentication during predicted attack periods increases.

Prominent online infrastructure provider Cloudflare uses AI-powered solutions to fend against DDoS assaults. Their machine learning algorithms look for irregularities by analyzing massive volumes of traffic data from their global network.

Their system immediately reroutes traffic and applies mitigation techniques when it detects an attack.

Data Encryption and Implementation:

Maintaining a secure and reliable environment within the Metaverse depends on ensuring secure networking for real-time interactions. This entails putting strong data encryption, authentication techniques, and user privacy safeguards into place.

To safeguard critical information sent during real-time conversations, data encryption is necessary. By making ensuring that data cannot be viewed by unauthorized outsiders, it protects user interactions and transactions (Networks et al., 1994).

Authentication Methods and Technique:

By confirming users' identities, secure authentication guards against potential security breaches and unauthorized access to the Metaverse. Two popular techniques to improve security are biometric verification and multi-factor authentication (MFA).

Privacy Preservation:

Due to the constant flow of sensitive and personal data in the Metaverse, user privacy protection is crucial. Adopting stringent data protection guidelines and granting people authority over their data are essential to ensuring privacy.

User data is managed securely by adhering to privacy-by-design principles, which incorporate privacy features into the system architecture from the start. Users can control their data visibility and consent preferences when explicit privacy settings are provided.

Security Concern in Cloud:

Maintaining a secure cloud infrastructure is necessary to keep the Metaverse running continuously. This section offers a thorough summary of the difficulties and recommended procedures related to cloud security and challenges shows in figure 1.

Figure 1. Security challenges and best Practices in Cloud

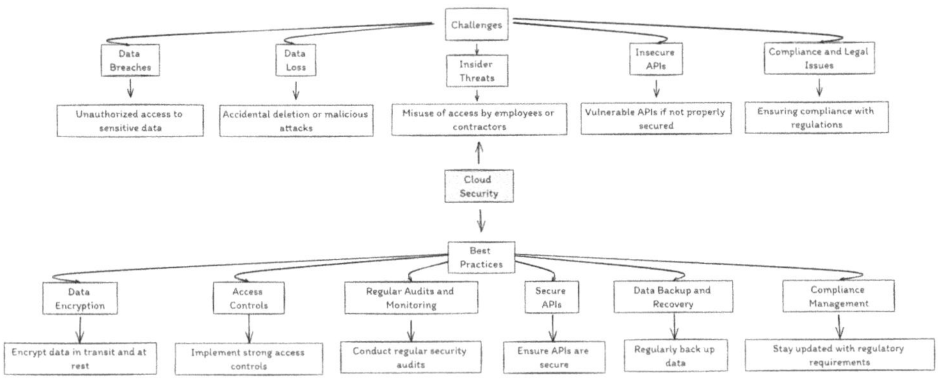

A secure cloud infrastructure in the Metaverse necessitates tackling serious issues like insider threats from staff members abusing their privileges, unintentional or malicious data loss, vulnerabilities in APIs that can be used to gain unauthorized access, and insider threats with sensitive data. It's also essential to adhere to intricate regulatory requirements (Dawood et al., 2023). Using strong access controls and multi-factor authentication, encrypting data while it's in transit and at rest, conducting frequent security audits and continuous monitoring, securing APIs with strong authentication and encryption, keeping regular data backups, and utilizing compliance management tools to ensure regulatory compliance are some best practices to reduce these risks. To preserve a dependable and safe cloud infrastructure and safeguard user data, the Metaverse must solve these issues and implement these best practices.

Securing the Metaverse Architecture, this section delves into the foundational aspect of Metaverse security – its architectural framework. It explores the various layers of the Metaverse architecture, from user interface components to backend databases, and discusses the security challenges associated with each layer. Emphasis is placed on implementing robust security protocols to protect against vulnerabilities in software coding, data storage, and user interaction points. The section also addresses the complexity of integrating multiple platforms and technologies within the Metaverse and the need for a unified security approach to protect the integrity and privacy of user data.

Mitigating DDoS Attacks in Virtual Worlds, Recognizing the susceptibility of virtual worlds to Distributed Denial of Service (DDoS) attacks, this part of the chapter examines the strategies and technologies necessary to mitigate such threats. It covers the techniques used by attackers to overwhelm virtual world servers and disrupt services and discusses the implementation of advanced network security measures, including traffic analysis, real-time monitoring, and incident response protocols. The section also provides insights into proactive defense mechanisms, including AI-driven predictive models, to identify and counteract potential DDoS attacks preemptively.

Secure Networking for Real-Time Interactions, focusing on the real-time interactive aspect of the Metaverse, this section addresses the security challenges in ensuring safe and seamless communication between users. It discusses the encryption of data transmissions, secure authentication methods, and the protection of user anonymity and confidentiality during interactions. The section also highlights the importance of maintaining low latency in network communications while ensuring security, a critical factor for an immersive user experience in the Metaverse.

Cloud Security Considerations for the Metaverse, Given the significant role of cloud computing in powering the Metaverse, this final section delves into the security considerations for cloud-based Metaverse platforms. It discusses the challenges of securing cloud infrastructure, including data breaches, unauthorized access, and cloud service vulnerabilities. The section outlines best practices for cloud security in the Metaverse context, such as multi-factor authentication, end-to-end encryption, regular security audits, and compliance with data protection regulations.

Throughout the chapter, there is an emphasis on a multidisciplinary approach, incorporating insights from network engineering, cybersecurity, cloud computing, and digital ethics. By providing an in-depth exploration of infrastructure and network security, this chapter aims to equip developers, policymakers, and users with the necessary knowledge to navigate and fortify the security landscape of the Metaverse.

SECTION 1: SECURING THE ARCHITECTURAL FRAMEWORK

1.1. Interfaces for users

The main means of communication between users and the Metaverse are user interfaces, or UIs. To safeguard consumers from any dangers and offer a flawless experience, it is imperative to guarantee the security of these interfaces.

1.2. Security of User Interfaces Is Critical

Preserving user confidence and protecting personal data require trustworthy user interfaces. Users are exposed to phishing attempts, data breaches, and unauthorized access in the absence of secure user interfaces, which can result in serious security problems.

1.3. Basic Vulnerabilities and mitigation techniques:

Common vulnerabilities like SQL Injection, Man-in-the-Middle (MITM) attacks, and Cross-Site Scripting (XSS) must be addressed to secure user interfaces within the Metaverse. The mitigation of each of these vulnerabilities entails certain strategies and procedures that frequently make use of mathematical equations and cryptography principles. Together, these flaws offer serious hazards.

Vulnerability Cross-Site Scripting (XSS): XSS attacks happen when an attacker inserts harmful scripts into content that comes from websites that are otherwise reliable. This may result in further nefarious behaviors like session hijacking and data theft.

Techniques of Mitigation:

Validation: Verify that user inputs follow the required formats by doing validation.

Sanitization: Remove special characters from inputs to make them clean.

Mathematical Representation:

Let I be the user input,and $V(I)$ be the validation function:

$$V(I) = \begin{cases} I \text{ if } I \text{ is Valid} \\ error \text{ if } I \text{ is invalid} \end{cases}$$

For sanitization, let $S(I)$ be the sanitization function:

$S(I) = I'$ where all special characters in I are escaped.

Content Security Policy:Script loading sources can be limited by implementing Content Security Policy (CSP).

As an example:

default – src'self'; script – src'self' is the content security policy set. script – src'self'; default – src'self' Content – Security – Policy : https://trusted.cdn.com ;

SQL Injection: An attacker can modify a database by inserting malicious SQL commands into an entry field and then executing them. This is known as the SQL Injection vulnerability.

Strategies for Mitigation:

Parameterized Queries and Prepared Statements when defining SQL code and binding parameters independently, using prepared statements.

Let P be the parameters and Q be the SQL query:

Q stands for "*SELECT * FROM users WHERE username* = ? *AND password* = ?"

Q="SELECT * FROM users WHERE username = ? AND password = ?"

P = (u ser n a m e, password)

P= (password, username)

Subsequently, the database engine securely inserts the parameters P into Q.

Input validation: Check that inputs follow expected formats, same as with XSS.

Let be the user input,and be the validation function:

1.4. Backend Database:

Because they house vital user and transactional data, backend databases play a key role in the design of the Metaverse. This renders them highly vulnerable to attackers. Safeguarding these databases is vital to guarantee data security and integrity, which in turn safeguards user confidence and system dependability.

Requirements for backend databases include:

i. Save user profiles with private information and preferences.
ii. Keeping track of transactional data is crucial to preserving the accuracy and consistency of financial and other user-related transactions.
iii. Act as the foundation for real-time interactions by securely and swiftly storing and retrieving data.

SQL Injection Attacks:

Vulnerability: SQL injection attacks are made when an attacker uses a database query execution vulnerability to introduce malicious SQL code into a query.

1.5. Protocols and Requirements

Protocols as well as requirements are crucial for guaranteeing secure communication and data management within the Metaverse. They offer principles and processes that safeguard the integrity, confidentiality, and validity of data exchanges. An successful method entails the utilization of Elliptic Curve Cryptography (ECC) and the Elliptic Curve Digital Signature Algorithm (ECDSA) for the establishment of secure protocols.

1.6. Enforcing Resilient Security Protocols

Ensuring strong security measures is essential for preserving the reliability, secrecy, and accessibility of data in the Metaverse. This entails implementing industry-leading methodologies, performing routine security evaluations, and guaranteeing thorough employee instruction.

Implementing the most effective methods and strategies used by the industry.

Following well-established security standards, such as ISO/IEC 27001 and the NIST Cybersecurity Framework, offers a systematic method for monitoring and safeguarding information systems.

The ISO/IEC 27001 standard is a globally recognized benchmark for the implementation and operation of information security management systems (ISMS). It offers a methodical strategy to overseeing confidential company data, guaranteeing its protection.

Man-in-the-Middle (MITM) Attack

Vulnerability:

MITM attacks involve intercepting and potentially altering communications between two parties without their knowledge.

Mitigation Techniques:

1. Use of HTTPS:

Encrypting data in transit using HTTPS to protect against eavesdropping and tampering.

Mathematical Representation:

HTTPS relies on SSL/TLS protocols, which use asymmetric cryptography to establish a secure Sessions.

Let represent the encryption of the message with the public key , and represent the decryption of ciphertext with the private key .

Establishing a secure session involves:

2. Digital Certificates:

Using digital certificates issued by trusted Certificate Authorities (CAs) to authenticate the server.

Mathematical Representation:

A digital certificate contains the public key and a signature from CA:
Clients verify the certificate by:

Regular Security Audits

Importance:
Conducting frequent security audits helps identity and fix vulnerabilities before they can be exploited.
Mitigation Techniques:

1. Automated Scanning Tools:

Using automated tools to scan for common Vulnerabilities.
Example:
Tools like OWASP ZAP or Nessus can systematically check for known security issues.
Security experts manually test the system for vulnerabilities that automated tools might miss.
Example:
Let be the set of automated checks and M be the set of manual tests:
Where is the comprehensive set of security tests /ensuring thorough coverage.
By implementing these mitigation techniques, we can significantly reduce the risk of XSS, SQL injection, and MITM attacks, thereby enhancing the security of user interfaces in the Metaverse.

Security Challenges in Database Management

SQL Injection Attacks

Vulnerability:

SQL injection occurs when an attacker inserts or "injects" a malicious SQL query into an input field, which is then executed by the backend database. This can lead to unauthorized data access, data manipulation, or even deletion.

Example Scenario:

Consider a login from where a user inputs their username and password. The backend SQL query might look like this:

If an attacker enters 'username=' OR '1'='1' and password=' OR '1'='1', the query becomes:

This query always returns true, allowing attacker to bypass authentication.

Mitigation Techniques:

1. Parameterized Queries:

Use parameterized queries to separate SQL code from data, preventing the execution of malicious SQL.

Mathematical Representation:

Let be the SQL query template and be the parameters:

The database engine safely substitutes the parameters into .

2. Stored Procedure:

Use stored procedures, which are predefined SQL statements stored in the database, to handle user input securely.

Mathematical Representation:

Let be a stored procedure.

3. Input Validation:

Validate input to ensure they conform to expected formats before using them in SQL Queries.

Mathematical Representation:

Let be the input validation function:

Unauthorized Access

Vulnerability:

Unauthorized access occurs when individuals gain access to the database without proper authorization, potentially leading to data breaches and unauthorized data manipulation.

Mitigation Techniques:

1. Access Control:

Implement strict access control mechanisms to ensure only authorized users can access the database.

Mathematical Representation:

Let be the set of users and be the access level of user :

2. Role-Based Access Control (RBAC):

Assign roles to users and grant permissions based on their roles.

Mathematical Representation:

Let be the set of roles,) be the permissions of the role , and be the role of the user :

3. Encryption:

Encrypt sensitive data to protect it even if unauthorized access is gained.

Mathematical Representation:

Let be the data and be the encryption of using key :

Data Leakage

Vulnerability:

Data leakage refers to the unintentional exposure of sensitive data, which can occur through various channels, such as improper data disposal, inadequate access controls, or inadvertent data sharing.

Mitigation Techniques:

1. Data Masking:

Mask sensitive data to prevent unauthorized users from viewing it.

Mathematical Representation:

Let be the original data and be the masked data:

2. Data Encryption:

Encrypt sensitive data both at rest and in transit to protect it from being exposed during data breaches.

Mathematical Representation:

Let be the data and be the encryption of using key :

3. Access Audits:

Regularly audit data access logs to detect and respond to unauthorized data access attempts.

Mathematical Representation:

Let be the set of access logs and be the audit function:

By addressing these security challenges with effective mitigation techniques, we can ensure that backend databases in the Metaverse remain secure, maintaining the integrity and confidentiality of critical user data and transactional information.

Mathematical Representation:

Consider a vulnerable SQL query:

If an attacker enters 'username=' OR '1'='1' and password=' OR '1'='1', the query becomes:

This always evaluates to true, allowing unauthorized access.

Mitigation Techniques:

1. Parameterized Queries:

Use parameterized queries to separate SQL code from data, preventing the execution of malicious SQL.

Equation:

Let be the SQL query template and be the parameters:

The database engine safely substitutes the parameters into .

2. Stored Procedure:

Use stored procedures to handle user inputs securely.

Equation:

Let be a stored procedure:

3. Input Validation:

Validate inputs to ensure they conform to expected formats before using them in SQL queries.

Equation:

Let V(I) be the input validation function:

Unauthorized Access

Vulnerability:

Unauthorized access occurs when individuals gain access to the database without proper authorization, potentially leading to data breaches and unauthorized data manipulation.

Mitigation Techniques:

1. Access Control:

Implement strict access control mechanisms to ensure only authorized users can access the database.

Mathematical Representation:

Let be the set of users and be the access level of user :

2. Role-Based Access Control (RBAC):

Assign roles to users and grant permissions based on their roles.

Mathematical Representation:

Let be the set of roles,) be the permissions of the role , and be the role of the user :

3. Encryption:

Encrypt sensitive data to protect it even if unauthorized access is gained.

Mathematical Representation:

Let be the data and be the encryption of using key :

Data Leakage

Vulnerability:

Data leakage refers to the unintentional exposure of sensitive data, which can occur through various channels, such as improper data disposal, inadequate access controls, or inadvertent data sharing.

Mitigation Techniques:

1. Data Masking:

Mask sensitive data to prevent unauthorized users from viewing it.

Mathematical Representation:

Let be the original data and be the masked data:

2. Data Encryption:

Encrypt sensitive data both at rest and in transit to protect it from being exposed during data breaches.

Mathematical Representation:

Let be the data and be the encryption of using key :

3. Access Audits:

Regularly audit data access logs to detect and respond to unauthorized data access attempts.

Mathematical Representation:

Let be the set of access logs and be the audit function:

By addressing these security challenges with effective mitigation techniques, we can ensure that backend databases in the Metaverse remain secure, maintaining the integrity and confidentiality of critical user data and transactional information.

Best Practices for Database Security

Ensuring the security of backend databases is critical for protecting the integrity and confidentiality of data within the Metaverse. Implementing best practices such as encryption, access control, and regular updates and patching can mitigate various security risks.

Encryption:

Encrypting data at rest ensures that stored data is unreadable to unauthorized users.

Mathematical Representation:

Let be the data and be the encryption key used for data at rest. The encrypted data is given by:

Decryption:

To read the data, it must be decrypted using the same key

Encryption in Transit:

Encrypting data in transit protects data being transmitted over the network from eavesdropping and tampering.

Mathematical Representation:

Let be the message and be the encryption key used for data in transit. The encrypted message is given by:

Decryption:

To read the message, it must be decrypted using the same key

Role-Based Access Control (RBAC):

RBAC is a method of restricting access based on the roles of individual users within an organization.

Mathematical Representation:

Let be the set of users, be the set of roles, and be the set of permissions. Define:

Access Determination:

A user has access to a resource if:
Example:
If user has role and role has permissions, then

Multi-Factor Authentication (MFA):

MFA adds an additional layer of security by requiring multiple forms of verification.

Mathematical Representation:

Let be the identity factors provided by the user. Access is granted if all factors are verified:

Regular Updates and Patching

Importance:

Regular updates and patching address known vulnerabilities and reduce the risk of exploitation.

Mathematical Representation:

Let be the software state and be the set of patches. Define:

Patch Application:

For each patch in :
Example:
If the initial software state is vulnerable, applying a series of patches results in an updated and more secure state

Summary:

Implementing these best practices ensures that backend databases in the Metaverse are secure and resilient against attacks.

1. **Encryption:** Protects data at rest and in transit, ensuring confidentiality and integrity
2. **Access Control:** Uses RBAC and MFA to ensure only authorized users can access the database.
3. **Regular Updates and Patching:** Keeps the database software up to date to protect against known vulnerabilities.

By adhering to these practices, organizations can significantly enhance the security of their backend databases, ensuring the protection of critical user data and transactional information.

Protocol Mechanism using ECC and ECDSA

Overview of ECC and ECDSA

- **ECC:** Utilizes the algebraic structure of elliptic curves over finite fields to create cryptographic keys.
- **ECDSA**: A variant of the Digital Signature Algorithm (DSA) which uses ECC to generate and verify digital signatures, ensuring data authenticity and integrity.

Key components

1. Elliptic Curve Parameters:
    - Curve Equation:
    - Base Point:
    - Order of the group:
    - Private Key: (a randomly selected integer)
    - Public Key:

Protocol Steps

1. Key Generation:

- Both the sender (Alice) and the receiver (Bob) agree on the elliptic curve parameters.
- Alice generated her private key and public key
- Bob generates his private key and public key

2. Digital Signature Creation (by Alice):
    - Alice wants to send a message to Bob.
    - Alice hashes the message to produce .
    - Alice selects a random integer and calculates:
    -

- Alice sends to Bob.

3. Signature verification (by Bob):

- Bob receives and Alice's public key .
- Bob verifies the signature by computing:
- The signature is valid if:

4. Secure Data Transmission:
    - To ensure confidentiality, Alice can encrypt the message using a shared secret derived from Bob's public key and her private key.
    - Shared Secret:
    - Encrypted Message:
5. Decryption (by Bob):
    - Bob computes the shared secret using Alice's public key and his private key.
    - Shared Secret
    - Decrypted Message: (C)

Summary

By following this ECC and ECDSA–based protocol mechanism, secure communication, and data handling within the Metaverse can be achieved. The use of elliptic curves provides robust security with smaller key sizes, ensuring efficiency and strong cryptographic guarantees.

1. Key Generation:
2. Signature Creation:
3. Signature Verification:
4. Encryption and Decryption:

Mathematical Representation:

Let be the set of security controls, be the set of risks, and be the set of assets Define

The goal is to minimize the risks by applying appropriate controls to protect assets

NIST Cybersecurity Framework:

The NIST Cybersecurity Framework provides guidelines for managing and reducing cybersecurity risks. It consists of five core functions: Identity, Protect, Detect, Respond, and Recover.

Mathematical Representation:

Let F represent the Framework Functions:

For each function

Vulnerability Assessments:

Vulnerability assessments identify, quantify, and prioritize vulnerabilities in a system.

Mathematical Representation:

Let be the set of vulnerabilities, be the set of severity scores, and be the set of priorities:

Each vulnerability is assigned a severity score and a priority

Employee Training

Ensuring all personnel are trained in security best practices and awareness is vital for maintaining a strong security posture.

Security Awareness Training:

Training programs educate employees about security policies, threat recognition, and safe practices.

Mathematical Representation:

Let be the set of training modules and be the set of employees:

Each employee completes training modules

Adopting Industry Best Practices

Regular Security Assessments

Employee Training

By adhering to these practices, organizations can ensure a robust security framework, protecting their assets and maintaining trust within the Metaverse.

For each function :

Regular Security Assessments

Regular security assessments, including audits and vulnerability assessments, help identify and mitigate potential security weaknesses.

Security Audits:

Security audits systematically evaluate the effectiveness of security measures and compliances with policies and regulations.

Mathematical Representation:

Let be the set of audit activities and be the set of evaluation criteria:

Each audit activity is evaluated against criteria :

SECTION 2: MITIGATING DDOS ATTACKS

I. Detecting DDoS Threats

Attacks known as DDoS (Distributed Denial of Service) overload a target system with a deluge of traffic from several sources, disrupting its functionality. These attacks take use of holes in infrastructure and network protocols to drain resources, rendering services unusable for authorized users.

ii. DDoS Attack Types

Attacks using volumetrics: Create a lot of traffic to fill the available bandwidth.

Protocol Attacks: Take use of flaws in network protocols, such as SYN flooding.

Application Layer Attacks: To interfere with services, target particular applications (such as HTTP floods).

iv. Effects on the Metaverse Infrastructure

DDoS attacks have the potential to cause significant disruptions to the Metaverse due to: Excessive server load resulting in service unavailability. Impairing user satisfaction as a result of sluggish or unresponsive services. Rising expenses associated with the efforts to reduce and recover from negative impacts.

iv. Enhanced Network Security Protocols

Advanced network security techniques are crucial for safeguarding against DDoS attacks. These methods encompass proactive defenses that have the capability to detect and neutralize threats prior to causing substantial harm.

Firewalls and Intrusion Detection Systems:

Firewalls function as barriers that selectively block harmful network traffic by applying predetermined criteria.

Intrusion Detection Systems (IDS):Intrusion Detection Systems are designed to monitor network traffic in order to detect and identify any suspicious activity. When such actions are detected, IDS create alerts to notify the appropriate personnel.

vi. Techniques for analyzing and filtering traffic:

Traffic analysis entails the surveillance and examination of network traffic to detect irregular trends. Filtering methods, such as rate limitation and blacklisting, are employed to obstruct or alleviate malevolent network traffic.

vii. Artificial Intelligence-Powered Predictive Models:

AI-powered predictive models utilize machine learning algorithms to examine traffic trends and forecast probable DDoS attacks. These models iteratively acquire knowledge from fresh data to enhance their precision and efficacy. The Function of Artificial Intelligence in Identifying and Mitigating Distributed Denial of Service (DDoS) Attacks. Artificial intelligence (AI) plays a crucial role in identifying and thwarting Distributed Denial of Service (DDoS) attacks through the following methods:

1.Implementing automated reactions to identified threats.
2.Improving the effectiveness and precision of mitigating methods.

viii. Illustrative Examples and Practical Implementations

Practical uses of artificial intelligence (AI) in reducing the impact of distributed denial-of-service (DDoS) assaults include:

1.Cloudflare: employs artificial intelligence to scan network traffic and identify distributed denial-of-service (DDoS) attacks, automatically implementing measures to counteract them.
2.Google Cloud Protection:Employs machine learning techniques to safeguard apps from DDoS attacks by accurately detecting and blocking harmful network traffic.

SECTION 3: SECURE NETWORKING FOR REAL-TIME INTERACTIONS

Data encryption is a security technique in which data is converted into a cipher or inaccessible form, making the original information inaccessible to anybody without the necessary decryption keys. This procedure protects data while it's in transit and at rest, and it forms the basis of contemporary data security. Two fundamental components of the system are the encryption algorithm and the keys that are utilized for both encryption and decryption.

Mathematical formulas or procedures known as encryption algorithms are used to transform plaintext into ciphertext. Popular algorithms consist of:

Symmetric Key: Employ the same key for encryption and decryption when using symmetric key algorithms. Data Encryption Standard (DES) and Advanced Encryption Standard (AES) are two examples. For big data volumes, they are quick and effective.

Asymmetric Key: Use a pair of keys, one for encryption (public key) and another for decryption (private key) when utilizing asymmetric key algorithms. Rivest-Shamir-Adleman (RSA) and elliptic curve cryptography (ECC) are two examples. Usually, these are utilized for digital signatures and safe key exchanges.

Key Management: It's essential to manage keys effectively. Key creation, storage, delivery, and destruction are all included. Robust encryption techniques can be undermined by bad key management, which can result in data leaks.

Applications: Data encryption is typically used for two types of data: data in transit (data traveling across a network) and data at rest (data kept on a device or server). HTTPS, for example, uses SSL/TLS protocols to encrypt data sent back and forth between a web browser and a server, guaranteeing safe online interactions.

Virtual reality, augmented reality, and Internet of Things (IoT) devices are just a few of the interactive components that make up the Metaverse, a sophisticated digital ecosystem that exchanges enormous volumes of user data on a continuous basis. To protect user security and privacy in such a situation, encryption is essential:

Confidentiality: Encryption guarantees the privacy of sensitive information, including financial data, private messages, and personal details. The information can only be accessed in its intended format by those who have the decryption key.

Integrity: It contributes to the preservation of data integrity by shielding it from unwanted changes. Technology that helps confirm that data has not been altered while in transit includes cryptographic hash functions and digital signatures, which are essential parts of encryption methods.

Authentication: Before allowing access to critical information or functions in the Metaverse, it is essential to confirm the identity of users or devices. By using digital signatures and certificates, encryption helps to verify that the entities are who they say they are.

Encryption protocols are a collection of regulations that govern the process of encrypting and decrypting data. Essential protocols consist of:

SSL/TLS: SSL and its successor, TLS, are protocols designed to secure internet communications. Encryption is used to secure the transmission of data via networks, guaranteeing the confidentiality and integrity of sensitive information such as credit card numbers and personal data. Implementation entails the configuration of SSL/TLS certificates on servers. These certificates verify the identity of the server and enable a secure connection through a handshake procedure.

Advanced Encryption Standard (AES): Advanced Encryption Standard, is a symmetric key encryption technique that has been selected by the U.S. government as the standard for encrypting secret material. AES is commonly employed due to its high efficiency across a range of hardware and software settings. Implementing AES requires the selection of key sizes (128, 192, or 256 bits) based on the desired security level and the implementation of strong key management methods.

Rivest Shamir Adleman (RSA): RSA is an encryption technique that is mostly utilized for safe transfer of data. It is an asymmetric encryption algorithm. The system operates based on the premise of employing a pair of keys: a public key for encryption and a private key for decryption. RSA is frequently utilized in digital signatures and SSL/TLS protocols to ensure safe key transfers.

Secure Authentication:

- Secure authentication mechanisms are implemented to validate the identity of users in order to safeguard systems against illegal access.

- Credential Verification involves the process of comparing user-provided credentials, such as usernames and passwords, with the stored credentials.
- Session Management refers to the process of ensuring the security and privacy of user sessions once they have been authenticated.

Security Protocols:

Implementing safeguards against brute force assaults, phishing, and other potential hazards.

Multi-factor Authentication:

Multi-factor authentication improves security by mandating the use of two or more verification factors, hence substantially reducing the likelihood of illegal access. Typical MFA methods include:

- Knowledge Factors: Information that the user possesses, such as passwords and PINs.
- Possession Factors: Items that the user possesses, such as security tokens and smartphones.
- Inherent Factors: User's biometric characteristics.

Biometric and behavioral authentication refers to the process of verifying an individual's identity using unique physical or behavioral characteristics. Biometric Authentication refers to the use of physical traits, such as fingerprints, facial recognition, or iris scans, to verify and confirm the identities of individuals. While biometric technology offers the advantages of being challenging to counterfeit and user-friendly, it necessitates meticulous management and secure storage of biometric data to avoid compromising privacy.

Behavioral authentication involves the analysis of users' behavior patterns, such as typing speed, mouse movements, and even walking behaviors. The system provides ongoing verification and can identify irregularities that may suggest unauthorized efforts to get access.

Ensuring User Privacy in Digital Platforms Encompasses:

- Data Protection: Ensuring that personal data is only accessed by authorized entities and solely for allowed reasons.
- Compliance involves conforming to privacy rules and regulations such as GDPR and CCPA, which stipulate the appropriate handling of user data.

- Transparency refers to the act of providing users with clear and comprehensive information regarding the collection and utilization of their data.

Issues of Privacy in Live Interactions

Instantaneous interactions, especially in settings such as the Metaverse, are prone to eavesdropping and the unauthorized release of data. To safeguard these conversations, it is imperative to employ encryption, establish secure channels, and maintain persistent surveillance.

- Data anonymization refers to the process of eliminating personally identifiable information (PII) from data collections.
- End-to-End Encryption guarantees that data is encrypted throughout its entire journey, starting from the moment it is sent until it reaches its intended recipient, and can only be accessed by the people involved in the communication.
- Access controls involve limiting data access according to user roles and specific requirements.

Privacy-Enhancing Technologies (PETs) are technologies that aim to reduce the amount of personal data used while maintaining the functionality of the system. Examples of PETs include differential privacy and zero-knowledge proofs.

Preventing Data Breaches and spying: Encryption serves as the first line of defense against potential threats from hackers and spying. It guarantees that information stays unreadable even if data traffic is intercepted, and one does not have the necessary decryption keys. Encryption plays an increasingly important role in safeguarding these virtual areas as the Metaverse develops. To provide a secure and reliable environment for users, developers and stakeholders need to give strong encryption techniques top priority.

Significance of encryption in the Metaverse: To safeguard private information and preserve user confidence, encryption is essential in the Metaverse. It guarantees that information exchanged in real-time exchanges is protected against manipulation and eavesdropping.

Figure 2. Data Encryption and Privacy in the Metaverse

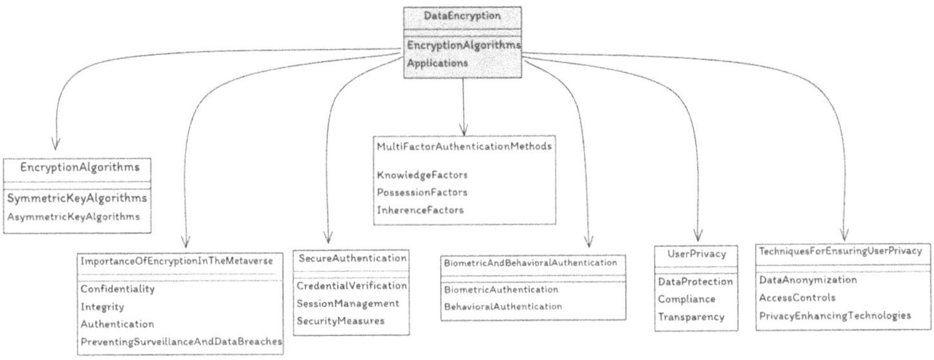

The Application of Encryption Protocols:

Transmission Layer Security which encrypts data traveling between clients and servers.

Computable Representation:

Where, the plaintext message is denoted by , the session key is denoted by , the encryption function is represented by , and the ciphertext is represented by .

Advanced Encryption Standard (AES): Data encryption in transit and at rest is frequently accomplished using AES.

where is the ciphertext, is the AES encryption function, is the message, and is the key.

TLS encrypts data in Metaverse applications when a user sends a message:

Identity Verification:

Methods of Multi-Factor Authentication (MFA) increases security by forcing users to provide two different kinds of verification.

Behavioral and Biometric Verification:

- Biometrics: Makes use of physical traits (such as a fingerprint or facial recognition system).
- Behavioral: Examines user patterns of activity, such as typing cadence.

In a Metaverse setting, entry to a forbidden place may need:

Concerns about User Privacy in Real-Time Interactions:

Unauthorized data access, tracking, and user profiling are among the privacy issues in the Metaverse for Protecting the Privacy of Users:

Erase personally identifying information from data sets through data anonymization.

The anonymization function is represented by the .

End-to-end encryption: Makes sure that only users who are in communication can access data.

Where, is the ciphertext, is the encryption function, is the decryption function, is the message, and is the encryption key.

Real-Time Illustration:

End-to-end encryption in a Metaverse virtual conference guarantees that discussions are confidential and available to participants only:

The Metaverse can offer its users safe and reliable real-time interactions by putting these encryption protocols, authentication strategies, and privacy mechanisms into practice.

SECTION 4: CLOUD SECURITY CONSIDERATIONS

Among the many difficulties facing cloud security in the Metaverse are insider attacks, misconfigurations, and data breaches. Both improper cloud resource design and unauthorized access to private data can leave systems highly vulnerable. Since attackers can take advantage of insecure APIs to obtain illegal access, they are another serious worry. Both user trust and service integrity are seriously threatened by data loss, whether it is from breaches, unintentional deletion, or malicious attacks. Furthermore, possible security holes can result from the restricted management and visibility over cloud resources. An ongoing danger, account hijacking compromises user accounts and results in illegal activities and data theft. Complicating cloud security even more are compliance and regulatory concerns, particularly when it comes to guaranteeing that data protection laws are followed in many jurisdictions. Further hazards can be introduced by shared technology vulnerabilities that result from shared infrastructure and multi-tenancy. Important risks are also insider misuse, when authorized staff utilize cloud resources improperly, and DDoS attacks, which interfere with cloud services and reduce availability. The intricacy and importance of protecting cloud settings in the Metaverse are highlighted along by weak identity management rules, inadequate disaster recovery planning, insufficient due diligence during cloud adoption, and third-party risks posed by service providers and partners.

Table 1. Challenges of Cloud Security in the Metaverse

No.	Challenge	Description
1	Data Breaches	Unauthorized access to sensitive data stored in the cloud.
2	Misconfigurations	Incorrect setup of cloud resources exposing systems to vulnerabilities.
3	Insider Threats	Employees or contractors misusing access to sensitive information.
4	Insecure APIs	Vulnerable application programming interfaces (APIs) that can be exploited by attackers.
5	Data Loss	Loss of data due to breaches, accidental deletion, or malicious attacks.
6	Lack of Visibility and Control	Limited oversight over cloud resources, leading to potential security gaps.
7	Account Hijacking	Compromise of user accounts leading to unauthorized actions and data theft.
8	Compliance and Regulatory Issues	Difficulties in ensuring compliance with data protection regulations across different jurisdictions.
9	Shared Technology Vulnerabilities	Risks arising from multi-tenancy and shared infrastructure in cloud environments.
10	DDoS Attacks	Distributed Denial of Service attacks that disrupt cloud services and affect availability.
11	Insider Misuse	Unauthorized or inappropriate use of cloud resources by insiders.
12	Weak Identity Management	Inadequate identity and access management policies leading to unauthorized access.
13	Limited Disaster Recovery	Insufficient disaster recovery planning and execution capabilities in cloud environments.
14	Insufficient Due Diligence	Failure to understand and mitigate cloud-specific risks during cloud adoption and deployment.
15	Third-Party Risks	Security risks introduced by third-party service providers and partners.

Following best practices is crucial to provide strong cloud security in the Metaverse. First, encryption of data is essential since it keeps sensitive information private and safe from unwanted access while it is in transit or at rest. Protecting data integrity can be achieved by using encryption protocols like TLS (Transport Layer Security) and secure communication channels like AES (Advanced Encryption Standard). Strict access management regulations must also be put in place. By limiting the possibility of unapproved data access, role-based access control (RBAC) makes sure that users have just the rights required for their responsibilities. By requiring many forms of verification, including a password plus a biometric scan or a security token, multi-factor authentication (MFA) increases security even further.

Audits and vulnerability evaluations are two types of routine security assessments that assist find and fix possible security flaws. Prolonged surveillance of cloud operations by sophisticated threat detection systems guarantees prompt reactions to any unusual activity or possible intrusions. Protection of data and prompt recovery in the event of data loss or breaches depend on secure storage options and strong backup plans. In the case of an attack or failure, putting in place thorough disaster recovery plans also helps to preserve company continuity.

Upholding cloud security requires initiatives for employee awareness and training. Human mistake and insider threats can be greatly reduced by making sure that all employees are aware of security best practices, possible threats, and the need of adhering to procedures. Moreover, the security posture of Metaverse platforms can be improved by keeping up with new developments in cloud security, such AI-driven threat detection and zero trust security scenarios. Organizations may give users of the Metaverse a safe, dependable, and reliable environment by incorporating these best practices.

The cloud security landscape is in a state of perpetual evolution, influenced by the emergence of new technologies and trends that are designed to improve resilience and protection. The adoption of Zero Trust Security models is one of the most significant trends. Zero trust architecture is based on the principle that no entity, regardless of its location within or outside the network, should be presumed to be trustworthy by default. Users are granted the minimum amount of privilege necessary, and each access request undergoes a thorough verification process. This method mitigates the likelihood of illicit access and insider threats.

Another critical advancement is the growing utilization of Artificial Intelligence (AI) and Machine Learning (ML) in cloud security. The real-time analysis of enormous amounts of data by AI and ML algorithms can identify patterns and anomalies that may indicate security threats. These technologies facilitate predictive analytics, which can predict and mitigate assaults prior to their occurrence. For instance, security information and event management (SIEM) systems that are driven by AI can identify and respond to anomalous activities, thereby offering a proactive defense against cyber threats.

Cloud-native security solutions are also garnering popularity. These solutions are specifically engineered for cloud environments, seamlessly integrating with cloud platforms to offer improved security. They encompass features such as infrastructure as code (IaC) security, continuous monitoring, and automated compliance checks, which guarantee that security policies are implemented consistently across all cloud resources.

Recent Developments in Cloud Security:

Protection of data and infrastructure has been substantially enhanced by recent developments in cloud security technology. One such advancement is Confidential Computing, which is designed to safeguard data in use by executing computations in a hardware-based trusted execution environment (TEE). This technology provides an additional layer of security by maintaining the encryption of data during the processing process.

Another cutting-edge advancement is quantum-resistant cryptography. Traditional encryption methods are at risk of becoming obsolete as quantum computing capabilities continue to develop. Quantum-resistant algorithms are engineered to resist attacks from quantum computers, thereby guaranteeing the long-term security of data.

Automated Threat Detection and Response (ATDR) systems have also undergone development. To detect and mitigate hazards in real time, these systems employ sophisticated AI and ML. ATDR systems can respond to assaults much more quickly by reducing the need for manual intervention, thereby minimizing potential damage.

Recent Advancement:

Blockchain technology is currently being investigated for cloud security applications, with a particular emphasis on the improvement of data integrity and the security of transactions. The decentralized nature of blockchains and their cryptographic protections can offer a transparent and tamper-proof method for recording transactions and administering identities.

Another significant advancement is the Secure Access Service Edge (SASE), which integrates wide area network (WAN) capabilities with network security functions (including secure web gateways, firewalls, and zero trust network access) to meet the dynamic, secure access requirements of organizations.

The Metaverse's Cloud Security Future Outlook:

The Metaverse's cloud security future appears to be encouraging, as ongoing developments guarantee enhanced protection mechanisms. The integration of these emergent trends and technologies will be essential in addressing the unique security challenges of the Metaverse as it expands. The primary focus will likely be on the development of more robust, AI-driven security measures, the enhancement of user privacy through advanced cryptographic techniques, and the assurance of seamless, secure interactions within this expansive virtual world. To guarantee a secure and dependable environment for all users, the Metaverse must remain ahead of these technological advancements.

CONCLUSION

This chapter has comprehensively examined the multifarious aspects of securing the Metaverse's infrastructure and network. Important areas of emphasis included safeguarding communication protocols, backend databases, and user interfaces. To protect against common vulnerabilities such as SQL injection, cross-site scripting, and man-in-the-middle attacks, the Metaverse can employ robust security measures, including input validation, encryption, and regular security audits. Discussions regarding the implementation of encryption protocols such as TLS and AES, as well as multi-factor authentication and biometric verification, were conducted to emphasize the importance of data encryption, secure authentication methods, and user privacy measures to guarantee secure and reliable real-time interactions within the Metaverse.

To detect and mitigate DDoS threats, it is essential to implement advanced network security measures and AI-driven predictive models. The availability and stability of services are essential in the presence of such assaults, and techniques such as traffic analysis, firewalls, and intrusion detection systems are essential for protecting them. The challenges of securing cloud infrastructure, such as data intrusions, insider threats, and compliance with regulatory requirements, were also addressed. The implementation of best practices, including data encryption, access control, regular updates and upgrading, and continuous monitoring, was advised to mitigate these risks and guarantee a resilient cloud environment.

The Metaverse security landscape is constantly changing, necessitating a comprehensive approach that incorporates insights from network engineering, cybersecurity, cloud computing, and digital ethics. The security landscape of the Metaverse can be effectively navigated and fortified by developers, policymakers, and users by adhering to industry best practices, undertaking regular security assessments, and organizing comprehensive employee training. As the Metaverse continues to expand and integrate into our digital lives, it will be essential to maintain a proactive and adaptive security posture to protect its infrastructure and guarantee a secure, immersive experience for all users.

This chapter has provided a thorough overview of the Metaverse's network security and infrastructure, paying special emphasis to the user interfaces, backend databases, and communication protocols. To protect against vulnerabilities like SQL injection, cross-site scripting, and man-in-the-middle attacks, robust security measures like input validation, encryption, and regular audits are essential. Multi-factor authentication, biometric verification, and encryption technologies like TLS and AES ensure secure interactions. Reducing DDoS attacks requires advanced network security measures and AI-driven models. The chapter also covers the challenges of cloud security and recommends best practices such data encryption, access control, and continuous monitoring. A comprehensive technique combining network engineering, cybersecurity, cloud computing, and digital ethics is needed to traverse and fortify the Metaverse's security environment. A proactive and flexible security posture is essential as the Metaverse expands to ensure that every user has a secure and engaging experience.

ACKNOWLEDGEMENT

This research work is supported by National Science and Technology Council (NSTC), Taiwan Grant No. NSTC112-2221-E-468-008-MY3 and NSTC 113-2811-E-468-002 .

REFERENCES

Al-Emran, M., & Deveci, M. (2024). Unlocking the potential of cybersecurity behavior in the metaverse: Overview, opportunities, challenges, and future research agendas. *Technology in Society*, 77, 102498. 10.1016/j.techsoc.2024.102498

Ali, M., Naeem, F., Kaddoum, G., & Hossain, E. (2023). Metaverse communications, networking, security, and applications: Research issues, state-of-the-art, and future directions. *IEEE Communications Surveys and Tutorials*.

Alzoubi, Y. I., Mishra, A., & Topcu, A. E. (2024). Research trends in deep learning and machine learning for cloud computing security. *Artificial Intelligence Review*, 57(5), 132. 10.1007/s10462-024-10776-5

Chen, Z., Gan, W., Wu, J., Lin, H., & Chen, C.-M. (2024). Metaverse for smart cities: A survey. *Internet of Things and Cyber-Physical Systems*, 4, 203–216. 10.1016/j.iotcps.2023.12.002

Dawood, M., Tu, S., Xiao, C., Alasmary, H., Waqas, M., & Rehman, S. U. (2023). Cyberattacks and Security of Cloud Computing: A Complete Guideline. *Symmetry*, 15(11), 11. Advance online publication. 10.3390/sym15111981

Dwivedi, Y. K., Hughes, L., Baabdullah, A. M., Ribeiro-Navarrete, S., Giannakis, M., Al-Debei, M. M., Dennehy, D., Metri, B., Buhalis, D., Cheung, C. M. K., Conboy, K., Doyle, R., Dubey, R., Dutot, V., Felix, R., Goyal, D. P., Gustafsson, A., Hinsch, C., Jebabli, I., & Wamba, S. F. (2022). Metaverse beyond the hype: Multidisciplinary perspectives on emerging challenges, opportunities, and agenda for research, practice and policy. *International Journal of Information Management*, 66, 102542. 10.1016/j.ijinfomgt.2022.102542

Garba, U. H., Toosi, A. N., Pasha, M. F., & Khan, S. (2024). SDN-based detection and mitigation of DDoS attacks on smart homes. *Computer Communications*, 221, 29–41. 10.1016/j.comcom.2024.04.001

Han, J., Yang, M., Chen, X., Liu, H., Wang, Y., Li, J., Su, Z., Li, Z., & Ma, X. (2022). Paradefender: A scenario-driven parallel system for defending metaverses. *IEEE Transactions on Systems, Man, and Cybernetics. Systems*, 53(4), 2118–2127. 10.1109/TSMC.2022.3228928

Han, J., Yang, M., Chen, X., Liu, H., Wang, Y., Li, J., Su, Z., Li, Z., & Ma, X. (2022). Paradefender: A scenario-driven parallel system for defending metaverses. *IEEE Transactions on Systems, Man, and Cybernetics. Systems*, 53(4), 2118–2127. 10.1109/TSMC.2022.3228928

Kaur, D., Singh, B., & Rani, S. (2023). Cyber Security in the Metaverse. In *Handbook of Research on AI-Based Technologies and Applications in the Era of the Metaverse* (pp. 418–435). IGI Global., 10.4018/978-1-6684-8851-5.ch023

Networks, I. of M. (US) C. on R. H. D., Donaldson, M. S., & Lohr, K. N. (1994). Confidentiality and Privacy of Personal Data. In *Health Data in the Information Age: Use, Disclosure, and Privacy*. National Academies Press (US). https://www.ncbi.nlm.nih.gov/books/NBK236546/

Pyae, A., Ravyse, W., Luimula, M., Pizarro-Lucas, E., Sanchez, P. L., Dorado-Diaz, I. P., & Thaw, A. K. (2023). Exploring User Experience and Usability in a Metaverse Learning Environment for Students: A Usability Study of the Artificial Intelligence, Innovation, and Society (AIIS). *Electronics (Basel)*, 12(20), 20. Advance online publication. 10.3390/electronics12204283

Saracoglu, D. (2023). Metaverse and New Cybersecurity Threats. In *Metaverse: Technologies, Opportunities and Threats* (pp. 99–121). Springer Nature Singapore. 10.1007/978-981-99-4641-9_7

Sharma, S., Singh, J., Gupta, A., Ali, F., Khan, F., & Kwak, D. (2024). User Safety and Security in the Metaverse: A Critical Review. *IEEE Open Journal of the Communications Society*, 1–1. 10.1109/OJCOMS.2024.3397044

Tariq, U., Ahmed, I., Bashir, A. K., & Shaukat, K. (2023). A Critical Cybersecurity Analysis and Future Research Directions for the Internet of Things: A Comprehensive Review. *Sensors (Basel)*, 23(8), 8. Advance online publication. 10.3390/s2308411737112457

Tukur, M., Schneider, J., Househ, M., Dokoro, A. H., Ismail, U. I., Dawaki, M., & Agus, M. (2023). The metaverse digital environments: A scoping review of the challenges, privacy and security issues. *Frontiers in Big Data*, 6, 1301812. 10.3389/fdata.2023.130181238074486

Wang, Y., Su, Z., Zhang, N., Xing, R., Liu, D., Luan, T. H., & Shen, X. (2022). A survey on metaverse: Fundamentals, security, and privacy. *IEEE Communications Surveys and Tutorials*.

Yu, B., Liu, Y., Ren, S., Zhou, Z., & Liu, J. (2023). METAseen: Analyzing network traffic and privacy policies in Web 3.0 based Metaverse. *Digital Communications and Networks*. Advance online publication. 10.1016/j.dcan.2023.11.006

Chapter 6
Standardization and Regulatory Challenges in Modern Cryptography

Boy Firmansyah
IBI Kosgoro 1957, Indonesia

Ritika Bansal
Insights2Techinfo, India

ABSTRACT

The field of modern cryptography faces significant standardization and regulatory challenges due to the rapid advancement of technology and the increasing importance of secure communication in various sectors. This abstract delves into the complexities surrounding the standardization and regulation of cryptographic algorithms and protocols.Standardization plays a crucial role in ensuring interoperability, security, and trustworthiness in cryptographic systems. However, the process of developing and implementing cryptographic standards is fraught with challenges such as balancing security requirements with usability, addressing evolving threats, and accommodating diverse stakeholder interests. One of the primary challenges in cryptographic standardization is the tension between the need for transparency and the desire to protect sensitive information. Openness and transparency are essential for building trust and verifying the security properties of cryptographic algorithms and protocols. However, excessive transparency can also expose vulnerabilities and aid adversaries in exploiting weaknesses. Regulatory challenges further complicate the landscape of modern cryptography. Governments and regulatory bodies seek to balance the interests of national security, law enforcement, and individual privacy rights. This often leads to debates over encryption backdoors, key escrow mechanisms, and export controls on cryptographic technologies. Navigating these chal-

DOI: 10.4018/979-8-3693-3824-7.ch006

lenges requires collaboration between cryptographic experts, policymakers, industry stakeholders, and civil society organizations. It involves striking a delicate balance between security, privacy, and regulatory compliance while fostering innovation and advancing the state-of-the-art in cryptography.In conclusion, standardization and regulatory challenges in modern cryptography highlight the intricate interplay between security, technology, and policy. By addressing these challenges through multi-stakeholder collaboration, the cryptographic community can promote the development and adoption of robust cryptographic standards that enhance security and privacy in the digital age.

INTRODUCTION

Cryptography, once shrouded in secrecy and employed primarily by military and intelligence agencies, has now permeated nearly every aspect of modern life. From securing online transactions to safeguarding sensitive communications, cryptographic techniques underpin the security of digital systems in an increasingly interconnected world. However, as the importance and complexity of cryptography have grown, so too have the challenges surrounding its standardization and regulation.

The title of this paper, "Standardization and Regulatory Challenges in Modern Cryptography," underscores the dual nature of the issues at hand. On one hand, standardization refers to the process of establishing uniform practices, protocols, and algorithms within the field of cryptography. Standardization is crucial for ensuring interoperability, compatibility, and security across diverse systems and platforms. On the other hand, regulatory challenges pertain to the legal and policy frameworks governing the use of cryptographic technologies. Regulatory measures are intended to balance competing interests such as national security, law enforcement, individual privacy, and technological innovation.

The evolution of cryptography can be traced back thousands of years to ancient civilizations such as the Egyptians and Greeks, who employed rudimentary cryptographic techniques to protect sensitive information. However, it was not until the 20th century that cryptography witnessed significant advancements with the advent of mechanical and electronic encryption machines. The invention of the Enigma machine during World War II, for instance, demonstrated the power of cryptography in both securing communications and breaking enemy codes.

The post-war era saw cryptography transition from the realm of military intelligence to academia and industry. Pioneering works by cryptographers such as Claude Shannon laid the theoretical foundations for modern cryptographic algorithms and protocols. The widespread adoption of computers in the latter half of the 20th century further accelerated the development of cryptographic techniques, leading to the emergence of public-key cryptography and digital signatures.

The proliferation of the internet in the late 20th and early 21st centuries brought cryptography to the forefront of cybersecurity efforts. The need to secure online communications, protect sensitive data, and authenticate users drove the demand for robust cryptographic solutions. Today, cryptography plays a pivotal role in securing e-commerce transactions, safeguarding sensitive information, and enabling secure communication over the internet.

However, alongside its widespread adoption, cryptography has also attracted the attention of policymakers, regulators, and law enforcement agencies. The dual-use nature of cryptographic technologies—capable of both securing communications and concealing illicit activities—has posed unique challenges for regulatory oversight. Governments around the world have grappled with striking a balance between promoting innovation and ensuring national security, often leading to divergent approaches to cryptographic regulation.

In addition to regulatory challenges, the standardization of cryptographic algorithms and protocols presents its own set of complexities. The process of developing and implementing cryptographic standards involves multiple stakeholders, including government agencies, industry consortia, standards organizations, and academic researchers. Conflicting interests, proprietary technologies, and the rapid pace of innovation can hinder efforts to establish universally accepted standards, leading to fragmentation and interoperability issues within the cryptographic ecosystem.

Furthermore, the emergence of novel technologies such as blockchain, quantum computing, and the Internet of Things (IoT) has introduced new challenges and opportunities for cryptographic standardization and regulation. These technologies present unique security requirements and vulnerabilities that must be addressed through innovative cryptographic solutions and adaptive regulatory frameworks.

COMPREHENSIVENESS OF HISTORICAL CONTEXT

Strengths:

1. **Historical Background**: The chapter provides a historical overview of cryptography, tracing its evolution from classical methods to modern algorithms like RSA and AES. This sets a solid foundation for understanding the significance of standardization in cryptography.
2. **Development of Standards**: It discusses the development of cryptographic standards over time, including milestones such as the establishment of the Data Encryption Standard (DES) and the Advanced Encryption Standard (AES).

Weaknesses:

1. **Limited Historical Depth**: The historical context could benefit from a more detailed exploration of the key events and figures that influenced the evolution of cryptographic standards. This would help readers appreciate the socio-political and technological factors that shaped modern cryptography.

Recommendations:

1. **Expand Historical Analysis**: Include more detailed accounts of pivotal moments in cryptographic history, such as the work of Alan Turing during WWII, the creation of public key cryptography by Diffie and Hellman, and the role of organizations like NIST and ISO in standard development.

DEPTH OF THE LITERATURE REVIEW

Strengths:

1. **Key Publications**: The chapter cites several seminal papers and standards documents, providing a good starting point for readers new to the topic.
2. **Regulatory Documents**: It includes references to important regulatory frameworks and guidelines, such as the General Data Protection Regulation (GDPR) and the Federal Information Processing Standards (FIPS).

Weaknesses:

1. **Insufficient Literature Coverage**: The literature review could be more comprehensive. It appears to focus mainly on well-known standards and regulations without delving into the broader academic discourse on the subject.
2. **Lack of Critique**: There is little critical analysis of the existing literature. The chapter could benefit from a discussion on the strengths and weaknesses of different cryptographic standards and regulatory approaches.

Recommendations:

1. **Broaden Literature Scope**: Include a wider range of academic articles, books, and conference papers that discuss the challenges and debates surrounding cryptographic standardization and regulation.

2. **Critical Analysis**: Add a section that critically evaluates the literature, highlighting areas of consensus and contention, and identifying gaps that future research could address.

CLARITY AND RELEVANCE OF INFORMATION

Strengths:

1. **Clear Definitions**: The chapter clearly defines key concepts related to cryptographic standards and regulation, making it accessible to readers with varying levels of expertise.
2. **Relevant Case Studies**: It includes case studies that illustrate the practical challenges of implementing cryptographic standards and complying with regulations.

Weaknesses:

1. **Technical Jargon**: Some sections are dense with technical jargon, which might be challenging for readers who are not cryptography specialists.
2. **Contextual Examples**: While case studies are provided, there could be more real-world examples that show the impact of standardization and regulation on different industries.

Recommendations:

1. **Simplify Language**: Where possible, simplify technical language or provide additional explanations to ensure that the content is accessible to a broader audience.
2. **Diversify Examples**: Include more diverse examples from various industries (e.g., finance, healthcare, government) to show the wide-ranging implications of cryptographic standardization and regulation.

HISTORICAL PERSPECTIVES ON CRYPTOGRAPHY

Cryptography, the art and science of secure communication, has a rich and storied history that spans thousands of years. From ancient civilizations to the digital age, cryptographic techniques have evolved in response to the needs of society, from protecting military communications to securing financial transactions and preserving individual privacy. Understanding the historical context of cryptography is essential for grasping its contemporary significance and the challenges it faces in terms of standardization and regulation. (Csenkey and Bindel, 2023)

Ancient Cryptography

The origins of cryptography can be traced back to ancient civilizations such as Egypt, Mesopotamia, and Greece, where rudimentary encryption techniques were used to conceal sensitive information. One of the earliest known examples of cryptography is the ancient Egyptian hieroglyphs, which often featured symbolic representations of animals and objects to convey messages. The Greeks employed a substitution cipher known as the Atbash cipher, where each letter of the alphabet was replaced with its reverse counterpart.

Ancient cryptography encompassed a variety of techniques and methods for encoding and decoding messages, ranging from simple substitution ciphers to more complex systems of symbols, codes, and hidden meanings. One of the earliest known examples of cryptography is the Caesar cipher, attributed to Julius Caesar, who used it to communicate secretly with his generals during military campaigns.

Figure 1. Hieroglyphics

(source: https://www.britannica.com/topic/hieroglyphic-writing/Relationship-of-writing-and-art)

In the Caesar cipher, each letter in the plaintext is shifted a certain number of positions down the alphabet to create the ciphertext. For example, with a shift of three positions, the letter “A” would be encrypted as “D,” “B” as “E,” and so on. While the Caesar cipher is relatively easy to implement, it can be easily broken through frequency analysis, where the frequency of letters in the ciphertext is analyzed to deduce the shift value.

Ancient cryptography played a significant role in military, diplomatic, and political affairs throughout history. From ancient civilizations such as Egypt, Greece, and Rome to medieval Europe and the Renaissance, cryptographic techniques were employed to safeguard military plans, diplomatic correspondence, and royal decrees from interception and espionage.

For example, the Spartan military used a scytale, a wooden rod with a strip of parchment wrapped around it, to encrypt and decrypt messages. The parchment would only reveal the plaintext when wrapped around a rod of the same diameter, serving as a form of transposition cipher that relied on the physical properties of the rod for encryption and decryption.

Similarly, during the Renaissance, polymaths and cryptographers such as Leon Battista Alberti and Johannes Trithemius developed innovative cryptographic systems based on mathematical principles and secret keys. These systems laid the groundwork for modern cryptography by introducing concepts such as polyalphabetic substitution and polygraphic substitution, which significantly strengthened the security of encrypted communication.

While ancient cryptography may seem primitive by modern standards, its legacy and influence are evident in contemporary cryptographic practices and techniques. Many of the fundamental principles and concepts of cryptography, such as encryption, decryption, key management, and cryptanalysis, originated from ancient civilizations and have been refined and expanded over time.

Moreover, the study of ancient cryptography provides valuable insights into the evolution of human communication and the enduring quest for privacy, secrecy, and security. The techniques and methods devised by ancient cryptographers laid the foundation for the development of modern cryptographic algorithms, protocols, and systems that underpin the digital infrastructure of the 21st century.

Classical Cryptography

The development of classical cryptography reached its zenith during the Renaissance and Enlightenment periods. One of the most famous examples of classical cryptography is the Caesar cipher, named after Julius Caesar, who reportedly used it to communicate with his generals. The Caesar cipher involves shifting each letter of the alphabet by a fixed number of positions. While simple, it provided a degree of security against casual eavesdroppers.

Figure 2. Caesar cipher

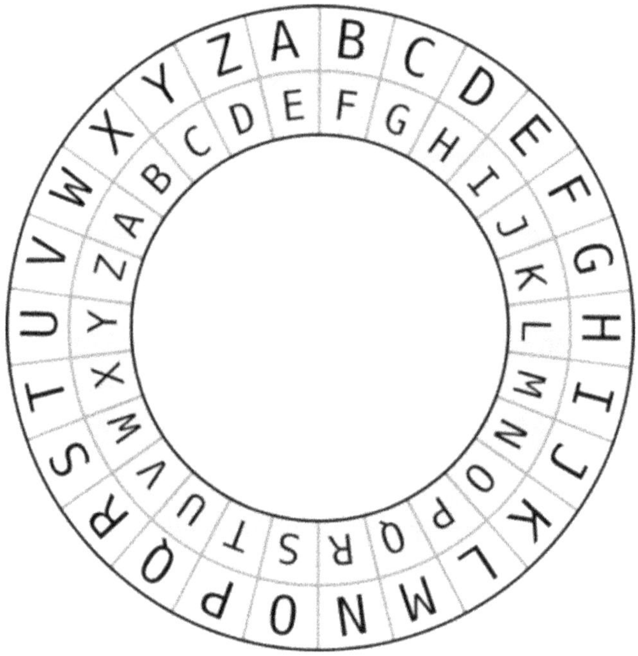

(source: http://www.thealmightyguru.com/Wiki/index.php?title=File:Caesar_Cipher_-_Ring.svg)

During the Renaissance, European cryptographers began to develop more sophisticated cryptographic techniques, including polyalphabetic ciphers such as the Vigenère cipher, which used multiple cipher alphabets to encrypt messages. These advancements laid the groundwork for modern cryptographic principles, including the concept of key-based encryption and frequency analysis.

The Renaissance era witnessed a resurgence of interest in cryptography, driven by advancements in mathematics, linguistics, and the arts. Polymaths such as Leon Battista Alberti and Johannes Trithemius made significant contributions to classical cryptography by introducing innovative cryptographic systems based on mathematical principles and secret keys.

One of the most notable examples of classical cryptography is the Vigenère cipher, developed by the French cryptographer Blaise de Vigenère in the 16th century. The Vigenère cipher is a polyalphabetic substitution cipher that uses a keyword to encrypt plaintext, with each letter of the keyword corresponding to a different Caesar cipher.

The Vigenère cipher provided a significant improvement in security over previous substitution ciphers, as it introduced variability and complexity into the encryption process. However, it was eventually broken by Charles Babbage and Friedrich Kasiski in the 19th century through frequency analysis and other cryptanalytic techniques.

Classical cryptography laid the foundation for many of the principles and techniques that are still used in modern cryptography today. The development of polyalphabetic substitution ciphers, secret key cryptography, and cryptanalysis techniques paved the way for the evolution of cryptographic algorithms and protocols in the digital age.

For example, the principles of secret key cryptography, where both the sender and receiver share a secret key for encrypting and decrypting messages, form the basis of symmetric encryption algorithms such as the Data Encryption Standard (DES) and the Advanced Encryption Standard (AES). These algorithms are widely used in modern encryption systems to secure data transmission and storage.

Moreover, classical cryptanalysis techniques, such as frequency analysis and Kasiski examination, laid the groundwork for modern cryptanalysis methods used to break cryptographic systems and algorithms. Cryptanalysts today employ mathematical, statistical, and computational techniques to analyze encrypted data and uncover vulnerabilities in cryptographic systems.

The legacy of classical cryptography is evident in the enduring importance of security, privacy, and trust in modern communication systems. While classical cryptographic techniques may seem rudimentary compared to modern algorithms, they represent significant milestones in the evolution of cryptographic principles and practices.

Furthermore, classical cryptography serves as a reminder of the ongoing arms race between cryptographers and cryptanalysts, where advances in encryption are met with corresponding advances in cryptanalysis. The cat-and-mouse game between encryptors and decryptors continues to drive innovation and research in cryptography, pushing the boundaries of what is possible in secure communication.

Military and Diplomatic Use

Cryptography played a pivotal role in military and diplomatic communications throughout history. During times of war, encrypted messages were used to relay strategic information, coordinate troop movements, and deceive adversaries. Perhaps the most famous cryptographic device of the 20th century was the German Enigma machine, used by the Axis powers during World War II to encrypt military communications. The Allied cryptanalysts, including Alan Turing and his team at Bletchley Park, played a crucial role in breaking the Enigma code, contributing to the Allied victory.

Figure 3. German Enigma machine

(source: https://www.theverge.com/2012/4/16/2953044/german-enigma-machine-1936-photos)

In addition to its military applications, cryptography has long been used in diplomatic communications to protect sensitive diplomatic correspondence and negotiations. Diplomatic codes and ciphers were employed by governments to maintain secrecy and confidentiality in their interactions with foreign powers.

Throughout history, cryptography has played a crucial role in military and diplomatic affairs, enabling secure communication and intelligence gathering in times of conflict and peace. Military and diplomatic organizations have leveraged cryptographic techniques to protect sensitive information, safeguard national security, and maintain diplomatic secrecy. This section explores the historical significance and contemporary relevance of cryptography in military and diplomatic contexts.

The use of cryptography in military and diplomatic contexts dates back to ancient civilizations, where rulers and generals employed secret codes and ciphers to convey orders, plans, and strategic intelligence securely. In ancient Greece, for example, the Spartan military used a scytale, a wooden rod with a strip of parchment wrapped around it, to encrypt and decrypt messages.

During World War II, cryptography played a pivotal role in shaping the outcome of the war, with both Allied and Axis powers employing sophisticated cryptographic systems and code-breaking efforts. The British cryptanalysts at Bletchley Park, led by Alan Turing, famously cracked the German Enigma machine, providing critical intelligence that helped turn the tide of the war in favor of the Allies.

In the modern era, cryptography remains essential for military and diplomatic organizations to protect classified information, secure communication channels, and prevent unauthorized access to sensitive data. Governments and military agencies worldwide invest heavily in cryptographic research, development, and deployment to maintain a technological edge in cyberspace and ensure national security.

Diplomatic communications between governments and international organizations also rely on cryptography to safeguard sensitive negotiations, treaties, and diplomatic agreements. Diplomatic cables, telegrams, and electronic communications are encrypted using secure cryptographic protocols and algorithms to prevent interception, eavesdropping, and espionage by foreign adversaries.

Cryptography has strategic implications for military and diplomatic operations, influencing decision-making, intelligence gathering, and conflict resolution in complex geopolitical environments. Secure communication channels and encrypted data transmission enable military commanders and diplomats to coordinate operations, exchange intelligence, and negotiate agreements with confidence.

Moreover, cryptographic techniques such as digital signatures and cryptographic hashes provide mechanisms for verifying the authenticity, integrity, and non-repudiation of electronic documents and communications. This enhances trust and accountability in diplomatic exchanges and legal proceedings, reducing the risk of fraud, forgery, and manipulation.

Despite the critical importance of cryptography in military and diplomatic contexts, regulatory challenges abound, particularly concerning the export, import, and use of cryptographic technologies and algorithms. Governments impose export controls and licensing requirements on cryptographic products and technologies to prevent their proliferation to hostile actors and adversaries.

Moreover, international agreements and treaties, such as the Wassenaar Arrangement and the Missile Technology Control Regime (MTCR), impose restrictions on the export of cryptographic technologies and dual-use goods with military applications. Compliance with these regulations poses challenges for cryptographic researchers, developers, and vendors seeking to innovate and collaborate across borders.

Modern Cryptography

The advent of the computer age in the mid-20th century revolutionized the field of cryptography. With the rise of digital computing, cryptographers began to develop more sophisticated encryption algorithms and protocols capable of withstanding brute-force attacks and cryptographic analysis. One of the most significant developments in modern cryptography was the invention of public-key cryptography by Whitfield Diffie and Martin Hellman in 1976. Public-key cryptography introduced the concept of asymmetric encryption, where a pair of keys—public and private—are used for encryption and decryption, respectively.

Figure 4. Public-key Cryptography

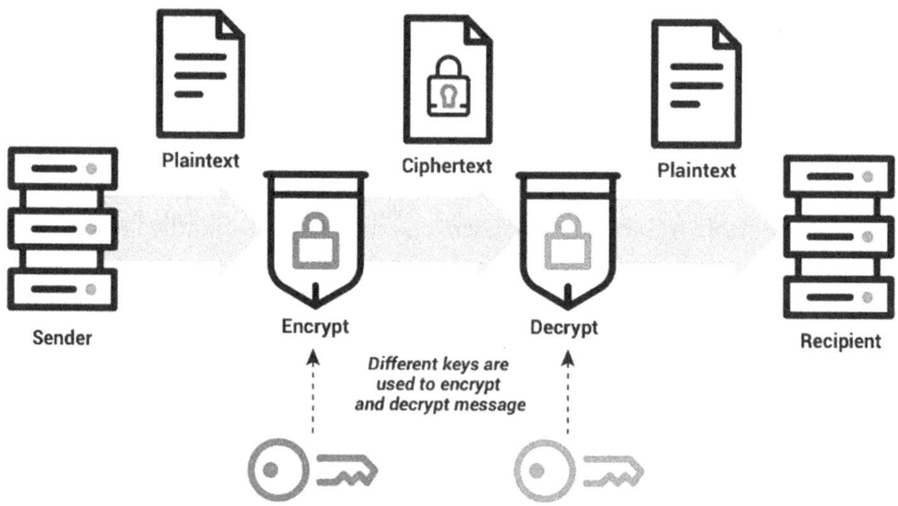

(source: https://www.sectigo.com/resource-library/public-key-vs-private-key)

The widespread adoption of the internet in the late 20th century brought cryptography to the forefront of cybersecurity efforts. Secure communication protocols such as SSL/TLS and SSH enabled encrypted data transmission over the internet, paving the way for e-commerce, online banking, and secure communication platforms.

Modern cryptography represents the culmination of centuries of cryptographic research, development, and innovation, harnessing advanced mathematical principles and computational techniques to secure digital communication and protect sensitive information in the digital age. From symmetric and asymmetric encryption algorithms to digital signatures and cryptographic protocols, modern cryptography encompasses a diverse range of techniques and methods for ensuring confidentiality, integrity, and authenticity in electronic communication. This section explores the principles, applications, and regulatory challenges of modern cryptography.

At the heart of modern cryptography are cryptographic algorithms, mathematical functions, and protocols designed to encrypt plaintext into ciphertext and vice versa, ensuring that only authorized parties can access and interpret the original message. Symmetric encryption algorithms, such as the Data Encryption Standard (DES) and the Advanced Encryption Standard (AES), use a single secret key to encrypt and decrypt data, making them efficient for bulk data encryption.

Asymmetric encryption algorithms, such as RSA and Elliptic Curve Cryptography (ECC), utilize a pair of keys – a public key for encryption and a private key for decryption – to facilitate secure communication and digital signatures. Digital signatures enable parties to verify the authenticity and integrity of electronic documents and messages, providing non-repudiation and accountability in digital transactions.

Despite the widespread adoption and importance of modern cryptography, regulatory challenges persist, particularly concerning the export, import, and use of cryptographic technologies and algorithms. Governments impose export controls and licensing requirements on cryptographic products and technologies to prevent their proliferation to hostile actors and adversaries, posing challenges for cryptographic researchers, developers, and vendors seeking to innovate and collaborate across borders.

Moreover, regulatory frameworks such as data protection laws and privacy regulations impose requirements for the secure storage, transmission, and processing of personal and sensitive data, necessitating the use of cryptographic techniques and mechanisms to achieve compliance. However, conflicting regulations and jurisdictional differences pose challenges for organizations operating in multiple countries or regions.

Challenges in Historical Cryptography

Throughout history, cryptography has faced numerous challenges, ranging from technological limitations to regulatory constraints. In the ancient world, cryptographic techniques were often rudimentary and vulnerable to cryptanalysis. The development of more sophisticated cryptographic methods in the Renaissance and Enlightenment periods introduced new challenges, as cryptanalysts sought to break increasingly complex ciphers.

During times of war, cryptographic systems were subject to intense scrutiny by enemy cryptanalysts, leading to the continuous arms race between code makers and code breakers. The widespread adoption of computers in the 20th century brought new challenges and opportunities for cryptography, as encryption algorithms became more complex and computationally intensive.

The history of cryptography is a testament to humanity's enduring quest for secrecy, security, and privacy. From ancient ciphers to modern encryption algorithms, cryptographic techniques have evolved in response to the changing needs of society. Understanding the historical context of cryptography is essential for appreciating its contemporary significance and the challenges it faces in terms of standardization and regulation. As we navigate the complexities of modern cryptography, we must draw upon the lessons of history to develop robust cryptographic standards and regulatory frameworks that promote security, privacy, and innovation.

The evolution of cryptography throughout history has been marked by various challenges, ranging from technological limitations to vulnerabilities in cryptographic systems. Historical cryptographers faced numerous obstacles in their quest to develop secure methods of communication and protect sensitive information. This section delves into some of the key challenges encountered in historical cryptography and their implications for the development of cryptographic techniques and practices.

One of the primary challenges in historical cryptography was the limited technological capabilities available to cryptographers. Ancient civilizations relied on manual methods of encryption, such as substitution ciphers and transposition techniques, which were labor-intensive and susceptible to human error. Without access to advanced computing technology, cryptanalysts had to rely on manual decryption methods, such as frequency analysis and pattern recognition, to break encrypted messages.

Moreover, the lack of standardized cryptographic techniques and protocols hindered interoperability and communication between different civilizations and cultures. Each civilization developed its own unique cryptographic systems and methods, making it challenging to decipher messages without knowledge of the specific encryption technique used.

Another challenge in historical cryptography was the absence of a formal mathematical foundation for cryptographic techniques. Ancient cryptographers lacked the mathematical knowledge and understanding of number theory, probability theory, and algebraic structures that underpin modern cryptographic algorithms and protocols. As a result, many historical cryptographic systems were based on ad hoc methods and empirical observations rather than rigorous mathematical principles.

Without a solid mathematical foundation, cryptographers struggled to develop secure encryption algorithms and assess the strength of cryptographic systems against cryptanalysis. The lack of mathematical rigor in historical cryptography contributed to the vulnerability of many cryptographic systems to attack and exploitation by adversaries.

In addition to technological and mathematical limitations, historical cryptographers faced challenges related to communication and transmission of encrypted messages. In ancient times, long-distance communication relied on physical couriers, messengers, and unreliable transportation methods, making it difficult to transmit encrypted messages securely over long distances.

Furthermore, the risk of interception, theft, or loss of encrypted messages posed significant challenges for maintaining the confidentiality and integrity of sensitive information. Without secure communication channels and authentication mechanisms, cryptographers had to rely on physical security measures, such as seals, tamper-evident packaging, and trusted couriers, to protect encrypted messages from unauthorized access and tampering.

The challenges encountered in historical cryptography have profound implications for the development and evolution of modern cryptographic techniques and practices. By learning from the mistakes and limitations of historical cryptographers, modern cryptographers have been able to design more secure, efficient, and robust cryptographic algorithms and protocols.

The advent of modern computing technology has revolutionized cryptography, enabling the development of complex encryption algorithms and cryptographic systems that offer unprecedented levels of security and reliability. Mathematical techniques such as number theory, probability theory, and computational complexity theory provide a rigorous foundation for analyzing the security of cryptographic algorithms and assessing their resilience against cryptanalysis.

Moreover, advancements in communication technology, such as the internet and digital networks, have facilitated the widespread adoption of cryptographic techniques for securing electronic communication, protecting data transmission, and ensuring the integrity of digital transactions. Cryptographic standards and protocols developed by international organizations, such as the National Institute of Standards and Technology (NIST) and the International Organization for Standardization (ISO), promote interoperability and compatibility among different cryptographic systems and platforms.

THE IMPORTANCE OF STANDARDIZATION IN CRYPTOGRAPHY

Standardization plays a pivotal role in ensuring the effectiveness, interoperability, and security of cryptographic systems in the digital age. Cryptography, the art and science of secure communication, relies on standardized algorithms, protocols, and key management practices to facilitate secure data transmission, protect sensitive information, and enable trusted communication across diverse platforms and applications. This section delves into the significance of standardization in cryptography, exploring its role in fostering interoperability, enhancing security, and facilitating innovation. (Mohajerani *et al.*, 2023)

Interoperability and Compatibility

One of the primary benefits of cryptographic standardization is the promotion of interoperability and compatibility among diverse systems and applications. Standardized cryptographic algorithms and protocols enable different software, hardware, and network components to communicate securely with each other, regardless of their underlying technologies or implementations. This interoperability is essential for enabling seamless communication, data exchange, and collaboration in the digital ecosystem.

For example, standardized encryption algorithms such as AES (Advanced Encryption Standard) and RSA (Rivest-Shamir-Adleman) are widely supported by software libraries, operating systems, and network devices, allowing developers to integrate encryption capabilities into their applications without compatibility issues. Similarly, standardized cryptographic protocols such as TLS (Transport Layer Security) and IPSec (Internet Protocol Security) facilitate secure communication over the internet by ensuring that client and server implementations can negotiate secure connections using mutually supported cryptographic algorithms and parameters.

Figure 5. Advanced Encryption Standard

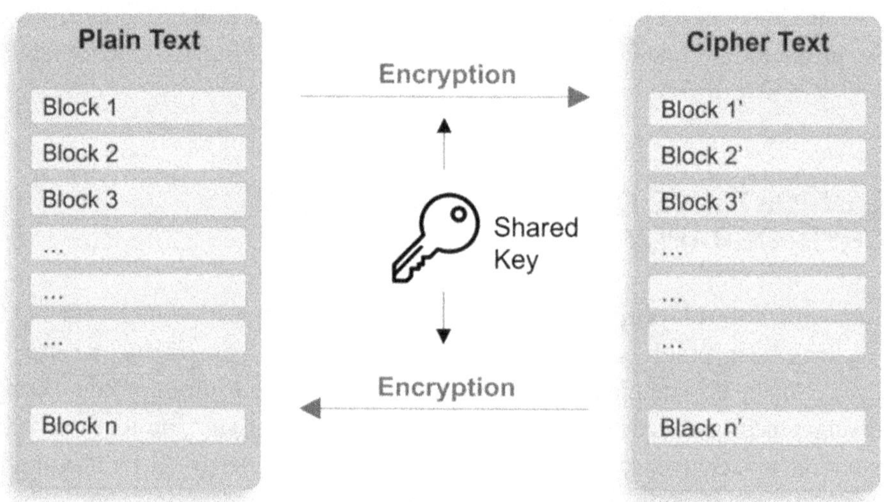

(source: https://www.pufsecurity.com/technology/aes-the-advanced-encryption-standard/)

Figure 6. Rivest-Shamir-Adleman

(source: https://www.splunk.com/en_us/blog/learn/rsa-algorithm-cryptography.html)

Figure 7. Transport Layer Security

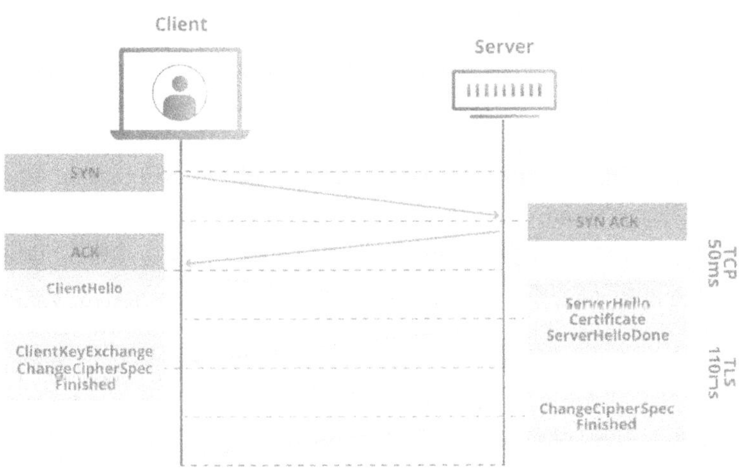

(source: https://www.cloudflare.com/learning/ssl/transport-layer-security-tls/)

Figure 8. Internet Protocol Security

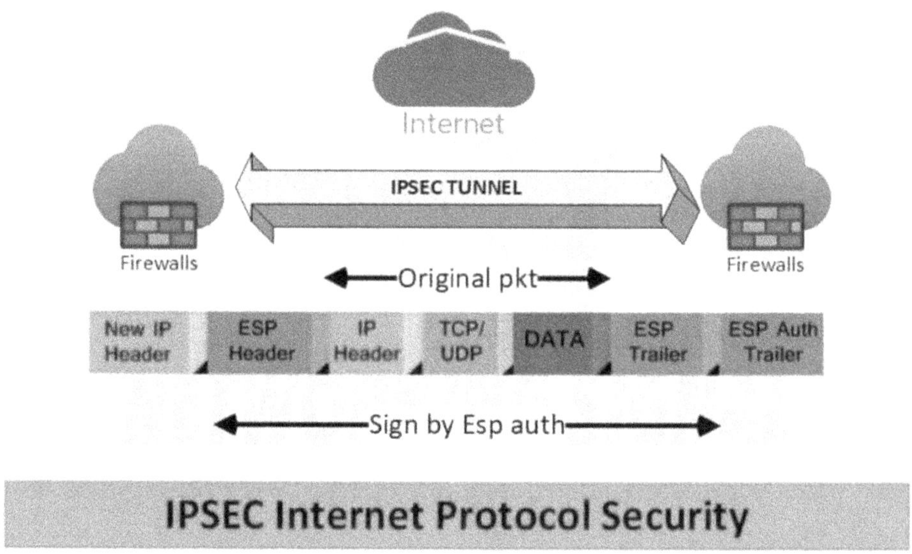

(source: https://www.networkingsignal.com/ipsec-internet-protocol-security/)

Interoperability and compatibility are critical considerations in modern cryptography, ensuring that cryptographic systems, algorithms, and protocols can communicate seamlessly across diverse platforms, devices, and networks. Interoperability refers to the ability of different cryptographic systems to work together and exchange data effectively, while compatibility ensures that cryptographic implementations adhere to common standards and specifications. This section explores the importance of interoperability and compatibility in modern cryptography and the challenges associated with achieving them.

Interoperability is essential for enabling secure communication and data exchange between different cryptographic systems and applications. In today's interconnected world, where digital communication spans across multiple platforms and devices, interoperable cryptographic solutions are crucial for ensuring seamless integration and interoperability among diverse systems and networks.

Interoperability enables organizations to deploy heterogeneous cryptographic solutions that meet their specific security requirements while ensuring compatibility and interoperability with existing systems and infrastructure. It allows for the integration of cryptographic functionalities, such as encryption, decryption, digital signatures, and key management, into a wide range of applications and services, including email, messaging, e-commerce, and cloud computing.

Achieving interoperability in modern cryptography presents several challenges, including differences in cryptographic algorithms, protocols, key management practices, and implementation standards. Cryptographic systems developed by different vendors or organizations may use proprietary algorithms or protocols that are incompatible with each other, making it difficult to establish secure communication and data exchange.

Moreover, variations in cryptographic implementations, such as key lengths, padding schemes, and encryption modes, can further complicate interoperability efforts. Differences in software and hardware platforms, operating systems, and programming languages may also introduce compatibility issues, requiring additional efforts to ensure compatibility and interoperability across diverse environments.

Compatibility ensures that cryptographic implementations adhere to common standards and specifications, enabling seamless integration and interoperability among different systems and applications. Standardized cryptographic algorithms, protocols, and formats facilitate compatibility by providing a common framework for implementing cryptographic functionalities and exchanging cryptographic data.

Compliance with industry standards and best practices, such as those established by organizations like the National Institute of Standards and Technology (NIST), the International Organization for Standardization (ISO), and the Internet Engineering Task Force (IETF), promotes compatibility and interoperability among cryptographic solutions developed by different vendors and organizations.

Despite the importance of compatibility, achieving compatibility in modern cryptography presents its own set of challenges. Rapid advancements in cryptographic research and technology may result in the proliferation of new algorithms, protocols, and standards, leading to fragmentation and divergence in cryptographic implementations.

Moreover, differences in interpretation, implementation, and enforcement of cryptographic standards and specifications may lead to inconsistencies and ambiguities that hinder compatibility and interoperability. Lack of coordination and collaboration among standards organizations, industry stakeholders, and cryptographic researchers may further exacerbate compatibility challenges, resulting in incompatible cryptographic solutions and fragmented ecosystems.

In conclusion, interoperability and compatibility are essential considerations in modern cryptography, enabling secure communication, data exchange, and integration across diverse platforms, devices, and networks. Despite the challenges posed by differences in algorithms, protocols, and standards, concerted efforts from standards organizations, industry stakeholders, and cryptographic researchers can overcome these obstacles and promote interoperability and compatibility in the digital ecosystem. By adopting open standards, implementing interoperability testing and certification programs, fostering collaboration and cooperation, and raising awareness, stakeholders can ensure that cryptographic solutions remain interoperable, compatible, and effective in safeguarding digital communication and data exchange in the modern world.

Security and Trust

Standardization also plays a critical role in enhancing the security and trustworthiness of cryptographic systems. By defining clear and well-vetted cryptographic algorithms and protocols, standardization bodies such as the National Institute of Standards and Technology (NIST) and the International Organization for Standardization (ISO) help mitigate the risk of vulnerabilities, weaknesses, and implementation errors that could compromise the security of cryptographic systems.

For instance, the rigorous evaluation and validation processes employed by standardization bodies help identify and address cryptographic weaknesses, such as algorithmic biases, side-channel attacks, and cryptographic flaws, before they are widely deployed in practice. This proactive approach to security helps build trust and confidence in standardized cryptographic solutions, fostering adoption and deployment across various industries and sectors.

Moreover, standardized cryptographic algorithms and protocols undergo extensive scrutiny and analysis by the cryptographic community, including academic researchers, cryptographers, and security experts, which further enhances their security and resilience against attacks. The peer review process ensures that cryptographic standards are robust, well-designed, and resistant to known cryptographic attacks, thereby providing a solid foundation for building secure and trustworthy cryptographic systems.

Compliance and Regulatory Requirements

Standardization also plays a crucial role in enabling organizations to comply with regulatory requirements and industry standards related to data security and privacy. Many regulatory frameworks, such as the General Data Protection Regulation (GDPR) in Europe and the Health Insurance Portability and Accountability Act (HIPAA) in the United States, mandate the use of standardized cryptographic algorithms and protocols to protect sensitive data, ensure confidentiality, integrity, and authenticity, and mitigate the risk of data breaches and cyber attacks.

For example, GDPR requires organizations to implement appropriate technical and organizational measures to ensure the security of personal data, including the use of encryption and pseudonymization techniques. By adhering to cryptographic standards endorsed by regulatory bodies and industry associations, organizations can demonstrate compliance with legal and regulatory requirements, thereby reducing the risk of non-compliance penalties, legal liabilities, and reputational damage.

Facilitating Innovation and Collaboration

Standardization also serves as a catalyst for innovation and collaboration within the cryptographic community by providing a common framework and language for designing, implementing, and evaluating cryptographic solutions. By establishing standardized interfaces, data formats, and interoperability requirements, cryptographic standards enable researchers, developers, and vendors to build upon existing technologies, leverage reusable components, and collaborate on new cryptographic innovations and breakthroughs.

Moreover, cryptographic standardization promotes competition and interoperability in the marketplace by ensuring a level playing field for vendors and service providers. By adhering to open and transparent standards, organizations can avoid vendor lock-in, promote vendor diversity, and foster healthy competition, which ultimately benefits end-users through lower costs, increased choice, and improved quality of cryptographic products and services.

CHALLENGES IN CRYPTOGRAPHIC STANDARDIZATION

Standardization is crucial for ensuring interoperability, security, and trust in cryptographic systems. However, the process of cryptographic standardization is fraught with challenges, ranging from technical complexities to political and economic considerations. This section explores the key challenges in cryptographic standardization, including conflicting interests among stakeholders, the pace of technological innovation, and the need for international collaboration. (Zhang *et al.*, 2022)

Conflicting Interests Among Stakeholders

One of the primary challenges in cryptographic standardization arises from the conflicting interests among stakeholders, including government agencies, industry consortia, standards organizations, and academic researchers. Each stakeholder group may have different priorities, objectives, and perspectives on cryptographic standards, leading to divergent opinions and competing proposals.

For example, government agencies may prioritize national security and law enforcement needs, advocating for cryptographic standards that include backdoors or escrow mechanisms to facilitate access to encrypted data for surveillance purposes. In contrast, privacy advocates and civil liberties organizations may oppose such proposals, citing concerns about the erosion of individual privacy rights and the potential for abuse by authoritarian regimes.

Similarly, industry stakeholders may prioritize commercial interests and market competitiveness, advocating for cryptographic standards that promote interoperability, innovation, and vendor diversity. However, proprietary technologies and intellectual property considerations may hinder efforts to develop consensus-based standards that are open, transparent, and royalty-free.

Pace of Technological Innovation

Another challenge in cryptographic standardization is the rapid pace of technological innovation, which often outpaces the standardization process. As cryptographic techniques evolve and new vulnerabilities are discovered, standardization bodies must adapt quickly to address emerging threats and ensure the security and resilience of cryptographic systems.

For example, the emergence of quantum computing poses significant challenges for cryptographic standardization, as quantum computers have the potential to break many existing cryptographic algorithms, such as RSA and ECC (Elliptic Curve Cryptography), which rely on the difficulty of factoring large integers or solving discrete logarithm problems. Standardization bodies are actively researching and developing quantum-resistant cryptographic algorithms, such as lattice-based cryptography and hash-based signatures, to mitigate the threat posed by quantum adversaries.

Figure 9. Quantum-Resistant Cryptographic Algorithms

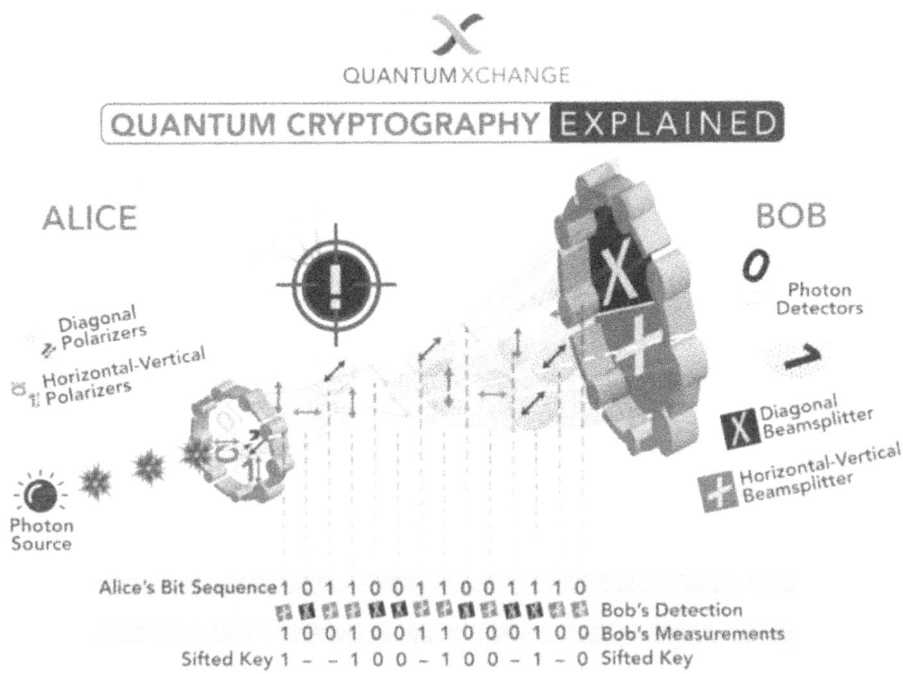

(source: https://techbooks.org/recommended-cryptographic-algorithms/)

Similarly, advancements in cryptanalysis and side-channel attacks necessitate ongoing revisions and updates to cryptographic standards to address newly discovered vulnerabilities and weaknesses. Standardization bodies must balance the need for security with the desire for stability and backward compatibility, ensuring that cryptographic standards remain robust and resilient in the face of evolving threats.

Lack of International Collaboration

A significant challenge in cryptographic standardization is the lack of international collaboration and coordination, particularly in the absence of a unified global framework for cryptographic regulation and governance. Cryptography is a global technology that transcends national boundaries, making it essential for standardization efforts to be inclusive, transparent, and consensus-driven across jurisdictions.

However, geopolitical tensions, trade disputes, and national security concerns can impede international collaboration on cryptographic standardization, leading to fragmentation and divergence in cryptographic policies and practices. For example, export controls on cryptographic technologies, such as encryption algorithms and key lengths, vary widely between countries, creating barriers to trade and hindering interoperability.

Moreover, differences in legal and regulatory frameworks, such as data protection laws and government surveillance practices, can complicate efforts to harmonize cryptographic standards and interoperability requirements across jurisdictions. Standardization bodies must navigate these complex geopolitical dynamics and engage with stakeholders from diverse backgrounds to develop globally applicable cryptographic standards that promote security, privacy, and trust in the digital ecosystem.

REGULATORY FRAMEWORKS FOR CRYPTOGRAPHY

Regulatory frameworks for cryptography play a crucial role in shaping the use, development, and deployment of cryptographic technologies. With the proliferation of digital communication, online transactions, and data storage, governments and regulatory bodies have sought to balance competing interests such as national security, law enforcement, individual privacy, and technological innovation. This section explores the diverse approaches to cryptographic regulation, ranging from strict controls to more permissive frameworks, and discusses their implications for security, privacy, and digital rights. (Alamati, 2020)

Government Regulation and Oversight

Government regulation of cryptography varies widely between countries and regions, reflecting differences in legal traditions, political ideologies, and national security priorities. Some countries, such as China and Russia, have implemented strict controls on cryptographic technologies, requiring government approval for the use and deployment of encryption algorithms and cryptographic products.

For example, China's State Encryption Management Bureau (SEMB) oversees the regulation of cryptographic technologies in China, imposing stringent requirements on the use of encryption algorithms, key management practices, and cryptographic products. Similarly, Russia's Federal Security Service (FSB) regulates the use of encryption technologies in Russia, requiring companies to register cryptographic products and obtain FSB approval for their deployment.

In contrast, other countries, such as the United States and European Union, have adopted more permissive frameworks for cryptographic regulation, emphasizing the importance of encryption for protecting privacy, promoting cybersecurity, and fostering digital innovation. The United States, for example, has historically taken a relatively hands-off approach to cryptographic regulation, allowing cryptographic technologies to be freely developed, distributed, and used by individuals and businesses.

Export Controls and Dual-Use Technologies

One area of cryptographic regulation that remains contentious is the export controls on cryptographic technologies, particularly those classified as dual-use technologies with both civilian and military applications. Many countries impose export controls on cryptographic technologies, limiting the export of encryption algorithms, key lengths, and cryptographic products to countries deemed friendly or trustworthy.

For example, the Wassenaar Arrangement, an international export control regime, regulates the export of dual-use technologies, including cryptographic software and hardware, to prevent their proliferation to hostile actors and rogue states. Under the Wassenaar Arrangement, member countries agree to control the export of cryptographic technologies based on their cryptographic strength and intended end-use.

However, export controls on cryptographic technologies have been criticized for stifling innovation, impeding the global adoption of strong encryption, and undermining digital privacy rights. Critics argue that export controls on cryptographic technologies disproportionately impact legitimate users and hinder the development of secure communication tools and platforms.

Law Enforcement Access and Encryption Backdoors

One of the most contentious issues in cryptographic regulation is the debate over law enforcement access to encrypted data and the use of encryption backdoors to facilitate access. Law enforcement agencies argue that encrypted communications and devices hinder their ability to investigate and prevent crimes, including terrorism, organized crime, and child exploitation.

As a result, some governments have proposed or implemented legislation mandating the inclusion of encryption backdoors or escrow mechanisms in cryptographic systems, allowing law enforcement agencies to access encrypted data under certain circumstances. However, encryption backdoors have been widely criticized by technologists, cybersecurity experts, and privacy advocates, who argue that they undermine the security and integrity of cryptographic systems, weaken digital privacy rights, and create vulnerabilities that can be exploited by malicious actors.

Data Protection and Privacy Laws

In response to growing concerns about data privacy and security, many countries have enacted comprehensive data protection laws that govern the collection, processing, and storage of personal data, including cryptographic requirements for securing sensitive information. For example, the European Union's General Data Protection Regulation (GDPR) requires organizations to implement appropriate technical and organizational measures, including encryption, to ensure the security and confidentiality of personal data.

Similarly, the California Consumer Privacy Act (CCPA) and other state-level privacy laws in the United States impose obligations on organizations to implement reasonable security measures, including encryption, to protect personal information from unauthorized access, disclosure, and misuse. These regulatory frameworks recognize the importance of encryption as a fundamental tool for safeguarding individual privacy rights and mitigating the risk of data breaches and cyber attacks.

BALANCING SECURITY AND PRIVACY

In the digital age, the interplay between security and privacy has become increasingly complex, particularly in the realm of cryptography. While cryptographic techniques are essential for ensuring the security of digital communications and transactions, they also raise significant concerns about individual privacy and civil liberties. This section explores the challenges of balancing security and privacy in cryptographic systems, examining the ethical, legal, and technical considerations at stake. (Gorva and Anandachar, 2022)

The Dual Nature of Cryptography:

Cryptography is often described as having a dual nature—it can be used to both secure communications and protect privacy, as well as to facilitate surveillance and undermine privacy. On one hand, cryptographic techniques such as encryption, digital signatures, and anonymity protocols are essential for safeguarding sensitive information, preserving confidentiality, and protecting individual privacy rights.

For example, encryption ensures that only authorized parties can access and decrypt sensitive data, preventing unauthorized interception and eavesdropping by adversaries. Similarly, digital signatures provide a means of verifying the authenticity and integrity of digital documents and transactions, enhancing trust and accountability in electronic communications and commerce.

On the other hand, cryptographic techniques can also be exploited for surveillance purposes, enabling governments, corporations, and malicious actors to monitor, intercept, and analyze digital communications without the knowledge or consent of the parties involved. Encryption backdoors, key escrow systems, and metadata analysis techniques are examples of cryptographic tools that can be used for surveillance purposes, raising concerns about mass surveillance, government overreach, and violations of privacy rights.

Ethical and Legal Considerations

The use of cryptographic techniques for surveillance purposes raises significant ethical and legal questions about the balance between security and privacy, individual rights and collective interests, and democratic principles and national security imperatives. At the heart of the debate is the tension between the need for effective security measures to protect against cyber threats and the desire to preserve individual privacy rights and civil liberties.

From an ethical standpoint, proponents of privacy argue that individuals have a fundamental right to privacy and autonomy, which encompasses the right to control their personal information and communications. Encryption is seen as a crucial tool for protecting privacy rights and ensuring that individuals can communicate, transact, and express themselves freely without fear of surveillance or interference.

Conversely, proponents of security argue that effective security measures are essential for safeguarding national security, public safety, and the rule of law, particularly in the face of evolving cyber threats, terrorism, and organized crime. They contend that law enforcement agencies and government authorities must have the necessary tools and capabilities to investigate and prevent criminal activities, including the lawful interception of communications when authorized by judicial oversight and due process.

Technical Challenges

From a technical perspective, balancing security and privacy in cryptographic systems poses significant challenges due to the inherent trade-offs between security, usability, and performance. Strong encryption algorithms that offer high levels of security and privacy may also impose computational overhead, increase latency, and complicate key management and usability.

For example, end-to-end encryption, which ensures that only the communicating parties can access the plaintext of their messages, requires complex key exchange protocols and secure key management practices to establish secure communication channels. While end-to-end encryption provides robust security and privacy protections, it can also make it difficult for service providers to comply with lawful interception requests and regulatory requirements.

Figure 10. Anonymous Cryptocurrencies

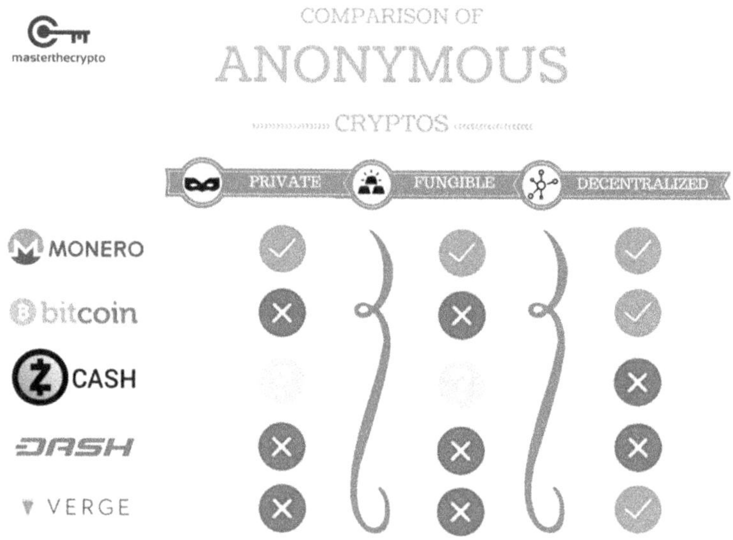

(source: https://masterthecrypto.com/privacy-coins-anonymous-cryptocurrencies/)

Similarly, cryptographic protocols that provide anonymity and unlinkability, such as mix networks and anonymous cryptocurrencies, face challenges in balancing privacy with the need to prevent abuse and criminal activities, such as money laundering, terrorist financing, and illicit transactions.

Regulatory Responses

Regulatory responses to the challenges of balancing security and privacy in cryptography vary widely between countries and regions, reflecting differences in legal traditions, political ideologies, and cultural norms. Some governments have adopted strict regulations and surveillance measures to combat cyber threats and maintain national security, while others have taken a more privacy-focused approach, prioritizing individual rights and civil liberties.

For example, countries such as China and Russia have implemented stringent regulations on cryptographic technologies, requiring government approval for the use and deployment of encryption algorithms and cryptographic products. These regulations are often justified on national security grounds, with authorities citing the need to combat terrorism, extremism, and cybercrime.

In contrast, countries such as the European Union and the United States have adopted more privacy-centric approaches to cryptographic regulation, emphasizing the importance of encryption for protecting individual privacy rights, promoting cybersecurity, and fostering digital innovation. The European Union's General Data Protection Regulation (GDPR), for example, mandates the use of encryption and other security measures to protect personal data from unauthorized access and disclosure.

CRYPTOGRAPHY IN EMERGING TECHNOLOGIES

Cryptography, the art and science of secure communication, is undergoing rapid evolution driven by emerging technologies that are reshaping the digital landscape. From blockchain and quantum computing to the Internet of Things (IoT) and artificial intelligence (AI), these technologies present both new opportunities and challenges for cryptographic standardization and regulation. This section explores the role of cryptography in emerging technologies, examining its applications, implications, and regulatory considerations. (Sedat Sonko *et al.*, 2024)

Blockchain and Cryptocurrencies

Blockchain technology, best known as the underlying technology behind cryptocurrencies such as Bitcoin and Ethereum, has revolutionized the way digital assets are transferred, verified, and secured. At the heart of blockchain technology is cryptography, which ensures the integrity, immutability, and security of transactions recorded on the blockchain.

Cryptography is used in blockchain systems to secure transactions through techniques such as digital signatures, hash functions, and consensus mechanisms. Digital signatures ensure that transactions are authentic and have not been tampered with, while hash functions create unique identifiers for each block of transactions, linking them together in a chain that is resistant to modification.

However, while blockchain technology offers unprecedented levels of transparency and decentralization, it also poses challenges for cryptographic standardization and regulation. The anonymity and pseudonymity afforded by blockchain systems raise concerns about money laundering, terrorist financing, and other illicit activities, prompting regulators to develop frameworks for combating financial crime while preserving privacy rights. (Cretarola, Figà-Talamanca and Grunspan, 2021)

Quantum Computing

Quantum computing, a revolutionary technology that leverages the principles of quantum mechanics to perform complex calculations at speeds far surpassing classical computers, poses significant challenges for cryptographic standardization and regulation. Quantum computers have the potential to break many existing cryptographic algorithms, including RSA and ECC, which rely on the difficulty of factoring large integers or solving discrete logarithm problems.

As quantum computing continues to advance, standardization bodies are actively researching and developing quantum-resistant cryptographic algorithms that are immune to attacks by quantum adversaries. Post-quantum cryptography, also known as quantum-safe or quantum-resistant cryptography, aims to ensure the long-term security of digital communication and data protection in the face of quantum threats.

Regulatory responses to the advent of quantum computing vary, with some governments investing in quantum research and development to maintain competitiveness in the global technology race, while others focus on mitigating the potential risks posed by quantum adversaries. International collaboration and coordination are essential for addressing the challenges of quantum computing and developing globally applicable standards for quantum-resistant cryptography. (Fernandez-Carames and Fraga-Lamas, 2020)

Internet of Things (IoT)

The Internet of Things (IoT), a network of interconnected devices and sensors that communicate and exchange data over the internet, presents new opportunities and challenges for cryptographic standardization and regulation. IoT devices collect, transmit, and process vast amounts of sensitive data, ranging from personal health information to industrial control systems, making security and privacy paramount concerns.

Cryptography is essential for securing IoT devices and networks against a wide range of threats, including unauthorized access, data breaches, and cyber attacks. Cryptographic techniques such as encryption, authentication, and key management help protect IoT devices from tampering, eavesdropping, and spoofing attacks, ensuring the integrity and confidentiality of data transmitted over IoT networks.

However, the sheer scale and heterogeneity of IoT deployments pose challenges for cryptographic standardization and regulation. Standardizing cryptographic algorithms and protocols for IoT devices requires considering factors such as resource constraints, power consumption, and interoperability, while also addressing emerging threats and vulnerabilities unique to IoT environments. (Hanafi and Bokhari, 2023)

Artificial Intelligence (AI)

Artificial intelligence (AI), encompassing machine learning, deep learning, and neural networks, is transforming the way data is analyzed, interpreted, and utilized across various domains, including cybersecurity and cryptography. AI-powered algorithms and techniques offer new opportunities for enhancing cryptographic security, improving threat detection, and optimizing cryptographic operations.

For example, AI algorithms can be used to analyze cryptographic protocols and detect vulnerabilities or weaknesses that may be overlooked by traditional methods. AI-powered intrusion detection systems can identify anomalous patterns in network traffic and alert administrators to potential security breaches or cyber attacks. AI can also optimize cryptographic operations, such as key generation and encryption, to improve efficiency and performance.

However, the use of AI in cryptography raises concerns about the potential for adversarial attacks and algorithmic bias. Adversarial attacks leverage AI techniques to bypass cryptographic defenses or exploit vulnerabilities in AI-powered systems, posing challenges for both cryptographic standardization and cybersecurity. Algorithmic bias, resulting from biased training data or flawed algorithms, can undermine the fairness and integrity of AI-powered cryptographic systems, highlighting the need for transparency, accountability, and ethical oversight. (Sood and Kim, 2023)

Regulatory Considerations

Regulating cryptography in emerging technologies requires a balanced approach that promotes innovation, fosters security, and protects individual privacy rights. Regulatory frameworks must adapt to the evolving technological landscape, addressing the unique challenges and opportunities presented by blockchain, quantum computing, IoT, and AI.

International collaboration and coordination are essential for developing harmonized regulatory standards and interoperability requirements for cryptographic technologies. Standardization bodies, government agencies, industry stakeholders, and the cryptographic community must work together to establish globally applicable standards that promote security, privacy, and trust in emerging technologies.

Regulatory frameworks should also prioritize transparency, accountability, and ethical considerations to ensure that cryptographic technologies are used responsibly and ethically. Privacy-enhancing technologies, such as zero-knowledge proofs and differential privacy, can help protect individual privacy rights while enabling secure and trusted communication in emerging technologies.

CASE STUDIES AND PRACTICAL IMPLICATIONS

Examining case studies and practical implications of standardization and regulatory challenges in modern cryptography provides valuable insights into real-world scenarios where cryptographic technologies intersect with legal, ethical, and technical considerations. This section explores notable case studies and their implications, highlighting key lessons learned and potential pathways for addressing standardization and regulatory challenges.

Case Study 1: Apple vs. FBI Encryption Battle

One of the most high-profile cases involving cryptography and regulatory challenges was the legal battle between Apple Inc. and the Federal Bureau of Investigation (FBI) in 2016. The FBI sought Apple's assistance in unlocking an iPhone used by one of the perpetrators of the San Bernardino terrorist attack. Apple refused to comply, citing concerns about user privacy, security, and the potential precedent for government-mandated backdoors in encryption.

The case sparked a heated debate over the balance between national security, law enforcement needs, and individual privacy rights. It underscored the importance of encryption as a fundamental tool for protecting sensitive information and preserving civil liberties, while also highlighting the challenges of reconciling conflicting interests and priorities in the digital age. (Schulze, 2017)

Practical Implications

The Apple vs. FBI encryption battle highlighted the need for clear legal frameworks and regulatory guidelines for law enforcement access to encrypted data. It emphasized the importance of transparency, accountability, and due process in government requests for assistance from technology companies.

From a technical perspective, the case underscored the importance of robust encryption and security measures in protecting user data from unauthorized access and exploitation. It demonstrated the potential risks and consequences of implementing encryption backdoors or weakening cryptographic standards for surveillance purposes.

Case Study 2: European Union's General Data Protection Regulation (GDPR)

The implementation of the General Data Protection Regulation (GDPR) in the European Union (EU) in 2018 has had significant implications for cryptographic standardization and regulatory compliance. GDPR mandates the use of appropriate technical and organizational measures, including encryption, to protect personal data from unauthorized access, disclosure, and misuse.

GDPR's emphasis on encryption as a fundamental tool for data protection has driven increased adoption of cryptographic technologies by organizations handling personal data. It has also raised awareness of the importance of encryption in safeguarding privacy rights and mitigating the risk of data breaches and cyber attacks. (Aseri, 2020)

Practical Implications

GDPR's requirements for encryption highlight the importance of developing standardized cryptographic algorithms and protocols that meet the security and privacy requirements of regulatory frameworks. Organizations subject to GDPR must implement encryption solutions that are robust, interoperable, and compliant with regulatory standards.

The GDPR has also led to increased scrutiny of encryption practices and technologies by regulatory authorities, requiring organizations to demonstrate compliance with encryption-related requirements through documentation, audits, and risk assessments. This has prompted investments in encryption technologies, security controls, and data protection measures to mitigate regulatory risks and liabilities.

Case Study 3: Quantum Computing and Post-Quantum Cryptography

The emergence of quantum computing poses significant challenges for cryptographic standardization and regulatory compliance. Quantum computers have the potential to break many existing cryptographic algorithms, such as RSA and ECC, which rely on the difficulty of factoring large integers or solving discrete logarithm problems.

Table 1. The Different RSA and ECC Algorithms

Security in bits	Minimum key size in bits for this security level		Performance based on Microchip speed comparison
	RSA	ECC	
112	**2048**	224	no data
128	3072	**256**	**ECC is 10x faster than RSA**
192	7680	384	no data
256	15360	512	**ECC is 50-100x faster than RSA**

(source: https://www.microsec.hu/en/pki-blog/rsa-or-ecc-frequently-asked-questions)

The development of post-quantum cryptography, also known as quantum-safe or quantum-resistant cryptography, aims to address the threat posed by quantum adversaries. Post-quantum cryptographic algorithms are designed to be secure against attacks by both classical and quantum computers, ensuring the long-term security of digital communication and data protection. (Kan and Une, 2021)

Practical Implications

The advent of quantum computing underscores the importance of investing in research and development of post-quantum cryptographic algorithms and protocols. Standardization bodies and cryptographic researchers are actively working to develop and evaluate post-quantum cryptographic solutions that offer robust security and interoperability across diverse applications and platforms.

From a regulatory perspective, the rise of quantum computing highlights the need for flexible, adaptive regulatory frameworks that can accommodate technological advancements and emerging threats. Regulators must consider the implications of quantum computing on encryption standards, export controls, and data protection laws to ensure that cryptographic systems remain secure and resilient in the face of quantum adversaries.

DETAILED DISCUSSION ON "CYBERSECURITY FUNDAMENTALS" CHAPTER IN RELATION TO "STANDARDIZATION AND REGULATORY CHALLENGES IN MODERN CRYPTOGRAPHY"

Constructive and Analytical Assessment

The chapter on "Cybersecurity Fundamentals" provides a foundational understanding of cybersecurity principles and practices. However, assessing its effectiveness in illustrating the specific issues, problems, and trends related to "Standardization and Regulatory Challenges in Modern Cryptography" reveals several strengths and areas for improvement.

Strengths:

1. **Foundational Knowledge**: The chapter lays a solid foundation for understanding key cybersecurity concepts, such as authentication, malware, and phishing attacks. This background is crucial for comprehending the broader context of cryptographic standardization and regulation.

2. **Relevance of Topics**: The inclusion of sections on authentication, integrity, availability, and other cybersecurity principles is relevant, as these areas often intersect with cryptographic practices. Understanding these principles helps readers appreciate why standardization and regulatory measures are necessary.
3. **Broad Overview**: By covering a wide range of cybersecurity issues, the chapter sets the stage for discussing more specialized topics like cryptographic standards and regulatory challenges.

Weaknesses:

1. **Lack of Direct Focus**: The chapter does not directly address the theme of "Standardization and Regulatory Challenges in Modern Cryptography." There is an absence of explicit connections between general cybersecurity practices and the specific issues of cryptographic standards and regulations.
2. **Insufficient Detail on Cryptography**: While foundational cybersecurity concepts are well-covered, the chapter lacks in-depth discussion on cryptographic methods, their standardization, and related regulatory frameworks. This gap makes it difficult for readers to fully grasp the unique challenges in this area.
3. **Limited Coverage of Trends and Challenges**: The chapter does not adequately cover the latest trends and challenges in cryptographic standardization and regulation, such as the rise of quantum computing, the need for quantum-resistant algorithms, and the evolving regulatory landscape across different jurisdictions.

SUGGESTIONS FOR IMPROVEMENT AND ENHANCEMENT

To more effectively illustrate the issues, problems, and trends related to "Standardization and Regulatory Challenges in Modern Cryptography," the following enhancements could be made:

1. **Incorporate Direct References to Cryptographic Standards and Regulations**:
    - Include a dedicated section that discusses key cryptographic standards such as RSA, AES, and ECC. Explain their importance, how they became standards, and the organizations (like NIST and ISO) involved in their standardization.
    - Discuss major regulatory frameworks that impact cryptography, such as GDPR, HIPAA, and PCI-DSS. Explain how these regulations influence cryptographic practices and the challenges they pose.
2. **Detail the Challenges of Standardization**:

- Explain the process of developing cryptographic standards and the challenges involved, such as ensuring security, performance, and interoperability.
- Discuss the debate between proprietary vs. open standards and the implications for security and innovation.

3. **Explore Contemporary Issues and Trends**:
   - Add sections on emerging issues like quantum computing and its impact on current cryptographic standards. Discuss the need for developing and standardizing quantum-resistant algorithms.
   - Highlight trends such as the increasing use of blockchain technology and how its cryptographic foundations pose new regulatory and standardization challenges.
4. **Provide Case Studies and Examples**:
   - Use case studies to illustrate the real-world impact of cryptographic standards and regulations. Examples could include the fallout from weak cryptographic standards (e.g., the deprecation of MD5 and SHA-1) and the implementation challenges of complying with regulations like GDPR.
   - Discuss notable cryptographic breaches and what they reveal about the need for robust standards and regulations.
5. **Integrate a Global Perspective**:
   - Include discussions on how different countries and regions approach cryptographic regulation and standardization. Highlight key differences and the challenges of achieving global consensus.
   - Discuss international cooperation and the role of global organizations in developing cryptographic standards.
6. **Critical Analysis of Existing Literature**:
   - Add a literature review section that critically evaluates existing research on cryptographic standards and regulations. Highlight key findings, debates, and gaps in the literature.
   - Use this analysis to frame the discussion on current challenges and future directions.
7. **Interactive and Updated Content**:
   - Incorporate interactive elements such as diagrams, flowcharts, and timelines that visually depict the evolution of cryptographic standards and the regulatory landscape.
   - Ensure the content is regularly updated to reflect the latest developments in cryptography and cybersecurity regulations.

CONCLUSION

The standardization and regulatory challenges in modern cryptography underscore the intricate interplay between technology, policy, and society in the digital age. Through an exploration of various subtopics, including historical perspectives, the importance of standardization, challenges in cryptographic standardization, regulatory frameworks, international collaboration, case studies, and practical implications, we have gained valuable insights into the complexities and nuances of cryptographic standardization and regulation.

From its historical roots to its role in emerging technologies such as blockchain, quantum computing, IoT, and AI, cryptography continues to play a pivotal role in safeguarding security, privacy, and trust in the digital ecosystem. However, the rapid pace of technological innovation, conflicting interests among stakeholders, and divergent regulatory approaches pose significant challenges for cryptographic standardization and regulation.

One of the key takeaways from this exploration is the importance of international collaboration and harmonization in addressing standardization and regulatory challenges. By fostering cooperation between governments, industry stakeholders, standards organizations, and the cryptographic community, we can develop globally applicable standards and regulatory frameworks that promote security, privacy, and trust in the digital ecosystem.

Furthermore, the case studies and practical implications discussed highlight the real-world implications of cryptographic standardization and regulation. From high-profile legal battles over encryption to the implementation of data protection regulations and the emergence of quantum computing, these case studies provide valuable lessons learned and insights into navigating the complexities of modern cryptography.

In conclusion, addressing standardization and regulatory challenges in modern cryptography requires a multifaceted approach that balances technical innovation, policy considerations, and ethical principles. By embracing collaboration, fostering innovation, and upholding fundamental rights and values, stakeholders can overcome the challenges of cryptographic standardization and regulation to build a more secure and resilient digital future for all.

REFERENCES

Alamati, N. (2020) 'Algebraic Frameworks for Cryptographic Primitives'.

Aseri, A. M. (2020). The implication of the European union's general data protection regulation (GDPR) on the global data privacy. *Journal of Theoretical and Applied Information Technology*, 98(4), 692–702.

Cretarola, A., Figà-Talamanca, G., & Grunspan, C. (2021). Blockchain and cryptocurrencies: Economic and financial research. *Decisions in Economics and Finance*, 44(2), 781–787. 10.1007/s10203-021-00366-3

Csenkey, K., & Bindel, N. (2023). Post-quantum cryptographic assemblages and the governance of the quantum threat. *Journal of Cybersecurity*, 9(1), 1–19. 10.1093/cybsec/tyad001

Fernandez-Carames, T. M., & Fraga-Lamas, P. (2020). Towards Post-Quantum Blockchain: A Review on Blockchain Cryptography Resistant to Quantum Computing Attacks. *IEEE Access : Practical Innovations, Open Solutions*, 8, 21091–21116. 10.1109/ACCESS.2020.2968985

Gorva, S. K., & Anandachar, L. C. (2022). Effective Load Balancing and Security in Cloud using Modified Particle Swarm Optimization Technique and Enhanced Elliptic Curve Cryptography Algorithm. *International Journal of Intelligent Engineering and Systems*, 15(2), 190–199. 10.22266/ijies2022.0430.18

Hanafi, B. and Bokhari, M. (2023) 'Enhancement of Security in Connection establishment for IoT Infrastructure through Adversarial Neural Cryptography using GANs'. .10.4108/eai.24-3-2022.2318924

Kan, K., & Une, M. (2021) 'Recent Trends on Research and Development of Quantum Computers and Standardization of Post-Quantum Cryptography', *Monetary and Economic Studies*, 39(November), pp. 77–108. Available at: https://ideas.repec.org/a/ime/imemes/v39y2021p77-108.html%0Ahttps://ideas.repec.org//a/ime/imemes/v39y2021p77-108.html

Mohajerani, K., ... (2023) 'SCA Evaluation and Benchmarking of Finalists in the NIST Lightweight Cryptography Standardization Process', *Cryptology ePrint Archive*. Available at: https://cryptography.gmu.edu/athena/index.php?id=LWC

Schulze, M. (2017). Clipper meets apple vs. FBI—A comparison of the cryptography discourses from 1993 and 2016. *Media and Communication*, 5(1), 54–62. 10.17645/mac.v5i1.805

Sonko, S.. (2024). Quantum Cryptography and U.S. Digital Security: a Comprehensive Review: Investigating the Potential of Quantum Technologies in Creating Unbreakable Encryption and Their Future in National Security. *Computer Science & IT Research Journal*, 5(2), 390–414. 10.51594/csitrj.v5i2.790

Sood, S., & Kim, A. (2023). The Golden Age of the Big Data Audit: Agile Practices and Innovations for E-Commerce, Post-Quantum Cryptography, Psychosocial Hazards, Artificial Intelligence Algorithm Audits, and Deepfakes. *International Journal of Innovation and Economic Development*, 9(2), 7–23. 10.18775/ijied.1849-7551-7020.2015.92.2001

Zhang, L., Xiong, H., Huang, Q., Li, J., Choo, K.-K. R., & Li, J. (2022). Cryptographic Solutions for Cloud Storage: Challenges and Research Opportunities. *IEEE Transactions on Services Computing*, 15(1), 567–587. 10.1109/TSC.2019.2937764

Chapter 7
An Extensive Review of Farming in Metaverse

Adwaya Adhikary
University of Petroleum and Energy Studies, India

Anshul Mantri
University of Petroleum and Energy Studies, India

Anushree Sah
https://orcid.org/0000-0003-3444-5860
University of Petroleum and Energy Studies, India

Saurabh Rawat
Graphic Era University, India

ABSTRACT

The humans made graphical world which can be accessed and carved for multiple usage and opportunities, with endless possibilities and no limit. One such in this article is farm- ing and agriculture in the virtual world. How can it be commercialized and made scalable. Minecraft metaverse based game has generated a revenue over $161 million in 2022. Users love reality in graphics, rockstar has made open world and to add more reality they have created different looking people, proper California streets, a proper beaches, real race cars in, etc. GTA (Grand Theft Auto). If we can create a world where the characters have access to shops and services, where the avatars can enjoy in the virtual reality and can buy get access to products and services. In this article we can cultivate our own raw materials and trade them via cryptocurrency. The only thing the players have to maintain is a valid crypto wallet. This platform can be sold to other metaverse based games and generate revenue. The main idea behind buying raw product is to add another layer of reality

DOI: 10.4018/979-8-3693-3824-7.ch007

to it. Proper and different crops can be designed .Some avatars can choose to cultivate and breed cattle in the virtual world and generate revenue in form of crypto currencies and sell them to other avatars. This article provide a comprehensive a comprehensive overview of farming in metaverse with all its challenges opportunities and future aspects. The information contained within this article is intended to aid researchers and other practitioners in the field of AI to refine their approach and to the enhancement in this field. By exploring the various aspects in farming in metaverse will help both experts and non experts to develop various techniques to optimize researches and development.

INTRODUCTION

Since the rebranding of Facebook as meta, the marvelous concept has gained immense popularity and became a over social media. Recently, Microsoft announced its acquisition of Activision Blizzard, a leading video game company, for a staggering $68.7 billion. This acquisition is seen as a significant move for Microsoft to expand its presence in the metaverse by boosting its gaming offerings. Recently, Metaverse Group, which is a metaverse based company has brought a parcel of land in the metaverse for $2.43 million. Snoop Dog has brought a land in Sandbox metaverse where he holds his virtual concerts and musical festivals for an immersive audience in the virtual world via VR technology. The metaverse is alluring many game maker, online finance companies and various social media networks. The Seoul metropolitan has launched an ambitious new project which provides the citizen with wide range of city. From education to tourism, it includes almost everything, mainly to interact via virtual platform (Abibullaev & Zollanvari, 2019). Metaverse Seoul will provide offers for persons with disabilities via extended reality (XR) apart from providing all the civic rights. According to the report Bloomberg Intelligence research, the global metaverse revenue will increase from USD 500 Billion to USD of 800 billion with 3-4 years. Video games companies and studio have updated their existing plans to upgrade 3D games .The idea of metaverse has circulated heavily along with advancement and development of internet for mass crowd (Agushaka, Ezugwu, & Abualigah, 2022). The paper put forward an idea that how virtual farming can offer sustainable development. Let us look at the rice plantation; Rice is a primary food source for billions of people. 1kg of rice require 3000L of water to produce. This leads to the flooding of the paddy fields. While this process controls the proliferation of weeds, leads to an enormous production of methane in nature. We are all familiar with the potency of methane to cause the global warming.

Soybean plantation; Soybean is an important source of vegetarian protein. Apart from soy granules they are used to make soy milk and tofu. On one hand soy beans are important as the fix nitrogen to the soil but on the other hand they deplete the soil of phosphorous and potassium. Over plantation of soybeans can also cause acidification of the soil.

The virtual farming methodology leads us to a scope of study research and development which can help make the environment sustainable. For e.g. in rice plantation in virtual farming we predict the amount of methane produced by rice plantation and can narrow it down to a certain tolerance limit or we can channelize the methane and put to other use. Similarly we can study and predict the pH of the soil after several soy plantation and provide the required nutrients to the soil, ergo making the soil sustainable. We can also basify the soil or adapt to a better prediction of most suitable crop for crop rotation

2. METAVERSE

Metaverse consists of the terms ‘meta’ and ‘verse’. It literally means beyond universe. Metaverse is a blend of digitally crafted worlds into one platform, it is often consider as the idea of shared virtual space. The technology aims to formulate a “digital twin” where digital copies of the actual surrounding are created and explored by the user via avatars. Multiple Digital twins are created for the avatars to experience multiple virtual world. Tech companies are planning to merge real and virtual world to augment a Metaverse, which will create a opportunity of a deep immersive digital space of business and endless opportunities (Alkhalefah et al., 2021). This brings us to our field of farming and agriculture in order for the avatars to sustain in the Metaverse, also try to test our innovations in the world where it will not affect the real world and will not cause any health hazards. The scope of the metaverse can be experienced by AR cloud that provide a hybrid experience of the Meta world and physical world (Alsenwi et al., 2021).

3. AI FOR METAVERSE

Various DL algorithms are developed which consists of recurrence neural network(RNN), long short-term memory(LSTM), and convolutional neural network(CNN) has been proven immensely powerful and utmost useful. It recognizes various complex patterns and deal with large intricate and complex data. NVDIA has recently introduced a DL super Sampling(DLSS) which is a neural graphic technology that exploits DL algorithm and amplifies the frame rate to maintain sharp in game images and it also boosts the game balance in various other multiplayer games. In some specific domains, the performance in AI based system can be optimized by using metaheuristic algorithm, mainly 'Prairie dog optimization algorithm', 'dwarf mongoose optimization algorithm', and 'Ebola optimization search algorithm'. 3D design of the new generation is very much promising to create a mesmerising virtual reality, in metaverse, as complete and rich and diversifying as the real world. Although the XR/VR, metaverse helps user to interact with each other and with other object in the virtual world, seamlessly and immersive (Athiwaratkun, & Stokes, 2017). To make this possible, there are various technologies involved, such as head-mounted VR goggles and sensor-detected wands, which allow users to experience the virtual world in a more tangible way. However, the most important technology driving the Metaverse forward is AI. AI has the ability to create a more profound, seamless and beautiful virtual reality experience by providing the intelligence necessary to make the virtual world more realistic and engaging (Azamfar, Li, & Lee, 2020). Ultimately, AI is the key to unlocking the full potential of the Metaverse and creating a truly immersive virtual reality experience. It is the underlying technology that drives the Metaverse forward, and as AI continues to advance, we can expect to see even more realistic and engaging virtual worlds emerge. Many DL based methods have been proposed by researchers to execute very minute, accurate and minor details while presenting the real time interface and it is boosted by mainly two software's PyTorch3D and Tensor RT (Azari, Ozger, & Cavdar, 2019). Meta recently introduced AI based research supercluster (RSC) to boost the research in the field of AI and also build an optimize metaverse.RSC had helped researchers and scientists to develop accurate and optimized DL based algorithm which operated over massive stacks of data mainly speech, texts, videos and various services. Some basic ML algorithm and Dl framework are used for the development of virtual world. Fig 1 below shows the development and timeline of metaverse (Banos et al.,2015) AI integration is a crucial part. We can achieve this by training various ML models to diffent soil quality, crop health, and climate patterns, judging the optimize way to maximize out yields.

Case Study: A virtual farming platform uses AI to help users grow better crops. The AI simulates different farming methods to understand their impact on crop growth. It analyzes historical data, such as past weather patterns, soil conditions, and crop performance, to make accurate predictions. By running these predictive models, the AI provides users with recommendations on the best farming practices to maximize their virtual crop yield. This helps users make informed decisions and improve their virtual farming success. For example, Taranis uses AI-powered aerial images to keep an eye on crop health and soil conditions, spotting problems like nutrient shortages or pest infestations early.

Figure 1. Development of Metaverse

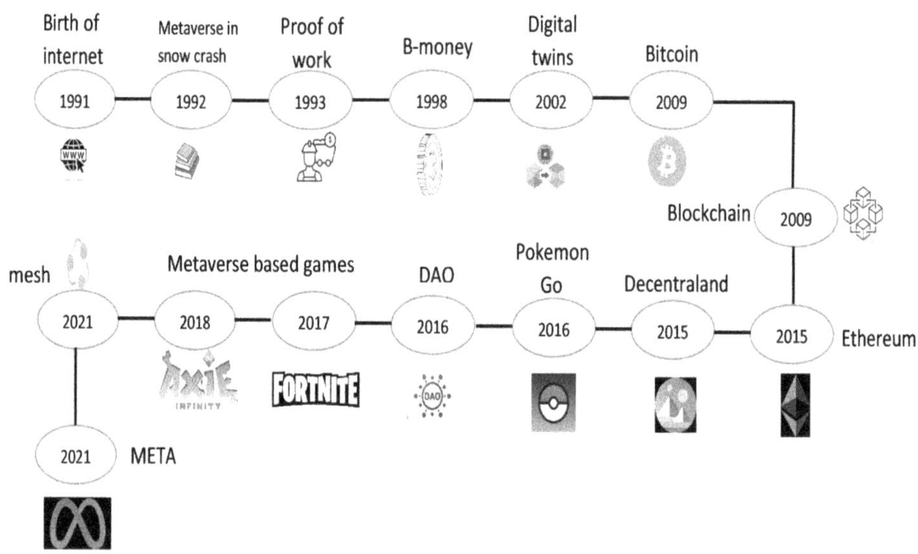

3.1. Natural Language Processing

The other name for NLS is computational linguistic, it auto analyze human speech and process it. NLP plays a vital role tin communication inside the virtual world. Particularly, NLP, play a vital role in designing; virtual assistant and AI based chatbots (Barba, MacIntyre, Mynatt, 2012). AI empowered chatbots can resolve and answer complex problems, they also provide multiple solution. NLP predicts word and develop Language modelling mainly, speaking character aware and word aware modelling techniques helps NLP and knowing the system to extract semantics information for several tasks and works in metaverse like tagging, named entity recognition (Benes, Baskar, & Burget, 2017). Apart from supervised learning, there are also other learning methods used in natural language processing. Unsupervised learning is one such method, which involves training models on unlabelled data to discover patterns and relationships within the data. This method is useful when labeled data is scarce or unavailable. For example, unsupervised learning can be used for topic modelling or clustering similar documents together. Reinforcement learning is another learning method, which involves training models to make decisions based on feedback from the environment. This method is useful for applications where the optimal outcome is not clear, such as in dialogue systems where the goal is to have a natural and engaging conversation with the user. Additionally, transfer learning is another approach that can be used in natural language processing. This involves using pre-trained models and transferring the knowledge gained from one task to another related task. For example, a sentiment analysis based model is useful to improve performance on related tasks such as emotion recognition. The fig 2 shows below the seven layers of AI that can empower metaverse(Bhat, & Huang, 2021).

Figure 2. 7 layers of AI in metaverse

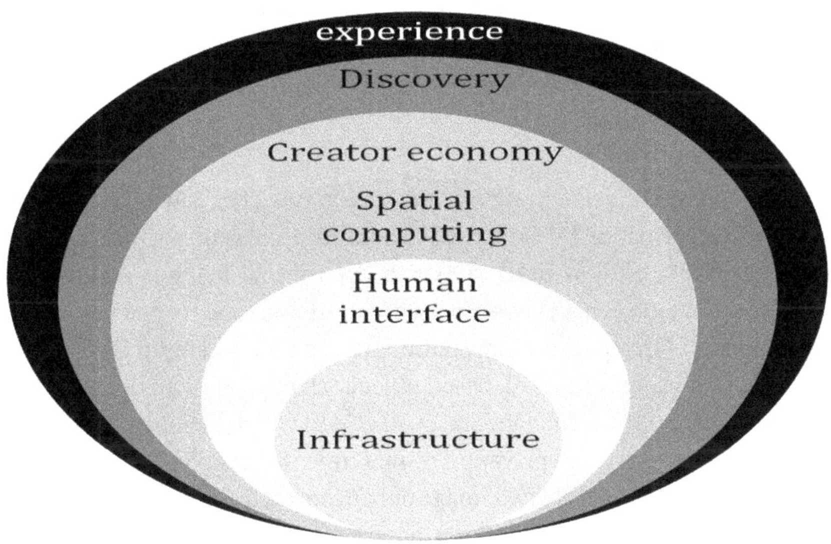

3.2 Extended reality

XR is a term that encompasses various technologies like VR, AR, and MR. AR technology allows users to experience graphics, video streaming, and generate holograms, while VR gives an experience of totally immersive digital surrounding. MR bridges the gap between both technologies, allowing users to experience a hybrid physical-virtual world. With the help of AI, these technologies can create more immersive and vivid realities with numerous features to explore. Compared to conventional two-dimensional videos, 360-degree videos provide an unlimited viewpoint suitable for VR performance. Some high-end VR goggles can even multitask, driven by AI automatically. AI algorithms are applied over VR gadgets.

It enhance Human to machine interaction, and neural networks are being used for human identification and authentication. This technology has potential in various scenarios, such as farming and shopping, and can be used to cultivate crops at a much faster rate with ease(Banyal et al., 2020). Machine learning and deep learning algorithms can be used in real-time VR/AR applications also. AR headsets, triboelectric gloves, joysticks, and tabletops are being used to access content in the metaverse. MR has more potential than VR and AR because it provides a hybrid physical-virtual experience. Holographic devices with see-through displays allow users to manipulate physical objects, while immersive devices allow users to interact with virtual objects. Using this technology, humans can explore the unexplored and see the unseen. They can interact with agricultural aspects in the metaverse and participate in other fun activities. Overall, XR and AI technologies have the potential to create an entirely new world of experiences for users (Cannavò, & Lamberti, 2021).

3.3. Computer vision

Recently, many DL related algorithms and approaches have tremendous improvement in performance by exploiting several deep learning when compared to traditional methods. CNN is used to extract deep visual features and multi scale resolution optimization, which has been used to design advance segmentation model. Metaverse is built of diversified single entities (e.g. single and multi Object module) therefore it is important for the AI-based objects identification to deal and process with complicated classes, (Sah, Dumka, et al., 2018) which includes real and virtual objects. The problems with deprivation of real time images like noise and blurring occur can be handled by mainly two image enhancement techniques- decomposition guided multi scale was presented, it removes haze of a single image, it uses deep residual structure and UNET learning frame that removes distorted components of an image. Other advance image optimization exploits CNN based architecture, which reduces image compression and saves undistorted clean images. Fig 3. Shows picture of farming in metaverse (Chen, Gong, & Xiang, 2011).

Figure 3. Farming in metaverse

3.4.Digital Twining

It can generate a replica of the real world, DT synchronizes assets, systems along with the real world and other actions, such as monitoring and predicting and it also processes along with several general actions such as monitoring, visualizing, analyzing and predicting . DT acts as a harbor in which real and virtual world interact with through IoT connection; so changing anything in the virtual world will not necessarily change the virtual world. These distinguished properties makes DT the foundation of metaverse creation, and create a gateway for the user to enter and interact inside the virtual world and have fun by exactly replicating the virtual reality world and including all structures and functionality(Sah et al., 2022). E.g. in industry 4.0, which is a DT framework that mainly aims at doing various tasks. ML methods with multi-level perception of the neural network which was deployed to validate sensory data. A DT framework is developed to monitor the welding action (Chen, Wang, Zhu, & Han, 2021). The data integration and synchronization problem:

Real time data feed can be achieved from various sources such as IoT sensors, weather stations, and agriculture databases to support and update the digital twinning process.

APIs can be used and integrated to fetch the real-world data to virtual database of the mode.

Synchronization updates can be event driven or periodic based on the requirement of data. Blockchain timestamping can also be used to ensure integrity and traceability of real time data. Now-a-days IoT sensors in real-world farms continuously monitor soil moisture levels and temperature. These sensor readings can be transmitted to the metaverse periodically through APIs. Latency management is an important issue.

3.5 Neural Interface

Technologies are developing and they are enriching the world, by filling the gap between man and machine, via metaverse. Vr and controllers are very important and immersive to interact within the metaverse (Rawat & Sah, 2013). BCI and neural interface is another new field of technology that is very promising and must be paid attention to. BCIs go beyond normal VR . These are mainly electrodes that are connected to the skull and receives electrical pulses from the brain. As per these noninvasive devices, they can only detect and control the thought process of the brain at the very root level. BMIs can only detect and manipulate thoughts via transcranial electromagnetic pulses. In processing stage. AI/ML helps analyze complicated neural signal and categorize emotion. The extremely critical spatial feature and correlation extracted from EEG via capsule and CaspNet has out performed several state-of-the art learning model. To Optimize the visual of the virtual farming, Convolutional neural networks are applied. The CNN models can be trained based on the synthetic data and the real world generated data, i.e. virtual and real world generated images. The training of data must undergo extensive preprocesing, including normalization, augmentation, and annotation, to ensure suitability for training of CNN.

Transfer learning techniques are utilized to adapt pre-trained CNN models to the world of virtual farming, while domain adaptation helps to bridge the gap between real-world and virtual world. The training process require to account a large and diverse datasets that includes wide range of synthetic farming scenarios, considering model across different type of soil condition and weather pattern.

The performance of CNN is supported using cross-validation, testing is various virtual environments.

By incorporating these methodological details CNN models can be trained specifically.

3.6 Ethical Consideration of Digital Divide

when we digitally divide the terrain of the whole earth and assign specific parts as per need for that region, we must interconnect various users, if a user needs to access someone other's land we can use the standard cyber ethics to maintains sanctity and discipline in the app. The standers established ethics will lay ground rules to manage transferred funds, keep records of transaction check the network penetration and firewall security to provide better more suitable environment. The regulations should be of international standards, considering all ethnicities. Ones identity and data must be preserved and should not be disclodes in public. Virtual farming creates a digital asset, to protect the assets one can introduce intellectual protocols like trademarks, protocols and patents. Non Fungible Tokens can set property right of the virtual assets while smart contracts can be used to automate IP rights and distribute royalty ownership.

We can establish a digital market place where virtual goods like seeds, tools, pesticides and even customized AI generated guide are available for the users. Some reforms like taxations, anti money laundering, consumer protections laws, KYCs can be implemented to ensure safety. These regulations can also facilitate cross Boder trades among users.

4. BLOCKCHAIN IN THE METAVERSE

Blockchain technology has gained popularity due to its ability to securely record transactions and track assets using cryptographic techniques. In metaverse, large amounts of data are generated by VR devices that are transmitted over a large distance and stored in various data centres, blockchain is very useful and promising for the protection of that data, especially when combined with AI technologies. As more digital assets are created in the metaverse, smart contracts can play a very helpful role to track and maintain the transparency of the transactions. However, one challenge with blockchain is the privacy issues of data sharing in blockchain networks. Federated learning (FL) emerged with a promising solution to handle this problem(Sah et al., 2020). AI models can be trained by multiple user over their local available data and collaboratively learn over the server globally. FL was integrated in a noble unity mechanism. We can use this to maintain the high privacy in data but with lesser computational speed and communicational cost which is generated by heterogeneous IoT devices(Sah, Bhadula, et al., 2018). Another important concern in blockchain is interoperability; it requires merging and collaborating with other groups over different infrastructure. The integration of blockchain and AI technologies in various application domains has shown great potential to improve data security, privacy, and interoperability, and is expected to have significant impacts on the metaverse and other areas in the future. The ability to securely record transactions and track assets using blockchain, combined with AI and FL technologies, could significantly enhance data privacy and security in the metaverse, enabling more transparent and secure digital transactions. blockchain integrated with AI technologies can transform the metaverse and other domains by improving data privacy, security, and interoperability. Smart contracts: smart contract can be used to automate process inside the virtual world such as plantation, watering and harvesting of the crops based on AI driven insights. Each virtual good, land or farming equipment can be tokenized using NFTs. These tokens can be used to represent ownership and transaction history that each of the virtual items have a specific origin and ownership can be verified.

Smart contracts can be used to automate and enforce agreements among various users. This reduces the needs for intermediates and transaction cost for various distributed parties.

Decentralized marketplace powder by blockchain can enable users to buy and sell virtual farming necessities and goods

4.1 Interoperability Issues

Scenario: Traceability of virtual crop

Implementation: A virtual farmer uses a blockchain-powered farm to grow crops. Every step of the crop's lifecycle—from planting to harvesting—is recorded on the blockchain. When the crop is harvested, it becomes an NFT (non-fungible token) that contains information about its growth conditions, the inputs used, and the yield.

Validation: Consumers and other stakeholders can check the blockchain record to see where the crop came from and verify its quality. This ensures transparency and builds trust in the virtual agricultural supply chain.Blockchain Integration: blockchain can be used for secure tracking of virtual assets such as land, crops and machinery. Each transactional and ownership can be stored in a decentralized ledger.

We can Standardized formats of data are introduced for agricultural data, including crop information, soil quality metrics, and weather data. These standard sets ensure integration across different metaverse platforms.

Various interoperability protocols can be implemented such as cross-chain bridges, atomic swaps, and frameworks like Polkadot or Cosmos. We can also develop standardized smart contracts for common agricultural transactions. Decentralized identity standards can implement to manage and authenticate stake holders. Various consensus mechanisms can be used such as Proof of Stake (PoS) that facilitate cross-platform transaction while maintaining network security and efficiency.

4.2 Methods

With the development in the industustrial revolution, new technologies have evolved to connect man and machines. Various digital techniques are used to enhance the physical world via machine, the metaverse creates a virtual world that is translated onto the physical world based on the foundation of real interaction and persistence. Currently, AI with ML algorithms and DL architectures have immensely helped in the manufacturing domain via numerous industrial applications. In the metaverse farming can be achieved by exploiting various frame works of the AI and ML. Extended reality or virtual reality goggles are the tool to begin farming in the metaverse, we can culture and cultivate various crops. Those cultivated crops will not be explicit or specific to any region or climate(Rawat & Sah, 2012) .We can sell those crops to other avatars via bitcoin. Large plots of land in the metaverse can be bought or sold via bitcoin transaction. Farming can be achieved in metaverse without putting much effort, we can pre-design avatars via neural interface and NLP to design cultivate farm. Those crops can be sold to other persons in the metaverse. NLP and extended VR can also be used to socialize among other individual and we can sell assets and other amenities as per the need of the seller. This can be a great source of earning and meet new people. Many people hold concerts in metaverse and buy retail land and real estate.

Games are one of the most popular applications in the metaverse, providing users with immersive experiences and social interactions. In the metaverse, games can range from simple puzzle games to massive multiplayer online games (MMOs) with thousands of players interacting in the same virtual world. One of the key advantages of games in the metaverse is the ability to create and customize avatars, allowing users to express themselves and stand out in a virtual world. Games can also provide a platform for social interactions, allowing users to meet and play with others from around the virtual world, games in the metaverse can incorporate blockchain technology to provide additional features such as ownership of in-game assets, allowing players to buy, sell, and trade virtual items with each other (Mathur, Sah, & Rawat2023). This creates a new economy within the game, with players able to earn real-world money by selling virtual items. If we make our own metaverse and sell it in other Metaverse companies, the reality and the advancement can be promising. Farming in metaverse can be used to try to test various crops and farming methods that can be hazardous in the real world. The effect of new pesticides cannot be studied without affecting the land or the wildlife surrounding the land metaverse can be an ideal place to test the impact and study the chemical effect without hampering the actual land or wildlife surrounding it. Climate change is a major issue nowadays that can be tackled by the use of metaverse. We can create our own virtual environment to coupe us with this change in climate that to some extent harmful for the study released to agriculture(Rawat & Kumar, 2020). With the development of metaverse, open vivid opportunities in the world of research and development. Any natural known architecture can be copied bit-by-bit into the metaverse via digital twining, their effects can be studied profoundly, and accurately which will help in further development in that field. .The virtual farming can be used in research and development, in education. We can create an app with enables VR and AR. The learning app will have real world exposers virtual modulated environment to try and test, we can add some features like commons fertilized their harms and benefits, AI driven guides and chatbots to apt most optimized methods and suggestions to maximize the yield in terms of per area growth.

A larger model can be created where the whole of the earth's terrain can be mapped in machine and the parts of the whole terrain can be accessed via VR. Scenario based validation to optimize virtual crop yield with AI and blockchain

Implementation:

We can create a virtual farming simulation using AI and ML techniques to optimize crop yield. Blockchain techniques can be used to trace and verify crops' lifecycle and development period. ML models can be used analyze collected data and recommend optimal farming techniques for maximum yield.

Validation:

Various simulation test runs can be done on multiple farming techniques under various conditions. The results of those conditions can be compared and can be optimized by various AI driven solutions.

Result and analysis:

The empirical data on the increase in crop yield can be compared using the AI driven methods and traditional methods. These changes can be incorporated in real farming techniques.

5. TECHNOLOGY LIMITATIONS

The AI may not always perform optimally. As AI is fully based on the underlying algorithm, under critical conditions the predicted data might not be absolutely. While the VR and AR fully depend on the hardware requirement and latency for seamless performance. To train an AI model the dataset should be big, and the quality of data must be very high. While the AR and VR modeling also require high resolution imager. Prolonged use of AR or VR might cause mental strain, motion sickness and psychological trauma.

The initial cost of development, deployment and maintenance is very high. The ROI in these products is quite hard to calculate as the development might take a prolonged period, also the outcomes might be intangible. Ther is a lack of skilled labor in the market who can develop such massive and high capital intensive projects. Overcoming challenges in AI, VR, and AR requires a comprehensive strategy. Investing in research and development is essential to improve these technologies. Creating ethical guidelines can address privacy, bias, and health concerns, ensuring responsible use. Public awareness and education will build trust and highlight benefits. Collaboration between governments and industry is necessary to develop balanced regulations that protect users and encourage innovation. Finally, fostering stakeholder cooperation and setting industry standards will ensure interoperability and ease of adoption.

6. HEALTH ANGLE TO THIS PERSPECTIVE

Prolonged used of the VR or AR headsets are highly as they can have lots of health hazards. Prolonged use of these headsets can cause strain in the eyes and hallucination. They can even cause addiction or isolation of an individual. Bad posture and ergonomics can have body related pain. We can have set timeout of the app, the headset has to be made comfortable and light to reduce the chances of neck pain provide better ergonomics. Ones virtual identity must be kept preserved and the data releated to the person must be kept safe.

7. RESULTS AND CONCLUSION

In the above graph the x-axis represent the years and the y-axis represent the no. of survey articles published in those years. Through this figure we can conclude that there had only been recent advancements in this field. In the late 2000s not much of development took place in this field of work, which infers some promising, advancements which are yet to be developed

Figure 4. Review of number of articles published in blockchain in metaverse

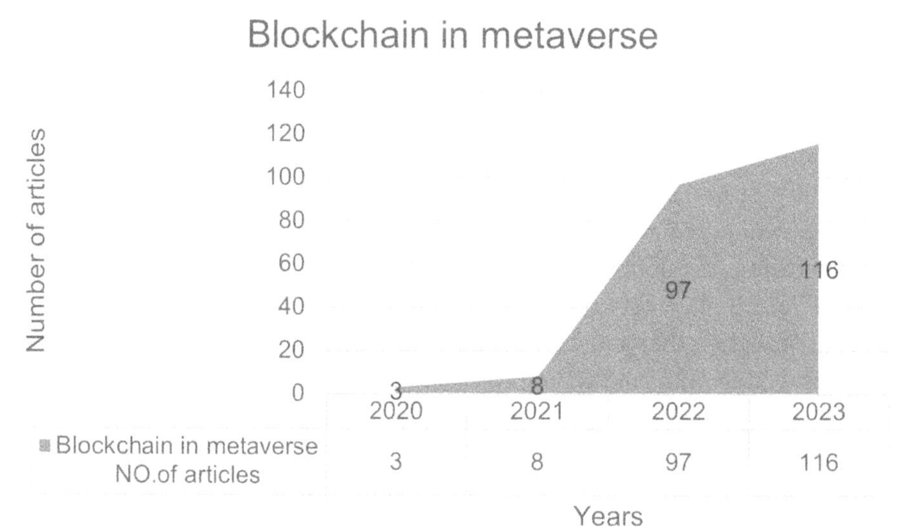

The Fig 4. Shows the review of number of articles published in blockchain in metaverse.

The data above is taken from sciencedirect. It can be seen that the research in blockchain field has increased many folds in the last few years. Blockchain is a new technology that is evolving exponentially. It has many implications in our field of work. As we are dealing with farming and real estate, blockchain plays a very important role. We can use blockchain to boost and secure our supply chain from manufacturer to customer. In real estate, we can securely handle our transaction via bitcoin or other digital ledger.

Figure 5. Review of number of articles published in AI in metaverse

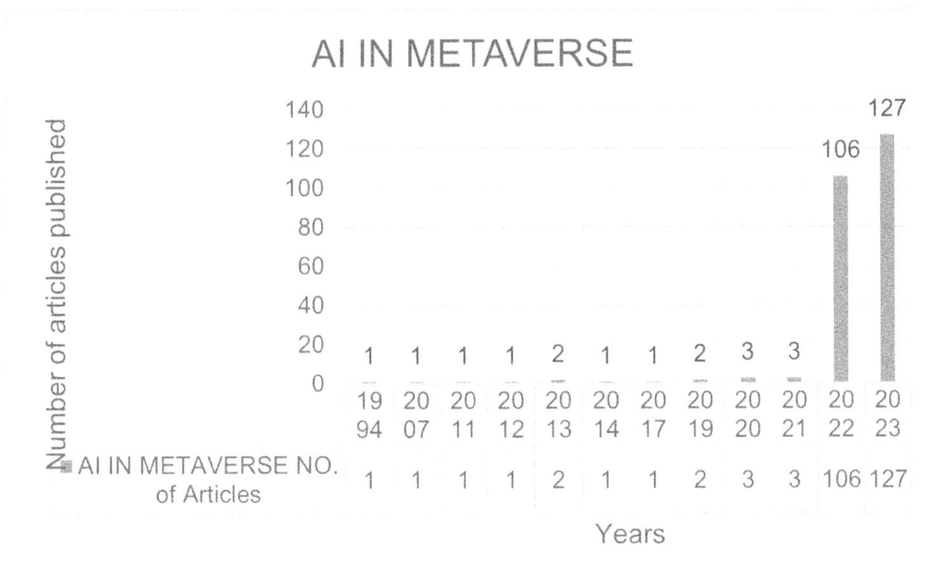

Fig 5. Shows Review of number of articles published in AI in metaverse. From the fig 5 above it can be seen the exponential growth in the field of AI and ML. With this rapid development, we are availed with immense amount of technology to implement diversified research and digital to digitally twin various scenarios and platforms to further develop and sell.

Figure 6. Review of number of articles published in Digital Twining in metaverse

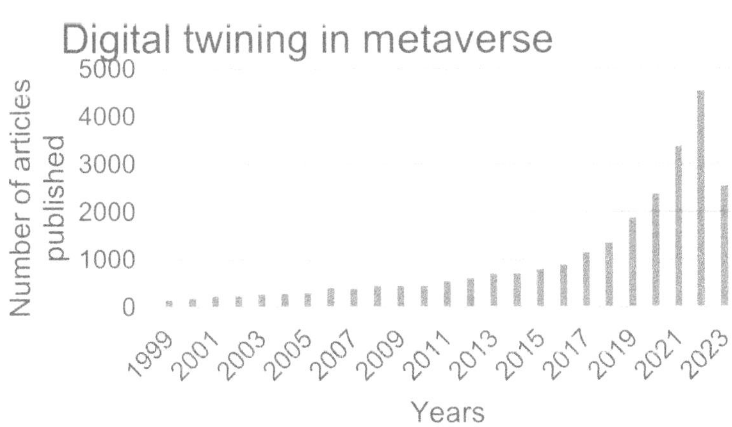

Fig 6. Shows Review of number of articles published in digital twining for metaverse. From the fig 6 above it can be seen the exponential growth in the field of AI and ML.

REFERENCES

Abibullaev, B., & Zollanvari, A. (2019). Learning discriminative spatiospectral features of ERPs for accurate brain–computer interfaces. *IEEE Journal of Biomedical and Health Informatics*, 23(5), 2009–2020. 10.1109/JBHI.2018.288345830668507

Agushaka, J. O., Ezugwu, A. E., & Abualigah, L. (2022). Dwarf mongoose optimization algorithm. *Computer Methods in Applied Mechanics and Engineering*, 391, 114570. 10.1016/j.cma.2022.114570

Alkhalefah, H., Qudeiri, J. E. A., Umer, U., Abidi, M. H., & Elkaseer, A. (2021). Development of an efficient prediction model for optimal design of serial production lines. *IEEE Access : Practical Innovations, Open Solutions*, 9, 61807–61818. 10.1109/ACCESS.2021.3074356

Alsenwi, M., Tran, N. H., Bennis, M., Pandey, S. R., Bairagi, A. K., & Hong, C. S. (2021). Intelligent resource slicing for eMBB and URLLC coexistence in 5G and beyond: A deep reinforcement learning based approach. *IEEE Transactions on Wireless Communications*, 20(7), 4585–4600. 10.1109/TWC.2021.3060514

Athiwaratkun, B., & Stokes, J. W. (2017). *Malware classification with LSTM and GRU language models and a character-level CNN. In 2017 IEEE international conference on acoustics, speech and signal processing (ICASSP)*. IEEE.

Azamfar, M., Li, X., & Lee, J. (2020). Deep learning-based domain adaptation method for fault diagnosis in semiconductor manufacturing. *IEEE Transactions on Semiconductor Manufacturing*, 33(3), 445–453. 10.1109/TSM.2020.2995548

Azari, A., Ozger, M., & Cavdar, C. (2019). Risk-aware resource allocation for URLLC: Challenges and strategies with machine learning. *IEEE Communications Magazine*, 57(3), 42–48. 10.1109/MCOM.2019.1800610

Banos, O., Bang, J., Hur, T., Siddiqi, M. H., Thien, H. T., Vui, L. B., . . . Lee, S. (2015, August). Mining human behavior for health promotion. In 2015 37th Annual International Conference of the IEEE Engineering in Medicine and Biology Society (EMBC) (pp. 5062-5065). IEEE.

Banyal, A., Sah, A., & Choudhury, T. (2020). Commitment of Traders Report: Angular-Based Graph Representation (Agriculture Contracts). In *Computational Intelligence in Pattern Recognition* (pp. 373–381). Springer. 10.1007/978-981-15-2449-3_32

Barba, E., MacIntyre, B., & Mynatt, E. D. (2012). Here we are! Where are we? Locating mixed reality in the age of the smartphone. *Proceedings of the IEEE*, 100(4), 929–936. 10.1109/JPROC.2011.2182070

Benes, K., Baskar, M. K., & Burget, L. (2017, August). Residual Memory Networks in Language Modeling: Improving the Reputation of Feed-Forward Networks. In INTERSPEECH (pp. 284-288).

Bhat, S. A., & Huang, N.-F. (2021). Big data and AI revolution in precision agriculture: Survey and challenges. *IEEE Access : Practical Innovations, Open Solutions*, 9, 110209–110222. 10.1109/ACCESS.2021.3102227

Cannavò, A., & Lamberti, F. (2021). How blockchain, virtual reality, and augmented re ality are converging, and why. *IEEE Consumer Electronics Magazine*, 10(5), 6–13. 10.1109/MCE.2020.3025753

Chen, D., Wang, D., Zhu, Y., & Han, Z. (2021). Digital twin for federated analytics using a Bayesian approach. *IEEE Internet of Things Journal*, 8(22), 16301–16312. 10.1109/JIOT.2021.3098692

Chen, K., Gong, S., & Xiang, T. (2011, November). Human pose estimation using structural support vector machines. In 2011 IEEE International Conference on Computer Vision Workshops (ICCV Workshops) (pp. 846-851). IEEE.

Mathur, A., Sah, A., & Rawat, S. (2023). Evolution of Cloud Computing With Blockchain and IoT. In Taghipour, A. (Ed.), *Blockchain Applications in Cryptocurrency for Technological Evolution* (pp. 14–32). IGI Global., 10.4018/978-1-6684-6247-8.ch002

Rawat, S., & Kumar, R. (2020). Direct-Indirect Link Matrix: A Black Box Testing Technique for Component-Based Software. *International Journal of Information Technology Project Management*, 11(4), 56–69. 10.4018/IJITPM.2020100105

Rawat, S., & Sah, A. (2012). An approach to Enhance the software and services of Health care centre. 3(7), 126–137.

Rawat, S., & Sah, A. (2013). An Approach to Integrate Heterogeneous Web Applications. *International Journal of Computer Applications*, 70(23), 7–12. 10.5120/12205-7639

Sah, A., Bhadula, S. J., Dumka, A., & Rawat, S. (2018). A software engineering perspective for development of enterprise applications. Handbook of Research on Contemporary Perspectives on Web-Based Systems, 1–23. 10.4018/978-1-5225-5384-7.ch001

Sah, A., Choudhury, T., Rawat, S., & Tripathi, A. (2020). A Proposed Gene Selection Approach for Disease Detection. *Advances in Intelligent Systems and Computing*, 1120, 199–206. 10.1007/978-981-15-2449-3_16

Sah, A., Dumka, A., & Rawat, S. (2018). Web technology systems integration using SOA and web services. Handbook of Research on Contemporary Perspectives on Web-Based Systems, 24–45. 10.4018/978-1-5225-5384-7.ch002

Sah, A., Rawat, S., Choudhury, T., & Dewangan, B. K. (2022). An Extensive Review of Web-Based Multi-Granularity Service Composition. *International Journal of Web-Based Learning and Teaching Technologies*, 17(4), 1–19. 10.4018/IJWLTT.285570

KEY TERMS AND DEFINITIONS

AI integration: is a crucial part. We can achieve this by training various ML models to diffent soil quality, crop health, and climate patterns, judging the optimize way to maximize out yields.

Case Study: A virtual farming platform uses AI to help users grow better crops. The AI simulates different farming methods to understand their impact on crop growth. It analyzes historical data, such as past weather patterns, soil conditions, and crop performance, to make accurate predictions. By running these predictive models, the AI provides users with recommendations on the best farming practices to maximize their virtual crop yield. This helps users make informed decisions and improve their virtual farming success. For example, Taranis uses AI-powered aerial images to keep an eye on crop health and soil conditions, spotting problems like nutrient shortages or pest infestations early.

Smart contracts: smart contract can be used to automate process inside the virtual world such as plantation, watering and harvesting of the crops based on AI driven insights.

Blockchain Integration: blockchain can be used for secure tracking of virtual assets such as land, crops and machinery. Each transactiona and ownership can be stored in a decentralized ledger.

Chapter 8

Navigating the Threat Landscape in the Metaverse: Emerging Risks and Security Strategies

Akshat Gaurav
https://orcid.org/0000-0002-5796-9424
Ronin Institute, USA

Brij B. Gupta
Department of Computer Science and Information Engineering, Asia University, Taichung, Taiwan

Priyanka Chaurasia
University of Ulster, UK

ABSTRACT

The metaverse, a convergence of digital and physical realities, presents unprecedented opportunities for interaction and commerce, but also introduces unique security vulnerabilities. This chapter explores the nature of these virtual environments, analyzing inherent weaknesses and the impact of user-generated content. It examines prevalent cyber threats, including malware, phishing, identity theft, and DDoS attacks, providing real-world examples of security breaches. By investigating notable incidents, the chapter highlights the impact on users and platforms and offers mitigation strategies to enhance security measures. Understanding the evolving threat landscape is crucial for developing effective security strategies to safeguard the future of the metaverse.

DOI: 10.4018/979-8-3693-3824-7.ch008

1. INTRODUCTION

The metaverse is a virtual shared space that integrates digital and physical realities through technologies like augmented reality (AR) and virtual reality (VR) (Zuo and Shen 2023; Gupta et al. 2023a). It is characterized by persistent, multi-user, shared 3D virtual spaces that blend elements of the virtual and real worlds (Zuo and Shen 2023; Kumar et al. 2023). The metaverse represents a convergence of physical and digital lives, creating a unified virtual community where various activities such as work, play, socializing, and transactions can occur (Azhar and Dani 2022; Gupta et al. 2023b; **?**; Gaurav et al. 2021).

In the metaverse, there is an integration of the Internet, web technologies, virtual reality, and other advanced technologies like IoT, AR, VR, XR, and 3D technologies (Kabanda, Chipfumbu, and Chingoriwo 2022)(Kasiyanto and Kilinc 2022; Singla et al. 2022). It functions as a network of real-time 3D virtual worlds where users can interact synchronously and persistently with others, maintaining continuity of data such as identity, objects, and communications (Ng 2022; Upadhyay et al. 2023; Sharma et al. 2023). Users can have an immersive experience in the metaverse, feeling psychologically

Table 1. Key Opportunities and Security Concerns in the Metaverse

Aspect	Description	Examples
Opportunities	Vast social, entertainment, and commercial potential	Virtual meetings, gaming, e-commerce
Security Concerns	Unique vulnerabilities and cyber threats	Data breaches, identity theft, DDoS
Importance of Security	Ensuring safe and trusted interactions	Protecting user data and privacy

and emotionally immersed in an alternate reality that meets their expectations (Xu et al. 2023; Gokasar et al. 2023).

Moreover, the metaverse intertwines with the physical world through technologies like the Internet of Things and Extended Reality (XR) (Turchet 2023; Gupta et al. 2023c). It offers a hybrid experience where digital elements interact with the actual environment, incorporating components of both AR and VR (Felice et al. 2023; Singh, Malhotra, and Sharma 2022). The metaverse is envisioned as a vast, unified, persistent, and shared realm on the Internet, providing users with an extended digital self and immersive virtual experiences (Manushri et al. 2022; Kozinets 2022; Gupta and Panda 2022).

Understanding the threat landscape in the metaverse is crucial due to the unique risks and challenges it presents in terms of cybersecurity (Dekker and Alevizos 2023). The metaverse introduces a new dimension to traditional cybersecurity concerns, ne- cessitating a comprehensive understanding of the evolving cyber threats that arise within this virtual environment (Saharan 2023; Tiwari 2023). The vastness of the metaverse, coupled with the integration of advanced technologies like AI, machine learning, and quantum computing, creates a fertile ground for cyber threats (Allimia 2024; GUPTA and CHUI 2022).

By illuminating the threat landscape, security experts can identify adversaries, their tools, techniques, and motives, enabling them to develop robust cybersecurity measures to safeguard users and assets in the metaverse (Dekker and Alevizos 2023; Arya 2023). The metaverse's convergence of physical and digital realities through technologies like IoT and XR further emphasizes the importance of comprehending the cyber threat landscape to mitigate risks effectively.

Moreover, financial cybercrime in the metaverse has become a significant challenge, necessitating the establishment of new regulatory frameworks and innovative cyber- security mechanisms to combat these crimes (Katterbauer, Syed, and Cleenewerck 2022). The integration of artificial intelligence, blockchain, and cloud computing in the metaverse underscores the need for integrated cybersecurity measures to address vulnerabilities and protect against cyber threats (Radanliev 2024).

In conclusion, a deep understanding of the threat landscape in the metaverse is es- sential to proactively address cybersecurity challenges, protect against hacking, iden- tity theft, financial fraud, and other cybercrimes, and ensure a secure and trustworthy virtual environment for users.

2. UNIQUE VULNERABILITIES OF VIRTUAL WORLDS

2.1. *Nature of Virtual Worlds*

Virtual worlds are digital environments that simulate physical spaces, allowing users to interact with each other and with virtual objects through avatars Hua and Haughton (2009). These worlds are designed using the place metaphor, providing networked envi- ronments for users to inhabit and engage within (Gu and Tsai 2010). The architecture of virtual worlds is characterized by flexible and dynamic infrastructures that sup- port various tasks transparently (Garc´ıa-Pen˜alvo et al. 2014).

These environments are highly interactive and dynamic, enabling users to have immersive experiences through the manipulation of 3D models (Gu and Maher 2003).

The architecture of virtual worlds is crucial for ensuring scalability, realism, inter- operability, and ubiquity (Jaber 2022). Commercial virtual worlds typically rely on client/server architectures, although these architectures may have scalability limita- tions (Varvello, Diot, and Biersack 2009). Innovative approaches, such as peer-to-peer architectures, have been explored to address scalability challenges in massive multi- player online games (Hampel, Bopp, and Hinn 2006). Additionally, the integration of distributed virtual environments using Metabots has been proposed as an alternative to traditional client-server models (Kotsilieris et al. 2014).

Virtual worlds also play a significant role in social and cultural innovation, providing stable and persistent digital infrastructures for users to engage in collaborative activities (Jensen, Phillips, and Strand 2012). The design of virtual environments in- volves structuring and experiencing space in unique ways, offering designers various architectural paradigms to create immersive experiences for users (Gladden 2018). Furthermore, the development of virtual worlds requires consideration of evolving fea- tures and emerging requirements, such as infrastructure mobility, content diversity, and immersive environments (Shen et al. 2020).

Virtual environments distinguish themselves from traditional digital platforms in various ways (Table 2). Firstly, virtual environments enable remote interactions among geographically dispersed individuals without the need for physical contact, facilitating collaboration and communication in a virtual space Effah (2019). This capability sets virtual environments apart from traditional digital platforms by offering users a more immersive and interactive experience.

Secondly, virtual environments, including digital twin platforms, broaden accessibil- ity to diverse stakeholder groups, enabling real-time collaboration on a shared digital platform (H¨am¨al¨ainen 2021). This collaborative feature enhances functionality by al- lowing multiple users to engage simultaneously in a virtual space, promoting innovation and cooperation across different domains.

Furthermore, virtual environments present distinct security challenges compared to traditional digital platforms. The dynamic nature of virtual environments, like virtual worlds, necessitates robust security measures to mitigate cyber threats and uphold data integrity (Guedes et al. 2022). The complexity of virtual environments, encom- passing digital proximity and adoption, underscores the importance of establishing secure digital infrastructures to mitigate potential vulnerabilities (Guedes et al. 2022). Moreover, virtual environments offer enhanced functionality for immersive expe- riences, as seen in virtual world libraries, where users can access information and interact with digital resources in innovative ways (Oladokun 2023). This functionality surpasses traditional digital platforms by providing users with interactive and engaging experiences that replicate real-world interactions.

Table 2. Difference Between Digital Platforms and Virtual Environments

Dimension	Digital Environments	Virtual Environments
Interaction	Text, audio, and video com- munication	Immersive and interactive ex- periences (VR, AR)
Accessibility	Access primarily through standard devices (computers, smartphones)	Real-time collaboration in shared digital spaces (digital twins, virtual worlds)
Security	Standard cybersecurity mea- sures	Robust security measures for dynamic environments
Functionality	Static web pages, basic collab- oration tools	Enhanced, immersive experi- ences (virtual libraries, inter- active simulations)
User Experi- ence	Limited to traditional inter- faces and static content	Immersive, engaging experi- ences replicating real-world interactions
Content Cre- ation	Content typically created and managed by platform providers	User-generated content with real-time interactions
Scalability	Often limited by physical hardware and server capabil- ities	Scalable virtual spaces sup- porting a large number of con- current users
Examples	Email, video conferencing, static websites	Virtual meetings, virtual real- ity games, digital twins

2.2. *Inherent Vulnerabilities*

In the design and implementation of virtual worlds, several inherent security weak- nesses exist that pose significant risks to the integrity and confidentiality of data. These vulnerabilities stem from various factors, including the complex nature of vir- tualization technologies and the dynamic interactions within virtual environments.

One key security weakness in virtual worlds is the disconnection between logical and physical situations, which can lead to security issues related to attacks on virtual machines Turki, Zwiad, and Almuttairi (2019). This disconnection creates a gap that attackers can exploit to compromise the security of virtual environments, potentially gaining unauthorized access to sensitive data.

Additionally, vulnerabilities in hypervisors, which are crucial components in virtualization environments, pose a significant risk to the security of virtual machines (Ishiguro and Kono 2020). Attackers target hypervisors because a vulnerability in these systems can undermine the security of all virtual machines running on the same infrastructure, making them an attractive target for malicious actors.

Moreover, the shared and open nature of virtualized environments, such as cloud computing platforms, introduces security challenges related to tampering with network policies and leaking sensitive processing states (Wang et al. 2021). Running in a shared environment without the protection of proprietary hardware can expose virtualized systems to potential security breaches and data leaks.

Furthermore, the complexity of hypervisors, which often have large lines of source code, increases the likelihood of vulnerabilities being present and makes it challenging to maintain their security (Alnaim 2022). These complexities can create opportunities for attackers to exploit weaknesses in the hypervisor architecture, compromising the overall security of virtualized environments.

User-generated content significantly impacts the security of virtual environments due to the inherent risks associated with content creation and sharing by users. The introduction of user-generated content in virtual worlds introduces various security vulnerabilities that can compromise the integrity, confidentiality, and availability of data within these environments.

One of the primary security concerns related to user-generated content is the poten- tial for malicious content to be uploaded, posing risks such as malware distribution, phishing attacks, and data breaches Liu et al. (2010). Malicious users may exploit the openness of virtual environments to upload harmful content, leading to security incidents that can impact the entire virtual community.

Moreover, user-generated content can introduce privacy risks, as users may inad- vertently share sensitive information or personal data while creating and interacting with content in virtual worlds (Lei, Duan, and Song 2021). This can lead to privacy violations, data leaks, and unauthorized access to personal information, highlighting the importance of implementing robust privacy protection measures in virtual envi- ronments.

Additionally, the sheer volume of user-generated content in virtual worlds can over- whelm security mechanisms and make it challenging to monitor and regulate all up- loaded content effectively (Guo and Gong 2011). This can create opportunities for cybercriminals to exploit weaknesses in content moderation processes and bypass se- curity controls to distribute malicious content.

Furthermore, the dynamic and interactive nature of user-generated content in virtual environments can complicate security efforts, as content may change rapidly, making it difficult to assess and mitigate potential risks in real-time (Reinhard and Amsterdam 2013). This dynamic environment requires continuous monitoring and proactive security measures to detect and respond to security threats effectively.

2.3. *Technological and Social Challenges*

Integrating advanced technologies like Virtual Reality (VR), Augmented Reality (AR), and blockchain into virtual worlds introduces a range of security challenges that must be addressed to ensure the integrity and confidentiality of data within these environ- ments. The convergence of these technologies in virtual worlds amplifies the complexity of security considerations and necessitates specialized measures to mitigate potential risks effectively.

One of the primary security challenges posed by integrating VR, AR, and blockchain into virtual worlds is the increased attack surface resulting from the interconnected nature of these technologies Truong, Le, and Niyato (2023). The integration of VR and AR technologies introduces new points of vulnerability that can be exploited by mali- cious actors to compromise the security of virtual environments. Similarly, blockchain technology, while offering benefits such as decentralized data storage and enhanced transparency, presents unique security risks related to smart contract vulnerabilities and consensus algorithm weaknesses (Akram et al. 2022).

Moreover, the immersive nature of VR and AR technologies in virtual worlds can create privacy concerns related to the collection and processing of user data (Wu and Kim 2022). The use of VR headsets and AR devices may inadvertently capture sensitive information, raising privacy implications that must be carefully managed to protect user confidentiality and comply with data protection regulations.

Additionally, the decentralized and immutable nature of blockchain technology in- troduces challenges related to data governance and access control within virtual en- vironments (Akram et al. 2022). Ensuring the secure integration of blockchain into virtual worlds requires robust authentication mechanisms, encryption protocols, and secure smart contract development practices to prevent unauthorized access and data manipulation.

Furthermore, the dynamic and interactive nature of VR and AR content in vir- tual worlds can complicate security efforts, as user-generated content may introduce vulnerabilities that can be exploited by threat actors (Wu and Kim 2022). Implement- ing effective content moderation, access controls, and threat detection mechanisms is essential to mitigate the risks associated with user-generated content in immersive virtual environments.

Integrating advanced technologies like Virtual Reality (VR), Augmented Reality (AR), and blockchain into virtual environments introduces unique security challenges, particularly concerning social engineering risks and the human factor. Social engi- neering exploits human psychology to manipulate individuals into divulging sensitive information or performing actions that compromise security. In virtual environments, the human factor plays a crucial role in susceptibility to social engineering attacks due to limited ability to detect deception, especially in the context of social networking sites (Algarni 2019).

The immersive nature of VR and AR technologies in virtual environments can en- hance the effectiveness of social engineering attacks by creating realistic scenarios that deceive users into disclosing confidential information or engaging in risky behaviors. The human tendency to trust virtual interactions and environments can be exploited by malicious actors to gain unauthorized access to sensitive data or systems (Algarni 2019).

Furthermore, the integration of blockchain technology in virtual environments introduces additional security considerations related to social engineering risks. Blockchain's decentralized and immutable nature can create a false sense of security, leading users to trust transactions and interactions without fully understanding the underlying technology. This trust can be exploited through social engineering tactics to manipulate users into making fraudulent transactions or revealing private keys.

The human factor in virtual environments also contributes to security vulnerabilities through factors such as social stability risks, social conflicts, and disharmony caused by various risk factors. These social risks can escalate into social crises, impacting social stability and order within virtual communities (He, Huang, and Fang 2021). Malicious actors may exploit social instability to sow discord, manipulate user behavior, or spread misinformation, leading to security breaches and compromised virtual environments.

3. TYPES OF CYBER THREATS IN THE METAVERSE

3.1. *Malware and Ransomware*

In virtual environments, various types of malware and ransomware threats pose sig- nificant risks to the security and integrity of data. Ransomware, in particular, has emerged as one of the most prevalent and damaging forms of malware, causing billions of dollars in losses for organizations worldwide (Kapoor et al. 2021). Ransomware en- crypts user data upon system infection, denying access until a ransom is paid, making it a major cybersecurity threat (Ahmed and Aldabbagh 2021). Figure 1 presents the ransomware attack on virtual market place.

Figure 1. Ransomware Attack on Virtual Market Place

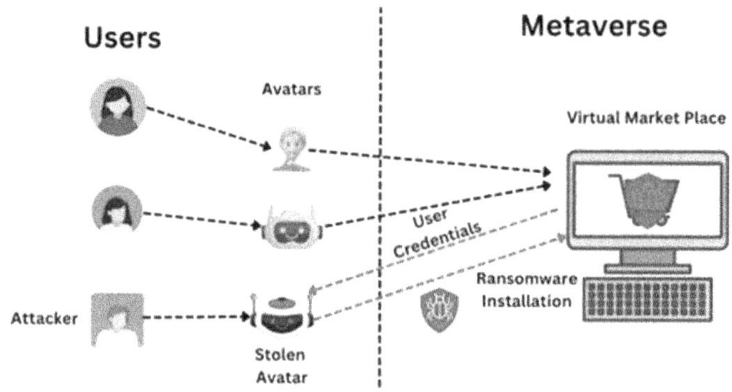

Some common ransomware families that are particularly threatening include Wan- naCry/WannaCryptor, Locky, Cerber, CryptoWall, Petya, NotPetya, GandCrab, Bad Rabbit, and CryptoLocker (Naik et al. 2019). These ransomware variants target both end users and organizations, encrypting valuable data and demanding ransom pay- ments for decryption.

The integration of advanced technologies like VR, AR, and blockchain into virtual environments can exacerbate the impact of ransomware attacks by creating realistic and immersive scenarios that deceive users into disclosing sensitive information or engaging in risky behaviors. Additionally, the decentralized and immutable nature of blockchain technology can create a false sense of security, leading users to trust transactions without fully understanding the underlying risks.

To combat ransomware threats in virtual environments, organizations and individ- uals must implement robust cybersecurity measures, such as backup sys- tems, encryp- tion analysis, and ransomware detection systems (Kapoor et al. 2021) (Maim´o et al. 2019)(Homayoun et al. 2020). Early-stage detection techniques, machine learning al- gorithms, and digital forensic techniques can help identify and mitigate ransomware infections before they cause significant damage (Coglio et al. 2023)(Thomas et al. 2019).

3.2. *Phishing and Social Engineering*

Common phishing techniques and social engineering attacks in the metaverse leverage the immersive and interactive nature of virtual environments to deceive users and manipulate their behavior. Attackers exploit human psychology and trust to trick individuals into divulging sensitive information or performing actions that compromise security.

One prevalent phishing technique in the metaverse is impersonation, where attack- ers pretend to be authorized entities to gain access to services or systems Wang et al. (2023). By impersonating trusted entities, attackers can deceive users into sharing login credentials, personal information, or financial details, leading to unauthorized access and data breaches. Another common social engineering attack in the metaverse involves social networking manipulation, where attackers exploit social interactions, teamwork, and persona discourse to deceive users (Kabanda, Chipfumbu, and Chin- goriwo 2022). By building trust and rapport with individuals in virtual environments, attackers can manipulate users into disclosing confidential information or engaging in risky behaviors.

Figure 2. Fake Profiles and Fake Events at Virtual World

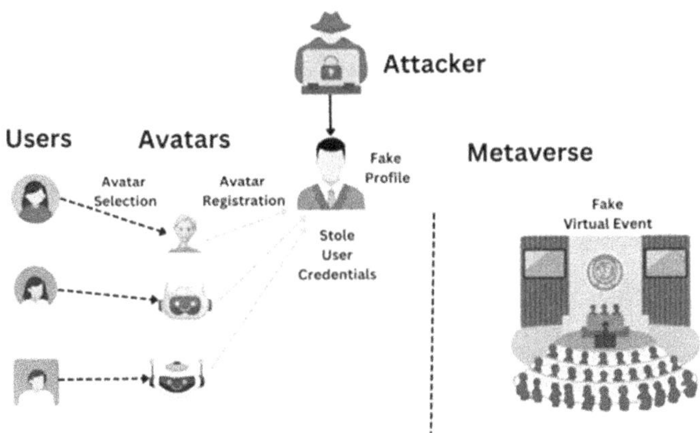

Moreover, in the context of virtual worlds, attackers may use social engineering tactics to create fake personas, establish false relationships, and manipulate user emo- tions to elicit sensitive information. These tactics exploit the human factor in virtual environments, where users may be more susceptible to deception due to the immersive and engaging nature of the metaverse.

To mitigate phishing and social engineering risks in the metaverse, users and orga- nizations should prioritize cybersecurity awareness, education, and training to recog- nize and respond to suspicious activities. Implementing multi-factor au- thentication, encryption, and secure communication channels can also help protect against social engineering attacks and phishing attempts in virtual environments.

Attackers exploit user trust in virtual environments to obtain sensitive information through various social engineering tactics. One common technique is impersonation, where attackers pretend to be trusted entities to deceive users into sharing confidential data Shariff and Zhang (2014). By impersonating authorized entities, attackers exploit user trust to gain access to sensitive information or systems.

Another prevalent social engineering attack involves social networking manipulation, where attackers build trust and rapport with users to manipulate them into dis- closing personal information or engaging in risky behaviors (Xu, Li, and Shao 2012). By leveraging social interactions and persona discourse in virtual communities, attackers can deceive users and exploit their trust to obtain sensitive information.

Moreover, attackers may create fake personas, establish false relationships, and ma- nipulate user emotions in virtual environments to elicit confidential data (Li, Helou, and Gillet 2010). These tactics exploit the immersive and interactive nature of virtual environments, where users may be more susceptible to deception due to the engaging and realistic experiences offered by the metaverse.

To mitigate social engineering attacks in virtual environments, users should be ed- ucated on recognizing and responding to suspicious activities, implementing multi- factor authentication, and using secure communication channels (Huang 2020). By raising awareness and implementing security best practices, users can protect them- selves against social engineering tactics that exploit trust in virtual environments.

3.3. *Identity Theft and Account Hijacking*

In virtual environments, the risks of identity theft and account hijacking are significant, posing serious threats to users' personal information and security. Attackers ex- ploit vulnerabilities in virtual worlds to obtain sensitive data through various means, including phishing, social engineering, and account hijacking techniques.

Phishing attacks in virtual environments involve deceptive tactics to trick users into revealing personal information, such as login credentials or financial details. Attackers may impersonate trusted entities, send fraudulent messages, or create fake websites to lure users into disclosing sensitive data, leading to identity theft and unauthorized account access Tirumala, Sathu, and Naidu (2015)(Alam, Muqeem, and Khan 2018). Social engineering attacks exploit human psychology and trust to manipulate users into divulging confidential information. In the metaverse, attackers may use social net- working manipulation, create fake personas, or establish false relationships to deceive users and obtain sensitive data (Gavrilova and Yampolskiy 2011)(Jordan, Leskovar, and Mariˇc 2018). These tactics exploit the immersive and interactive nature of virtual environments to exploit user trust and compromise security.

Account hijacking is another prevalent threat in virtual environments, where attack- ers gain unauthorized access to user accounts to steal personal information, financial data, or virtual assets. Account hijackers may extend their crimes by sending spam emails, spreading malware, or impersonating the account holder to deceive contacts and spread further attacks (Bendiab, Shiaeles, and Boucherkha 2018)(Madarie et al. 2019).

To mitigate the risks of identity theft and account hijacking in virtual environments, users should be vigilant against phishing attempts, avoid sharing sensitive informa- tion with unknown entities, and use strong authentication methods to protect their accounts. Organizations should implement robust security measures, such as multi- factor authentication, encryption, and regular security audits, to safeguard user data and prevent unauthorized access (Iqbal and Matulevi˘cius 2019)(Sanders and Marchang 2016).

The repercussions of phishing attacks and social engineering in the metaverse can be severe for users and the community. These attacks can lead to identity theft, financial losses, data breaches, and compromised security within virtual environments. When users fall victim to phishing attacks, they may permanently lose valuable information, including personal data, login credentials, and financial details Sharma, Dash, and Ansari (2022).

Phishing attacks in the metaverse can result in users being redirected to illegitimate websites that mimic legitimate platforms, leading to the theft of sensitive information and credentials. Despite awareness efforts, users continue to be affected by these at- tacks, as attackers evolve their tactics to create convincing phishing websites and emails that appear authentic (Hema* 2020).

The consequences of phishing attacks extend beyond individual users to impact the entire metaverse community. These attacks can lead to the spread of fraudulent mes- sages, data breaches, and financial fraud, affecting the trust and security of virtual environments. Phishing attacks are viewed as serious crimes that can result in iden- tity theft, intellectual property theft, financial fraud, cyber espionage, and hacktivism (Chou, Chen, and Lo 2021).

Account hijacking and identity theft in the metaverse can have far-reaching implications, including the loss of sensitive information, financial fraud, and compromised virtual assets. Attackers may use stolen credentials to impersonate users, access their accounts, and engage in fraudulent activities that harm both individuals and the broader metaverse community (Islam et al. 2023).

3.4. *DDoS Attacks and Network Exploits*

Distributed Denial of Service (DDoS) attacks and network exploits are significant cybersecurity threats that can have detrimental effects on users and the metaverse community. DDoS attacks involve overwhelming a network or system with a flood of traffic, rendering it inaccessible to legitimate users. These attacks disrupt services, cause downtime, and impact the overall performance of virtual environments Maggi, Pozza, and Sisto (2008).

Network exploits, on the other hand, involve taking advantage of vulnerabilities in network systems to gain unauthorized access, steal data, or compromise secu- rity. Attackers exploit weaknesses in network configurations, software, or protocols to launch cyberattacks, infiltrate systems, and cause damage to virtual environments (Amezziane, Al-Shaer, and Ali 2012).

The consequences of DDoS attacks and network exploits for users and the metaverse community can be severe (Figure 3). Users may experience service disruptions, loss of data, financial losses, and compromised privacy as a result of these attacks. DDoS attacks can disrupt virtual activities, communication, and transactions, leading to frustration and distrust among users (Conti, Gaspari, and Mancini 2020).

For the metaverse community, DDoS attacks and network exploits can have broader implications, including reputational damage, financial repercussions, and legal conse- quences. These attacks can undermine the trust and security of virtual environments, impacting user engagement, community interactions, and the overall integrity of the metaverse (Ammann, Wijesekera, and Kaushik 2002).

DDoS attacks and network exploits can disrupt virtual environments and have a significant impact on user experience. These attacks can lead to service interruptions, system downtime, and degraded performance, affecting users' ability to access and in- teract within virtual environments. DDoS attacks overwhelm network resources, caus- ing slowdowns or complete unavailability of services, which can disrupt communication, collaboration, and transactions in the metaverse Wang and Zhao (2022).

Network exploits, on the other hand, exploit vulnerabilities in network systems to gain unauthorized access, steal data, or compromise security. These exploits can lead to data breaches, unauthorized access to sensitive information, and system compro- mise, impacting the confidentiality, integrity, and availability of virtual environments (Veinovi´c 2016).

The consequences of DDoS attacks and network exploits for users and the metaverse community include financial losses, data breaches, compromised security, and reputa- tional damage. Users may experience frustration, inconvenience, and loss of trust in virtual environments due to service disruptions and security breaches. The community may suffer from reputational harm, financial repercussions, and legal consequences as a result of these attacks (Patterson, Hobbs, and Zhu 2017).

Figure 3. DDoS Attack in Metaverse

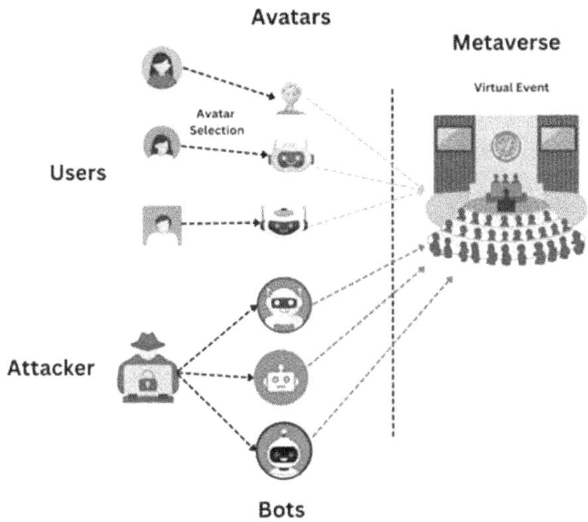

To mitigate the impact of DDoS attacks and network exploits in virtual environments, organizations should implement robust security measures, such as intrusion detection systems, firewalls, and network monitoring tools. User awareness, education, and proactive security practices are essential to protect against these threats and ensure a secure and reliable virtual experience for all users (Irwin et al. 2012).

4. CYBERSECURITY BEST PRACTICES

4.1. *Notable Security Breaches*

(1) What are some notable security breaches that have occurred in virtual environ- ments?
(2) How did these breaches occur, and what vulnerabilities were exploited?

Some notable security breaches that have occurred in virtual environments include:

- The Cloud Security Alliance (CSA) identified the top security threats in cloud computing for 2013 as data breaches resulting from vulnerability of shared virtual resources Almutairi, Sarfraz, and Ghafoor (2018).

- discussed the security vulnerabilities of various virtualization techniques applied in virtual machines, particularly in healthcare records maintenance (Saravanan and Umamakeswari 2018).
- Abu-Alhaija et al. highlighted the security issues raised by hypercalls in virtualized environments and proposed a Xen-based distributed intrusion detection system to enhance security (Zhang and Xin 2017).
- emphasized the security vulnerability analysis in virtualized computing environments, recognizing seven areas of virtualization security that require special consideration (Brooks, Caicedo, and Park 2012).
- Jouini and Rabai pointed out that interoperability in mediator-free environments can lead to security and privacy breaches (Shehab, Bertino, and Ghafoor 2008).

5. CONCLUSION

The metaverse's rapid expansion necessitates robust security measures to address its unique vulnerabilities and cyber threats. Analyzing the nature of virtual worlds and prevalent cyber threats reveals critical weaknesses and the significant impact of se- curity breaches. Case studies illustrate the real-world consequences and underscore the need for continuous vigilance. Effective mitigation strategies and proactive secu- rity protocols are essential to protect users and ensure the integrity of virtual envi- ronments. As the metaverse evolves, ongoing innovation and adaptation in security strategies will be vital to maintaining a safe and secure digital landscape.

ACKNOWLEDGEMENT

This research work is supported by National Science and Technology Council (NSTC), Taiwan Grant No. NSTC112-2221-E-468-008-MY3.

REFERENCES

Ahmed, O., & Aldabbagh, O. (2021). Ransomware detection system based on machine learning. *Journal of Education and Science*, 30(5), 86–102. 10.33899/edusj.2021.130760.1173

Akram, S., Malik, P., Singh, R., Gehlot, A., Juyal, A., Ghafoor, K., & Shrestha, S. (2022). Imple- mentation of digitalized technologies for fashion industry 4.0: Opportunities and challenges. *Scientific Programming*, 2022, 1–17. 10.1155/2022/7523246

Alam, S., Muqeem, M., & Khan, S. (2018). Review on security aspects for cloud archi- tecture. *International Journal of Electrical and Computer Engineering (Ijece)*, 8(5), 3129. 10.11591/ijece.v8i5.pp3129-3139

Algarni, A. (2019). What message characteristics make social engineering successful on face- book: The role of central route, peripheral route, and perceived risk. *Information (Basel)*, 10(6), 211. 10.3390/info10060211

Allimia, H., Baror, S., & Venter, H. (2024, March). Cybersecurity Implications of Virtual Currency Reward Systems in the Metaverse. In *International Conference on Cyber Warfare and Security* (Vol. 19, No. 1, pp. 1-9).

Almutairi, A., Sarfraz, M., & Ghafoor, A. (2018). Risk-aware management of virtual resources in access controlled service-oriented cloud datacenters. *IEEE Transactions on Cloud Computing*, 6(1), 168–181. 10.1109/TCC.2015.2453981

Alnaim, A. (2022). Misuse patterns from the threat of modification of non-control data in net- work function virtualization. *Future Internet*, 14(7), 201. 10.3390/fi14070201

Amezziane, M., Al-Shaer, E., & Ali, M. Q. (2012, April). On stochastic risk ordering of network services for proactive security management. In *2012 IEEE Network Operations and Management Symposium* (pp. 994-1000). IEEE.

Ammann, P., Wijesekera, D., & Kaushik, S. (2002, November). Scalable, graph-based network vulnerability analysis. In *Proceedings of the 9th ACM Conference on Computer and Communications Security* (pp. 217-224).

Arya, V. (2023). “Metaverse Ecosystems and Smart Mobil- ity: A Symbiotic Relationship.” https://insights2techinfo.com/ metaverse-ecosystems-and-smart-mobility-a-symbiotic-relationship/. Accessed: 2024-01-30.

Azhar, A., & Dani, I. (2022). Interpersonal communication with the deaf in the metaverse age. *Muharrik Jurnal Dakwah Dan Sosial*, 5(2), 285–291. 10.37680/muharrik.v5i2.1682

Bendiab, K., Shiaeles, S., & Boucherkha, S. (2018, February). A new dynamic trust model for" on cloud" federated identity management. In 2018 9th IFIP International Conference on New Technologies, Mobility and Security (NTMS) (pp. 1-5). IEEE.

Brooks, T., Caicedo, C., & Park, J. (2012). Security vulnerability analysis in virtualized computing environments. *International Journal of Intelligent Computing Research*, 3(4), 263–277. 10.20533/ijicr.2042.4655.2012.0034

Chou, F., Chen, A., & Lo, V. (2021). Mindless response or mindful interpretation: Exam- ining the effect of message influence on phishing susceptibility. *Sustainability (Basel)*, 13(4), 1651. 10.3390/su13041651

Coglio, F., Lekssays, A., Carminati, B., & Ferrari, E. (2023, March). Early-stage ransomware detection based on pre-attack internal API calls. In *International Conference on Advanced Information Networking and Applications* (pp. 417-429). Cham: Springer International Publishing.

Conti, M., Gaspari, F., & Mancini, L. (2020). A novel stealthy attack to gather sdn configuration-information. *IEEE Transactions on Emerging Topics in Computing*, 8(2), 328–340. 10.1109/TETC.2018.2806977

Dekker, M., & Alevizos, L. (2023). A threat-intelligence driven methodology to incorporate uncertainty in cyber risk analysis and enhance decision-making. *Security and Privacy*, 7(1), e333. Advance online publication. 10.1002/spy2.333

Effah, J. (2019). Brightening Physical University Admission Through Digital Process Virtualization: An Action Case Study in Ghana. In ICT Unbounded, Social Impact of Bright ICT Adoption: IFIP WG 8.6 International Conference on Transfer and Diffusion of IT, TDIT 2019, Accra, Ghana, June 21–22, 2019, Proceedings (pp. 170-179). Springer International Publishing.

Garc’ıa-Pen˜alvo, F., Cruz-Benito, J., Maderuelo, C., P’erez-Blanco, J., & Mart’ın-Su’arez, A. (2014). Usalpharma: A cloud-based architecture to support quality assurance training pro- cesses in health area using virtual worlds. *TheScientificWorld-Journal*, 2014, 1–10. 10.1155/2014/659364

Gaurav, A., Gupta, B. B., Hsu, C. H., Castiglione, A., & Chui, K. T. (2021). Machine learning technique for fake news detection using text-based word vector representation. In Computational Data and Social Networks: 10th International Conference, CSoNet 2021, Virtual Event, November 15–17, 2021 [Springer International Publishing.]. *Proceedings*, 10, 340–348.

Gavrilova, M. L., & Yampolskiy, R. (2011). Applying biometric principles to avatar recognition. Transactions on computational science XII: Special issue on cyberworlds, 140-158.

Gladden, M. (2018). A phenomenological framework of architectural paradigms for the user- centered design of virtual environments. *Multimodal Technologies and Interaction*, 2(4), 80. 10.3390/mti2040080

Gokasar, I., Pamucar, D., Deveci, M., Gupta, B. B., Martinez, L., & Castillo, O. (2023). Metaverse integration alternatives of connected autonomous vehicles with self-powered sensors using fuzzy decision making model. *Information Sciences*, 642, 119192.

Gu, N., & Tsai, J. (2010). Interactive graphical representation for collaborative 3d virtual worlds. *Computer-Aided Civil and Infrastructure Engineering*, 25(1), 55–68. 10.1111/j.1467-8667.2009.00613.x

Guedes, A., Faria, S., Gouveia, S., & Rebelo, J. (2022). The effect of virtual proximity and digital adoption on international tourism flows to southern europe. *Tourism Economics*, 29(6), 1643–1661. 10.1177/13548166221116704

Guo, J., & Gong, Z. (2011). Measuring virtual wealth in virtual worlds. *Information Technology and Management*, 12(2), 121–135. 10.1007/s10799-011-0082-9

GUPTA. (2022). *A. K., & CHUI, K. T.* Blockchain-Based Decentralized Data Management for the Metaverse.

Gupta, B. B., Gaurav, A., Albeshri, A. A., & Alsalman, D. (2023a). New paradigms of sustainable entrepreneurship in metaverse: A micro-level perspective. *The International Entrepreneurship and Management Journal*, 19(3), 1449–1465. 10.1007/s11365-023-00875-0

Gupta, B. B., Gaurav, A., Chui, K. T., & Arya, V. (2023b). “Revolutioniz- ing Human-Machine Interaction through Hand Gesture Recognition in 6G-Enabled Meta- verse Environments.” In *2023 IEEE International Conference on Advanced Networks and Telecommunications Systems (ANTS)*, 1–6. IEEE.

Gupta, B. B., Gaurav, A., Chui, K. T., Le Wang, V. A., Shukla, A., & Perakovi'c, D. (2023c). "Ddos attack detection through digital twin technique in metaverse." In *2023 IEEE International Conference on Consumer Electronics (ICCE)*, 1–5. IEEE. 10.1109/ICCE56470.2023.10043433

Gupta, T., & Panda, S. P. (2022). Cloudlet and virtual machine performance enhancement with CLARA and evolutionary paradigm. [IJCAC]. *International Journal of Cloud Applications and Computing*, 12(1), 1–16. 10.4018/IJCAC.298322

H¨am¨al¨ainen, M. (2021). Urban development with dynamic digital twins in helsinki city. *IET Smart Cities*, 3(4), 201–210. 10.1049/smc2.12015

Hampel, T., Bopp, T., & Hinn, R. (2006, October). A peer-to-peer architecture for massive multiplayer online games. In *Proceedings of 5th ACM SIGCOMM workshop on Network and system support for games* (pp. 48-es).

He, Z., Huang, D., & Fang, J. (2021). Social stability risk diffusion of large complex engineering projects based on an improved sir model: A simulation research on complex networks. *Complexity*, 2021, 1–17. 10.1155/2021/7998655

Hema, D. (2020). "A dynamic and combined phishing detection technique." *International Journal of Innovative Technology and Exploring Engineering* 9: 1421–1425. .10.35940/ijitee.E2819.039520

Homayoun, S., Dehghantanha, A., Ahmadzadeh, M., Hashemi, S., & Khayami, R. (2020). Know abnormal, find evil: Frequent pattern mining for ransomware threat hunting and intelligence. *IEEE Transactions on Emerging Topics in Computing*, 8(2), 341–351. 10.1109/TETC.2017.2756908

Hua, G., & Haughton, D. (2009). Virtual worlds adoption: A research framework and empirical study. *Online Information Review*, 33(5), 889–900. 10.1108/14684520911001891

Huang, Y. (2020). Exploration of influencing factors on mechanism of chinese usersamp;39; continuous trust in transactional virtual community. *Asian Social Science*, 16(11), 80. 10.5539/ass.v16n11p80

Iqbal, M., & Matulevičius, R. (2019). Blockchain-based application security risks: A systematic literature review. In Advanced Information Systems Engineering Workshops: CAiSE 2019 International Workshops, Rome, Italy, June 3-7, 2019 [Springer International Publishing.]. *Proceedings*, 31, 176–188.

Irwin, A., Slay, J., Choo, K., & Liu, L. (2012). Are the financial transactions conducted inside virtual environments truly anonymous? *Journal of Money Laundering Control*, 16(1), 6–40. 10.1108/13685201311286832

Ishiguro, K., & Kono, K. (2020). Instruction filters for mitigating attacks on instruction emulation in hypervisors. *IEICE Transactions on Information and Systems*, 103(7), 1660–1671.

Islam, M., Sajjad, M., Hasan, M., & Mazumder, M. (2023). Phishing attack detecting system using dns and ip filtering. *Asian Journal of Computer Science and Technology*, 12(1), 16–20. 10.51983/ajcst-2023.12.1.3552

Jaber, T. (2022). Security risks of the metaverse world. *International Journal of Interactive Mobile Technologies (Ijim)*, 16(13), 4–14. 10.3991/ijim.v16i13.33187

Jensen, S., Phillips, L., & Strand, D. (2012). Virtual worlds as sites for social and cultural in- novation. *Convergence (London)*, 18(1), 3–10. 10.1177/1354856511419911

Jordan, G., Leskovar, R., & Marič, M. (2018). Impact of fear of identity theft and perceived risk on online purchase intention. *Organizacija*, 51(2), 146–155. 10.2478/orga-2018-0007

Kabanda, G., Chipfumbu, C., & Chingoriwo, T. (2022). A cybersecurity model for a roblox- based metaverse architecture framework. *British Journal of Multidisciplinary and Advanced Studies*, 3(2), 105–141. 10.37745/bjmas.2022.0048

Kapoor, A., Gupta, A., Gupta, R., Tanwar, S., & Davidson, I. (2021). Ransomware detection, avoidance, and mitigation scheme: A review and future directions. *Sustainability (Basel)*, 14(1), 8. 10.3390/su14010008

Kasiyanto, S., & Kilinc, M. (2022). Legal conundrums of the metaverse. *Journal of Central Banking Law and Institutions*, 1(2). Advance online publication. 10.21098/jcli.v1i2.25

Katterbauer, K., Syed, H., & Cleenewerck, L. (2022). Financial cybercrime in the Islamic finance metaverse. *Journal of Metaverse*, 2(2), 56–61.

Kozinets, R. (2022). Immersive netnography: A novel method for service experience research in virtual reality, augmented reality and metaverse contexts. *Journal of Service Management*, 34(1), 100–125. 10.1108/JOSM-12-2021-0481

Kumar, A., Shankar, A., Behl, A., Gupta, B. B., & Mavuri, S. (2023). Lights, camera, metaverse!: Eliciting intention to use industrial metaverse, organizational agility, and firm performance. [JGIM]. *Journal of Global Information Management*, 31(8), 1–20. 10.4018/JGIM.333169

Lei, Y., Duan, Y., & Song, M. (2020, October). Technical implementation framework of AI governance policies for cross-modal privacy protection. In *International Conference on Collaborative Computing: Networking, Applications and Worksharing* (pp. 431-443). Cham: Springer International Publishing.

Li, N., El Helou, S., & Gillet, D. (2010, April). Trust-based rating prediction for recommendation in web 2.0 collaborative learning social software. In 2010 9th International Conference on Information Technology Based Higher Education and Training (ITHET) (pp. 208-212). IEEE.

Madarie, R., Ruiter, S., Steenbeek, W., & Kleemans, E. (2019). Stolen account credentials: An empirical comparison of online dissemination on different platforms. *Journal of Crime and Justice*, 42(5), 551–568. 10.1080/0735648X.2019.1692418

Maggi, P., Pozza, D., & Sisto, R. (2008, June). Vulnerability modelling for the analysis of network attacks. In *2008 Third International Conference on Dependability of Computer Systems DepCoS-RELCOMEX* (pp. 15-22). IEEE.

Maim'o, L., & Celdr'an, A. (2019). Intelligent and dynamic ransomware spread detection and mitigation in integrated clinical environments. *Sensors (Basel)*, 19(5), 1114. 10.3390/s1905111430841592

Manushri, S., Santhiya, J., & Roobasri, A. (2022). Metaverse - the future of virtual world. *International Journal of Engineering Technology and Management Sciences*, 6(5), 779–783. 10.46647/ijetms.2022.v06i05.121

Naik, N., Jenkins, P., Savage, N., & Yang, L. (2019, June). Cyberthreat hunting-part 2: Tracking ransomware threat actors using fuzzy hashing and fuzzy c-means clustering. In 2019 IEEE international conference on fuzzy systems (FUZZ-IEEE) (pp. 1-6). IEEE.

Ng, D. (2022). What is the metaverse? definitions, technologies and the com- munity of inquiry. *Australasian Journal of Educational Technology*, 38(4), 190–205. 10.14742/ajet.7945

Oladokun, B., Yahaya, D. O., & Enakrire, R. T. (2023). Moving into the metaverse: Libraries in virtual worlds. *Library Hi Tech News*, 40(9), 18–21. 10.1108/LHTN-08-2023-0147

Patterson, N., Hobbs, M., & Zhu, T. (2017). A cyber-threat analytic model for autonomous detection of virtual property theft. *Information and Computer Security*, 25(4), 358–381. 10.1108/ICS-11-2016-0087

Radanliev, P. (2024). Integrated cybersecurity for metaverse systems operating with ar- tificial intelligence, blockchains, and cloud computing. *Frontiers in Blockchain*, 7, 1359130. Advance online publication. 10.3389/fbloc.2024.1359130

Reinhard, C., & Amsterdam, P. (2013). Virtual world television products and practices: Comparing television production in second life to traditional television production. *Journal of Virtual Worlds Research*, 6(2). Advance online publication. 10.4101/jvwr.v6i2.7042

Saharan, S., Singh, S., Bhandari, A. K., & Yadav, B. (2024). The future of Cyber-Crimes and cyber war in the metaverse. In *Forecasting cyber crimes in the age of the metaverse* (pp. 126–148). IGI Global.

Sanders, B., & Marchang, J. (2016, November). A novel taxonomy of opportunities and risks in massively multiplayer online role playing games. In *Proceedings of the 8th International Conference on Management of Digital EcoSystems* (pp. 90-98).

Saravanan, N., & Umamakeswari, A. (2018). Security vulnerabilities of virtu- alization technique. *IACSIT International Journal of Engineering and Technology*, 7(2.24), 478. 10.14419/ijet.v7i2.24.12140

Shariff, S. M., & Zhang, X. (2014, June). A survey on deceptions in online social networks. In *2014 International Conference on Computer and Information Sciences (ICCOINS)* (pp. 1-6). IEEE.

Sharma, A., Gupta, B. B., Singh, A. K., & Saraswat, V. K. (2023). A novel approach for detection of APT malware using multi-dimensional hybrid Bayesian belief network. *International Journal of Information Security*, 22(1), 119–135. 10.1007/s10207-022-00631-5

Sharma, P., Dash, B., & Ansari, M. (2022). Anti-phishing techniques – a review of cyber defense mechanisms. *International Journal of Advanced Research in Computer and Communication Engineering*, 11(7). Advance online publication. 10.17148/IJARCCE.2022.11728

Shehab, M., Bertino, E., & Ghafoor, A. (2008, September). Proactive role discovery in mediator-free environments. In *2008 Eighth International Conference on Peer-to-Peer Computing* (pp. 150-159). IEEE.

Shen, B., Wei-ming, T., Guo, J., Cai, H., Wang, B., & Zhuo, S. (2020). A study on design requirement development and satisfaction for future virtual world systems. *Future Internet*, 12(7), 112. 10.3390/fi12070112

Singh, G., Malhotra, M., & Sharma, A. (2022). An adaptive mechanism for virtual machine migration in the cloud environment. [IJCAC]. *International Journal of Cloud Applications and Computing*, 12(1), 1–10. 10.4018/IJCAC.311504

Singla, A., Gupta, N., Aeron, P., Jain, A., Garg, R., Sharma, D., & Arya, V. (2022). Building the metaverse: Design considerations, socio-technical elements, and future research directions of metaverse. [JGIM]. *Journal of Global Information Management*, 31(2), 1–28.

Thomas, J., Galligher, R., Thomas, M., & Galligher, G. (2019). Enterprise cybersecurity: Inves- tigating and detecting ransomware infections using digital forensic techniques. *Computer and Information Science*, 12(3), 72. 10.5539/cis.v12n3p72

Tirumala, S. S., Sathu, H., & Naidu, V. (2015, December). Analysis and prevention of account hijacking based incidents in cloud environment. In 2015 international Conference on Information Technology (ICIT) (pp. 124-129). IEEE.

Tiwari, H. (2023). “Metaverse Federated Learning in Music Streaming: Rev- olutionizing Personalization and Privacy.” https://insights2techinfo.com/ metaverse-federated-learning-in-music-streaming-revolutionizing-personalization-and-privacy/. Accessed: 2024-01-30.

Truong, V., Le, L., & Niyato, D. (2023). Blockchain meets metaverse and dig- ital asset management: A comprehensive survey. *IEEE Access : Practical Innovations, Open Solutions*, 11, 26258–26288. 10.1109/ACCESS.2023.3257029

Turchet, L. (2023). Musical metaverse: Vision, opportunities, and challenges. *Personal and Ubiquitous Computing*, 27(5), 1811–1827. 10.1007/s00779-023-01708-136685785

Turki, A., Zwiad, A., & Almuttairi, R. (2019). Security issues, attacks and vulnerabilities for virtualization in cloud computing and their solutions. *Journal of Engineering and Applied Sciences (Asian Research Publishing Network)*, 14, 9509–9518. 10.36478/jeasci.2019.9509.9518

Upadhyay, U., Kumar, A., Sharma, G., Gupta, B. B., Alhalabi, W. A., Arya, V., & Chui, K. T. (2023). Cyberbullying in the metaverse: A prescriptive perception on global information systems for user protection. [JGIM]. *Journal of Global Information Management*, 31(1), 1–25. 10.4018/JGIM.325793

Varvello, M., C. Diot, and E. Biersack. 2009. “A walkable kademlia network for virtual worlds.” .10.1109/INFCOMW.2009.5072106

Veinovi´c, M. 2016. “Privileged identities - threat to network and data security.” .10.15308/Sinteza-2016-154-160

Wang, J., Yu, Y., Li, Y., Fan, C., & Hao, S. (2021). Design and implementation of virtual security function based on multiple enclaves. *Future Internet*, 13(1), 12. 10.3390/fi13010012

Wang, Y., Su, Z., Zhang, N., Xing, R., Liu, D., Luan, T., & Shen, X. (2023). A survey on metaverse: Fundamentals, security, and privacy. *IEEE Communications Surveys and Tutorials*, 25(1), 319–352. 10.1109/COMST.2022.3202047

Wang, Y., & Zhao, J. 2022. "Mobile edge computing, metaverse, 6g wireless communications, artificial intelligence, and blockchain: survey and their convergence." https://doi.org//arxiv.2209.14147.10.48550

Wu, Y., & Kim, E. (2022). Users' perceptions of technological features in augmented reality (ar) and virtual reality (vr) in fashion retailing: A qualitative content analysis. *Mobile Information Systems*, 2022, 1–13. 10.1155/2022/3080280

Xu, B., Li, D., & Shao, B. (2012). Knowledge sharing in virtual communities: A study of citizenship behavior and its social-relational antecedents. *International Journal of Human-Computer Interaction*, 28(5), 347–359. 10.1080/10447318.2011.590121

Xu, Y., Liu, W., He, T., & Tsai, S. (2023). Buzzword or fuzzword: An event study of the metaverse in the chinese stock market. *Internet Research*, 34(1), 174–194. 10.1108/INTR-07-2022-0526

Zhang, R., & Xin, X. (2017). Study of immune-based intrusion detection technology in vir- tual machines for cloud computing environment. *Mobile Information Systems*, 2017, 1–15. 10.1155/2017/2301970

Zuo, M., & Shen, Y. (2023). How features and affordances of a metaverse portal engage users? evidence from exergames. *Internet Research*, 34(1), 239–261. 10.1108/INTR-08-2022-0618

Chapter 9
Metaverse Security Paradigms

Sreerakuvandana
Jain University (Deemed), India

Princy Pappachan
Asia University, Taiwan

Ritika Bansal
Insights2Techinfo, India

ABSTRACT

The User Education and Awareness chapter in Metaverse Security Paradigms tackles the essential aspects of user education and awareness in safeguarding against the myriad security risks. Beginning with an in-depth analysis of common security threats such as data breaches, identity theft, and phishing attacks, the chapter catalogues these risks. Then, it explores the influential roles of community leaders and the adoption of innovative approaches like gamification to establish security as a collective responsibility. The practical implementation of these strategies across diverse virtual platforms is also thoroughly examined. Next, the chapter delves into the processes for reporting and responding to security incidents in the Metaverse. It details the establishment of efficient reporting channels, the formation of rapid response teams, and the use of automated systems for early threat detection. Concluding with a guide on best practices, the chapter equips users with strategies for personal protection, from basic digital hygiene to advanced tactics against complex threats.

DOI: 10.4018/979-8-3693-3824-7.ch009

1. INTRODUCTION

Metaverse is not a new concept anymore. It is a term that is awes the imagination of many tech-giants, the corporate industries, the government and even the education sector. The predominant reason why it has garnered a lot of attention is because of its truly immersive experience that leads to the development of a new kind of applications and also business categories. There has been a period of relative stagnation and a declining internet traffic dividend as a result of the widespread use of mobile internet. The internet industry has not grown as much as it could have because of a lack of innovation in communication, engagement, and content delivery (Liu, 2023). "Metaverse" eventually became a solution to combat this and companies became to recognize this as a way to integrate multiple technologies. The term metaverse does not refer to anything specific, but rather to a broad shift in the way we interact with technology. These technologies can include virtual reality; which is characterized by a persistent virtual world entity that exists even when you are not working with it, augmented reality; that is a combination of the digital and the physical world, Internet of Things (IoT), advanced communication such as 5G. A lot of businesses that have joined the metaverse bandwagon also hope to create a new digital marketplace where people can produce, purchase, and trade goods. Though it's more difficult than it seems, in the more idealistic conceptions of the metaverse, it becomes possible to move virtual goods like cars or clothes from one platform to another.

The need of user awareness and education in preserving strong security cannot be emphasized in the always changing environment of the Metaverse. Within the framework of Metaverse Security Paradigms, the chapter on User Education and Awareness highlights the vital part vigilant and educated users perform in preventing a range of security hazards. Understanding and reducing risks such data breaches, identity theft, and phishing attempts is essential as the Metaverse gets more and more included into daily life.

Starting with a thorough investigation of common security concerns, this chapter travels with a thorough list of problems users could run into in virtual environments. It then shifts to looking at the important part community leaders and creative learning strategies like gamification play in encouraging a society of communal security responsibility. These leaders and approaches help to ensure that all users are involved and proactive in their security procedures, therefore changing security from a single duty into a group effort. Examined closely is the pragmatic implementation of these teaching techniques across several virtual platforms, providing understanding of how varied settings might adapt and use these approaches successfully. The chapter also explores the systems for Metaverse security issue reporting and response. It describes the creation of fast reaction teams, the installation of effective reporting lines, and the application of automated technologies meant for early danger identification, thereby building a strong basis for incident management.

Finally addressing with some guidance on recommended practices, this chapter gives readers a whole toolset for personal safety. Readers are given practical ideas to improve their safety on the internet from basic ideas of digital hygiene to sophisticated measures meant to resist difficult attackers. By means of this all-encompassing strategy, the chapter seeks to empower consumers so that they may traverse and safely negotiate their virtual experiences in the Metaverse.

2. CONCEPT OF THE METAVERSE

Evidently, metaverse is not a singular concept, rather, it is a combination of an ecosystem driven by technology that has hardware devices, proprietary software and also frameworks (Jeon, 2021). While various attempts can be made to build a monopoly in the metaverse space, the true potential can only be realized when there is a multi-stakeholder model where there are multiple parties involved and various space providers who work together to a offer a value spectrum for the end user. Metaverse is a term that encompass the real and virtual internet ecosystems that have their own autonomous transaction system and also clearly defined property rights. Blockchain, AI, and VR/AR technologies combine to create three-dimensional, immersive virtual environments that allow users to alter their surroundings and add content. This results in a tightly knit social network that connects the virtual and real worlds .Cyber-Physical System called "Metaverse" combines blockchain, cloud computing, virtual reality, artificial intelligence, and other cutting-edge technologies. These systems are susceptible to logical and physical failures due to vulnerabilities in both the hardware and software. It is also important to note that there should not currently be any expectation of privacy rights in VR experiences as a whole; privacy rights are more secure in AR environments because they have a foothold in the real world.

From a macro perspective, the development of the metaverse typically occurs in three stages, as shown in Fig. 1: (i) digital twins, (ii) digital natives, and finally (iii) surreality. In the first stage, a mirror world made up of large-scale, highly accurate digital twins of people and objects in virtual settings is created with the goal of creating a realistic digital depiction of the real world. During this stage, reality and virtuality exist as two parallel spaces, and virtual attributes and activities, like user emotion and movement, mimic their physical counterparts. The creation of native content is the primary focus of the second phase. Here, digital natives, embodied by avatars, can generate novel ideas and insightful perspectives within virtual environments, which may be exclusive to those virtual realms. During this stage, the vast amounts of content produced in the digital world are on par with those produced in the physical world. Additionally, the digital world can innovate and change the way the physical world produces content, increasing the intersections between the two worlds. In the final stage, the metaverse reaches maturity and becomes a persistent, self-sustaining surreal reality world that absorbs reality into itself. This phase will see the seamless merging and mutual symbiosis of the physical and virtual worlds realised, with the virtual world having a larger scope than the real world and the ability to contain more scenes and lives that do not exist in reality.

2.1. Impact of Human Errors

A significant share of organizational information security incidents that we hear about are due to human errors, which are sometimes the direct or indirect cause, including intentional and unintentional behaviours (Siponen and Vance, 2010). Also, ENISA (2019) showed that about 77% data breaches at the companies are caused by the exploitation of human vulnerabilities. Additionally, it was previously discovered that employees' inadequate information security compliances accounted for more than half of all information security breaches. With this in mind, employees' Information Security Awareness (ISA) places a greater onus on information security behaviour and employees' security compliance (Bulgurcu et al., 2010; DeGroot et.al., 2012). According to Ingham (2018), sensitive data was most frequently sent to the incorrect person by email, mail, or fax. Other common errors were losing or stealing documents, failing to redact data, or storing data in an unsafe place, like a public cloud server. According to Ernstand and Young's 2018-2019 Global Information Security Survey, around 34% of organisations state that employees who were unaware were the major vulnerable ones. Such vulnerabilities cost huge financial loss and also damage the reputation of the business, even more seen after the advent of strict data protection laws such as EU's General Data Protection Regulation (GDPR). This is also one of the key explanations for why senior management of organisations prioritise cybersecurity, according to the most recent Cyber Security Breaches Survey 2019 (Vaidya, 2019). The majority of employees of the company are seen to be unaware of information security threats and issues, even though research and practice have long emphasised the importance of Information Security Awareness (ISA) (Lim et al., 2010). According to ENISA (2019), for instance, nearly 90% of cybersecurity professionals reported that the company they work for felt vulnerable to insider threats. Research on information security awareness is still an evolving field with many uncharted areas to be explored, according to Jaeger (2018). Furthermore, despite a large number of studies on ISA, there was a lack of a comprehensive understanding of the concept and its relationship with other constructs (Jaeger, 2018). Additional research (Abawajy, 2014; Annetta, 2010; Cone et al., 2007) supports this, indicating that ISA campaigns and training are failing to alter employees' behaviour for a variety of reasons.

Yeom et al., (2020) point out that the vulnerability of the many security systems in an organisations comes from the users' lack of knowledge on the usage of technology and hence, information leak by insiders is a common problem. In the past, cyberattacks typically had no particular target and were random in nature. But today's cyberattacks are more focused on achieving specific objectives against preselected targets (Kim et al., 2019a, 2019b). They have also developed and grown more sophisticated. Phishing is one type of serious cyberattack in this day and age. Phishers typically use phoney email addresses and/or websites in these attacks in an attempt to obtain users' login credentials (Chaudhry et al., 2016). Thirty percent of victims of phishing emails read the emails, according to a Verizon data breach report (Cranor, 2018). Furthermore, it was revealed that 12% of those victims clicked on phoney attachments or websites (Chen et al., 2018), and roughly 50,000, or 20%, of the 250,000 employees in one renowned company clicked on a malicious link. According to Verizon's announcement in 2019, roughly 10% of the breaches involved the financial industry. These breaches resulted in significant financial losses for the financial companies, as well as their customers and employees. It was also found that gender and age had an effect on cybersecurity awareness (Farooq et al., 2015; Fatokun et al., 2019). Cybercriminals also have the potential to exploit health data in many newer ways. As a result, there is a possibility of multiple fraudulent activities, such as identity theft, insurance fraud, prescription forgery, and associated offences. It is also seen that healthcare organisations are at a greater risk to data breaches when compared to other industries (Gordon, Fairhall & Landman, 2017). This vulnerability occurs when multiple actors in healthcare settings have access to patient health information for treatment purposes, raising the possibility of privacy breaches due to human error. Inadequate technology investment, IT security staffing, and funding all add to the increased risk that healthcare organisations must deal with. Apart from the possible harm to impacted individuals, data breaches lead to serious financial and organisational repercussions, such as fines and harm to the company's reputation (Goode et al., 2017, McLeod and Dolezel, 2018). The value of safeguarding personal data and privacy is becoming more widely acknowledged (Esmaeilzadeh, 2020, Miltgen and Smith, 2015). As a testament to this acknowledgment, new policy regulations such as EU's General Data Protection Regulation (GDPR), California's Consumer Privacy Act (CCPA), China's Personal Information Protection Law (PIPL), India's Digital Personal Data Protection Act (DPDPA) 2023 were introduced.

Figure 1. Development Stages of Metaverse

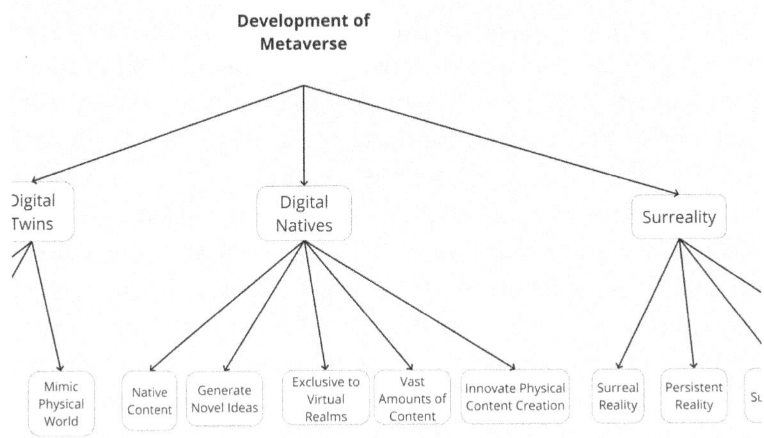

3. ROLE OF CYBERSECURITY IN THE METAVERSE

With the development of the aforementioned critical technologies, it is anticipated that the security space will expand and provide new avenues for cybercriminals to target organisations and people. These days, cybersecurity is a horizontal technology that impacts numerous industries and spheres of life. It is also a vital part of systems for national defence and security. The world is becoming more and more digital, and the Metaverse is one reason why the cybersecurity industry is expanding. The physical and cyber layers are merging as almost every device, including medical and military equipment, is going digital and interacting with cyberspace. In this context, cybersecurity technologies are regarded as one of the fundamental technologies of the Metaverse. It is estimated that countries failing to prioritise the field of cybersecurity in light of these swift advancements will suffer catastrophic consequences. Organisations are racing to produce metadata as the Metaverse takes shape, and cybercriminals are taking advantage of this to launch cyberattacks by taking advantage of the weaknesses in blockchain, cryptocurrencies, IoT, AR, and VR. Thus, advanced risk assessment features for infrastructure and connected devices are required for organisations investigating metadata storage.

3.1. Impact of Data Breaches

In the Metaverse, where numerous virtual environments house a wealth of user data and interactions, cybersecurity is essential. As the Metaverse keeps growing and changing, so do the hazards and difficulties related to cybersecurity. Gaining an understanding of the relationship between cybersecurity and data breaches is crucial to preventing threats and guaranteeing users' privacy and safety in virtual environments. First and foremost, cybersecurity acts as a defence against malevolent intrusions, illegal access, and Metaverse data breaches. Platform providers can prevent cyber threats to sensitive user data by implementing strong security measures like intrusion detection systems, authentication protocols, and encryption. By constructing layers of defence against potential attacks, these methods lessen the possibility that data breaches will be successful. Second, cybersecurity plays a critical role in anticipating and reacting to data breaches. Even with the greatest of intentions to stop breaches, hackers might still find weaknesses to take advantage of. In these situations, platform providers can quickly detect and contain breaches by using cybersecurity tools and techniques like threat monitoring, incident response, and forensic analysis. This reduces the impact of the breaches on users and prevents additional harm. Preventing data breaches in the Metaverse requires raising awareness of cybersecurity issues and providing education on the subject. Users need to be aware of the dangers of disclosing personal information online and have the know-how to effectively protect themselves. By educating users about privacy settings, phishing awareness, and best practices for password management, you can help them make more informed decisions and less vulnerable to online dangers.

3.2. Types of Cyber Threats

Despite the metaverse's encouraging signs, security and privacy concerns are the main obstacles preventing further development. In the metaverse, there could be a wide range of security lapses and privacy violations, ranging from handling enormous data streams, ubiquitous user profiling, unfair AI algorithmic results, to safeguarding human bodies and physical infrastructures. First off, the metaverse may inherit the vulnerabilities and inherent defects of the various modern technologies and systems that it integrates as its foundation. Emerging technology-related incidents have included the theft of virtual currencies, the hacking of wearables or cloud storage, and the misuse of artificial intelligence to fabricate news. Second, because different technologies are entwined, the effects of current threats can intensify and become more serious in virtual worlds, and new threats that do not exist in real-world or online contexts can emerge, like virtual stalking and virtual espionage (Leenes, 2008). In particular, the metaverse can use personal data that is more detailed and remarkably common to create a digital replica of reality, which creates new opportunities for crimes involving private big data (Falchuk, 2018). For instance, users will unavoidably wear wearable AR/VR devices with built-in sensors to thoroughly collect speech, facial expressions, eye movements, hand movements, brain wave patterns, and biometric features, as well as the surrounding environment, in order to build a virtual scene using AI algorithms.

There are a range of common threats that happen as a part of cyber exploitation. For instance, users will unavoidably wear wearable AR/VR devices with built-in sensors to thoroughly collect speech, facial expressions, eye movements, hand movements, brain wave patterns, and biometric features, as well as the surrounding environment, in order to build a virtual scene using AI algorithms. Furthermore, since users in the metaverse must be uniquely identified, it is possible to track users' actual locations illegally using headsets, VR glasses, or other devices (Shang et al., 2022). Last but not least, hackers can use device compromises and system flaws as entry points to break into actual equipment, posing a threat to people's safety. They can even use advanced persistent threat (APT) attacks to threaten vital infrastructure, including high-speed rail, water supply, and power grid systems (Hu et al., 2015). Fig (2) outlines some of the most common types of cyberattacks are listed below.

Figure 2. Most common types of cyberattacks

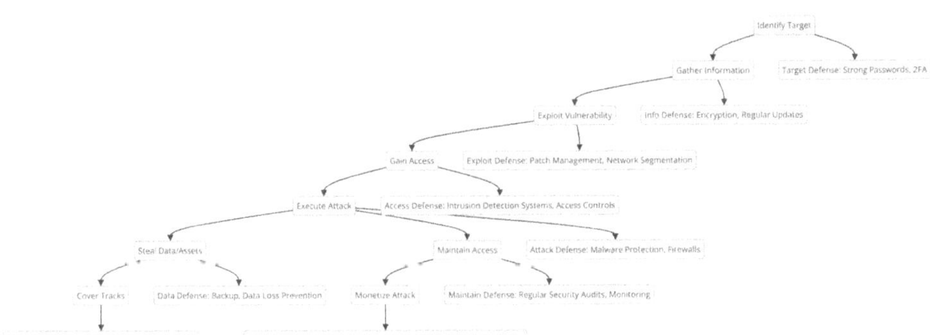

a. **Data Breaches:** One of the significant threat to the users in the Metaverse come from data breach. In this, the virtual environment host huge amounts of data that contains personal information that may be susceptible to unauthorized access. These security lapses happen when malevolent actors break into protected networks and steal private information, such as contact records, payment information, and user profiles. In order to safeguard their data, users need to understand how important it is to use strong security measures. This entails using two-factor authentication, creating strong, one-of-a-kind passwords, and actively monitoring privacy settings on Metaverse platforms. Through the implementation of these security measures, users can considerably lower the probability of unauthorised access to their personal data.

b. **Identity Theft:** The most common of all is the identity theft, which is of greater concern in metaverse universe. Users can customise their digital avatars in the metaverse and use them as a virtual proxy to communicate with other users and the metaverse environment. It helps to consider this digital persona as a virtualized version of the user. This twin can be used for fraudulent purposes and the situation will further worsen with the use of artificial intelligence enables functions such as deep fakes. Deep fakes mimic a person as closely as possible that it sometimes becomes difficult to tell the person and deep fake apart.

c. **Phishing attack:** The next major and a common problem is that of phishing attack. Phishing involves deceptive emails, messages and fraudulent advertisements that ask the user to take action, messages that trick the customer into revealing their login credentials. The cybercriminals pose as legitimate institutions, generally via email, in order to procure sensitive information such as bank passwords etc.

d. **Malware attacks:** Malware is the short for malicious attack and it refers to any software that is designed with an intention to cause damage to the computer system, to its server or client, or even the computer network. This damage can be in the form of viruses, ransomware, spyware etc. When any kind of these malwares enter the system, it can potentially corrupt the files, steal all sensitive information by way of an unauthorized entry into the system. The repercussions can range from system damage to huge financial loss. Sometimes, these malware go undetected for long periods which can lead to continuous exploitation of the system in question.

e. **Clickjack:** This is a procedure where the invader deceives a user to click on a certain link or page. The attacker loads another page over the page in which the user actually intended to go to. This false page stands on top as a transparent layer. A variant of this is the cursorjacking where instead of the cursor, an image of the cursor appears on the screen which deceives the user into using the fake cursor to click on any malicious site with smart positioning of the elements in the page.

Given these, it is crucial to research the effects of low user awareness and the advantages of knowledgeable practices in cyber exploitation in order to reduce risks, safeguard people and organisations, minimise financial losses, maintain privacy and confidentiality, and promote digital trust and resilience. We can provide users the tools they need to navigate cyberspace safely and securely by increasing awareness and promoting cybersecurity education.

4. CREATING A CULTURE OF SECURITY IN METAVERSE

The establishment of a proactive security culture is critical in the dynamic environment of virtual communities, where security threats are commonplace. According to Liu et al. (2018), a strong security culture must be established to develop a comprehensive overall security, IT, and business strategy. Staff members need to be educated about acceptable practices and security threats through training and awareness programmes. This may include security drills and phishing simulations, among other training activities aimed at raising awareness of security issues.

Undoubtedly, "culture" is one of the cornerstones of a proactive strategic framework, like the Cybersecurity Target Operating Model (TOM), and it is the key to achieving security maturity. Within the field of cybersecurity, culture refers to a set of common values that influence how people within an organisation approach, view, and think about security. It highlights that cybersecurity shouldn't be seen as an isolated function within the IT department, but rather as a component of every level of the organisation. In the end, building a strong cybersecurity environment and laying the foundation for an organization's defences comes down to culture. Cybersecurity and culture go hand in hand. It's about our thoughts, feelings, and behaviours as much as it is about laws and regulations. The human element is at play here. Cybersecurity encompasses more than just encryption and firewalls. It has to do with consciousness, participation, accountability, ownership, and wellbeing. It's also critical to realise that a solid cybersecurity culture is based on shared values that influence everyone in an organisation, regardless of role or position, in terms of how they think and behave. Beyond the fundamental security awareness training course, true security culture is more profound. It emphasises how important it is for each person to keep up a strong defence against online attacks. It involves establishing a work environment in which every employee has the information and tools necessary to participate in routine preventative actions, like reporting incidents on their own, spotting malicious files, and reporting phishing emails. In addition, staff members must accept responsibility for the stewardship that accompanies their roles.

This section explores the importance of security culture, the critical role that developers, influencers, and community leaders play in creating a culture where security is a shared responsibility. It looks at creative ways to use gamification, incentive programmes, and community-driven projects to foster security-focused community norms. It also looks at how well these controls are applied in various virtual contexts, such as professional networks and gaming platforms.

4.1. Importance of a Security Culture

There are a plenty of reasons why security culture is important.

It is easier to recognise and address security threats before they are exploited when there is a strong security culture in place.

Inspiring staff to take responsibility for their security and protect both the business and them from external and occasionally internal threats.

safeguarding corporate assets and data.

A security breach that results in the loss of intellectual property or confidential information can be extremely costly and damage one's reputation.

A security culture helps safeguard assets and data by promoting best practices like access controls and strong passwords.

A community's or organization's security culture is the culmination of all of its members' shared beliefs, behaviours, and attitudes towards security-related issues. In today's connected and digital environment, protecting an organization's data and assets is crucial. The complexity and regularity of cyberthreats mean that every company is vulnerable to cyberattacks. The entire company needs to create a security culture; the IT department is not the only one who has to do this. Therefore, companies must instill a security mindset among all parties involved. Everyone in the organisation will be committed to protecting the company's online assets and will understand the importance of security if there is a security culture in place.

To make sure that everyone in the organisation is aware of and complies with security policies, procedures, and best practices, effective communication between your security team and the rest of the business is crucial. This includes transparent, unambiguous, easy to follow, and understand procedures for reporting security incidents and other security-related issues.

Another essential component of any security culture is risk management. This is a crucial component in identifying potential security threats and weaknesses. An effective risk management programme must be put in place before threat mitigation plans can be developed and put into action.

4.2. Promoting Security Awareness

A security culture is a separate entity that constitutes to more than just cyber awareness. It must incorporate a more comprehensive corporate culture that promotes employees' deliberate decision-making in line with security policies on a daily basis. It must also be made mandatory for employees to understand the security risk and the procedures for mitigating it. This means, a security culture comes with a combination of knowledge and a good understanding of daily work tasks. Despite the diversity in the communication channels that exists today, social Internet services

(SNSs) are the most common of mass communication. Today, the SNSs not simply consolidate the tools used for messaging and for multimedia content, but they also are used for self-organising of the society into the many virtual communities. Geotagged photos are very popular these days. People upload photos to the internet, adding geolocation metadata to them. Certain applications possess a feature called geotagging, which records the user's current location inside a picture until they manually disable it. This exposes personal information, such as one's residence and travel destinations, and invites criminals who may target the victim for theft. A frequent update on where they are could put their life in danger by opening them up to potential robbery and stalker situations. A Heimdal Security report states that approximately 6 lakh Facebook accounts are compromised every day (2015). Like-jacking, which happens when attackers add phoney Facebook like buttons to websites, phishing sites, and spam emails, is the most common type of social media attack. The percentage of American internet users who, as of May 2020, the entire survey shows that 74% of participants who are 65 years of age or older do not share their online passwords with friends and family (Jain et al., 2021). Existing literature has demonstrated the security concern related to metaverse games using case studies (Bono et al., 2009) and also qualitative studies (Shang et al., 2022). Bono et al., 2009 present two case studies; *Second Life* and *Anarchy Online,* demonstrate how a hacker exploits the features and other vulnerabilities of metaverse games in order to fully take over players' device such as the laptop. Lebeck et al, 2018, conduct a qualitative lab study with the Microsoft HoloLen augmented reality headset. The findings reveal a number of security, privacy, and safety concerns as well as the ease with which users can become fully immersed in AR experiences and treat virtual objects as real. Shang et al., 2022 figure out a new user's location tracking attack in location based AR games such as Pokemon Go. They do this by exploiting the traffic of the network that the player is connected to.

4.3. Importance of Influencers and Platforms

Community members' attitudes and behaviours are greatly influenced by community leaders and influencers. By supporting security awareness campaigns, promoting best practices, and setting a high standard for behaviour, they create a solid basis for a culture that is security-conscious. To increase awareness and encourage members to take preventative security measures, leaders can organise informative events, produce interesting content, and start a conversation about cybersecurity issues. For instance, Twitch is an American video live-streaming service, focuses on video game live streaming. A streamer with a reputation for playing competitive multiplayer games, for instance, might host a special stream on cybersecurity awareness. They could talk about frequent security risks that affect gamers during the stream, like phishing schemes that target in-game items or account takeovers. Additionally, they might invite professionals in cybersecurity as guests to share their knowledge and respond to audience queries (Deveci et al., 2023). Twitch streamers may educate viewers about cybersecurity concerns unique to the gaming community and encourage them to adopt best practices for safeguarding their accounts and personal data by utilising their platform and interacting with their followers directly.

Apart from this, LinkedIn influencers can also help promote cyber hygiene. Influential thought leaders and business specialists have the chance to influence their peers' and followers' cybersecurity practices. Through webinars, articles, and posts, these influencers frequently provide insightful advice, cybersecurity resources, and tips. For example, a well-known cybersecurity expert on LinkedIn might write articles on a regular basis about new developments in cybersecurity, how to secure remote work environments, or how important it is to update software. They might also hold online seminars or webinars for professionals from different industries that cover the basics of cybersecurity.

In order to keep users safe and secure, Discord, a well-liked communication tool for communities and gamers, mainly depends on server administrators and community moderators. These people, who are frequently volunteers or dependable community members, are essential in upholding rules and handling security-related concerns (Kumar et al., 2023). For instance, moderators may be assigned to oversee chat channels, spot and delete questionable or harmful content, and instruct users on security best practices on a Discord server catering to a particular gaming community. They might plan frequent security awareness campaigns, disseminate advice on how to spot malware and phishing scams, and offer help with account and device security (Rahaman, et al., 2024).

Companies also these days send out phishing awareness email that look just like scam emails. They are however educational tools which alert employees to the many common tactics used by cybercriminals in these attacks. When the staff of the company are exposed to such emails, they become adept at recognizing and ignoring the real threats. While these emails may be rudimentary, they are critical components in helping strengthen the organisation's first line of defense (Jensen et al., 2017). Also, staff members who receive phishing education are better able to recognise and steer clear of malicious attempts, which lowers the likelihood of data theft and security breaches (Gokasar et al., 2023).

5. BEST PRACTICES FOR USERS

To keep yourself safe in the Metaverse, you need to educate and be aware of security risks like data breaches, identity theft, and phishing attacks. The first thing that needs to be done to make a place safe is to teach people about these common threats and how they might affect things. Creating a culture of security knowledge depends on the support of community leaders and the use of new approaches, like making things more like games (Rahaman, Lin, et al., 2024). These techniques help people understand and remember important information about security practices by giving examples and making the learning process fun. Making educational material fit different online sites makes it easier for a wide range of users to access and makes it more useful (Al-Emran & Deveci, 2024).

For security to stay high in the Metaverse, there must be good ways to report problems and get answers. There should be clear and quick ways for users to report security events, and they should know how to find and report them right away (Sharma et al., 2024). Automated threat detection systems and the creation of fast reaction teams can help quickly stop threats (Khorshed et al., 2012). By using these tactics together, users can better understand and protect their online experiences, making the internet a safer place for everyone. Using strong passwords, turning on two-factor login, and using encryption tools are also basic best practices for personal safety (Rahaman et al., 2023).

5.1. Incident Reporting

Incidents involving cyber security are becoming common in many organisations. One could argue that the likelihood of future security incidents of a similar nature will decrease for those who are able to learn from them and address the root causes.

Organisations in the modern era must accept that incidents will happen and be ready to respond, learn from, and move on. Along with the increase in incidents, many organisations now have to deal with stricter security laws, increased customer demands, and new reporting guidelines pertaining to infrastructure resilience and data privacy. They therefore can't just put in more effort to handle the elevated incident risks, especially since many lack the necessary cyber security skills (de Zan, 2019). Connolly and Wall (2019) assert that gaining knowledge from incidents is an essential tactic for enhancing risk awareness, preventative measures, and organisational response capability. Systemic thinking is necessary for an organisation to learn, and incidents must be acknowledged to have several, sometimes obscure, causes (Schein, 2017). Security teams can control their workload by stopping the increase in incidents by addressing the root causes (Gonzalez, 2005).

The computer Security Resource centre states the glossary of security incident as thus "*an occurance that results in actual or potential jeopardy to the confidentiality, integrity, or availability of an information system or the information the system processes, stores, or transmits or that constitutes a violation or imminent threat of violation of security policies, security procedures, or acceptable use policies*". Acknowledging the occurrence of an incident is the first step towards mitigating its damage in a cyber security attack. Organisations are more resilient to the effects of cyber security when they are aware of impending danger. According to an IBM survey, it takes 287 days on average to find and stop a data breach. According to the same IBM study, companies that act promptly after an incident save 30% of expenses and cut the time it takes to contain a threat to less than 200 days.

The following are the reasons why there must be a robust incident reporting process shown in Fig. 3.

a. **A Culture of Security Is Encouraged by Incident Reporting**: A culture of security is based on the idea that everyone is "in this together." Reporting incidents should not be something to be feared but rather a routine procedure. Include reporting incidents in the company's standard operating procedures and employee expectations for when something concerning occurs. By offering a quick and simple method for reporting issues, employers enable staff members to participate in the defence against cyberattacks. This promotes a sense of community in the fight against fraud and cybercrime.
b. **Creates a Simplified Procedure to Stop Events from Turning Into Serious Attacks:** The reporting infrastructure needs to use automated workflows, be tailored to your organization's needs, and be built on an incident reporting framework. An incident reporting system ought to be adjustable to facilitate the escalation of security incidents from reporting to triage to mitigation, all the while guaranteeing that the right person is notified as soon as the process starts.
c. **Implements Security Procedures:** Implementing a security incident procedure aids in upholding the security policy of your business. An incident can be taken from triage to mitigation using a reporting system that employs incident workflows and security policy advisories.
d. **Preservation of Evidence:** Reporting security incidents aids in the preservation of vital evidence that can be used in cybercrime investigations and prosecutions. In-depth incident reports that contain timestamps, logs, and pertinent information are helpful in determining the extent and character of security breaches. They also make it easier to assign blame and conduct forensic analysis.

Figure 3. Robust incident reporting process

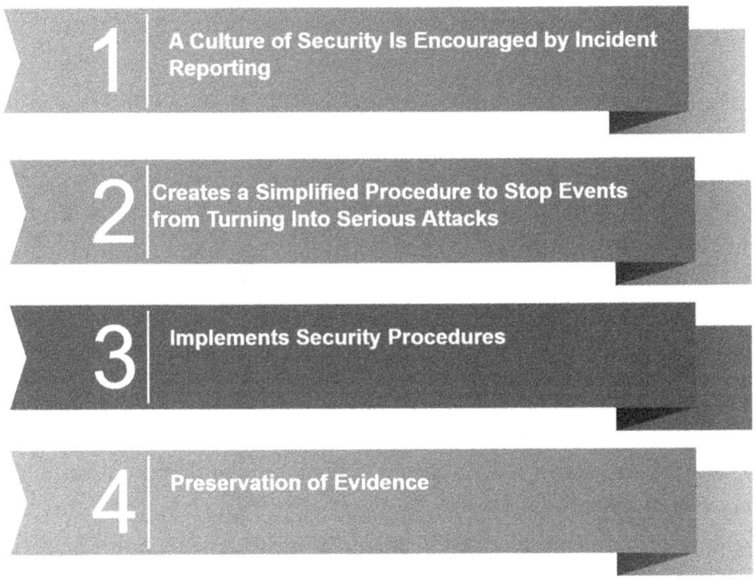

In a recent incident, Uber's Internal system was compromised by an 18-year-old. The attacker was able to take control of the company's Slack account, hack its HackerOne account, and get full administrator access to its GCP and AWS Web Services accounts. The entry attack used a social engineering campaign to target Uber employees. Uber is currently looking into the incident, and the hack caused some temporary disablement of internal systems.

5.2. Risk Management in Security Policy

Since total security is unachievable, risk management is the foundation of today's security policy and architecture approaches. The most comprehensive examination of the potential sources and techniques of system attack is the first step in any typical security architecture. The security architect then proceeds methodically in choosing and implementing security measures, making sure that the system can continue to serve its intended purpose with acceptable consequences for long-term evolution, cost, performance, and reliability. To achieve an acceptable level of security risk, security design frequently makes use of products with defined assurance levels as well as design patterns, security protocols, and standards.

Threat agents of cyber-attack come in a range of forms as indicated below.

a. The most dangerous individuals are those who are already inside system defences and have access to targeted assets. These individuals may be malicious (intentionally trying to cause harm, steal, etc.) or inadvertent (careless, ill-trained, etc.).
b. Hackers, thrill seekers, and lone criminals are people or small groups whose motives can be anything from monetary gain to a rush of adrenaline from breaking into a system.
c. groups trying to break into systems in order to steal information, extort money, demand ransom, or accomplish other illegal goals; On the Dark or Black Web, a collection of covert peer-to-peer networks (also known as "darknets") that use the public Internet but have access controls in place to keep users anonymous, stolen data is frequently traded (Borky & Bradley, 2019).

The security architect uses tested designs, mechanisms, products, and procedures to achieve a cyber- resilient system architecture and implementation while maintaining acceptable system performance, cost, and reliability. Too often, managers and organisations believe that cybersecurity is limited to technical measures like firewalls. In actuality, all three components are necessary for an efficient security solution. These include:

I. Employees at all levels of management, system users, and system support personnel who have received the necessary training, motivation, and authority to carry out their responsibilities in a secure and dependable manner
II. Mechanisms and protocols that carry out a security policy and preserve the efficacy of protective measures
III. Technologies that put security measures in place and adapt to a constantly shifting threat landscape

To describe the security controls or safeguards used to protect a system, a second threefold taxonomy is helpful. It usually takes a combination of technical, physical, and procedural security measures to secure a system that involves human interaction. The following are some of the technical measures that can be taken.

a. To prevent unauthorised information from entering or leaving the system, firewalls and other security measures should be placed at the system boundary.
b. Intrusion detection systems are used to identify, record, and examine unauthorised attempts to access a system. They frequently trigger alarms, allowing defensive actions to be taken quickly.
c. Public Key Infrastructure (PKI)

d. Activity log auditing, system configuration modifications, and other events are monitored for unusual or forbidden behaviour so that it can be addressed.

Security testing to confirm the strength of data protection and find flaws that need to be fixed, including simulated hostile attacks

e. Policy servers that automate the rules controlling how security mechanisms operate

Access control systems to limit unauthorised use of data and resources and enforce user privileges

Apart from these, there are also *physical measures* and *procedural measures.* The *physical measures* include all the measures taken to place sensitive information safe guarded against barriers that range from controls such as badges, door locks to guarded enclosures. *Procedural measures* which cover safe operations and procedures meant to preserve the efficacy of security measures and get rid of mistakes made by people. One common instance would be an obligation to remove private software and data from a computer at the end of a workday or assignment. Others include scheduling frequent, timely system scans to look for unusual activity or changed system configurations, and automatically locking computers after a certain amount of inactivity. Teaching system users to practise good security "hygiene," such as regularly changing passwords and recognising and thwarting "phishing" attacks that attempt to fool a user into divulging sensitive information or loading malicious software, is a crucial component of procedural security. Besides, always turn on two-factor authentication for all accounts. By requiring a second form of verification—like a code sent to your phone or email—in addition to your password, this increases security. Another emerging security strategy aims to be proactive by continuously monitoring user behaviour and cybersecurity events, even in real-time, and responding dynamically to reduce or contain attempted intrusions (Hershey & Silo, 2012). This might involve deploying of agents in various locations which has information to measure events like password change attempts or even failed log-in attempts. Agent reports can notify operational staff of unusual circumstances and start automated reactions, like network address blocking, when they are received.

6. CONCLUSION

Threats like data breaches, identity theft, and scam attacks must be understood and stopped as virtual settings become more and more important to daily life. To build a sense of shared duty for safety, this part has stressed the role of community leaders and new ways of teaching, such as gaming. People can better understand and follow necessary security practices if there is a culture of security and relevant training material that is easy to find and use on a variety of virtual platforms. For managing security events, the chapter also stresses how important it is to have effective ways to report and respond to them. To handle incidents quickly, it is important to set up clear ways for people to report them, quick reaction teams, and automated danger detection systems. Finally, the chapter talks about the best ways to keep yourself safe online, from basic safety tips to more complex security strategies. This way, readers will be fully equipped to safely explore the Metaverse and enjoy their time there. To make the internet a safer place for everyone, this all-around method gives people the information and tools they need to keep themselves safe.

Working on making smarter, more dynamic learning tools that can change with the Metaverse should be the main goal of future work in this area. Combining AI and machine learning should be looked into as a way to make security training more personalized based on how each user acts and the threats they face. Plus, studies need to keep going to see how well the current teaching methods and ways of telling things work, with a focus on always getting better and adapting to new security problems. To improve user education and knowledge and make the Metaverse safe for everyone, it will be important for all parties to work together. This includes platform providers, cybersecurity experts, and instructors.

REFERENCES

Abawajy, J. (2014). User preference of cyber security awareness delivery methods. *Behaviour & Information Technology*, 33(3), 237–248. 10.1080/0144929X.2012.708787

Al-Emran, M., & Deveci, M. (2024). Unlocking the potential of cybersecurity behavior in the metaverse: Overview, opportunities, challenges, and future research agendas. *Technology in Society*, 77, 102498. 10.1016/j.techsoc.2024.102498

Annetta, L. A. (2010). The "I's" have it: A framework for serious educational game design. *Review of General Psychology*, 14(2), 105–113. 10.1037/a0018985

Anstett, A. (2021). *What is spear phishing?* Wandera, Retrieved Jul 27, 2021, from https://www.wandera.com/what-is-spear-phishing/ [Ref list]

Bono, S., Caselden, D., Landau, G., & Miller, C. (2009, May/June). Reducing the attack surface in massively multiplayer Online role-playing games. *IEEE Security and Privacy*, 7(3), 13–19. 10.1109/MSP.2009.75

Borky, J. M., Bradley, T. H., Borky, J. M., & Bradley, T. H. (2019). Protecting information with cybersecurity. Effective Model-Based Systems Engineering, 345-404.

Bulgurcu, B., Cavusoglu, H., & Benbasat, I. (2010). Information security policy compliance: An empirical study of rationality-based beliefs and information security awareness. *Management Information Systems Quarterly*, 34(3), 523–548. 10.2307/25750690

Chaudhry, A. J., Chaudhry, A. S., & Rittenhouse, G. R. (2016). Phishing Attacks and Defenses. *International Journal of Security and Its Applications*, 10(1), 247–256. 10.14257/ijsia.2016.10.1.23

Chen, Y., YeckehZaare, I., & Zhang, A. F. (2018). YeckehZaare I, Zhang AF. Real or bogus: Predicting susceptibility to phishing with economic experiments. *PLoS One*, 13(6), 1–18. 10.1371/journal.pone.019821329949585

Cone, B. D., Irvine, C. E., Thompson, M. F., & Nguyen, T. D. (2007). A video game for cyber security training and awareness. computers & security, 26(1), 63-72.

Connolly, L. Y., & Wall, D. S. (2019). The rise of crypto-ransomware in a changing

Connolly, L. Y., & Wall, D. S. (2019). The rise of crypto-ransomware in a changing cybercrime landscape: Taxonomising countermeasures. *Computers & Security*, 87, 101568.

Content, C. S. R. C. (Ed.). (n.d.-b). *Computer Security Incident - Glossary | CSRC*. https://csrc.nist.gov/glossary/term/computer_security_incident

De Zan, T. (2019). Mind the gap: the cyber security skills shortage and public policy interventions.

DeGroot, H.III, Uzunishvili, S., Weir, R., Al-omari, A., & Gomes, B. (2012). Intra-articular injection of hyaluronic acid is not superior to saline solution injection for ankle arthritis: A randomized, double-blind, placebo-controlled study. *The Journal of Bone and Joint Surgery. American Volume*, 94(1), 2–8. 10.2106/JBJS.J.0176322218376

Deveci, M., Pamucar, D., Gokasar, I., Köppen, M., Gupta, B. B., & Daim, T. (2023). Evaluation of Metaverse traffic safety implementations using fuzzy Einstein based logarithmic methodology of additive weights and TOPSIS method. *Technological Forecasting and Social Change*, 194, 122681. 10.1016/j.techfore.2023.122681

ENISA. (2019). ENISA threat landscape report 2018: 15 Top Cyber-Threats and Trends. Heraklion: european Network and Information Security Agency (ENISA). 10.2824/622757

Esmaeilzadeh, P. (2021). How does IT identity affect individuals' use behaviors associated with personal health devices (PHDs)? An empirical study. *Information & Management*, 58(1), 103313. 10.1016/j.im.2020.103313

Falchuk, B., Loeb, S., & Neff, R. (2018, June). The social metaverse: Battle for privacy. *IEEE Technology and Society Magazine*, 37(2), 52–61. 10.1109/MTS.2018.2826060

Farooq, A., Isoaho, J., Virtanen, S., & Isoaho, J. (2015). Information security awareness in educational institution: An analysis of students' individual factors. *Proceedings - 14th IEEE International Conference on Trust, Security and Privacy in Computing and Communications, TrustCom 2015, 1*, 352–359. 10.1109/Trustcom.2015.394

Fatokun, F. B., Hamid, S., Norman, A., & Fatokun, J. O. (2019). The Impact of Age, Gender, and Educational level on the Cybersecurity Behaviors of Tertiary Institution Students: An Empirical investigation on Malaysian Universities. *Journal of Physics: Conference Series*, 1339(1), 012098. Advance online publication. 10.1088/1742-6596/1339/1/012098

Gokasar, I., Pamucar, D., Deveci, M., Gupta, B. B., Martinez, L., & Castillo, O. (2023). Metaverse integration alternatives of connected autonomous vehicles with self-powered sensors using fuzzy decision making model. *Information Sciences*, 642, 119192. 10.1016/j.ins.2023.119192

Gonzalez, J. J. (2005, September). Towards a cyber security reporting system–a quality improvement process. In *International Conference on Computer Safety, Reliability, and Security* (pp. 368 380). Berlin, Heidelberg: Springer Berlin Heidelberg. 10.1007/11563228_28

Goode, S., Hoehle, H., Venkatesh, V., & Brown, S. A. (2017). User compensation as a data breach recovery action. *Management Information Systems Quarterly*, 41(3), 703–A16. 10.25300/MISQ/2017/41.3.03

Gordon, W. J., Fairhall, A., & Landman, A. (2017). Threats to information security—Public health implications. *The New England Journal of Medicine*, 377(8), 707–709. 10.1056/NEJMp170721228700269

Heimdal Security. (n.d.). *Heimdal® - One Platform. Total Cyber Security.* https://heimdalsecurity.com/

Hershey, P., & Silo, C. (2012) Procedure for detection of and response to distributed denial of service cyber attacks on complex enterprise systems. In Proceedings of 6th Annual 10.1109/SysCon.2012.6189438

Hu, P., Li, H., Fu, H., Cansever, D., & Mohapatra, P. "Dynamic defense strategy against advanced persistent threat with insiders", *Proc. IEEE Conf. Comput. Commun. (INFOCOM)*, pp. 747-755, 2015. 10.1109/INFOCOM.2015.7218444

Ingham, L. (2018). *88% of UK data breaches caused by human error, not cyberattacks*. The Verdict Magazine.

International Systems Conference, Vancouver, 19–22 March 2012, p 85–90

Jaeger, L. (2018). Information security awareness: literature review and integrative framework.

Jain, A. K., Sahoo, S. R., & Kaubiyal, J. (2021). Online social networks security and privacy: Comprehensive review and analysis. *Complex & Intelligent Systems*, 7(5), 2157–2177. 10.1007/s40747-021-00409-7

Jaipong, P., Siripipattanakul, S., Sriboonruang, P., Sitthipon, T., Jaipong, P., Siripipattanakul, S., & Sitthipon, T. (2023). A review of metaverse and cybersecurity in the digital era. *International Journal of Computing Sciences Research*, 7, 1125–1132. 10.25147/ijcsr.2017.001.1.122

Jensen, M., Dinger, M., Wright, R., & Thatcher, J. (2017). Training to Mitigate Phishing Attacks Using Mindfulness Techniques. *Journal of Management Information Systems*, 34(2), 597–626. 10.1080/07421222.2017.1334499

Jeon, J.-E. (2021). The effects of user experience-based design innovativeness on user-metaverse platform channel relationships in South Korea. *J. Distrib. Sci.*, 19, 81–90.

Khorshed, M., Ali, A. B. M. S., & Wasimi, S. A. (2012). A survey on gaps, threat remediation challenges and some thoughts for proactive attack detection in cloud computing. *Future Generation Computer Systems*, 28(6), 833–851. 10.1016/j.future.2012.01.006

Kim, E., Yoon, J. K., Kwon, J., Liaw, T., & Agogino, A. M. (2019a). From innocent irene to parental patrick: Framing user characteristics and personas to design for cybersecurity. *Proceedings of the International Conference on Engineering Design, ICED, 2019-Augus*(August), 1773–1782. 10.1017/dsi.2019.183

Kim, H., Kwon, H. J., & Kim, K. K. (2019). Modified cyber kill chain model for multimedia service environments. *Multimedia Tools and Applications*, 78(3), 3153–3170. 10.1007/s11042-018-5897-5

Kumar, A., Shankar, A., Behl, A., Gupta, B. B., & Mavuri, S. (2023). Lights, Camera, Metaverse!: Eliciting Intention to Use Industrial Metaverse, Organizational Agility, and Firm Performance. [JGIM]. *Journal of Global Information Management*, 31(8), 1–20. 10.4018/JGIM.333169

Lebeck, K., Ruth, K., Kohno, T., & Roesner, F. "Towards security and privacy for multi-user augmented reality: Foundations with end users", *Proc. IEEE Symp. Security Privacy (SP)*, pp. 392-408, 2018. 10.1109/SP.2018.00051

Leenes, R. (2008). Privacy in the metaverse: Regulating a complex social construct in a virtual world. *Proc. Future Identity Inf. Soc.*, (Jul), 95–112.

Lim, J. S., Ahmad, A., Chang, S., & Maynard, S. (2010). Embedding information security culture emerging concerns and challenges.

Liu, L., De Vel, O., Han, Q. L., Zhang, J., & Xiang, Y. (2018). Detecting and preventing cyber insider threats: A survey. *IEEE Communications Surveys and Tutorials*, 20(2), 1397–1417. 10.1109/COMST.2018.2800740

Liu, S. Y. (2023). The security challenges of the "Metaverse". *Secur Saf*, 2, 2023010.

McLeod, A., & Dolezel, D. (2018). Cyber-analytics: Modeling factors associated with healthcare data breaches. *Decision Support Systems*, 108, 57–68. 10.1016/j.dss.2018.02.007

Miltgen, C. L., & Smith, H. J. (2015). Exploring information privacy regulation, risks, trust, and behavior. *Information & Management*, 52(6), 741–759. 10.1016/j.im.2015.06.006

Rahaman, M., Lin, C.-Y., & Moslehpour, M. (2023). SAPD: Secure Authentication Protocol Development for Smart Healthcare Management Using IoT. *2023 IEEE 12th Global Conference on Consumer Electronics (GCCE)*, 1014–1018. 10.1109/GCCE59613.2023.10315475

Rahaman, M., Lin, C.-Y., Pappachan, P., Gupta, B. B., & Hsu, C.-H. (2024). Privacy-Centric AI and IoT Solutions for Smart Rural Farm Monitoring and Control. *Sensors (Basel)*, 24(13), 13. Advance online publication. 10.3390/s2413415739000936

Rahaman, M., Tabassum, F., Arya, V., & Bansal, R. (2024). Secure and sustainable food processing supply chain framework based on Hyperledger Fabric technology. *Cyber Security and Applications*, 2, 100045. 10.1016/j.csa.2024.100045

Schein, E. H. (2010). *Organizational culture and leadership* (Vol. 2). John Wiley & Sons.

Shang, J., Chen, S., Wu, J., & Yin, S. (2022, February). ARSpy: Breaking location-based multi-player augmented reality application for user location tracking. *IEEE Transactions on Mobile Computing*, 21(2), 433–447. 10.1109/TMC.2020.3007740

Sharma, S., Singh, J., Gupta, A., Ali, F., Khan, F., & Kwak, D. (2024). User Safety and Security in the Metaverse: A Critical Review. *IEEE Open Journal of the Communications Society*, 1–1. *IEEE Open Journal of the Communications Society*, 1. Advance online publication. 10.1109/OJCOMS.2024.3397044

Siponen, M., & Vance, A. (2010). Neutralization: New insights into the problem of employee information systems security policy violations. *Management Information Systems Quarterly*, 34(3), 487–502. 10.2307/25750688

Uchendu, B., Nurse, J. R., Bada, M., & Furnell, S. (2021). Developing a cyber security culture: Current practices and future needs. *Computers & Security*, 109, 102387. 10.1016/j.cose.2021.102387

Vaidya, R. (2019). Cyber security breaches survey 2019. Department for Digital, Culture, Media and Sport, 66.

Verizon. (2019). *2019 Verizon Data Breach Investigations Report: First impressions from the perimeter*. Verizondigitalmedia, Retrieved Jul 27, 2021, from https://www.verizondigitalmedia.com/blog/2019-verizon-data-breach-investigations-report-first-impressions/

What's new in the 2021 Cost of a Data Breach Report - Security Intelligence. (2023b, August 23). Security Intelligence. https://securityintelligence.com/posts/whats-new-2021-cost-of-a data-breach-report

Yeom, S., Shin, D., & Shin, D. (2021). Scenario-based cyber attack· defense education system on virtual machines integrated by web technologies for protection of multimedia contents in a network. *Multimedia Tools and Applications*, 80(26), 34085–34101. 10.1007/s11042-019-08583-0

Chapter 10
The Future of Metaverse Security:
Anticipating Challenges and Developing Advanced Protective Measures

Brij B. Gupta
https://orcid.org/0000-0003-4929-4698
Department of Computer Science and Information Engineering, Asia University, Taichung, Taiwan

Arcangelo Castiglione
University of Salerno, Italy

ABSTRACT

The metaverse, an evolving digital frontier integrating VR, AR, blockchain, 5G, and quantum computing, presents both opportunities and security challenges. This chapter explores these emerging technologies, their security implications, and the innovative measures developed to mitigate associated risks. The role of AI in enhancing metaverse security is examined, highlighting effective algorithms and future prospects. Challenges in scaling security, regulatory and ethical considerations, and collaborative approaches are discussed. A vision for a secure and inclusive metaverse is proposed, emphasizing key characteristics and strategies for accessibility. The chapter concludes with essential takeaways and future directions for metaverse security.

DOI: 10.4018/979-8-3693-3824-7.ch010

1. INTRODUCTION

The metaverse, a virtual reality space where users can interact with a computer-generated environment and other users, presents a myriad of security concerns that need to be addressed to ensure a safe and trustworthy digital environment (wang et al. 2022; Gupta et al. 2023d). There are many security concerns in metaverse (Table 1) One of the fundamental challenges in securing the metaverse is its inherent characteristics, such as immersive realism, hyper spatiotemporality, sustainability, and heterogeneity, which can lead to issues like scalability and interoperability (wang et al. 2022; Setia et al. 2024). These challenges can complicate security provisioning in the metaverse, making it crucial to develop robust security measures to protect users and data within this complex environment.

Privacy and security issues are at the forefront of concerns surrounding the metaverse, with a focus on formulating rules and principles, addressing privacy threats, and managing data effectively (Tukur 2023; Zhou et al. 2021). The ability for users to create multiple avatars in the metaverse introduces internal security issues, as these avatars can be manipulated to deceive or harm others (Kim 2023; Gupta et al. 2023c). Additionally, the growing complexity and diversity of functionalities in the metaverse,

Table 1. Overview of the Metaverse and Security Concerns

Aspect	Description	Examples/Details
Definition of the Metaverse	A virtual universe combining VR, AR, and the internet	Immersive virtual environments, digital economies
Evolution of the Metaverse	Development stages and future trends	Early VR platforms, integration of blockchain and AI
Primary Security Concerns	Key security issues faced in the metaverse	Data privacy, identity theft, cyber attacks
Importance of Security	Reasons why robust security is crucial	User trust, safe transactions, protection against breaches

coupled with the increasing demand for network bandwidth and computational re- sources, contribute to heightened security threats that need to be mitigated (Han et al. 2023; Mishra, Gupta, and Gupta 2023).

Augmented Reality (AR) has been identified as a significant contributor to security risks in the metaverse, particularly concerning user privacy (Jaber 2022; Gupta et al. 2023b). Uneven power distribution, cybersecurity issues, privacy threats, and potential negative impacts on users' mental health are among the various concerns associated with the metaverse (Ghazal et al. 2022; Gupta et al. 2023a). Furthermore, when considering the use of the metaverse in education, risks such as cyberattacks, data breaches, and threats to student safety must be carefully managed to ensure a secure learning environment (Bhardwaj 2024d; Aldweesh et al. 2023).

As the metaverse continues to evolve and integrate into various sectors, including healthcare, concerns about cybersecurity risks, data management, privacy issues, and AI bias become more pronounced (Bhardwaj 2023; Kumbhojkar and Menon 2022). The development and integration of metaverse technologies face obstacles related to data management, privacy, cybersecurity, AI bias, and cultural and social access barriers (Cheng 2024; Gaurav 2023). Establishing robust security parameters is essential before introducing the metaverse into critical sectors like medicine to safeguard sensitive data and ensure user privacy (Sinha 2023; Sethi 2022).

Authentication and authorization play crucial roles in protecting users and their data within the metaverse, highlighting the importance of implementing strong security measures to prevent unauthorized access and data breaches (Bhardwaj 2024c; Hasan 2023). The complexity of the metaverse raises new challenges related to privacy and security, necessitating a comprehensive approach to address these issues effectively (Sebastian 2022). Privacy attacks, defenses, and the safeguarding of digital assets and transactions through Blockchain technology are key concerns in ensuring the security of metaverse applications (Kabanda, Chipfumbu, and Chingoriwo 2022).

2. EMERGING TECHNOLOGIES AND THEIR IMPACT ON SECURITY

2.1. Introduction to Emerging Technologies

The metaverse, a virtual reality space where users can interact with a computer-generated environment and other users, is being shaped by a range of emerging technologies that are revolutionizing the way individuals engage with digital environments (Truong, Le, and Niyato 2023). One key technology driving the development of the metaverse is the advancement of communication and networking technologies, such as 5G and beyond wireless networks, which provide ultra-high speed, low latency, and reliable data communications among metaverse devices and networks (Truong, Le, and Niyato 2023). These technologies are essential for creating seamless and immersive experiences within the metaverse, enhancing user interactions and connectivity. Vir- tual human reconstruction (Figure 1) is a crucial undertaking in different Metaverse applications. Its objective is to employ sensory data to restore the three-dimensional structure and visual characteristics of humans, resulting in precise and lifelike reconstructions. Ultimately, the goal is to create compact 3D representations that can be easily transferred to different devices(Zhang et al. 2022).

Figure 1. Virtual Human Reconstruction in Metaverse

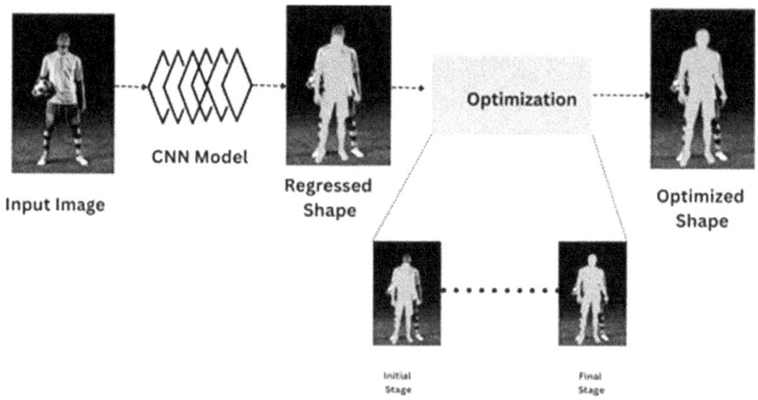

Big Data, the Internet of Things (IoT), and Digital Twins are among the innovative technologies that are playing a crucial role in shaping the metaverse (Allam et al. 2022). These technologies provide rich datasets and advanced computational understandings of human behavior, offering opportunities to redefine city designing activities and ser- vice provisioning in urban environments, thereby increasing efficiencies and quality performance within the metaverse (Allam et al. 2022). By leveraging these technolo- gies, the metaverse can enhance user experiences, create dynamic environments, and support a wide range of applications.

Blockchain technology is another significant innovation that is being integrated into the metaverse to maintain decentralization, transparency, and immutability (Aloqaily et al. 2023). By leveraging blockchain, the metaverse can ensure secure transactions, protect digital assets, and establish trust among users within the virtual environment (Aloqaily et al. 2023). The integration of blockchain technology in the metaverse is essential for creating a secure and reliable platform for users to engage with digital assets and conduct transactions.

The deployment of Internet of Things (IoT) and blockchain technologies in the metaverse can enhance energy efficiency and decentralized management and ownership within the virtual environment (Din 2023). By integrating IoT devices and blockchain technology, the metaverse can optimize energy consumption, improve resource man- agement, and enhance the overall sustainability of the virtual world (Din 2023). These technologies play a crucial role in mitigating energy demands and ensuring efficient operations within the metaverse.

Digital Twin technology, combined with advanced intelligent technologies, is being integrated into the metaverse to create scalable and immersive experiences (Aloqailyet al. 2023) (Figure 2). Digital Twins enable real-time mapping of physical entities, allowing users to simulate and test physical environments within the metaverse, en- hancing the overall user experience and interaction with virtual spaces (Aloqaily et al. 2023). By leveraging Digital Twins and intelligent technologies, the metaverse can offer realistic and dynamic environments for users to explore and engage with. In

Figure 2. Metaverse and Digital Twin

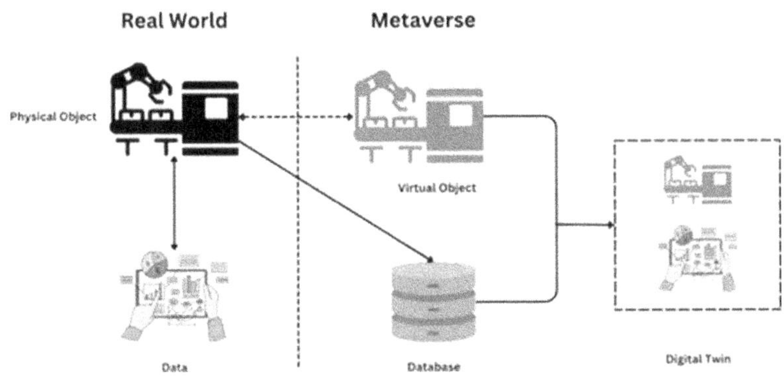

addition to these technologies, Artificial Intelligence (AI) is shaping the future of the metaverse by enabling intelligent interactions, personalized experiences, and immersive environments (Li et al. 2023). AI-driven technologies, such as intelligent cockpits for vehicles, are driving the development of interactive and empathetic systems within the metaverse, enhancing user engagement and emotional experiences (Li et al. 2023). By integrating AI into the metaverse, virtual environments can become more responsive, adaptive, and tailored to individual user preferences.

Overall, the convergence of technologies such as AI, blockchain, IoT, Digital Twins, and advanced networking technologies is shaping the metaverse into a dynamic and immersive digital environment (Zhao 2023). These technologies are revolutionizing the way users interact with virtual spaces, enabling new opportunities for creativity, collaboration, and exploration within the metaverse. By leveraging these emerging technologies, the metaverse is poised to redefine digital experiences, create innovative applications, and transform the way individuals engage with virtual worlds.

2.2. Security Implications

Security vulnerabilities introduced by Virtual Reality (VR) and Augmented Real- ity (AR) technologies pose significant risks that need to be addressed to ensure the safety and integrity of these immersive environments. One of the primary concerns highlighted in the literature is related to authentication challenges in AR and VR technologies, which can lead to security breaches and unauthorized access Duezguen et al. (2020). These authentication challenges can stem from the unique user interac- tions and interfaces in AR and VR environments, making it crucial to develop secure and usable authentication mechanisms to mitigate these vulnerabilities.

Furthermore, security and privacy risks in multi-user AR environments have been identified as a key concern, particularly when considering individual users or AR de- vices (Lebeck et al. 2018)(Figure 3). The collaborative nature of multi-user AR experiences can introduce vulnerabilities related to data privacy, user identifi- cation, and information sharing, emphasizing the need for robust security measures to protect user data and interactions within these shared environments.

Figure 3. Attack in Multi-user AR Environment

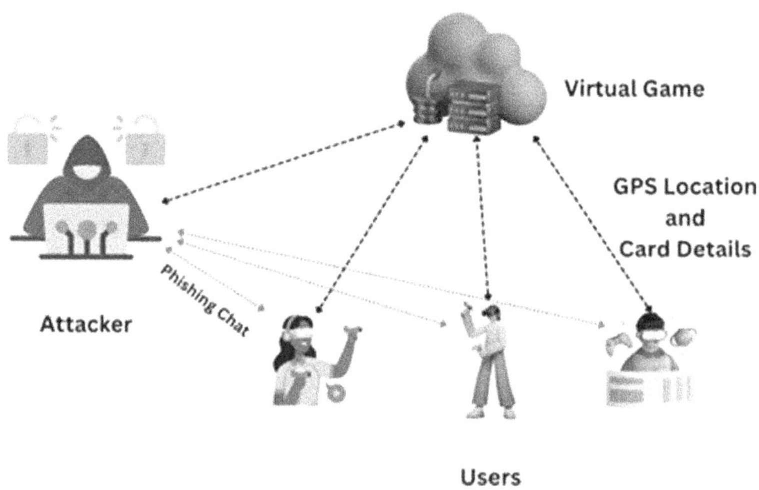

Moreover, the integration of IoT devices in AR and VR technologies can introduce security vulnerabilities related to software and hardware flaws, misconfigurations, and operational weaknesses (Nebbione and Calzarossa 2023). The diverse nature of IoT devices and their interconnectedness within AR and VR ecosystems can create entry points for cyberattacks and data breaches, highlighting the importance of implement- ing security protocols to safeguard these interconnected systems.

Additionally, the use of smart technologies in AR and VR applications can make these environments susceptible to security risks, particularly in on-farm data acquisi- tion technologies and other smart devices (Hazrati, Dara, and Kaur 2022). The reliance on smart technologies introduces vulnerabilities that can be exploited by malicious actors, necessitating comprehensive security measures to protect sen- sitive data and ensure the integrity of these systems.

Another significant security concern in AR and VR technologies is the potential for malicious attacks targeting vulnerabilities in networked devices and systems, including design defects and implementation flaws (Choudhary et al. 2022). These vulnerabilities can be exploited to compromise the security of AR and VR environments, underscoring the importance of conducting thorough security assessments and implementing robust security protocols to mitigate potential risks.

Blockchain technology significantly enhances the security of transactions within the metaverse by providing a secure and transparent framework for recording and verifying digital transactions (Tao et al. 2023). It serves as the primary transaction and payment channel in the metaverse, impacting the network security of the metaverse ecosystem and ensuring the integrity and authenticity of transactions (Tao et al. 2023). The integration of blockchain technology into the metaverse enables secure and tamper- resistant transactions through consensus mechanisms and public ledgers, making it computationally infeasible to distort published transactions (Xu et al. 2022a).

One of the key contributions of blockchain technology to transaction security in the metaverse is its ability to maintain decentralization, transparency, and immutability within the virtual environment (Aloqaily et al. 2023). Stakeholders can manage their

IoT data records in shared blockchain ledgers, resolving security issues and ensuring transaction integrity within the metaverse (Ahsani et al. 2023). Blockchain technol- ogy in the metaverse facilitates secure digital asset tracking and provides a secure mechanism for financial transactions (Hutson et al. 2023).

Moreover, blockchain technology enhances transaction security in the metaverse by enabling data transparency, openness, authenticity, and efficiency (Ryu et al. 2022). Stakeholders can track and trace transactions through blockchain technology, ensur- ing transparency and data authenticity within the metaverse environment (Ryu et al. 2022). The integration of blockchain technology into the metaverse ecosystem empow- ers decentralized finance (DeFi) and boosts decentralized market activities, enhancing security and trust in transactions (Yang et al. 2022).

Furthermore, blockchain technology in the metaverse enables secure computation techniques, including zero-trust environments, to ensure data security and privacy for users (Wang et al. 2022a). By incorporating blockchain technology into the metaverse, education is elevated to a new level, providing enhanced security and transparency in educational transactions (Cui et al. 2023). Secure storage of assets in blockchain-based frameworks within the metaverse addresses concerns related to asset security and data integrity (Ersoy and Gu¨rfidan 2022).

2.3. Protective Measures and Innovations

To address the security challenges posed by emerging technologies in the metaverse, new security protocols have been developed to enhance the safety and integrity of transactions and interactions within these immersive digital environments. One signif- icant development in response to these challenges is the implementation of encryption protocols, stringent access controls, and comprehensive data protection measures Ajani (2023). Access control is most important in metaverse events (Figure 4). These pro- tocols aim to secure data transmission, restrict unauthorized access, and safeguard sensitive information within the metaverse, ensuring the privacy and security of users.

Figure 4. Access Control in Metaverse Meeting

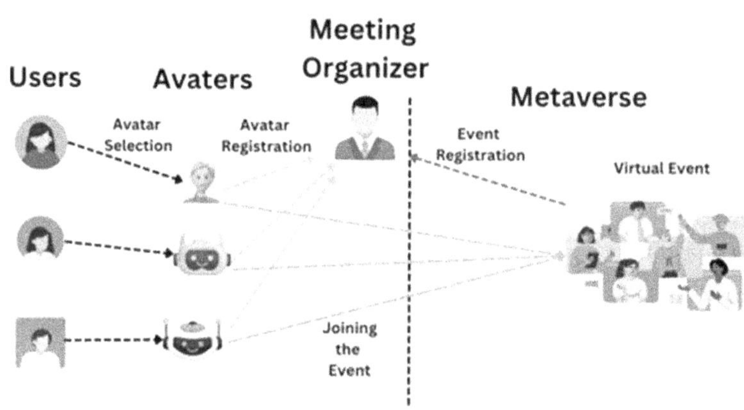

In addition, novel PHY layer security (PLS) schemes have been introduced as promising approaches to safeguard the security of metaverse access, offering information-theoretic security guarantees (Ahsani et al. 2023). These security protocols leverage advanced technologies to protect the physical layer of communication networks in the metaverse, enhancing the overall security posture of the virtual envi- ronment and ensuring secure data transmission and interactions.

Furthermore, evolving security protocols and digital ledger technologies like blockchain have been instrumental in increasing the transparency and cybersecurity of digital assets within the metaverse (Camilleri 2023). By leveraging blockchain tech- nology, the metaverse can enhance the security of transactions, protect digital assets, and ensure the integrity of data exchanges, fostering trust and reliability in virtual interactions.

Zero-trust architectures have also emerged as critical security protocols in ensuring the security and integrity of the metaverse system as it continues to develop and expand (Blowers 2023). These architectures operate on the principle of "never trust, always verify," requiring strict verification of all users and devices accessing the network, thereby minimizing security risks and vulnerabilities within the metaverse ecosystem. Moreover, the integration of secure mutual authentication schemes using biometric information and Elliptic Curve Cryptography (ECC) has been proposed to establish secure communication between users and platform servers in the metaverse (Ryu et al. 2022). These authentication protocols enhance the security of user interactions and transactions within the virtual environment, ensuring that only authorized entities can access and engage with metaverse platforms.

In the dynamic landscape of the metaverse, advancements in encryption, authentication, and access control are pivotal in addressing security concerns and ensuring the confidentiality and integrity of transactions and interactions within these immersive digital realms. Various new security protocols have been developed to harness these technologies and bolster the overall security framework of the metaverse.

Encryption protocols have played a critical role in securing data transmission and safeguarding sensitive information within the metaverse. Through the encryption of data at rest and in transit, these protocols guarantee that data remains confidential and protected, even in scenarios of unauthorized access or interception Upadhyay (2023). Robust encryption mechanisms are instrumental in upholding user privacy and thwarting unauthorized entities from accessing sensitive information, thereby fortifying the security of the metaverse ecosystem.

Authentication mechanisms, such as two-factor authentication and biometric au- thentication, have been integrated to authenticate user identities and ensure secure entry to metaverse platforms (Natarajan 2024). By necessitating multiple authentica- tion factors like passwords, biometric data, or security tokens, these protocols heighten the security of user accounts and prevent unauthorized access to sensitive data within the metaverse environment.

Access control strategies, encompassing Single Sign-On (SSO) solutions, blockchain- based access control, Attribute-Based Access Control (ABAC), and adaptive access control, have been deployed to regulate user permissions and curb unauthorized access to resources within the metaverse (Patwe 2024). These access control mechanisms enforce security policies, restrict user privileges based on roles and attributes, and deter unauthorized activities, thereby enhancing the overall security of the metaverse ecosystem.

Blockchain technology has significantly contributed to enabling secure and inter- operable authentication schemes within the metaverse (Turner et al. 2023). By lever- aging blockchain for access control and authentication, the metaverse can ensure the integrity and transparency of user identities and transactions, fostering trust and secu- rity within the virtual environment (Xu et al. 2022b). Blockchain offers a decentralized and tamper-resistant framework for managing access control and authentication pro- cesses, mitigating security risks and vulnerabilities in the metaverse.

Furthermore, the integration of Secure Socket Layer (SSL) encryption and Virtual Private Networks (VPNs) has been utilized to secure data transmission and communication channels within the metaverse, shielding sensitive information from unauthorized access and interception (Bhardwaj 2024a). These encryption proto- cols guarantee the confidentiality and integrity of data exchanged between users and platforms, enhancing the overall security of interactions within the metaverse.

3. THE ROLE OF AI IN ENHANCING SECURITY MEASURES

3.1. Introduction to AI in Security

AI plays a crucial role in enhancing security measures within the metaverse by lever- aging advanced algorithms and machine learning techniques to detect and prevent security threats, ensuring the integrity and confidentiality of data and transactions. Several studies have highlighted the significance of AI in fortifying security proto- cols within the metaverse ecosystem. As represented in Figure 5, AI can be used for authentication of avatars in metaverse.

Figure 5. AI Based Authentication of Avatars in Metaverse

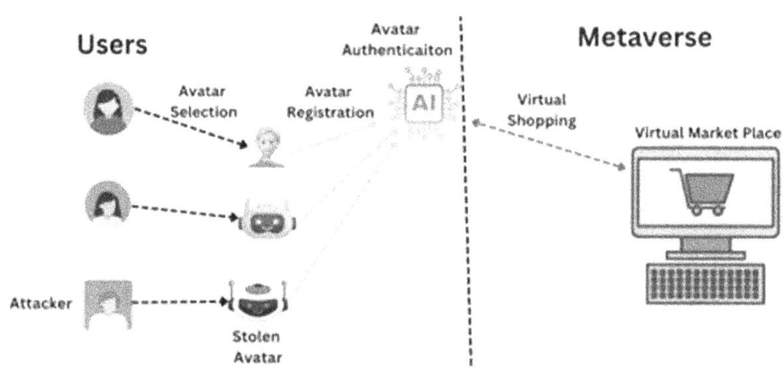

One study by Al-Suqri and Niaz (2022); Agrawal (2020) emphasizes how AI facili- tates secure information handling to mitigate threats and cyber-attacks, underscoring its role in bolstering security measures within the metaverse. Similarly, Siriwardhana et al. (2021) delve into the utilization of AI in securing 6G networks, shedding light on the opportunities and challenges associated with leveraging AI for enhancing security in advanced network environments.

Park, Siddiqui, and Qureshi (2022) explore the application of AI technology to address security challenges in the metaverse, showcasing how AI can be instrumental in solving security issues within virtual environments. Additionally, Truong, Le, and Niyato (2023) discuss securing AI models in the metaverse through blockchain-based "AI smart contracts," highlighting the integration of blockchain technology with AI for enhanced security measures.

The fusion of blockchain and AI technologies has been recognized as a promising approach to increasing cyber resilience and enhancing security within distributed envi-ronments, as outlined by (Salah et al. 2019). Furthermore, Abed and Anupam (2022) emphasize the role of AI in driving security solutions in IoT networks, showcasing the importance of AI-driven approaches in fortifying security measures in interconnected systems.

Integrating AI and blockchain technologies can significantly enhance the safety and inclusivity of the metaverse, particularly in combating hate speech and bolstering user engagement, as demonstrated by et al. (Sanghvi 2023). Moreover, the study by Gupta, Kumari, and Tanwar (2020) highlights the fusion of blockchain and AI for secure drone networking, showcasing the potential of AI-driven solutions in ensuring secure communication in drone systems.

3.2. AI-Driven Security Solutions

Analyzing user behavior and detecting anomalies to prevent security breaches in the metaverse is a critical application of artificial intelligence (AI) technologies. By leverag- ing advanced algorithms and machine learning techniques, AI can effec-tively monitor user activities, identify patterns, and detect deviations from normal behavior that may indicate potential security threats. Several studies have explored the role of AI in enhancing security measures within the metaverse through anomaly detection and behavior analysis.

Wang et al. (2022b) discuss implementing anomaly detection by building nor-mal behavior models and identifying abnormal behaviors based on their deviation from es- tablished norms. This approach allows AI to detect unusual activities or patterns that may indicate security breaches or malicious intent within the metaverse environment. Pan, Li, and Zhao (2009) highlight the merit of anomaly detection in comparing normal behavior profiles with actual program behaviors to uncover potential attacks.

By analyzing deviations from expected behavior, AI can proactively identify security threats and prevent breaches in executable programs within the metaverse.

Saurabh and Verma (2014) emphasize the importance of anomaly detection in iden- tifying abnormal system behavior that violates established policies. AI-driven anomaly detection mechanisms can help maintain security protocols and prevent unauthorized activities within the metaverse ecosystem.

Protogerou et al. (2022) introduce a mitigation engine employing a distributed neu- ral network algorithm to handle detected anomalies effectively. By leveraging AI al- gorithms, the metaverse can respond to anomalous events and mitigate threats in a timely and optimal manner.

Cunha et al. (2021) propose an AI-based module to detect and diagnose anomalies among services deployed on virtualized infrastructure in 5G and beyond network environments. AI technologies can assist administrators and users in identifying and addressing security anomalies within network slices in the metaverse.

Guo et al. (2022) highlight the role of AI in cybersecurity, including user access au- thentication, network situation awareness, dangerous behavior monitoring, and abnor- mal traffic identification. AI technologies can enhance security measures by monitoring user behavior and detecting anomalies that may pose security risks in the metaverse.

3.3. Benefits and Limitations

Artificial Intelligence (AI) offers several advantages over traditional security measures in the metaverse, leveraging advanced algorithms and machine learning techniquesto enhance security protocols and protect user data and interactions within virtual environments. Several studies have highlighted the benefits of utilizing AI in fortifying security measures within the metaverse ecosystem.

Enhanced Threat Detection: AI algorithms can analyze vast amounts of data in real-time to detect anomalies and identify potential security threats more effec- tively than traditional security measures Yang (2023). By continuously monitor- ing user behavior and network activities, AI can proactively identify suspicious patterns and behaviors that may indicate security breaches, enabling swift re- sponses to mitigate risks.

Dynamic Security Measures: AI-powered security solutions can adapt and evolve based on emerging threats and changing attack patterns in the metaverse (Wang, Zhou, and Yan 2023). By utilizing machine learning models, AI systems can con- tinuously learn from new data and adjust security protocols to address evolv- ing cybersecurity challenges, providing dynamic and robust protection against emerging threats.

Improved Accuracy and Efficiency: AI algorithms can analyze complex datasets and identify security vulnerabilities with high accuracy and efficiency, reduc- ing false positives and false negatives in threat detection (Chen et al.

2023). By automating security processes and leveraging AI-driven analytics, organiza- tions can enhance the effectiveness of security measures and streamline incident response procedures.

Personalized Security Solutions: AI technologies can provide personalized secu- rity solutions tailored to individual user behaviors and preferences within the metaverse (Park, Siddiqui, and Qureshi 2022). By analyzing user interactions and behaviors, AI systems can customize security settings and access controls to meet specific user needs, enhancing overall security while ensuring a seamless user experience.

Predictive Security Analytics: AI can leverage predictive analytics to anticipate and prevent security breaches before they occur, enabling proactive threat mit- igation and risk management in the metaverse (Jaber 2022). By analyzing his- torical data and identifying patterns indicative of potential security incidents, AI systems can preemptively address vulnerabilities and enhance overall security posture.

6. Integration with Blockchain Technology: AI can be integrated with blockchain technology to enhance security measures in the metaverse, leveraging the transparency and immutability of blockchain to secure transactions and data exchanges. By combining AI and blockchain, organizations can establish secure and tamper-proof systems that protect user data and ensure the integrity of transactions within virtual environments.

4. CHALLENGES AND OPPORTUNITIES IN SCALING SECURITY

4.1. Scalability Issues

Scaling security measures to accommodate the growing metaverse presents several challenges that need to be addressed to ensure the safety and integrity of virtual envi- ronments. Several studies have highlighted the obstacles and complexities associated with scaling security measures in the metaverse ecosystem.

Scalability and Interoperability: One of the fundamental challenges in scaling security measures in the metaverse is the need to ensure scalability and interoperability of security solutions across diverse virtual environments Wang et al. (2023); Law et al. (2021). As the metaverse expands and evolves, security mea- sures must be able to adapt and scale effectively to protect a growing number of users, devices, and interactions within virtual spaces.

Complexity of Security Solutions: The complexity of security solutions required to safeguard the metaverse poses a significant challenge in scaling security mea- sures (Cavanaugh et al. 2000). Implementing comprehensive security protocols that can address diverse threats and vulnerabilities within virtual environments while maintaining usability and performance is a complex task that requires careful planning and execution.

Integration with Emerging Technologies: The integration of security measures with emerging technologies such as artificial intelligence, blockchain, and edge computing poses challenges in scaling security solutions in the metaverse (Venu- gopal, Subramanian, and Peatchimuthu 2023). Ensuring seamless integration and compatibility between different technologies while maintaining security stan- dards is crucial for protecting user data and interactions within virtual environ- ments.

Security in Communication Networks: The deployment of advanced communication networks, such as beyond-the-fifth and sixth-generation wireless networks, presents challenges for scaling traditional security solutions in the metaverse (Ahsani et al. 2023). Ensuring the security of communication networks and data transmissions within the metaverse requires innovative security measures that can address the unique challenges posed by advanced network technologies.

Data Privacy and Sensitivity: Protecting sensitive data and ensuring user privacy in the metaverse presents challenges in scaling security measures to accommo- date the growing volume of data and interactions within virtual environments (Kang et al. 2022). Implementing robust data protection measures and privacy- enhancing technologies is essential to safeguard user information and prevent unauthorized access or data breaches.

Ethical and Governance Challenges: Addressing ethical considerations, governance issues, and regulatory compliance in scaling security measures for the metaverse poses challenges related to AI regulation, privacy enforcement, and governance scalability (Blowers 2023). Ensuring ethical use of AI technologies, protecting user rights, and enforcing security policies across diverse virtual en- vironments are critical challenges that need to be addressed.

4.2. Regulatory and Ethical Considerations

The legal and ethical implications of metaverse security are multifaceted and require careful consideration to ensure the protection of user rights, data privacy, and compli- ance with regulatory frameworks. Several studies have explored the legal and ethical challenges associated with metaverse security and the implications for governance, privacy, and user protection.

Regulatory Compliance: Ensuring compliance with existing and emerging regu- lations, such as data protection laws and consumer privacy regulations, is a key legal consideration in metaverse security (Huang, Li, and Cai 2023). Organiza- tions operating in the metaverse must adhere to legal requirements to protect user data, prevent data breaches, and uphold privacy standards.

Ethical Use of Data: The ethical implications of metaverse security encompass issues related to data collection, storage, and usage within virtual environments (Ford et al. 2023). Ensuring ethical data practices, transparency in data handling, and user consent for data processing are essential ethical considerations in metaverse security to protect user privacy and rights.

Governance Challenges: The governance of security measures in the metaverse involves establishing policies, guidelines, and procedures to safeguard user data and ensure compliance with legal requirements (Kasiyanto and Kilinc 2022). Addressing governance challenges, such as defining roles and responsibilities for security management and enforcing security protocols, is crucial for maintaining a secure and ethical metaverse ecosystem.

Corporate Social Responsibility: Considerations of corporate social responsibility (CSR) in metaverse security involve promoting ethical business practices, pro- tecting user rights, and upholding moral principles within virtual environments (Papagiannidis, Bourlakis, and Li 2008). Organizations operating in the meta- verse must prioritize CSR initiatives to ensure ethical conduct and responsible use of technology.

Privacy and Data Protection: Safeguarding user privacy and protecting sensitive data are critical ethical considerations in metaverse security (Huang, Li, and Cai 2023). Implementing robust data protection measures, encryption protocols, and access controls is essential to ensure the confidentiality and integrity of user information within virtual environments.

Legal Protections and Terms of Service: Establishing legal protections, terms of service agreements, and user agreements for transactions occurring in the metaverse is essential.

5. VISION FOR A SECURE AND INCLUSIVE METAVERSE

5.1. Defining a Secure Metaverse

A secure metaverse should exhibit characteristics such as immersive realism, hyper spa- tiotemporality, sustainability, heterogeneity, scalability, interoperability, privacy pro- tection, user interaction enhancement, innovative technologies, secure authentication, data security and privacy, and ethical use of technology. By incorporating these key characteristics into security measures, the metaverse can provide a safe and secure environment for users to engage in virtual experiences.

Immersive Realism: A secure metaverse should provide immersive experiences that mimic real-world interactions while ensuring the security and privacy of user data and interactions (Wang et al. 2023).
Hyper Spatiotemporality: The metaverse's security measures should address the challenges of hyper spatiotemporality, ensuring real-time security monitoring and response to threats within virtual environments (Wang et al. 2023).
Sustainability: Security measures in the metaverse should be sustainable, ensur- ing long-term protection of user data, privacy, and interactions while adapting to evolving cybersecurity threats (Wang et al. 2023).
Heterogeneity: The diverse nature of the metaverse, including different platforms, technologies, and user interactions, requires security measures that can accommodate heterogeneity and ensure comprehensive protection across virtual environments (Wang et al. 2023).
Scalability: Security solutions in the metaverse should be scalable to accommodate the growing number of users, devices, and interactions within virtual spaces while maintaining robust protection against security threats (Venugopal, Subramanian, and Peatchimuthu 2023).
Interoperability: Ensuring interoperability of security measures across different platforms and technologies within the metaverse is essential for seamless protec- tion of user data and interactions (Venugopal, Subramanian, and Peatchimuthu 2023).
Privacy Protection: A secure metaverse should prioritize data privacy and protec- tion, implementing robust encryption, access controls, and data anonymization techniques to safeguard user information (Kaa, Viardot, and McCarthy 2022). User Interaction and Experience: Security measures should enhance user interac- tion and experience within the metaverse while ensuring that security protocols do not hinder usability or accessibility (Lee 2023).

Innovative Technologies: Leveraging innovative technologies such as artificial in- telligence, blockchain, and edge computing can enhance security measures in the metaverse, providing advanced threat detection and response capabilities (Ahsani et al. 2023).
Secure Authentication: Implementing secure authentication mechanisms, such as biometric authentication and blockchain-based authentication, can enhance the security of user access and interactions within the metaverse (Huynh-The et al. 2022).
Data Security and Privacy: Ensuring robust data security and privacy measures, including encryption, data anonymization, and secure data storage, is essential for protecting user information within the metaverse (Otoum 2024).
Ethical Use of Technology: Adhering to ethical principles and guidelines in the development and deployment of security measures is crucial for maintaining user trust and ensuring responsible use of technology within the metaverse (Patwe 2024).

5.2. Roadmap for the Future

Effective Management of Human Digital Identities: In the future metaverse era, the effective management of human digital identities will become a significant issue for governments, given concerns regarding network information security and information disorder Li (2024).
Technological Developments Impacting Security: To aid in forecasting potential crimes, it is important to consider current trends and technological developments that may impact the future of metaverse security, such as the growth of decen- tralized technologies, the increasing prevalence of artificial intelligence, and the potential for quantum computing (Bhardwaj 2023).
Immersive and Multidimensional Virtual Space: The metaverse aims to establish an immersive and multidimensional virtual space in which global users can interact with one another, similar to interactions in the real world (Zhang 2023). Open Research Directions: Future metaverse systems will need to address open research directions to enhance security measures and ensure the safety and in- tegrity of virtual environments (Wang et al. 2023).

- New Laws for Healthcare Metaverse: While the future of the metaverse in health-care looks promising, it is essential to create new metaverse-specific laws to ad- dress potential downsides and ensure user safety (Hulsen 2023).

Transformative Potential of Virtual Economies: Virtual economies within the metaverse have transformative potential, offering opportunities for growth and complexity, while also presenting challenges that need to be addressed (Bhardwaj 2024b).
Enhanced Security Measures: The increasing adoption of multifactor authentication underscores the importance of safeguarding access to the virtual environment, highlighting the need for robust security measures (Catagua 2023).
Balancing Technological Advancements with Environmental Stewardship: As the metaverse gains momentum, companies will need to prioritize sustainability and explore ways to balance technological advancements with environmental stew- ardship (Nleya 2024).
Security Challenges in the Metaverse Era: Predicting future cybercrime trends and addressing security challenges in the metaverse era will be crucial for pre- venting or mitigating cybercrime in virtual environments (Shafik 2023).
Ethical Use of Technology: Ensuring the ethical use of technology, protecting user rights, and upholding moral principles within virtual environments will be essential for maintaining user trust and ensuring responsible use of technology within the metaverse (Bhaskar 2023).

6. CONCLUSION

The metaverse's rapid evolution necessitates robust security measures to ensure its successful adoption. Emerging technologies introduce unique vulnerabilities, while AI offers promising solutions for enhanced security. Addressing scalability challenges, reg- ulatory implications, and fostering industry collaboration are crucial for a secure meta- verse. An inclusive approach to security design is essential to maintain accessibility. This chapter underscores the importance of continuous innovation and vigilance in se- curing the metaverse, outlining a strategic roadmap for future advancements in meta- verse security.

REFERENCES

Abed, A., & Anupam, A. (2022). Review of security issues in internet of things and artificial intelligence-driven solutions. *Security and Privacy*, 6(3), e285. Advance online publication. 10.1002/spy2.285

Agrawal, D. P. (2020). *Recent Advances in Security, Privacy, and Trust for Internet of Things (IoT) and Cyber-Physical Systems*. CPS.

Ahsani, V., Rahimi, A., Letafati, M., & Khalaj, B. H. (2023). Unlocking metaverse-as-a-service the three pillars to watch: Privacy and security, edge computing, and blockchain. arXiv preprint arXiv:2301.01221.

Ajani, Y., Enakrire, R. T., Oladokun, B. D., & Bashorun, M. T. (2023). Reincarnation of libraries via metaverse: A pathway for a sustain- able knowledge system in the digital age. *Business Information Review*, 40(4), 191–197. 10.1177/02663821231208044

Al-Suqri, M., & Niaz, H. (2022). A comparative analysis of information and artificial intelligence toward national security. *IEEE Access : Practical Innovations, Open Solutions*, 10, 64420–64434. 10.1109/ACCESS.2022.3183642

Aldweesh, A., Alauthman, M., Al Khaldy, M., Ishtaiwi, A., al-Qerem, A., Almoman, A., & Gupta, B. B. (2023). The Meta-Fusion: A Cloud-Integrated Study on Blockchain Technology Enabling Secure and Efficient Virtual Worlds. [IJCAC]. *International Journal of Cloud Applications and Computing*, 13(1), 1–24. 10.4018/IJCAC.331752

Allam, Z., Sharifi, A., Bibri, S., Jones, D., & Krogstie, J. (2022). The metaverse as a virtual form of smart cities: Opportunities and challenges for environmen- tal, economic, and social sustainability in urban futures. *Smart Cities*, 5(3), 771–801. 10.3390/smartcities5030040

Aloqaily, M., Bouachir, O., Karray, F., Ridhawi, I., & Saddik, A. (2023). Integrating digital twin and advanced intelligent technologies to realize the metaverse. *IEEE Consumer Electronics Magazine*, 12(6), 47–55. 10.1109/MCE.2022.3212570

Bhardwaj, A. (2023). “Navigating the metaverse.” 33–65. .10.4018/979-8-3693-0220-0.ch003

Bhardwaj, A. (2024a). “Cyber fraud use cases in the metaverse.” 106–130. .10.2174/9789815238457124010007

Bhardwaj, A. (2024b). “Evolution of virtual economies: from cryptocurrencies to digital assets.” 201–241. .10.2174/9789815238457124010010

Bhardwaj, A. (2024c). "Securing the infinite: traversing cybersecurity challenges in the meta- verse." 131–156. .10.2174/9789815238457124010008

Bhardwaj, A. (2024d). "Stepping into the metaverse: exploring the potential of virtual worlds in education while safeguarding privacy and security." 60–84. .10.2174/9789815238457124010005

Bhaskar, S. (2023). "A prelude to cybersecurity challenges in the metaverse." 149–170. .10.4018/979-8-3693-0220-0.ch008

Blowers, M. (2023). "Benefits and challenges of a military metaverse." .10.1117/12.2663772

Camilleri, M. (2023). Metaverse applications in education: A systematic review and a cost-benefit analysis. *Interactive Technology and Smart Education*, 21(2), 245–269. 10.1108/ITSE-01-2023-0017

Catagua, G. (2023). Information security in the metaverse: A systematic and prospective review. *C'odigo Cient'ıfico Revista De Investigaci'on*, 4(2), 781–817. 10.55813/gaea/ccri/v4/n2/257

Cavanaugh, M., Boswell, W., Roehling, M., & Boudreau, J. (2000). An empirical examination of self-reported work stress among u.s. managers. *The Journal of Applied Psychology*, 85(1), 65–74. 10.1037/0021-9010.85.1.6510740957

Chen, Y., Huang, S., Gan, W., Huang, G., & Wu, Y. (2023, April). Federated learning for metaverse: A survey. In Companion Proceedings of the ACM Web Conference 2023 (pp. 1151-1160).

Cheng, X., Mou, J., Shen, X.-L., de Vreede, T., & Alt, R. (2024). Guest editorial: Exploring the research opportunities and challenges in the metaverse. *Internet Research*, 34(1), 1–8. 10.1108/INTR-10-2023-0994

Choudhary, G., Sihag, V., Gupta, S., & Shandilya, S. (2022). Aviation attacks based on ils and vor vulnerabilities. *Journal of Surveillance Security and Safety*, 3, 27–40. 10.20517/jsss.2021.17

Cui, L., Zhu, C., Hare, R., & Tang, Y. (2023). MetaEdu: A new framework for future education. *Discover Artificial Intelligence*, 3(1), 10.

Cunha, V. A., Maroulis, N., Papagianni, C., Sacido, J., Jiménez, M., Ubaldi, F., . . . Garcia-Saavedra, A. (2021, June). 5 Growth: Secure and reliable network slicing for verticals. In 2021 Joint European Conference on Networks and Communications & 6G Summit (EuCNC/6G Summit) (pp. 347-352). IEEE.

Din, I. (2023). Integration of iot and blockchain for decentralized management and ownership in the metaverse. *International Journal of Communication Systems*, 36(18), e5612. Advance online publication. 10.1002/dac.5612

Duezguen, R., Mayer, P., Das, S., & Volkamer, M. (2020). Towards secure and usable authentication for augmented and virtual reality head-mounted displays. arXiv preprint arXiv:2007.11663.

Ersoy, M., & Gu¨rfidan, R. (2022). Blockchain-based asset storage and service mechanism to metaverse universe: Metarepo. *Transactions on Emerging Telecommunications Technologies*, 34(1), e4658. Advance online publication. 10.1002/ett.4658

Ford, T., Buchanan, D., Azeez, A., Benrimoh, D., Kaloiani, I., Bandeira, I., Hunegnaw, S., Lan, L., Gholmieh, M., Buch, V., & Williams, N. R. (2023). Taking modern psychiatry into the metaverse: Integrating augmented, vir- tual, and mixed reality technologies into psychiatric care. *Frontiers in Digital Health*, 5, 1146806. Advance online publication. 10.3389/fdgth.2023.114680637035477

Gaurav, A. (2023). "Navigating New Realities: Machine Learn- ing in the Metaverse." https://insights2techinfo.com/ navigating-new-realities-machine-learning-in-the-metaverse/. Accessed: 2024-01-30.

Ghazal, T., Issa, G., & Dmour, N., and H. AlzoubiZ. (. (2022). Studying the metaverse ef- fect on its users. *Pakistan Journal of Engineering Technology Science*, 10, 7–15. 10.22555/pjets.v10i1.838

Guo, Y., Yu, T., Wu, J., Wang, Y., Wan, S., Zheng, J., Fang, L., & Dai, Q. (2022). Artificial intelligence for metaverse: A framework. *Caai Artificial Intelligence Research*, 1(1), 54–67. 10.26599/AIR.2022.9150004

Gupta, B. B., Chui, K. T., Gaurav, A., & Arya, V. (2023a). "GRU-Based DDoS Detection for Enhanced Security in Consumer Electronics." In *2023 IEEE 13th International Conference on Consumer Electronics-Berlin (ICCE-Berlin)*, 1–4. IEEE. 10.1109/ICCE-Berlin58801.2023.10375584

Gupta, B. B., Gaurav, A., Arya, V., & Chui, K. T. (2023b). Machine Learning- Based DDoS Mitigation Framework for Unmanned Aerial Vehicles (UAV) Environment Using Software-Defined Networks (SDN). In *GLOBECOM 2023-2023 IEEE Global Com- munications Conference* (pp. 2178–2183). IEEE. 10.1109/GLOBECOM54140.2023.10437490

Gupta, B. B., Gaurav, A., Arya, V., & Kim, P. (2023c). "A Deep CNN-based Framework for Distributed Denial of Services (DDoS) Attack Detection in Internet of Things (IoT)." In *Proceedings of the 2023 International Conference on Research in Adaptive and Convergent Systems*, 1–6. 10.1145/3599957.3606239

Gupta, B. B., Gaurav, A., Chui, K. T., & Arya, V. (2023d). "Optimized Edge- cCCN Based Model for the Detection of DDoS Attack in IoT Environment." In *International Conference on Edge Computing*, 14–23. Springer.

Gupta, R., Kumari, A., & Tanwar, S. (2020). Fusion of blockchain and artificial intelligence for secure drone networking underlying 5g communications. *Transactions on Emerging Telecommunications Technologies*, 32(1), e4176. Advance online publication. 10.1002/ett.4176

Han, J., Yang, M., Chen, X., Liu, H., Wang, Y., Li, J., & Ma, X. (2022). Paradefender: A scenario-driven parallel system for defending metaverses. *IEEE Transactions on Systems, Man, and Cybernetics. Systems*, 53(4), 2118–2127.

Hazrati, M., Dara, R., & Kaur, J. (2022). On-farm data security: Practical recommendations for securing farm data. *Frontiers in Sustainable Food Systems*, 6, 884187. Advance online publication. 10.3389/fsufs.2022.884187

Huang, Y., Li, Y., & Cai, Z. (2023). Security and privacy in metaverse: A comprehensive survey. *Big Data Mining and Analytics*, 6(2), 234–247. 10.26599/BDMA.2022.9020047

Hulsen, T. (2024). Applications of the metaverse in medicine and healthcare. Advances in Laboratory Medicine/Avances en Medicina de Laboratorio, 5(2), 159-165.

Hutson, J., Banerjee, G., Kshetri, N., Odenwald, K., & Ratican, J. (2023). Architecting the metaverse: Blockchain and the financial and legal regulatory challenges of vir- tual real estate. *Journal of Intelligent Learning Systems and Applications*, 15(1), 1–23. 10.4236/jilsa.2023.151001

Huynh-The, T., Pham, Q. V., Pham, X. Q., Nguyen, T. T., Han, Z., & Kim, D. S. (2023). Artificial intelligence for the metaverse: A survey. *Engineering Applications of Artificial Intelligence*, 117, 105581.

Jaber, T. (2022). Security risks of the metaverse world. *International Journal of Interactive Mobile Technologies (Ijim)*, 16(13), 4–14. 10.3991/ijim.v16i13.33187

Kaa, G., Viardot, E., & McCarthy, I. (2022). Standardization for platform ecosystems. *Electronic Markets*, 32(4), 1807–1811. 10.1007/s12525-022-00611-6

Kabanda, G., Chipfumbu, C., & Chingoriwo, T. (2022). A cybersecurity model for a roblox- based metaverse architecture framework. *British Journal of Multidisciplinary and Advanced Studies*, 3(2), 105–141. 10.37745/bjmas.2022.0048

Kang, J., Ye, D., Nie, J., Xiao, J., Deng, X., Wang, S., & Niyato, D. (2022, August). Blockchain-based federated learning for industrial metaverses: Incentive scheme with optimal aoi. In *2022 IEEE International Conference on Blockchain (Blockchain)* (pp. 71-78). IEEE.

Kasiyanto, S., & Kilinc, M. (2022). Legal conundrums of the metaverse. *Journal of Central Banking Law and Institutions*, 1(2). Advance online publication. 10.21098/jcli.v1i2.25

Kim, M., Oh, J., Son, S., Park, Y., Kim, J., & Park, Y. (2023). Secure and privacy-preserving authentication scheme us- ing decentralized identifier in metaverse environment. *Electronics (Basel)*, 12(19), 4073. 10.3390/electronics12194073

Kumbhojkar, N. R., & Menon, A. B. (2022). Integrated predictive experience management framework (IPEMF) for improving customer experience: In the era of digital transformation. [IJCAC]. *International Journal of Cloud Applications and Computing*, 12(1), 1–13. 10.4018/IJCAC.2022010107

Law, K. M., Ip, A. W., Gupta, B. B., & Geng, S. (Eds.). (2021). *Managing IoT and mobile technologies with innovation, trust, and sustainable computing*. CRC Press.

Lebeck, K., Ruth, K., Kohno, T., & Roesner, F. (2018, May). Towards security and privacy for multi-user augmented reality: Foundations with end users. In *2018 IEEE Symposium on Security and Privacy (SP)* (pp. 392-408). IEEE.

Lee, M., & Chaney, D. (2023). The psychological and functional factors driving metaverse resistance. *Internet Research*, 34(1), 195–215. 10.1108/INTR-08-2022-0647

Li, P. (2024). "The impact of avatar identification on the attractiveness of vr games: the medi- ational role of immersion (preprint)." 10.2196/preprints.56704

Li, W., Wu, L., Xue, J., Hu, W., Li, S., Guo, G., & Cao, D. (2023). Intelligent cockpit for intelligent vehicle in metaverse: A case study of empathetic auditory regulation of hu- man emotion. *IEEE Transactions on Systems, Man, and Cybernetics. Systems*, 53(4), 2173–2187. 10.1109/TSMC.2022.3229021

Mishra, A., Gupta, N., & Gupta, B. B. (2023). Defensive mechanism against DDoS attack based on feature selection and multi-classifier algorithms. *Telecommunication Systems*, 82(2), 229–244. 10.1007/s11235-022-00981-4

Natarajan, T., Pragha, P., Dhalmahapatra, K., & Veera Raghavan, D. R. (2024). Unveiling metaverse sentiments using machine learning approaches. *Kybernetes*. Advance online publication. 10.1108/K-11-2023-2268

Nebbione, G., & Calzarossa, M. (2023). A methodological framework for ai-assisted security assessments of active directory environments. *IEEE Access : Practical Innovations, Open Solutions*, 11, 15119–15130. 10.1109/ACCESS.2023.3244490

Nleya, S. M., & Velempini, M. (2024). Industrial Metaverse: A Comprehensive Review, Environmental Impact, and Challenges. *Applied Sciences (Basel, Switzerland)*, 14(13), 5736.

Otoum, Y., Gottimukkala, N., Kumar, N., & Nayak, A. (2024). Machine learning in metaverse security: Current solutions and future chal- lenges. *ACM Computing Surveys*, 56(8), 1–36. 10.1145/3654663

Pan, W., Li, W., & Zhao, W. (2009, November). A Novel Anomaly Detection Approach for Executable Program Security. In *2009 International Conference on Multimedia Information Networking and Security* (Vol. 1, pp. 422-426). IEEE.

Papagiannidis, S., Bourlakis, M., & Li, F. (2008). Making real money in virtual worlds: Mmorpgs and emerging business opportunities, challenges and ethical im- plications in metaverses. *Technological Forecasting and Social Change*, 75(5), 610–622. 10.1016/j.techfore.2007.04.007

Park, W., Siddiqui, I., & Qureshi, N. (2022). Ai-enabled grouping bridgehead to se- cure penetration topics of metaverse. *Computers, Materials & Continua*, 73(3), 5609–5624. 10.32604/cmc.2022.030235

Patwe, S., & Mane, S. B. (2024). Blockchain-enabled secure and interoperable authentication scheme for meta- verse environments. *Future Internet*, 16(5), 166. 10.3390/fi16050166

Protogerou, A., Kopsacheilis, E., Mpatziakas, A., Papachristou, K., Theodorou, T., Papadopoulos, S., Drosou, A., & Tzovaras, D. (2022). Time series network data enabling distributed intelligence—A holistic iot security platform solution. *Electronics (Basel)*, 11(4), 529. 10.3390/electronics11040529

Ryu, J., Son, S., Lee, J., Park, Y., & Park, Y. (2022). Design of secure mutual authentication scheme for metaverse environments using blockchain. *IEEE Access : Practical Innovations, Open Solutions*, 10, 98944–98958. 10.1109/ACCESS.2022.3206457

Salah, K., Rehman, M., Nizamuddin, N., & Al-Fuqaha, A. (2019). Blockchain for ai: Review and open research challenges. *IEEE Access : Practical Innovations, Open Solutions*, 7, 10127–10149. 10.1109/ACCESS.2018.2890507

Sanghvi, H., Bhavsar, R., Hundlani, V., Gohil, L., Vyas, T., Nair, A., Desai, S., Jadav, N. K., Tanwar, S., Sharma, R., & Yamsani, N. (2023). metahate: Ai-based hate speech detection for secured online gaming in metaverse using blockchain. *Security and Privacy*, 7(2), e343. Advance online publication. 10.1002/spy2.343

Saurabh, P., & Verma, B. (2014). A novel immunity inspired approach for anomaly detection. *International Journal of Computer Applications*, 94(15), 14–19. 10.5120/16418-6034

Sebastian, G. (2022). A descriptive study on metaverse. *International Journal of Security and Privacy in Pervasive Computing*, 15(1), 1–14. 10.4018/IJSPPC.315591

Sethi, A. (2022). *Security and Privacy in Metaverse: Issues, Challenges, and Future Op- portunities*. Cyber Security Insights Magazine.

Setia, H., Chhabra, A., Singh, S. K., Kumar, S., Sharma, S., Arya, V., & Wu, J. (2024). Securing the road ahead: Machine learning-driven DDoS attack detection in VANET cloud environments. *Cyber Security and Applications*, 2, 100037.

Shafik, W. (2024). Predicting future cybercrime trends in the metaverse era. In *Forecasting cyber crimes in the age of the metaverse* (pp. 78–113). IGI Global.

Sinha, K. (2023). The Metaverse and Digital Libraries: Ensuring Safe and Secure Access to Information. In Handbook of Research on Advancements of Contactless Technology and Service Innovation in Library and Information Science (pp. 1-22). IGI Global.

Siriwardhana, Y., Porambage, P., Liyanage, M., & Ylianttila, M. (2021, June). AI and 6G security: Opportunities and challenges. In 2021 Joint European Conference on Networks and Communications & 6G Summit (EuCNC/6G Summit) (pp. 616-621). IEEE.

Tao, B., Dai, H. N., Xie, H., & Wang, F. L. (2023). Structural identity representation learning for blockchain-enabled metaverse based on complex network analysis. *IEEE Transactions on Computational Social Systems*, 10(5), 2214–2225.

Truong, V. T., Le, L., & Niyato, D. (2023). Blockchain meets metaverse and digital asset management: A comprehensive survey. *IEEE Access : Practical Innovations, Open Solutions*, 11, 26258–26288.

Tukur, M., Schneider, J., Househ, M., Dokoro, A. H., Ismail, U. I., Dawaki, M., & Agus, M. (2023). The metaverse digital environments: A scoping review of the challenges, privacy and security issues. *Frontiers in Big Data*, 6, 1301812. Advance online publication. 10.3389/fdata.2023.130181238074486

Turner, S., Karakus, M., Guler, E., & Uludag, S. (2023). A promising integration of sdn and blockchain for iot networks: A survey. *IEEE Access : Practical Innovations, Open Solutions*, 11, 29800–29822. 10.1109/ACCESS.2023.3260777

Upadhyay, U., Kumar, A., Sharma, G., Saini, A. K., Arya, V., Gaurav, A., & Chui, K. T. (2023). Mitigating risks in the cloud-based metaverse access control strategies and techniques. *International Journal of Cloud Applications and Computing*, 14(1), 1–30. 10.4018/IJCAC.334364

Venugopal, J., Subramanian, A., & Peatchimuthu, J. (2023). The realm of metaverse: A sur- vey. *Computer Animation and Virtual Worlds*, 34(5), e2150. Advance online publication. 10.1002/cav.2150

Wang, G., Badal, A., Jia, X., Maltz, J., Mueller, K., Myers, K., Niu, C., Vannier, M., Yan, P., Yu, Z., & Zeng, R. (2022a). Devel- opment of metaverse for intelligent healthcare. *Nature Machine Intelligence*, 4(11), 922–929. 10.1038/s42256-022-00549-636935774

Wang, W., Abbasi, O., Yanikomeroglu, H., Liang, C., Tang, L., & Chen, Q. (2022b). "Vhet- nets for ai and ai for vhetnets: an anomaly detection case study for ubiquitous iot." https://doi.org//arxiv.2210.08132.10.48550

Wang, Y., Su, Z., & Yan, M. (2023). Social metaverse: Challenges and solutions. *IEEE Internet of Things Magazine*, 6(3), 144–150.

Wang, Y., Su, Z., Zhang, N., Xing, R., Liu, D., Luan, T., & Shen, X. (2023). A survey on metaverse: Fundamentals, security, and privacy. *IEEE Communications Surveys and Tutorials*, 25(1), 319–352. 10.1109/COMST.2022.3202047

Wang, Y., Su, Z., Zhang, N., Xing, R., Liu, D., Luan, T. H., & Shen, X. (2022). A survey on metaverse: Fundamentals, security, and privacy. *IEEE Communications Surveys and Tutorials*, 25(1), 319–352.

Xu, H., Li, Z., Li, Z., Zhang, X., Sun, Y., & Zhang, L. (2022a). Metaverse native communication: A blockchain and spectrum prospective. In 2022 IEEE International Conference on Communications Workshops (ICC Workshops) (pp. 7-12). IEEE.

Xu, M., Ng, W. C., Lim, W. Y. B., Kang, J., Xiong, Z., Niyato, D., & Miao, C. (2022b). A full dive into realizing the edge-enabled metaverse: Visions, enabling technologies, and challenges. *IEEE Communications Surveys and Tutorials*, 25(1), 656–700.

Yang, K. 2023. "The future of the "metaverse": artificial intelligence and cybersecurity." 1627– 1632. $_2$46.10.2991/978-94-6463-040-4

Yang, Q., Zhao, Y., Huang, H., Xiong, Z., Kang, J., & Zheng, Z. (2022). Fusing blockchain and AI with metaverse: A survey. *IEEE Open Journal of the Computer Society*, 3, 122–136.

Zhang, H., Lee, S., Lu, Y., Yu, X., & Lu, H. (2022). A survey on big data technologies and their applications to the metaverse: Past, current and future. *Mathematics*, 11(1), 96. 10.3390/math11010096

Zhang, L., Du, Q., Lu, L., & Zhang, S. (2023). Overview of the integration of communications, sensing, computing, and storage as enabling technologies for the metaverse over 6g networks. *Electronics (Basel)*, 12(17), 3651. 10.3390/electronics12173651

Zhao, H., Zhao, J., Liu, W., Yan, Y., Huang, J., & Wen, F. (2023). Metaverse-based decentralised autonomous organisation in energy systems. *Energy Conversion and Economics*, 4(6), 379–386. 10.1049/enc2.12104

Zhou, Zhili, & Gaurav, Akshat, BB Gupta, Hedi Hamdi, and Nadia Nedjah. (2021). A statistical approach to secure health care services from DDoS attacks during COVID-19 pandemic. *Neural Computing & Applications*, 1–14.34511731

Chapter 11
Exploring Security and Privacy Challenges for Banks in the Evolving Landscape of the Metaverse

Mushtaq Ahmad Shah
https://orcid.org/0000-0002-3177-9622
Lovely Professional University, India

Furquan Uddin
https://orcid.org/0000-0001-6502-8854
Aliah University, India

ABSTRACT

The metaverse presents an unprecedented opportunity for banks to innovate and transform their services, offering immersive and interactive experiences to customers. However, this virtual frontier comes with a myriad of security challenges that must be meticulously addressed to safeguard sensitive information, prevent fraud, and ensure regulatory compliance. This chapter explores the transformative potential of the metaverse for banking and examines the key security challenges such as data breaches, cybersecurity threats and virtual property theft. It presents comprehensive strategies to address these issues, including robust encryption, multi-factor authentication, blockchain technology, and user education. By implementing these measures, banks can ensure a secure, resilient virtual banking environment, safeguarding sensitive information and maintaining regulatory compliance. The chapter emphasizes the importance of continuous monitoring and proactive security

DOI: 10.4018/979-8-3693-3824-7.ch011

practices in navigating the evolving digital landscape.

INTRODUCTION

Banks and other financial institutions have a huge opportunity to invest and participate in the metaverse. As per a McKinsey June 2022 report, with an estimated economic impact of around $5 trillion by 2030 for consumer and enterprise use cases, the metaverse has a tremendous potential to impact our commercial and personal lives (Sachdeva, 2023). Metaverse presents a dramatic shift in virtual interactions for individuals and organisations, including banks, and presents several opportunities and difficulties (Rosário, Lopes and Rosário 2023). The Metaverse provides great prospects for the banking sector, but it also represents significant obstacles, particularly in terms of security and privacy (Lyoussi and Kouchih, 2023). In the Metaverse, user identity authentication and compliance with Know Your Customer (KYC) regulations are complex since avatars and pseudonymous profiles are so widely used (Tan et al., 2023). This complexity stems from the immersive and interactive nature of the Metaverse, where users engage through virtual representations rather than real identities, raising concerns about verifying individuals' true identities and ensuring regulatory compliance in financial transactions (Huang & Cai 2023). Addressing these challenges necessitates innovative solutions that balance user privacy and security with regulatory requirements, highlighting the need for robust authentication mechanisms and enhanced KYC protocols tailored to the unique characteristics of the Metaverse. Data privacy and ownership are the critical issues within the Metaverse (Far & Rad, 2022). The virtual environment generates vast amounts of data, raising significant concerns about who owns this data and how it is managed. Currently, there is a lack of clear frameworks for data ownership and transparent privacy policies, leading to potential misuse and user mistrust. The significance of transparency in building trust is underscored, with technical developments like solid personal datastores offering a platform for negotiating privacy terms and enhancing transparency in data processing (Esteves et al., 2022). Addressing this gap involves implementing decentralized data storage solutions and developing comprehensive data privacy laws that ensure users have control over their personal information. Cybersecurity is another major concern as the metaverse is vulnerable to various threats, including data breaches, virtual asset theft, and malicious avatar behaviour such as harassment (Pooyandeh, Han & Sohn 2022). The current state of cybersecurity in the metaverse reveals inadequacies in proactive measures and real-time monitoring systems to detect and prevent these threats. Therefore, establishing advanced security protocols, conducting regular security audits, and deploying AI-driven threat detection systems are essential steps to safeguard virtual environments.

The decentralized and global nature of the metaverse further complicates regulatory compliance, as financial institutions must navigate varying international regulations. The absence of standardized regulatory frameworks across different jurisdictions creates challenges for banks operating in the Metaverse (Pandey & Gilmour 2024). Ethical considerations also play a crucial role in the Metaverse. The immersive nature of this virtual space raises ethical questions related to user behaviour, financial interactions, and the potential for addiction or manipulation. Currently, ethical guidelines and mechanisms to address predatory practices and ensure fair treatment are underdeveloped. Banks must develop and enforce ethical standards, offer clear terms and conditions, and provide robust dispute resolution mechanisms to protect users and maintain trust (Ionaşcu, Barbu & Popa 2023). There is a lack of comprehensive understanding of how traditional banking principles translate into the Metaverse, and inadequate frameworks for identity verification and privacy management in a decentralized virtual space. Empirically, there is limited research on the efficacy of current security and privacy measures in the metaverse, and various strategies to mitigate virtual banking security and privacy is sparse.

This chapter explores the transformative potential of the metaverse for banking and critically assess the security and privacy frameworks for banking in the metaverse, ensuring client trust and regulatory compliance, highlighting key security challenges such as data breaches, identity theft, and virtual property theft. As banks embrace the opportunities presented by the Metaverse, prioritizing security and privacy is essential for building trust, fostering innovation, and ensuring the long-term success of virtual banking services.

BACKGROUND OF THE STUDY

When Facebook renamed its corporate identity to Meta in October 2021 and announced intentions to invest at least $10 billion in the concept that year, Metaverse became a household term (Cheng, 2023). Google, Microsoft, Nvidia, and Qualcomm, in addition to Meta, are investing billions of dollars in the concept. McKinsey & Company, a management consulting firm, has optimistically forecast that the metaverse economy might reach $5 trillion by 2030. In addition to e-commerce, gaming, recreation, academia, and marketing are anticipated to become significant areas in the metaverse. For Stephenson's “metaverse” notion to become a reality, technology played the most significant role. The section (see figure 1) discusses the emerging technologies in the creation and development of the metaverse.

Machine learning: Using facial recognition technology that captures the face of a real-world user and integrates it into a virtual avatar that resembles the physical person, Metaverse avatars are generated from real users. This type of technology is a component of Machine Learning (ML). ML is a crucial discipline in artificial intelligence (AI) that enables the computer to effectively anticipate the outcomes of future events based on its trial-and-error experience with past occurrences (Dogan & Birant, 2021). Integration of ML in Metaverse apps is vital for preserving the comfort of the user's experience of the Metaverse application by enabling the machine to properly forecast and execute various difficult activities for users to aid them in making decisions in the virtual world.

Blockchain: As a technological, digitalization is vital to the metaverse. Blockchain technology incorporates various functions in the metaverse including computerized property verification, operations in assets, "affordability and information sharing" (Ali et al., 2022). Blockchain offers comprehensive transaction audit trails, enabling people and organisations to confirm all transactions (Xiong et al., 2022). This will improve the quality of data within the metaverse.

Cryptocurrency: Digital currencies, often known as virtual currencies, are an alternative form of currency based on encryption technology. Using encryption technology, cryptocurrencies serve both as a medium of commerce and a virtual accounting system. Bitcoin is the most widely recognised cryptocurrency. The introduction of Bitcoin spawned other alternative cryptocurrencies, such as Ethereum, NFTs, Dollar coins, etc., which may be integrated with other technologies like Metaverse (Park & Seo, 2022).

Figure 1. Metaverse Transformers

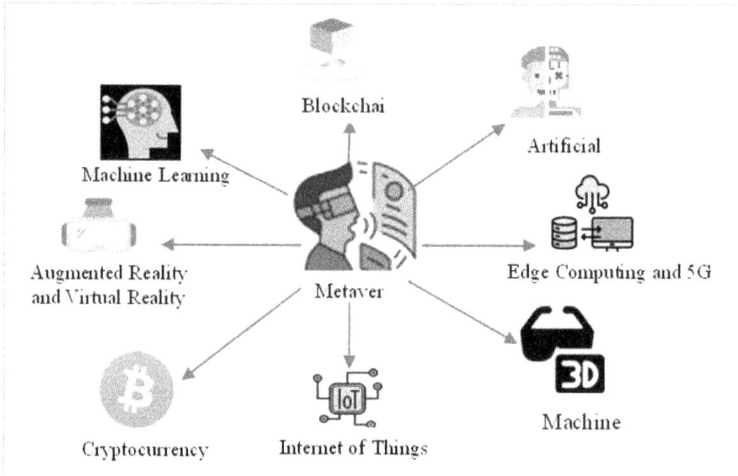

Source: Authors' Compilation

Augmented Reality and Virtual Reality: Technologies such as artificial intelligence (AI), augmented reality (AR), and virtual reality (VR) have strong connections to the notion of the metaverse (VR) (Mystakidis, 2022). Using the technology known as augmented reality, it is possible to integrate virtual things into the actual world. The VR technology facilitates the viewing of 3D simulations. AR technology, on the other hand, enables people to experience things through the creation of physical simulations. It assists users in hearing, sensing, and interacting with the metaverse.

Artificial Intelligence: Smart glasses and AI identify photos, detect faces, analyse data, and recognise voice in the Metaverse. Most augmented reality systems use vision. Marker-based, marker-less, and non-visual AR systems differs by registration technique. These systems use HMDs (Daşdemir 2022). This technique enhances metaverse immersion. It speeds up processing, decision-making, and the user experience. Several games and services use it for non-player characters. AI and Metaverse technologies provide Metaverse infrastructure stability and offer actionable data to highest levels. AI will be crucial to the development of Metaverse social places like NVIDIA technologies.

3D Reconstruction: This technology uses sophisticated 3D cameras and other reconstruction tools to construct realistic prototypes. For real-world structures, objects, and environments, we may use 3D reconstruction techniques to generate digital twins in the metaverse (Ma & Liu 2018). Users may construct 3D models using 3D modelling software such as 3ds Max10, Blender11, or Maya12; however, these modelling systems rely heavily on professional 3D modelling is a computer graphics approach for creating a digital three-dimensional representation of any surface or object. The 3D realism of the Metaverse is vital for the continued satisfaction of its clients. A 3D world requires a substantial amount of image collecting and visual design. In the majority of games similar to The Sandbox (SAND), the 3D graphics give the illusion that the player is actively participating in the game. The Metaverse must be built on the same foundation.

Internet of Things (IoT): represents the network of physical items, things, equipped with sensors, software, and other technologies to communicate and exchange data over the Internet ITU (2015). This technology links gadgets and sensors to the internet to collect user data (Shah, & Khang 2023). AI and machine learning can optimise the metaverse using device data to improve user experience. IoT will allow the Metaverse to study and interact with the actual world and serve as a 3D user interface for IoT devices, making them more customised. The Metaverse and Internet of Things will let enterprises make data-driven decisions quickly.

Edge Computing and 5G: Edge computing promotes quicker data transport with less latency (Xiang & Zhang 2022). Consequently, computers are able to efficiently manage intensive simulations. This lowers latency and an immersive experience is ensured in the metaverse. 5G technology has the ability to reduce the cost of utilising the metaverse.

Metaverse Market Size Projection

There is a significant increase in metaverse market size over the decade, reflecting the anticipated growth and investment in metaverse technologies and applications.

Figure 2. Metaverse Market Size (Billion USD)

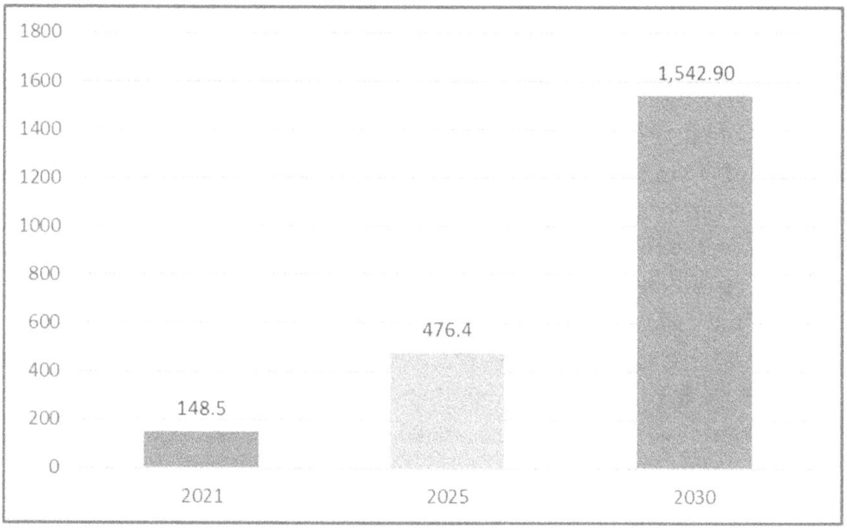

The figure 2 above illustrated the substantial projected increase in the size of the metaverse market over the next decade. Starting at $148.5 billion in 2021, the market is expected to more than triple to $476.4 billion by 2025. This growth trajectory continues exponentially, with the market size anticipated to reach $1,542.9 billion by 2030. The dramatic rise in market size reflects the increasing interest and investment in metaverse technologies, which encompass virtual and augmented reality, digital economies, and immersive online experiences. This growth is indicative of the expanding role of the metaverse in various sectors, including gaming, social media, e-commerce, and remote work, highlighting its potential to significantly influence the future digital landscape.

Metaverses incorporate virtual reality, augmented reality, and other immersive technologies as applications. The major income sources for metaverses are e-commerce and gaming. In addition, metaverses provide new revenue-generation potential in the education, recreation, health and fitness, and even telecommuting industries.

Figure 3. Global Metaverse Income

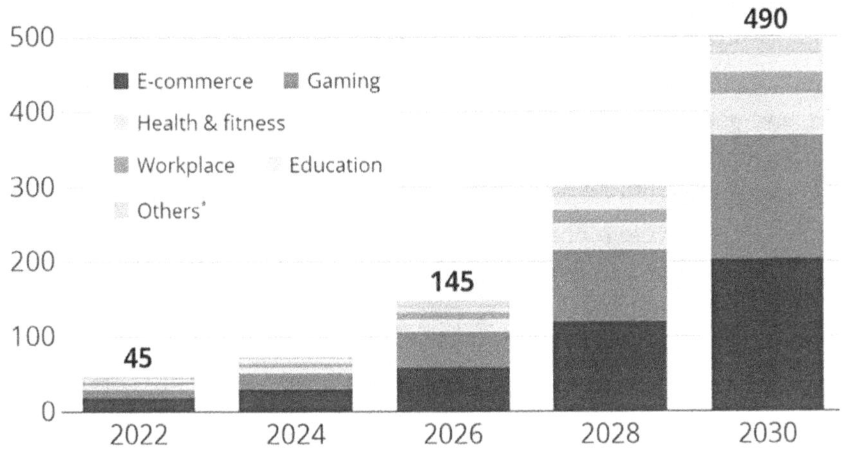

**Virtual Assets, adertising, AR & VR hardware, digital media*
Source: Statista Advertising & Media Markets Insights

Advertising & Media Markets Data from Statista projects that global metaverse income will reach $490 billion by 2030 figure 3. This forecast is rather cautious. Some analysis firms estimate a market volume of between 750 and 1,700 billion U.S. dollars. Metaverse e-commerce sales alone might surpass $200 billion by 2030, up from the current $20 billion. The gaming industry is anticipated to increase even further, from around $10 billion currently to over $163 billion by 2030. The next largest revenue-generating uses for the metaverse are health & fitness, the workplace, and education.

Evolution Phases of Metaverse Bank

The banking industry has indeed experienced a remarkable evolution from traditional brick-and-mortar setups to innovative digital-first experiences, driven by the rapid growth of digitalization (Rathnayake, 2023). This shift has been facilitated by the adoption of digital banking (DB) innovations, transforming traditional banking activities into a digital environment (Dutta et al., 2022). This evolution can be categorized into several distinct phases, each marked by its own unique characteristics and advancements. In this section a detailed explanation of these banking models is discussed

Traditional Banking Traditional banking forms the foundation of the banking sector, characterized by personal touch and direct customer engagement (Chiorazzo et al., 2018). While it ensures trust and relationship building, it often lacks the flexibility and convenience demanded by modern customers. Traditional banking primarily focuses on personal, face-to-face interactions between customers and bank staff. This model heavily relies on physical branches where customers can perform transactions, seek advice, and resolve issues. Services are generally standardized with limited customization options. The products and services offered are relatively uniform, and personalized banking solutions are not commonly available. Many processes in traditional banking involve paper-based transactions, including checks, receipts, and application forms, which can be time-consuming and less efficient. Banking services are often limited to branch operating hours, restricting customer access to financial services outside of these times (Colombo, 2017).

Internet Banking: Internet banking marks the beginning of digital transformation in banking. It offers increased accessibility and convenience, reducing the need for physical branch visits and catering to a growing demand for online services. Internet banking revolutionizes the customer experience by enabling access to banking services through digital channels such as mobile phones and computers. Customers can perform transactions, check balances, and manage accounts online without visiting a branch. The focus shifts to creating a seamless digital experience, prioritizing convenience and speed. The customer journey is redesigned to be intuitive and user-friendly, catering to the tech-savvy generation. Internet banking incorporates advanced security features, such as two-factor authentication, encryption, and secure login procedures to protect customer information and transactions. Internet banking offers round-the-clock access to financial services, allowing customers to conduct transactions and access their accounts at any time (Shah et al., 2024).

Open Banking: Open banking represents a significant shift towards interoperability and collaboration in the financial sector (Gozman, Hedman, & Sylvest 2018). By leveraging APIs, banks can offer enhanced services and foster innovation, providing customers with more choices and better experiences. Open banking allows banks to connect with third-party applications through Application Programming Interfaces (APIs). This connectivity fosters innovation and the development of new services, providing customers with a broader range of financial tools.

Table 1. Metaverse Bank Evolution and Key Characteristics

Banking Model	Key Characteristics
Traditional Banking	Reliance on one-on-one customer interactions
	Absence of customizations
	Paper-based processes
	Limited accessibility

continued on following page

Table 1. Continued

Banking Model	Key Characteristics
Internet Banking	Processes accessed through mobile & internet
	New digital-first customer journey
	Enhanced security measures
	24/7 availability
Open Banking	Connectivity with third-party apps through APIs
	Rise of neo-banks, digital-only banks
	Customer data portability
	Increased competition
Digitalized Finance Banking	Advent of Web3 for a secure & fast banking economy
	New assets in the financial market like art and gaming
	Smart contracts for automation
	Decentralized finance (DeFi)
Metaverse in Banking	Rise in virtual banking experience
	New marketing & revenue models
	Enhanced customer engagement
	Integration with digital currencies

Source: Authors' Compilation

The dawn of open banking gives rise to neo-banks, which operate exclusively online without any physical branches. These digital-only banks offer innovative services, often with better rates and lower fees compared to traditional banks. Customers can easily transfer their financial data between different banking service providers, enabling them to access better deals and more personalized services. Open banking fosters a more competitive market, encouraging traditional banks to innovate and improve their services to retain customers (Schneider, 2023).

Digitalized Finance Banking. Digitalized finance banking leverages cutting-edge technologies to create a more secure and efficient banking ecosystem. The inclusion of new asset classes reflects the evolving nature of investments and the financial market, catering to diverse customer interests. The integration of Web3 technologies, such as blockchain, enhances security, transparency, and speed in banking transactions. This technology enables decentralized financial systems, reducing reliance on traditional banking infrastructure. Digitalized finance expands the range of financial assets, incorporating digital and tokenized assets such as NFTs (Non-Fungible Tokens) in art and gaming. This diversification offers new investment opportunities and markets. The use of smart contracts allows for automated, self-executing contracts with the terms directly written into code, reducing the need for intermediaries and increasing efficiency (Nzuva, 2019). DeFi platforms enable users to access financial services such as lending, borrowing, and trading without traditional banks, using decentralized technology and protocols.

Metaverse in Banking: The integration of the metaverse in banking signifies the future of financial services, combining virtual experiences with traditional banking operations. This model provides new opportunities for customer engagement and revenue generation, positioning banks at the forefront of technological innovation (Dubey et al., 2022). The metaverse introduces a virtual dimension to banking, offering immersive experiences through virtual reality (VR) and augmented reality (AR). Customers can interact with bank representatives and services in a virtual environment. The metaverse opens up novel avenues for marketing and revenue generation. Banks can create virtual branches, host events, and offer unique digital products, engaging customers in innovative ways. Virtual environments allow for more interactive and engaging customer experiences, with personalized avatars and virtual assistance enhancing customer service (Basheer et al., 2023). The metaverse often integrates with digital currencies and cryptocurrencies, enabling seamless transactions within virtual environments and expanding financial services into new digital realms.

Cyber security concerns surrounding the metaverse

While the virtual platform promises to offer a plethora of opportunities for businesses to transform the way they operate, we cannot discuss the metaverse without addressing or including cyber security challenges. Although most of these threats are very similar to the ones we encounter on the internet today, tackling these problems in a virtual environment is an additional headache for many organisations. Some of the main issues that businesses could potentially encounter within this virtual space include:

Security challenges concerning currency exchanges: Much like the multiple national currencies that already exist in the real world, the metaverse will use its own currency or cryptocurrency. While crypto as a digital currency is set to develop over time, it could also lead to significant increase in "money laundering" attempts within the metaverse's virtual economy (Campbell 2018). As these digital currencies are set to evolve, uncertainties surrounding their transferability from one metaverse to another and a lack of provision for secure exchanges between buyers and sellers could lead to the exploitation of the newly developed financial system by threat actors.

Increase in scams and other fraudulent activities: At present, the metaverse poses significant security challenges as most of its user's value interconnectivity and their user experience over intrusive online safety measures (Saracoglu, 2023). This could exacerbate the security concerns or privacy issues that already exist within social media. Considering the inherent challenges imposed by web domains to govern or control areas beyond traditional national borders, the metaverse could also present itself as an unregulated environment to cyber criminals. Not having proper measures in place to protect the safety of its users means that it could become increasingly difficult for one to identify or recognise scammers or hackers who may use this as an opportunity to impersonate other entities or individuals.

Safeguarding young users or new generations of digital natives: As with online games, the metaverse's virtual environment is set to become very popular among children or young digital natives, who are also prone to being victimised by abusers and scammers present within these digital communities. In fact, a recent investigation conducted by BBC News found that the virtual design of the metaverse allows children to be easily exposed to racial abuse and sexual harassment. Although most of these virtual platforms are supposedly age restricted to prevent children from using it without adult supervision, it does not stop them from joining virtual worlds for shopping or entertainment. As applications are created to offer a real-life experience to their users Wang (2023), they also hold the potential to inflict emotional trauma amongst children by exposing them to grooming and other harmful experiences.

Challenges of banking in the metaverse

The topmost concerns for banks in the metaverse revolve around security, privacy, governance, and regulations (Huang, Li, & Cai 2023). Infosys research reveals this, with 55% of banks citing security and privacy as a key challenge, 47% citing governance, and 41% mentioning authentication and identity management. While none of the above are related only to banking, these are highly concerning for financial institutions. This is owing to the extreme caution needed when capturing, managing, and securing sensitive financial customer data

Transactions in the metaverse are facilitated largely by cryptocurrencies and NFTs. First, crypto wallets must be financed by fiat currencies, which are highly regulated. However, crypto regulations are still nascent, posing several security risks. Meta-banking customers often fear theft or devaluation of their cryptocurrency due to scams and crypto-volatility. Meta-avatars are twins of real users who may use biometric devices to mimic their faces along with tactile gloves for sensory feedback. While these devices certainly enhance the customer experience, they also help authenticate the identity of meta-avatars during banking transactions. Without rigorous identity authentication, banks are susceptible to bad actors posing as genuine customers to conduct fraud, scams, and money laundering. However, biometric devices present their own challenges, namely data ownership. It is vital to establish trusted entities to handle and govern such biometric data in order to prevent unfair monopolisation or unauthorised monetisation through data mining. Data privacy rules over ownership of such customer data must also be well-defined. This section outlines the various security and privacy challenges (see figure 4) present in the metaverse and corresponding strategies to address these challenges, ensuring a safer and more trustworthy virtual environment.

Data Breaches: Data breaches are a significant concern in the metaverse, where vast amounts of personal and financial information are stored and exchanged. Breaches can result from vulnerabilities in virtual platforms, leading to unauthorized access and potential identity theft (Zhang, & Smith, 2023). The impact of a data breach can be severe, including financial loss, reputational damage, and legal consequences. To mitigate this risk, it is crucial to implement robust encryption methods, conduct regular security audits, and employ strict access controls. Platforms must prioritize data security to maintain user trust and comply with regulatory requirements, ensuring that sensitive information is protected from unauthorized access (Adams, 2023).

Identity Theft: In the metaverse, identity theft involves the unauthorized use of a person's digital identity or avatar. This can lead to significant consequences, such as financial fraud and reputational damage (Elshenraki, 2023). As users create and interact with digital personas, the risk of identity theft increases. Advanced authentication measures, including multi-factor authentication and biometric verification, are essential to safeguard virtual identities (Zhang & Smith 2023). Additionally, platforms should educate users about the importance of protecting their digital identities and the potential risks of identity theft, fostering a secure virtual environment.

Figure 4. Impediments to banking in the metaverse

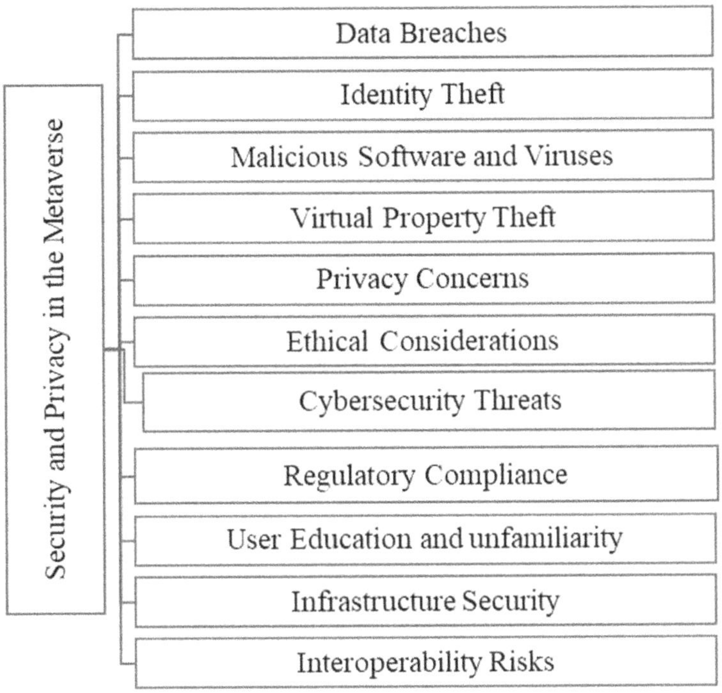

Malicious Software and Viruses: The metaverse, like the real world, is susceptible to malicious software and viruses. These threats can infiltrate virtual environments through seemingly harmless links or files, compromising digital devices and personal information (Saharan, et al., 2024). To combat these risks, users should employ reliable security software and remain vigilant about potential threats. Platforms must implement stringent security measures, such as regular updates and patches, to protect against malware and viruses. Educating users about safe practices, such as avoiding suspicious links and downloads, is also crucial in mitigating these threats.

Virtual Property Theft: Virtual property theft in the metaverse involves the unauthorized acquisition of virtual assets, such as real estate, items, or currency. This theft can occur due to vulnerabilities in the system or inadequate security measures (Adams, 2023). To prevent virtual property theft, users should secure their virtual assets with strong passwords and utilize platforms that implement reliable security protocols. Additionally, platforms should continuously update their security measures to address emerging threats and protect users' virtual assets. Educating users about the importance of securing their virtual property can also help mitigate the risk of theft.

Privacy Concerns: Privacy concerns in the metaverse stem from the collection and sharing of user data for purposes such as targeted advertising and user profiling. This can compromise user privacy and lead to unauthorized use of personal information (Huang & Cai 2023). Understanding and utilizing platform privacy policies and settings is crucial for protecting user privacy. Platforms must prioritize data protection by ensuring transparency in data collection practices and providing users with control over their personal information. Implementing robust privacy measures and educating users about data protection can help address these concerns.

Ethical Considerations: Ethical considerations in the metaverse encompass issues such as digital rights, inclusivity, accessibility, virtual harassment, algorithmic bias, and data protection (Zhang & Smith 2023). Ensuring ethical standards in the metaverse is essential to create a safe and supportive environment for all users. Platforms should implement robust moderation systems to address virtual harassment and cyberbullying. Promoting inclusivity and accessibility by offering customization options and support for diverse needs can enhance the user experience. Addressing algorithmic bias and ensuring transparency in data handling are also crucial ethical considerations in the metaverse.

User Education and Unfamiliarity: Many users in the metaverse may not fully understand the security risks and protection measures associated with virtual environments. Lack of user education can lead to increased vulnerability to threats such as identity theft and data breaches. Developing comprehensive user education programs is essential to raise awareness about potential threats and promote best practices for safeguarding personal and financial information. Platforms should provide resources and training to help users understand the importance of security measures and how to protect themselves in the metaverse.

Infrastructure Security: Infrastructure security plays a crucial role in ensuring the safe operation of metaverse platforms. The metaverse, as an emerging paradigm of the next-generation Internet, relies on a robust infrastructure to support its immersive and interactive nature (Liu et al., 2023). Infrastructure security is fundamental to the secure operation of metaverse platforms. Vulnerabilities in the underlying infrastructure, including servers and networks, can lead to widespread service outages, data loss, and increased risks of attacks. To maintain a secure infrastructure, platforms should invest in advanced security solutions and conduct regular vulnerability assessments. Fortifying infrastructure against potential attacks and breaches is crucial to ensure the stability and security of metaverse environments. Continuous monitoring and updating of security measures can help address emerging threats and protect the infrastructure.

Interoperability Risks: Interoperability risks arise from the integration of multiple platforms and systems within the metaverse. Ensuring secure interoperability while maintaining data integrity and security is challenging but essential (Blessing

& Anderson 2023). Poorly managed interoperability can introduce vulnerabilities, making it easier for attackers to exploit weaknesses across interconnected systems. Establishing strict security standards and protocols for interoperability is vital to mitigating these risks. Platforms should collaborate to develop secure integration methods and ensure that data is protected during interactions between different systems.

Cybersecurity Threats: The cybersecurity threat landscape in the metaverse is vast and evolving (Chow et al., 2022). As an emerging platform, the metaverse is an attractive target for cybercriminals who exploit its novelty and potential for high-value transactions. Phishing, malware, and ransomware attacks are prevalent, requiring banks and platforms to deploy advanced threat detection and response systems. Continuous monitoring and updating of cybersecurity measures are crucial in protecting against financial losses, operational disruptions, and loss of customer trust. Platforms should invest in advanced cybersecurity technologies to address these evolving threats.

Regulatory Compliance: Regulatory compliance in the metaverse is complex due to the nascent state of regulations governing virtual environments. Existing financial regulations may not fully address the unique aspects of metaverse banking, leading to potential legal challenges. Banks and platforms must engage proactively with regulatory bodies to develop and adhere to new guidelines that ensure compliance and protect against legal penalties and fines. Ensuring comprehensive regulatory compliance is essential to maintain trust and integrity in the metaverse. Platforms should stay updated with regulatory changes and implement necessary measures to comply with evolving regulations (Cherif et al., 2023)

Insecure Transactions: Insecure transactions within the metaverse involve the use of digital currencies and assets, which necessitate robust encryption and secure payment gateways. Insecure transactions can lead to financial fraud and loss of funds, compromising the integrity of the banking system (Adams, 2023). Banks and platforms must adopt secure blockchain technologies and develop reliable payment solutions to facilitate safe and seamless transactions. Ensuring robust encryption for transactions and continuously monitoring for potential vulnerabilities can help protect against financial fraud. Educating users about secure transaction practices is also crucial to prevent insecure transactions.

Strategies for Addressing Metaverse Security Challenges Faced by Banks

Addressing the wide range of security challenges in the metaverse requires banks to adopt a complex and proactive strategy. Firstly, ensuring robust encryption and secure data management practices is essential to protect sensitive information within virtual environments.

Robust encryption is essential for ensuring the confidentiality and integrity in metaverse, especially for banks that handle sensitive financial information. Implementing end-to-end encryption (E2EE) means that data is encrypted on the sender's device and only decrypted on the recipient's device, preventing unauthorized access during transmission. Banks should use advanced encryption standards like AES-256, which is widely regarded as unbreakable with current technology. This encryption should be applied to all data, including transaction details, personal information, and communication between users and banking platforms. To implement robust encryption, banks must establish comprehensive encryption protocols and policies. This includes encrypting data both at rest and in transit. Data at rest encryption involves securing data stored on servers and databases using encryption keys managed through a hardware security module (HSM). Data in transit encryption ensures that data exchanged over networks is protected, using protocols like TLS (Transport Layer Security) to encrypt data during transmission. Regularly updating encryption keys and conducting encryption audits are also critical practices to maintain security. Additionally, banks should educate their employees about the importance of encryption and proper handling of encrypted data to prevent accidental breaches

In Addition to robust encryption, Multi-Factor Authentication (MFA) is a critical component for securing access to banking services in the metaverse. MFA requires users to provide two or more verification factors to gain access to their accounts, significantly reducing the risk of unauthorized access. Typically, MFA involves something the user knows (password), something the user has (security token or mobile device), and something the user is (biometric verification such as fingerprint or facial recognition). Banks must implement multi-factor authentication (MFA) and advanced identity verification methods to prevent identity theft and unauthorized access. Regular security audits, vulnerability assessments, and an up-to-date incident response plan will help mitigate the risks of data breaches and cyberattacks. The deployment of comprehensive anti-malware solutions and consistent patch management across all platforms can safeguard against malicious software and viruses.

For virtual property theft, employing blockchain technology and smart contracts can offer secure and transparent transaction mechanisms. Blockchain technology offers a decentralized and secure method for recording transactions and managing digital assets in the metaverse. For banks, leveraging blockchain can enhance transparency, reduce fraud, and ensure the integrity of financial transactions. For Example, HSBC is using blockchain to revolutionize the gold market by creating a secure and transparent system. Transactions are recorded on a shared ledger, making them tamper-proof and reducing fraud risk. Ownership of gold is represented by digital tokens, which don't reveal sensitive information like account number. Privacy concerns can be addressed by adhering to data minimization principles, maintaining transparency about data usage policies, and ensuring compliance with data protection regulations such as GDPR or CCPA.

Collaborative Efforts Among Stakeholders

Collaborative efforts among stakeholders are essential for addressing metaverse security and privacy challenges. Banks, technology providers, regulatory bodies, and industry consortia must work together to develop comprehensive security frameworks. Collaboration focuses on developing interoperable security standards for seamless integration between platforms and systems. Banks and technology providers can create secure APIs and interfaces for safe data exchange and transaction processing, while joint efforts can develop secure identity verification systems leveraging blockchain for decentralized and tamper-proof digital identities.

Regulatory bodies play a crucial role by establishing guidelines and frameworks for compliance with security and privacy standards. They facilitate dialogues between banks and technology providers to address regulatory challenges and promote best practices through workshops and conferences. Industry consortia, like the Financial Services Information Sharing and Analysis Center (FS-ISAC), serve as platforms for information sharing and threat intelligence, enabling collective responses to cyber threats and enhancing the banking sector's resilience in the metaverse. Collaborative research and development initiatives drive innovation in security technologies. Banks, academic institutions, and technology companies can explore advanced encryption methods, biometric verification techniques, and blockchain security enhancements, pooling resources and expertise to accelerate the development and adoption of cutting-edge security solutions

Enhancing user education through continuous awareness campaigns and providing intuitive security features can help bridge the gap in user unfamiliarity and ensure secure interactions within the metaverse. Designing user-friendly security features and interfaces is crucial for ensuring effective metaverse security. By prioritizing ease of use, banks can encourage users to adopt robust security practices without compromising their experience. Intuitive interfaces for multi-factor authentication, clear prompts for secure transactions, and straightforward encryption tools can significantly reduce user errors and enhance overall security. Ensuring that security measures are accessible and understandable promotes user compliance and builds trust, making it easier to protect sensitive data and maintain privacy within the metaverse. Lastly, regulatory compliance must be maintained through regular audits, policy updates, and training employees on regulatory requirements, while secure transaction practices, including tokenization and real-time monitoring, will safeguard against insecure transactions. By integrating these strategies, banks can create a secure and resilient presence within the metaverse, protecting their assets and customer trust.

CONCLUSION AND FUTURE SCOPE THE STUDY

The metaverse presents an unprecedented opportunity for banks to innovate and transform their services, offering immersive and interactive experiences to customers. However, this virtual frontier comes with a myriad of security challenges that must be meticulously addressed to safeguard sensitive information, prevent fraud, and ensure regulatory compliance. By implementing robust encryption, multi-factor authentication, regular security audits, and advanced threat detection systems, banks can mitigate risks such as data breaches, identity theft, and malicious software attacks. Additionally, leveraging blockchain technology and smart contracts can secure virtual transactions, while comprehensive user education and continuous monitoring will enhance overall security.

Ensuring privacy and ethical considerations are embedded within the organizational culture is crucial to maintaining user trust and fostering a secure virtual environment. Infrastructure security, interoperability standards, and regulatory compliance must be prioritized to protect against the evolving threat landscape in the metaverse. By adopting these proactive strategies, banks can establish a secure and resilient presence in the metaverse, positioning themselves at the forefront of technological innovation and digital finance.

Future Scope

As the metaverse continues to evolve, the scope for future research and development in banking security is vast. Future advancements could explore the integration of artificial intelligence and machine learning to enhance threat detection and response capabilities, offering more predictive and adaptive security measures. Additionally, the development of standardized regulations and global frameworks for metaverse banking could provide clearer guidelines for compliance and data protection. The exploration of quantum computing's potential impact on encryption and cybersecurity within the metaverse is another area of interest, as it may revolutionize how security is approached in virtual environments. Furthermore, continuous innovation in biometric authentication and the use of decentralized finance (DeFi) platforms could offer new avenues for secure and efficient financial transactions. Collaboration between technologists, regulators, and financial experts will be essential to address emerging security challenges and ensure a safe, inclusive, and prosperous digital future. By staying ahead of technological advancements and evolving threats, banks can continue to innovate while maintaining robust security measures, ultimately enhancing their role in the dynamic landscape of the metaverse.

REFERENCES

Adams, A. (2023). *A Qualitative Inquiry Into the Security Concerns Affecting Cloud Adoption Rates of Healthcare Organizations* (Doctoral dissertation, Colorado Technical University).

Basheer, S., Walia, S., Farooq, S., Shah, M. A., & Mir, F. A. (2023). Exploring the Metaverse: The Future of Tourism Through AI and Virtual Reality. In *Influencer Marketing Applications Within the Metaverse* (pp. 195-204). IGI Globa

Blessing, J., & Anderson, R. (2023, March). One Protocol to Rule Them All? On Securing Interoperable Messaging. In *Cambridge International Workshop on Security Protocols* (pp. 174-192). Cham: Springer Nature Switzerland. 10.1007/978-3-031-43033-6_17

Campbell-Verduyn, M. (2018). Bitcoin, crypto-coins, and global anti-money laundering governance. *Crime, Law, and Social Change*, 69(2), 283–305. 10.1007/s10611-017-9756-5

Cheng, S. (2023). Metaverse. In *Metaverse: Concept, Content and Context* (pp. 1–23). Springer Nature Switzerland.

Cherif, A. N., Achir, Y., Youssfi, M., Elgarej, M., & Bouattane, O. (2023, May). Ensuring security and data integrity in Multi Micro-Agent System Middleware with Blockchain Technology. In *2023 3rd International Conference on Innovative Research in Applied Science, Engineering and Technology (IRASET)* (pp. 1-6). IEEE. 10.1109/IRASET57153.2023.10152950

Chiorazzo, V., D'Apice, V., DeYoung, R., & Morelli, P. (2018). Is the traditional banking model a survivor? *Journal of Banking & Finance*, 97, 238–256. 10.1016/j.jbankfin.2018.10.008

Chow, Y. W., Susilo, W., Li, Y., Li, N., & Nguyen, C. (2022). Visualization and cybersecurity in the metaverse: A survey. *Journal of Imaging*, 9(1), 11. 10.3390/jimaging901001136662109

Colombo, S. (2017). Traditional banks, online banks, and number of branches. *Economia e Politica Industriale*, 44(2), 175–197. 10.1007/s40812-016-0033-x

. Dubey, V., Mokashi, A., Pradhan, R., Gupta, P., & Walimbe, R. (2022). Metaverse and banking industry–2023 the year of metaverse adoption.

Dutta, S., Pramanik, H. S., Datta, S., & Kirtania, M. (2022). Imperatives, Trends and Dynamics of Digital Transformation as Banks Adopt Technology and Intelligent Systems. In *Intelligent Systems in Digital Transformation: Theory and Applications* (pp. 323–348). Springer International Publishing.

Elshenraki, H. N. (2023). *Forecasting Cyber Crimes in the Age of the Metaverse*. IGI Global. 10.4018/979-8-3693-0220-0

Esteves, B., Asgarinia, H., Penedo, A. C., Mutiro, B., & Lewis, D. (2022, December). Fostering trust with transparency in the data economy era: An integrated ethical, legal, and knowledge engineering approach. In *Proceedings of the 1st International Workshop on Data Economy* (pp. 57-63). 10.1145/3565011.3569061

Far, S. B., & Rad, A. I. (2022). Applying digital twins in metaverse: User interface, security and privacy challenges. *Journal of Metaverse*, 2(1), 8–15.

Gozman, D., Hedman, J., & Sylvest, K. (2018). Open banking: Emergent roles, risks & opportunities. In *26th European Conference on Information Systems, ECIS 2018*. Association for Information Systems. AIS Electronic Library (AISeL).

Huang, Y., Li, Y. J., & Cai, Z. (2023). Security and privacy in metaverse: A comprehensive survey. *Big Data Mining and Analytics*, 6(2), 234–247. 10.26599/BDMA.2022.9020047

Ionaşcu, A., Barbu, C. A., & Popa, A. (2023). Ethics in the banking sector. *LUMEN Proceedings, 19*, 137-145.

Liu, S., Zou, H., Zhao, X., Wang, C., & Fan, Y. (2023). Preface: Security and Safety in the "Metaverse". *Security and Safety*, 2, E2023014. 10.1051/sands/2023014

Lyoussi, D., & Kouchih, A. (2023). Metaverse and financial inclusion opportunities and risks for the banking ecosystem. In *Influencer Marketing Applications Within the Metaverse* (pp. 205–224). IGI Global. 10.4018/978-1-6684-8898-0.ch013

Mooij, A. (2024). *Regulating the Metaverse Economy: How to Prevent Money Laundering and the Financing of Terrorism*. Springer Nature. 10.1007/978-3-031-46417-1

Mystakidis, S. (2022). Metaverse. *Encyclopedia*, 2(1), 486–497. 10.3390/encyclopedia2010031

Nzuva, S. (2019). Smart contracts implementation, applications, benefits, and limitations. *Journal of Information Engineering and Applications*, 9(5), 63–75.

Ooi, K. B., Tan, G. W. H., Aw, E. C. X., Cham, T. H., Dwivedi, Y. K., Dwivedi, R., Hughes, L., Kar, A. K., Loh, X.-M., Mogaji, E., Phau, I., & Sharma, A. (2023). Banking in the metaverse: A new frontier for financial institutions. *International Journal of Bank Marketing*, 41(7), 1829–1846. 10.1108/IJBM-03-2023-0168

Pandey, D., & Gilmour, P. (2024). Accounting meets metaverse: Navigating the intersection between the real and virtual worlds. *Journal of Financial Reporting and Accounting*, 22(2), 211–226. 10.1108/JFRA-03-2023-0157

Pooyandeh, M., Han, K. J., & Sohn, I. (2022). Cybersecurity in the AI-Based metaverse: A survey. *Applied Sciences (Basel, Switzerland)*, 12(24), 12993. 10.3390/app122412993

Rathnayake, N. D. N. B. (2023). The Era of the Transition–From Traditional to Digital Banking. In *Transformation for Sustainable Business and Management Practices: Exploring the Spectrum of Industry 5.0* (pp. 41-55). Emerald Publishing Limited. 10.1108/978-1-80262-277-520231005

Rosário, A. T., Lopes, P. R., & Rosário, F. S. (2023). Metaverse in Marketing: Challenges and Opportunities. *Handbook of Research on AI-Based Technologies and Applications in the Era of the Metaverse*, 204-227.

Saharan, S., Singh, S., Bhandari, A. K., & Yadav, B. (2024). The Future of Cyber-Crimes and Cyber War in the Metaverse. In *Forecasting Cyber Crimes in the Age of the Metaverse* (pp. 126–148). IGI Global.

Saracoglu, D. (2023). Metaverse and New Cybersecurity Threats. In *Metaverse: Technologies, Opportunities and Threats* (pp. 99–121). Springer Nature Singapore. 10.1007/978-981-99-4641-9_7

Schneider, M. (2023). Open Banking and Digital Ecosystems. In *Digital Project Practice for New Work and Industry 4.0* (pp. 169–179). Auerbach Publications. 10.1201/9781003371397-12

Shah, V., & Khang, A. (2023). Metaverse-Enabling IoT Technology for a Futuristic Healthcare System. In *Handbook of Research on AI-Based Technologies and Applications in the Era of the Metaverse* (pp. 165–173). IGI Global. 10.4018/978-1-6684-8851-5.ch008

Tan, V. H., Lim, W. Y. B., Xiong, Z., & Niyato, D. (2023, June). Blockchain for Decentralized Know Your Customer (KYC) and Customer Due Diligence (CDD) Pipelines in the Metaverse. In *2023 IEEE International Conference on Metaverse Computing, Networking and Applications (MetaCom)* (pp. 433-440). IEEE. 10.1109/MetaCom57706.2023.00083

Wang, H., Ning, H., Lin, Y., Wang, W., Dhelim, S., Farha, F., Ding, J., & Daneshmand, M. (2023). A survey on the metaverse: The state-of-the-art, technologies, applications, and challenges. *IEEE Internet of Things Journal*, 10(16), 14671–14688. 10.1109/JIOT.2023.3278329

Zhang, Y., & Smith, T. (2023). The impact of customer firm data breaches on the audit fees of their suppliers. *International Journal of Accounting Information Systems*, 50, 100628. 10.1016/j.accinf.2023.100628

Chapter 12
Privacy-Preserving Techniques and User Anonymity in the Metaverse

Brij B. Gupta
https://orcid.org/0000-0003-4929-4698
Department of Computer Science and Information Engineering, Asia University, Taichung, Taiwan

Chunjia Han
Birkbeck, University of London, UK

Priyanka Chaurasia
University of Ulster, UK

ABSTRACT

Emphasizing sophisticated methods to safeguard user information and guarantee privacy, this chap- ter explores user anonymity and privacy-preserving technologies in the Metaverse. Important subjects include differential privacy for data exchange, federated learning for artificial intelligence, safe multi- party computing for group projects, and virtual world anonymity methods. This chapter also investigates the harmony between security and privacy, ethical issues and future developments in metaverse privacy protection. Moreover, this chapter offers a thorough review of Metaverse privacy-preserving techniques.

DOI: 10.4018/979-8-3693-3824-7.ch012

INTRODUCTION TO PRIVACY CHALLENGES IN THE METAVERSE

A major issue of privacy in the Metaverse has to be resolved if we are to guarantee users' confidentiality and security of data. Table 1, presents the key privacy challenges in metaverse. As investigated by Li et al. (2023), the confluence of physical and cyberspace in the Metaverse raises major security and privacy concerns that must be carefully investigated. This study carried out by sheds clarifies the need of knowing and addressing these issues to protect users' information and interactions in the Metaverse. As underlined by Verma et al. (2022), one of the main factors aggravating security issues in the Metaverse is the existence of many virtual systems on one actual hardware. This configuration adds several degrees of security needs to guarantee that every virtual device is segregated from illegal access and stays guarded. Maintaining user privacy in the Metaverse depends on strong security measures addressing these virtualization security issues being top priority.

Moreover, the impact of fusion display modes on users' perception of personal security in virtual immersion devices, as investigated by Hu et al. (2021); Gupta et al. (2023) emphasizes the complex link between privacy and user experience in virtual reality settings. Various interaction techniques may affect users' sense of security, which emphasizes the requirement of creating immersive experiences.

Table 1. Key Privacy Challenges in the Metaverse

Reference	Privacy Challenge	Description
Li et al. (2023)	**Convergence of Physical and Cyber Worlds**	**Integration of physical and virtual environments introduces complex privacy and security issues**
Verma (2022)	**Virtualization Security**	**Presence of multiple virtual systems on a single physical machine creates varying security needs**
Hu et al. (2021)	Fusion Display Modes	Different interaction methods in virtual systems impact users' perception of personal security
Abraham (2022)	Reality-Virtuality Con- tinuum	Security and privacy concerns vary across different points of the Reality-Virtuality contin- uum
Kong (2010)	Untrusted Hosts	Protecting virtual machines from internal threats to maintain data confidentiality
Muhla (2020)	Secure Virtual Reality Experiences	Ensuring safety and privacy in immersive VR environments for realistic and secure user en- gagement
Singh & Mishra (2019)	Privacy in Virtual Mental Health	Ensuring confidentiality in virtual mental health interventions to foster trust and adoption

Emphasizing the nature of security and privacy issues throughout the Reality-Virtuality continuum, Abraham et al. (2022) provide specifics on how extended reality (XR) affects behavior, privacy, and security. Although the whole scope of these questions may not be known, establishing successful privacy solutions in the

Metaverse depends on knowing the possible problems at many locations along this continuum.

Furthermore underlined by Kong (2010) the requirement of safeguarding virtualized environments from internal risks by means of protection of their confidentiality against untrusted users. Preventing il- legal access and data leaks that can jeopardize user information in the Metaverse depends on protecting personal and private information within virtual computers.

In the framework of virtual reality experiences, including those investigated by Muhla et al. (2020); Xie et al. (2023), establishing realistic and safe surroundings is crucial for increasing user involvement while thus guaranteeing privacy and safety. One may safely perform simulated real-life events within regulated virtual environments by using virtual reality technologies.

Examining the use of virtual reality in mental health under (Singh & Mishra, 2019) emphasizes the possibilities of virtual settings to assist mental health. Nonetheless, maintaining confidence and promoting general acceptance of these technologies depends critically on guaranteeing the secrecy and privacy of the people participating in such virtual mental health treatments.

DIFFERENTIAL PRIVACY FOR DATA SHARING

In the Metaverse, especially in relation to data sharing as shown in Figure 1, differential privacy is a basic idea in maintaining data confidentiality and privacy. Differential privacy is introduced in Nguyen et al. (2020) providing a formal privacy guarantee for metaverse users. But depending too much on reliable third parties in numerous differentially private systems might expose flaws in the information exchange system. Including secure hardware will help to solve this problem by improving metaverse privacy protection strategies.

Figure 1. Differential Privacy

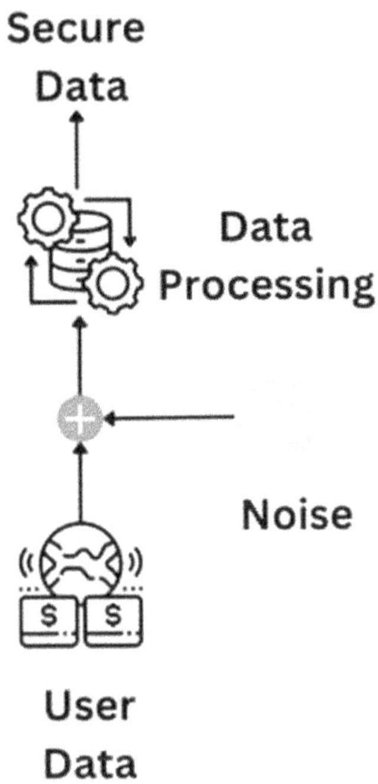

Within the Metaverse's data sharing issues, Gadekallu et al. (2022) draw attention to the dangers connected to centralized data exchange systems. Sharing sensitive user data on these sites could dis- close private information and seriously compromise security. Differential privacy turns out to be a way for identifying these hazards, hence preserving personal privacy during private and confident data exchange.

Ahsani et al. (2023) underline the need of security and methods in privatizing sensitive data char- acteristics and safeguarding deep learning algorithms within distributed settings in the virtual world. Differential privacy concepts help to anonymize sensitive data thus safeguarding individual user privacy throughout cooperative machine learning projects and data analysis.

Furthermore merging federated learning (FL) and blockchain technology, Kang et al. (2022); Agrawal (2020) provide a user-centric privacy-preserving mechanism for sensing data sharing in healthcare metaverses. While blockchain technology guarantees data security and reduces the possibility of a single point of failure, FL approaches provide users' privacy protection. This method shows how so- phisticated technology may be used to uphold privacy rules while enabling data exchange and joint study in delicate fields.

Emphasizing the need of addressing issues with data confidentiality and security, Musale (2024); Law et al. (2021) highlights society worries about security in the Metaverse. Differential privacy offers a methodical technique to safeguard private data in the metaverse as a strict mathematical framework for assessing and guaranteeing data privacy. Differential privacy methods help parties to properly negotiate privacy preservation challenges in the Metaverse environment by including into data sharing policies.

Nelson Garfinkel et al. (2018) addresses the difficulties in deploying differential privacy in the field of differential privacy research, including the need of suitable computing environments, qualified personnel, and mechanisms that fit users' needs.

FEDERATED LEARNING FOR PRIVACY-PRESERVING AI

Within the Metaverse, recently federated learning (FL) methods are used for privacy-preserving artifi- cial intelligence (AI) applications under Figure 2. FL presents a distributed architecture for maintain- ing norms of data privacy and cooperative model training. FL is presented in W. Wang (2024) as a distributed deep learning method enabling the cooperative training of models across a varied collection of connected devices, thereby enabling their collaborative learning and enhancement and so protecting of data privacy. This approach is especially important in the framework of the virtual worlds, where data sharing and joint artificial intelligence projects need for strict privacy policies to protect user data.

In the field of intelligent transportation, W. Wang (2024) underlines the need of FL in enabling safe and safe autonomy, stressing its part in improving model training without sacrificing data security. FL is a useful tool for privacy-preserving AI applications in the Metaverse as it allows model training locally on individual devices without exchanging raw data, hence efficiently addressing privacy issues. This strategy fits the key objective of preserving data secrecy while using collective knowledge to drive artificial intelligence developments.

Zeng et al. (2022); Himanshu (2023) explore the field of heterogeneous FL with memorable data semantics in the industrial Metaverse, thereby underlining federated learning as a privacy-preserving collaborative machine learning framework that enables edge intelligence. FL presents a potential path for privacy-preserving artificial intelligence applications in industrial environments inside the Meta- verse by allowing model training on dispersed dataset sets while maintaining data localization. This method guarantees that sensitive data stays private and confidential while using the dispersed character of data.

Figure 2. Federated Learning in Metaverse Environment

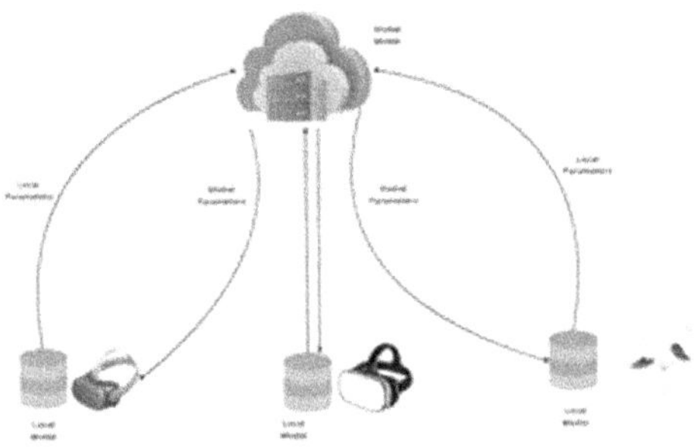

Furthermore covering the design, implementation, and difficulties of FL in distributed artificial intelligence systems, Shanmugam (2023) emphasizes its use in distributed user device collaborative model training. Preserving data privacy and allowing safe model training helps federated learning to become a viable paradigm for Metaverse privacy-preserving AI applications. By giving privacy in AI-driven interactions within virtual environments first priority, this method not only improves data security but also builds trust among users.

Within the scope of healthcare metaverses, Kang et al. (2022); Aiyaan (2023) provide a user-centric privacy-preserving blockchain-based FL architecture. This framework emphasizes the need of preserv- ing data security in sensitive fields by including distributed FL approaches, therefore guaranteeing pri- vacy protection for sensing information exchange. This user-centric approach emphasizes how FL may be applied to particular industrial demands within the Metaverse, therefore demonstrating its adaptabil- ity in tackling privacy issues across several uses.

SECURE MULTI-PARTY COMPUTATION FOR COLLABORATIVE TASKS

A cryptographic technique called Secure Multi-Party Computation (SMPC) allows many users to col- laboratively calculate functions on their private inputs without disclosing individual data, therefore guaranteeing data privacy and security (Jitkrittum et al., 2021). This approach is crucial for situations when entities must cooperate on computations while preserving the privacy of their inputs (Vaidya & Clifton, 2003). Table 2 presents the SMPC framworks.

By providing effective neural architectures for safe multi-party computing (Jit- krittum et al., 2021),

Table 2. SMPC Frameworks and Applications

Reference	Framework	Application
Jitkrittum et al. (2021)	HD-cos Networks	Efficient neural architectures for secure multi-party computation
Fan et al. (2022)	PoS4MPC	Automated security policy synthesis for SMPC deployment
Jarin & Eshete (2021)	PRICURE	SMPC for collaborative inference in multi-party settings

creative paradigms such as HD-cos Networks have improved the idea of SMPC. These developments raised SMPC's scalability and efficiency, therefore enabling it to be a useful tool for distributed jobs in the Metaverse needing sophisticated calculations while maintaining data security requirements.

PoS4MPC's automated security policy synthesis helps to automatically synthesize security rules (Fan et al., 2022), thereby streamlining the implementation to secure multi-party computing. This au- tomated system guarantees data security and safe calculations across many parties, therefore improving the execution of SMPC in Metaverse collaborative projects.

In multi-user environments, frameworks such as PRICURE provide safe multi-party computing by allowing participants to cooperatively calculate functions and thereby protect the privacy of their inputs for collaborative inference(Jarin & Eshete, 2021; Varsha, 2023).

As investigated in an incentive mechanism research, the combined integration of SMPC and blockchain technologies in distributed routing improves security and privacy in cooperative activities inside the Metaverse (C. Wang, 2024). This integration guarantees the preservation of private routing data and motivates safe user cooperation.

Furthermore, the efficacy of safe multi-user computing in building privacy-preserving distributed optimization frameworks is highlighted by SMPC's use in distributed frameworks as shown in privacy- preserving distributed optimization in power systems (Tian et al., 2022).

ANONYMITY TECHNIQUES IN VIRTUAL WORLDS

Maintaining privacy and secrecy in the Metaverse depends critically on anonymity strategies, as repre- sented in Figure 3. Protection of users' personal data and identities during virtual interactions depends on these methods. To solve privacy issues and improve user security, several research have investigated many facets of anonymity approaches in virtual environments.

By matching their avatar motions in the metaverse with auxiliary data from motion sensors, Sabra et al. (2023) illustrated the hazards of de-anonymizing faced by virtual reality users. This work high- lights the significance of knowing weaknesses in virtual environments and the requirement of strong anonymity policies to safeguard user identities.

Emphasizing the need of privacy protection research in virtual reality, Wu et al. (2023) underline the need of investigating and using successful techniques to preserve user seucrity within virtual worlds.

Figure 3. Anonymity Techniques

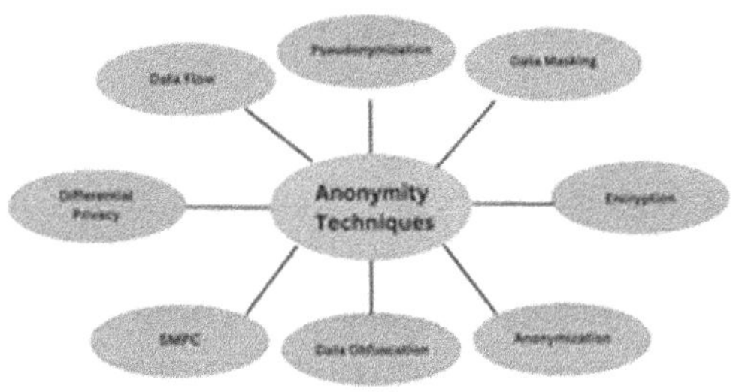

The changing terrain of privacy issues in virtual reality settings and the need of anonymity methods to reduce hazards were under discussion in this paper.

Emphasizing the part user navigation and interaction play in metaverse settings, Haggerty et al. (2018) investigate perceived navigation aid and affordances in virtual worlds. Effective anonymity approaches to safeguard user identities and activities depend on an awareness of how users negotiate and interact in virtual environments.

Sharma (2024) outlines main elements of privacy and security for guaranteeing a safe metaverse, therefore shedding light on user safety and security dimensions in virtual worlds. This work emphasizes the many aspects of user security issues and the need of anonymity methods in protection of user data.

Emphasizing the hazards connected with virtual property ownership in metaverse, Patterson et al. (2017) address cyber-threat analytic frameworks for identifying virtual property theft in metaverse. By using anonymous methods, one may improve user privacy and security by thereby reducing the possibility of theft and illegal access to virtual assets.

Within the framework of user rights in virtual reality systems, Wójtowicz & Cellary (2010) provide approach for utilizing object-oriented systems and user privileges to improve user interactions within metaverse. By means of efficient administration of user rights, these methods help to create safe and privacy-aware virtual environments.

Emphasizing the need of informed permission, privacy protection, and identity management in virtual educational environments, Girvan & Savage (2012) highlighted the ethical issues for educational research in metaverse. Maintaining ethical norms and guaranteeing user privacy in learning virtual environments depend much on anonymity techniques.

Advancing the knowledge of virtual and immersive environments, Hill & Meister (2013) investigate the adoption of virtual world tools and frameworks in the domain of virtual libraries in the Metaverse. In virtual libraries, anonymity strategies may improve user security and privacy, therefore protecting user interactions and data.

FUTURE DIRECTIONS IN PRIVACY PRESERVATION

Maintaining user data confidentiality and security in virtual settings depends on future approaches in safeguarding the Metaverse. Including cutting-edge technology and techniques as the Metaverse de- velops can help to solve growing security issues and properly safeguard user data. The protection of privacy in the Metaverse may be shaped going forward by many important research paths and ap- proaches.

Using blockchain technology to improve metaverse privacy preservation is one important future path Gadekallu et al. (2022). Blockchain lets consumers gain ownership over their data by providing a distributed and safe framework for data exchanges and storage, therefore guaranteeing immutability and openness. Blockchain integration with Metaverse systems helps users to get improved data security and privacy protection features.

Adoption of FL and blockchain-based solutions (Kang et al., 2022) promises yet another interesting path for privacy protection in the Metaverse. A user-centric privacy-preserving strategy may be con- structed for distributed work in several Metaverse fields by combining FL approaches with blockchain technology. This method not only guarantees user privacy but also guarantees data security and reduces the possibility of single points of data leaks, thereby improving the general efforts on privacy preservation.

Moreover, the idea of social Metaverse offers chances for interactions driven by privacy-preserving artificial intelligence (Y. Wang et al., 2023). Enabled by distributed model training and user data pro- tection, federated learning presents a paradigm change towards privacy-preserving AI applications to social Metaverse contexts. By emphasizing privacy-enhancing technologies like FL, social Metaverse platforms may give user privacy and data security top priority in further advancements.

Within the framework of Metaverse online social networks, developments in privacy protection technologies are crucial to secure user personal data P. Wang et al. (2016). Future avenues of study might include investigating creative privacy-preserving solutions for huge data settings, tackling pri- vacy leakage kinds, and improving current privacy preservation technologies to meet changing privacy issues in online social networks.

Furthermore improving user privacy protection in the Metaverse is the inclusion of privacy-preserving methods in recommender systems and data mining applications (Pramod, 2022). Stakeholders can guar- antee that user data is safe by creating cutting-edge privacy-preserving technologies and frameworks, therefore allowing tailored suggestions and metaverse data analysis.

Maintaining data security will depend on the Metaverse's expansion assuring privacy preservation in IoT devices and virtual settings.(Torre et al., 2023). Stakeholders may reduce privacy concerns and safeguard private data in linked virtual environments by investigating privacy-preservation methods for IoT devices and putting strong security policies into use.

CONCLUSION

Maintaining security and confidence in the Metaverse depends on measures of privacy preservation as well as user anonymity. Growing virtual environments depend on constant innovation and research in privacy-preserving techniques to protect user confidentiality. Future developments will improve these methods even more so guaranteeing a safe and private Metaverse experience for every user.

REFERENCES

Abraham, M., Saeghe, P., McGill, M., & Khamis, M. (2022). Implications of xr on privacy, security and behaviour: insights from experts. 10.1145/3546155.3546691

Agrawal, D. P. (2020). *Recent advances in security, privacy, and trust for internet of things (iot) and cyber-physical systems (cps)*. Chapman and Hall/CRC.

Ahsani, V., Rahimi, A., Letafati, M., & Khalaj, B. (2023). Unlocking metaverse-as-a-service the three pillars to watch: privacy and security, edge computing, and blockchain. doi: /arxiv.2301.0122110.48550

Aiyaan, H. (2023). *Preventing metaverse cyberattacks: Security issues and threat mitiga- tion.*https://insights2techinfo.com/preventing-metaverse-cyberattacks-security-issues-and-threat-mitigation/. (Accessed: 2024-01-30)

Fan, Y., Song, F., Chen, T., Zhang, L., & Liu, W. (2022). Pos4mpc: automated security policy synthesis for secure multi-party computation., 385-406. 10.1007/978-3-031-13185-1_19

Gadekallu, T., Huynh-The, T., Wang, W., Yenduri, G., Ranaweera, P., Pham, Q., . . . Liyanage, M. (2022). Blockchain for the metaverse: a review. doi: /arxiv.2203.0973810.48550

Garfinkel, S., Abowd, J., & Powazek, S. (2018). Issues encountered deploying differential privacy. 10.1145/3267323.3268949

Girvan, C., & Savage, T. (2012). Ethical considerations for educational research in a virtual world. *Interactive Learning Environments*, 20(3), 239–251. 10.1080/10494820.2011.641678

Gupta, B. B., Gaurav, A., & Arya, V. (2023). Secure and privacy-preserving decentralized federated learning for personalized recommendations in consumer electronics using blockchain and homomor- phic encryption. *IEEE Transactions on Consumer Electronics*.

Haggerty, K., Cosgrove, P., & Griffin, J. (2018). Using virtual worlds to investigate perceived affor- dances on learned navigation and objective location performance. *Proceedings of the Association for Information Science and Technology*, 55(1), 819–820. 10.1002/pra2.2018.14505501131

Hill, V., & Meister, M. (2013). Virtual worlds and libraries: Gridhopping to new worlds. *College & Research Libraries News*, 74(1), 43–47. 10.5860/crln.74.1.8887

Himanshu, T. (2023). *A federated learning approach to the metaverse: Unlocking the power of data privacy and collaboration.* https://insights2techinfo.com/ a-federated-learning-approach-to-the-metaverse-unlocking-the-power-of-data-privacy-and-collaboration/. (Accessed: 2024-01-30)

Hu, M., Weng, D., Guo, J., & Wang, Y. (2021). The influence of fusion display mode on the user's sense of personal security in virtual immersion system. *Journal of the Society for Information Display*, 29(4), 254–263. 10.1002/jsid.984

Jarin, I., & Eshete, B. (2021). Pricure: privacy-preserving collaborative inference in a multi-party setting. /arxiv.2102.0975110.1145/3445970.3451156

Jitkrittum, W., Lukasik, M., Suresh, A., Yu, F., & Wang, G. (2021). Hd-cos networks: efficient neural architectures for secure multi-party computation. doi: / arxiv.2110.1544010.48550

Kang, J., Ye, D., Nie, J., Xiao, J., Deng, X., Wang, S., . . . Niyato, D. (2022). Blockchain-based federated learning for industrial metaverses: incentive scheme with optimal aoi. 10.1109/Blockchain55522.2022.00020

Kong, J. (2010). Protecting the confidentiality of virtual machines against untrusted host. 10.1109/IPTC.2010.11

Law, K. M., Ip, A. W., Gupta, B. B., & Geng, S. (2021). *Managing iot and mobile technologies with innovation, trust, and sustainable computing*. CRC Press. 10.1201/9780367822750

Li, K., Cui, Y., Li, W., Lv, T., Yuan, X., Li, S., Ni, W., Simsek, M., & Dressler, F. (2023). When internet of things meets metaverse: Convergence of physical and cyber worlds. *IEEE Internet of Things Journal*, 10(5), 4148–4173. 10.1109/ JIOT.2022.3232845

Muhla, F., Clanché, F., Duclos, K., Meyer, P., Maïaux, S., Colnat-Coulbois, S., & Gauchard, G. (2020). Impact of using immersive virtual reality over time and steps in the timed up and go test in elderly people. *PLoS One*, 15(3), e0229594. 10.1371/ journal.pone.022959432168361

Musale, P. (2024). Demystifying the metaverse: a deep dive into characteristics, enabling technologies, key components, surmounting challenges, and unveiling boundless applications. *Interantional Jour- nal of Scientific Research in Engineering and Management, 08*, 1-5. 10.55041/IJSREM31625

Nguyen, P., Silence, A., Darais, D., & Near, J. (2020). Duetsgx: differential privacy with secure hardware. doi: /arxiv.2010.1066410.48550

Patterson, N., Hobbs, M., & Zhu, T. (2017). A cyber-threat analytic model for autonomous detection of virtual property theft. *Information and Computer Security*, 25(4), 358–381. 10.1108/ICS-11-2016-0087

Pramod, D. (2022). Privacy-preserving techniques in recommender systems: State-of-the-art review and future research agenda. *Data Technologies and Applications*, 57(1), 32–55. 10.1108/DTA-02-2022-0083

Sabra, M., Sureshkanth, N., Sharma, A., Maiti, A., & Jadliwala, M. (2023). Exploiting out-of-band motion sensor data to de-anonymize virtual reality users. doi: /arxiv.2301.0904110.48550

Shanmugam, L. (2023). Federated learning architecture: design, implementation, and challenges in distributed ai systems. *Journal of Knowledge Learning and Science Technology Issn 2959-6386 (Online), 2*, 371-384. 10.60087/jklst.vol2.n2.p384

Sharma, S., Singh, J., Gupta, A., Ali, F., Khan, F., & Kwak, D. (2024). User safety and security in the metaverse: A critical review. *IEEE Open Journal of the Communications Society*, •••, 1–1. 10.1109/OJCOMS.2024.3397044

Singh, M., & Mishra, K. D. (2019). Applications of virtual reality in mental health. *International Jour- nal of Recent Technology and Engineering, 8*, 3735-3739. 10.35940/ijrte.B1481.0982S1119

Tian, N., Guo, Q., Sun, H., & Zhou, X. (2022). Fully privacy-preserving distributed optimization in power systems based on secret sharing. *Ienergy*, 1(3), 351–362. 10.23919/IEN.2022.0045

Torre, D., Chennamaneni, A., & Rodriguez, A. (2023). Privacy-preservation techniques for iot devices: A systematic mapping study. *IEEE Access : Practical Innovations, Open Solutions*, 11, 16323–16345. 10.1109/ACCESS.2023.3245524

Vaidya, J., & Clifton, C. (2003). Leveraging the "multi" in secure multi-party computation. 10.1145/1005140.1005149

Varsha, A. (2023). *Metaverse security 2.0: Evolving attack detection in virtual environ- ments.*https://insights2techinfo.com/metaverse-security-2-0-evolving-attack-detection-in-virtual-environments/. (Accessed: 2024-01-30)

Verma, R., Rane, D., Jha, R., & Ibrahim, W. (2022). Next-generation optimization models and al- gorithms in cloud and fog computing virtualization security: The present state and future. *Scientific Programming*, 2022, 1–10. 10.1155/2022/2419291

Wang, C., & Peeta, S. (2024). Incentive mechanism for privacy-preserving collaborative routing using secure multi-party computation and blockchain. *Sensors (Basel)*, 24(2), 542. 10.3390/s2402054238257634

Wang, P., Wang, Z., & Chen, T. (2016). Privacy protection in online social network in the context of big data. 10.2991/icemaess-15.2016.103

Wang, W. (2024). Empowering safe and secure autonomy: Federated learning in the era of au- tonomous driving. *Applied and Computational Engineering*, 51(1), 40–44. 10.54254/2755-2721/51/20241158

Wang, Y., Zhou, S., & Yan, M. (2023). Social metaverse: challenges and solutions. doi: /arxiv.2301.1022110.48550

Wójtowicz, A., & Cellary, W. (2010). Representing user privileges in object-oriented virtual reality systems., 52-61. 10.1007/978-3-642-11628-5_6

Wu, C., Yang, L., Zhao, X., & Sun, Q. (2023). P-2.24: a survey of privacy protection research based on virtual reality. *Sid Symposium Digest of Technical Papers, 54*, 572-576. 10.1002/sdtp.16358

Xie, Y., Li, P., Nedjah, N., Gupta, B. B., Taniar, D., & Zhang, J. (2023). Privacy protection framework for face recognition in edge-based internet of things. *Cluster Computing*, 26(5), 3017–3035. 10.1007/s10586-022-03808-836415683

Zeng, S., Li, Z., Yu, H., Zhang, Z., Lu, L., Li, B., & Niyato, D. (2022). Hfedms: heterogeneous federated learning with memorable data semantics in industrial metaverse. doi: /arxiv.2211.0330010.48550

Chapter 13
Protection and Management of User Privacy System Data Security With the Metaserve Approach

Paryati Paryati Yati
UPN "Veteran" Yogyakarta, Indonesia

ABSTRACT

The metaserve world and architecture provide a glimpse into what connects the virtual to the real world. At a time discusses existing data security and personal data privacy. This is very important because it has high and urgent risks in the metaserve world. This paper discusses the issue of data security and personal data which is usually referred to as individual personal privacy. In this paper there are things that are very interesting about a metaserve representing the next generation, using the internet to change the way people live. As well as new forms of media in communicate with the system, which can give users their own avatar in work, socializing and in the world of entertainment with virtual games, and has the ability to integrate various technologies such as artificial intelligence technology, blockchain, virtual reality can be combined with augmented reality. So the metaserve can actually help activities humans, but can also cause side effects in various problems related to data security and data privacy system users, for example, data breaches and identity theft.

DOI: 10.4018/979-8-3693-3824-7.ch013

INTRODUCTION

The data collection in this research is based on digital literacy from previous research, thereby obtaining a contribution, namely revising the origins of the metaserve concept. It then presents its current background, which is useful for uncovering the first question of why the metaverse has become an interesting topic in recent years. This research focuses on security issues and personal data or individual privacy. Hopefully the results of the second question are why future metaserve examples may represent something different from what has been seen in the technology domain until now. There is exponential technological growth as an unprecedented capability in creating, collecting and analyzing data, as well as the convergence between the cyber world and the physical world. In this situation, it is hoped that it can be used to predict the development of the metaserve in the future. Risks related to security and personal data. The use of digital communications cannot be separated from the use of big data. This is because the world today cannot be separated from the role of data because everything is built on a data foundation. Today, large amounts of data are collected and generated every day offering a variety of analytical opportunities for organizations to uncover information that is beneficial to their operations. Like E- commerce requires large amounts of data, often called big data. Big data technology is a tool or technology used to process data efficiently. Big data technology has been proven effective in processing various types of data. The system will be designed and prepared for implementation. At advanced stages of development several technologies that represent the building blocks of the metaserve already exist. An explanation of the metaserve is needed to understand the core elements, characteristics and functions of the metaverse as a long-term direction in which the metaserve can further develop. It is also presented as a starting point for Zuckerberg's proposed metaserve vision, as it represents the most comprehensive of all that have been proposed so far. Metaserve is a combination of persistent, multi-user, shared 3D virtual spaces, intertwined with the physical world and joining together to create a unified and eternal virtual universe (P. Pramesti, A, etc all, 2022) Meta is positioned to drastically change the business landscape. Users enter the metaverse with avatars, which can interact with each other and with the items, applications, services, and businesses that exist in the metaserve. Metaserve refers to a virtual reality that exists outside of reality. Immediate feedback and quick replies from businesses save time, keep consumers happy and increase loyalty. It was originally attributed to Neal Stephenson's vision in his 1992 science fiction book Snow Crash but is practically an idea that can be found in many cultures and eras, at least since The Cave of Plato, as brilliantly explained by Ethan Zuckerman in the latest edition of The Atlantic metaverse periodically sparks heated debate among technology experts and the general public, following more or less successful attempts at implementing it for example Second Life. The development of information technology demands changes in roles. Recently, they made the news again, when some of the biggest tech companies announced major investments and ambitious plans for the development of new and futuristic metaserves (Iswanto, N.I, etc all, 2022) Among them are Microsoft, Epic Games, and Meta, the technology company that Facebook accidentally changed its name to. Mark Zuckerberg Meta and Facebook CEO, in particular, envision the metaverse as the next evolution of the Internet. Namely, cyber-physical Internet 3.0 empowered by technology that is able to go beyond the mobile Internet paradigm. His vision of the metaserve as the next evolutionary leap of our physical and digital networking capabilities and thus, also of our social lives perfectly explains the huge hype and spasmodic attention that has quickly built around the metaverse. To support this ambitious vision, the first example of a metaserve will build on several recent technological advances (P. Pramesti, et al., 2021). For example, virtual reality VR will be used to create immersive 3D spaces while augmented reality AR will enable close integration between the virtual world and the physical world. Digital twins will allow physical objects to be brought, visualized, and shared across the metaserve. Wearable sensors will allow avatars in virtual spaces to mimic real-world movements, while other sensors, such as those embedded into next-generation smart devices, will feed additional real-world data into the metaverse. Metasere will also feature a rich marketplace of physical goods and virtual goods. The latter will be tied to, and owned by, the avatar itself and will be implemented as a non-fungible token (S. Eyer, 2009). Ultimately, next-generation networking technologies and algorithms will make the metaverse more pervasive than today's social media and social networking platforms. While combining the latest technology, social media, advanced algorithms, a constant and unlimited supply of data from the system evolving sensors, and more, the metaverse will remain more comprehensive than can be described at the time of writing, due to its capacity to adapt and adopt any innovation (E. Zuckerman, 2022).

LITERATUR REVIEW

Based on the background of the problem, metaserve currently has a very important role in the real world and has enormous benefits in the world of digital transformation technology (N. I. Putri, et al., 2022). So as to reveal and prove that the metaverse is a very interesting topic nowadays. Mainly focuses on security issues and personal data or individual privacy. Everyone really needs the right and accurate solution to overcome data security problems and the need for large data storage. In creating, collecting data, and analyzing data, as well as convergence between the cyber world and the physical world, big data and metaserves are really needed (S. Nadella, 2021). Apart from that, it also discusses risks related to security and personal data. The use of digital communications cannot be separated from the use of big data because everything is built on a data foundation. Metaverse is a combination of persistent, multi-user, shared 3D virtual spaces, intertwined with the physical world and joining together to create a unified and eternal virtual universe (Z. Munawar, et al., 2021). Meta is positioned to drastically change the business landscape. Users enter the metaserve with avatars, which can interact with each other and with the items, applications, services, and businesses that exist in the metaverse. Metaserve refers to a virtual reality that exists outside of reality (D. Khairunnisa, et al., 2022). Immediate feedback and quick replies from businesses save time, keep consumers happy and increase loyalty. It was originally attributed to the vision of Neal Stephenson in his 1992 science fiction book Snow Crash but is practically an idea that can be found in many cultures and eras, at least since The Cave of Plato, as brilliantly explained by Ethan Zuckerman in the latest edition The Atlantic metaverse periodically sparks heated debate among technology experts and the general public, following more or less successful attempts at implementing it for example Second Life. The development of information technology demands changes in roles. Recently, they made the news again, when some of the biggest tech companies announced major investments and ambitious plans for the development of new and futuristic metaserves (Z. Munawar, 2018). Among them are Microsoft, Epic Games, and Meta the technology company that Facebook accidentally changed its name to. Mark Zuckerberg Meta and Facebook CEO, in particular, envision the metaverse as the next evolution of the Internet (Munawar, et al., 2021). Namely, cyber-physical Internet 3.0 empowered by technology that is able to go beyond the mobile Internet paradigm. His vision of the metaverse as the next evolutionary leap of our physical and digital networking capabilities and thus, also of our social lives perfectly explains the huge hype and spasmodic attention that has quickly built around the metaserve. To support this ambitious vision, the first example of a metaserve will build on several recent technological advances. For example, virtual reality VR will be used to create immersive 3D spaces while augmented reality AR will enable close integration between the virtual world and the physical world (Munawar, et al., 2019). Correspondingly, digital twins will enable physical objects to be brought, visualized and shared into the metaserve. We arable sensors will allow avatars in virtual spaces to mimic real-world movements, while other sensors, such as those embedded into next-generation smart devices, will feed additional real-world data into the metaserve. Metaserve will also feature a rich marketplace of physical goods and virtual goods (N. I. Putri, et al., 2022). The latter will be tied to, and owned by, the avatar itself and will be implemented as a non-fungible token. Ultimately, next-generation network technologies and algorithms will make the metaverse more pervasive than today's social media and social networking platforms. While combining the latest technology, social media, advanced algorithms, a constant and unlimited supply of data from the system evolving sensors, and more, the metaverse will remain more comprehensive than can be described at the time of writing, due to its capacity to adapt and adopt any innovation (Z. Munawar, 2017). In this context, it seems clear that security and privacy concerns will not only be magnified, but completely transformed. And with them, several other critical issues, as discussed below. The benefits of using digital technology have been felt in recent years. This is because technological developments are increasingly rapid day by day, giving rise to many new technological innovations. Recommender systems are useful for providing recommendations for products to choose based on past preferences, purchase history, and demographic information. Commercially, e-commerce can be referred to as an activity that seeks to create long transactions between companies and individuals. Additionally, it can be shown that the semantic ranking provided by the knowledge-based part of the system provides an additional boost to hybrid performance (Z. Munawar & N. I. Putri, 2020). This method is used to produce an application user interface that suits the user's needs.

METHOD

By collecting data according to digital literacy from previous research, we can get a contribution regarding the origin of the concept of the metaserve. The background serves to understand why the metaserve has become an interesting topic in recent times. Over the last ten years, we can see the internet revolution on mobile devices, enabling access to online applications and social ecosystems that can be done from virtually anywhere, this is due to its immersive nature (Z. Munawar, 2020). There are things that limit the use of screen devices to enter and enjoy virtual environments. Through AR and VR technology methods, access to online virtual spaces is also possible in the metaserve. Indeed, Pervasiveness and immersiveness are the two main and differentiating features of the metaverse, achieved through an unprecedented merging of the virtual world and the physical world. Various ways of using the metaserve, which involve how to access and interact with the metaverse, as well as how we receive feedback from it. For example, mobile immersive access to the metaverse will be possible thanks to AR-enabled smart devices such as compact smart glasses (Indah Putri et al., 2021. The transition from 2D interfaces to 3D virtual spaces will be accompanied by a number of additional possibilities that will further increase immersiveness. The number of 2D applications and services used every day, such as WhatsApp, Zoom, Google Meet, Google Drive, Dropbox, Facebook, Instagram, etc., will into applications embedded into the metaverse (Munawar, et al., 2022). Users will inhabit the metaverse in the form of avatars, thereby moving from static 2D profile images to interactive and personalized 3D avatars. Users will be able to represent themselves with photorealistic, cartoon or completely fictional avatars on the activities, applications or virtual spaces used. It is also possible for users to own and create virtual copies of physical items, namely digital twins, and share them in the metaserve, thereby further reducing the gap between virtual and physical dimensions. Finally, the use of sensors and wearable devices will strengthen the bond between our physical and virtual worlds by bringing more real-world data into the metaverse and by providing users with unprecedented sensory feedback. Virtual Reality VR and the availability of embedded messaging and video conferencing applications enable immersive meetings to take place in the metaserve. In addition, traditional and new forms of trade will be supported by one or more online marketplaces, which will feature physical and digital goods for sale. In particular the marketplace will connect independent content creators with potential customers as a recommender system, namely metaserve users, this allows business opportunities to be scaled to an unprecedented level (C. Bermejo & P. Hui, 2017). A recommendation system is needed because previously there were weaknesses in content-based systems. The original virtual form of the metaserve can be seen in many cases of concerts held in the virtual worlds of online games such as Roblox5, Minecraft, and Fortnite, there are even genuine physical concerts but they remain accessible through the metaserve, as in the case of real-world concerts that allow metaserve users to participate via Virtual Reality (Munawar, 2021). The field of sports and fitness is another group of activities that will clearly benefit from the cyber-physical integration made possible with the metaverse. In particular, wearable sensors with Augmented Reality AR/Virtual Reality VR will enable realistic and immersive virtual sports simulations, with unprecedented opportunities for personalization and customization (Munawar, et al., 2022). The same considerations can be made for learning and other educational activities, which will greatly benefit from the immersiveness and capabilities of 3D metaserves.

RESULT ANALYSIS

The largest and most frequent metaserve activities are games and other forms of entertainment, including the possibility of participating in art performances and concerts. Metaserve inherits some of the massive multiplayer characteristics of online games. Games or computer games continue to grow, both in terms of users and developer income. One of the activities that is often carried out is a combination of games and entertainment in general. Metaserve will also be used for work and business, as well as for ecommerce. Architecturally metaverse can be thought of as a framework that connects multiple applications with the services embedded in them. Thus, interoperability is another key feature of the metaserve and its users will experience it in various ways. For example, users can interact simultaneously with several applications, similar to what we usually do on our desktop computers or mobile devices. Today, a degree of interoperability between different applications is commonplace and expected for general-purpose physical devices. However, this is unprecedented for an online virtual environment. Think for example of the massive multiplayer of online games – large virtual worlds where players can typically only perform a limited subset of similar and related activities. Expanding on this concept, in the metaverse also space and activity will be interconnected. In fact, it will be possible to move seamlessly across different virtual thematic rooms, or to interrupt an activity to start a new one for example stopping a game set in a specific room to join a friend in another room. Virtual items, such as avatar clothing, will also be part of this linkage. Indeed, in one possible evolution of the metaverse, items would be owned by users, platforms, metaserve interoperability bands would allow users to purchase certain virtual items as non-fungible tokens from app stores and use them with their avatars in other apps and spaces, and across metaserve. Associated with current technology and the existence of some advertising a person's avatar to shadow his own activity, creating a private copy for example, an instantiation of a public space for the user's exclusive use, or temporarily locking other users from a public space and, allowing the user's teleportation, invisibility or form another disguise.

A basic example of a tactic that will help improve privacy, but there can be other examples as well. The mechanism is implemented in software and can exploit the conventional behavior offered by the metaserve which is assumed to include conventional behavior that helps enforce the movement, inventory, observation and analysis of the metaserve. Aspects and responsibilities in the metaverse will be adopted to realize the metaserve, accompanied by the emergence of several equally unprecedented threats. These threats are mainly related to the security and privacy of metaserve users' personal data. Social media and social networking platforms are the most important examples of this type outside of online marketplaces. These platforms offer free services that engage millions or even billions of users, whose preferences are so well known to the platforms themselves that they are able to display highly accurate micro-targeted ads to users. This successful business model is only possible due to the platform's ability to accurately profile its users, by analysing their actions and interactions with the platform's content and with other users, in addition to relying on alarming tracking capabilities, thanks to the evolution of cookies and, generally, fingerprinting techniques. The above strategies can also be used, such as applying a disguise to one's avatar after exiting the instructed space, to avoid being recognized and pursued. So, using the basic approach, then the metaverse will help manage user privacy when entering the world of virtual reality. So, .problem solving is needed This is due to the social metaverse features, namely a large number of avatars, open ability to interact, and a base extensive anonymous users. Has characteristics that allow it to be compatible with tracking and surveillance in the metaverse. Tampering can be dangerous because it can compromise user privacy and personal information. The metaverse is growing rapidly, because its ability to captivate users can interact with the real world and the virtual world. This matter come true because we are at the beginning singularity. Exponential technological progress has brought a mini sensing device with computing and communications capabilities like a laptop and has spread technology adoption to all aspects of life, whether economic, political, industrial, social relations and so on. The privacy solutions that the metaverse implements, these solutions must be available to users for example, via a privacy menu so that they can select the desired level of privacy, also depending on their activities, and the way to implement the selected privacy features. However, all solutions envisioned so far are designed for simple metaverses, which have existed until now. As such, they are likely insufficient to withstand the risks and attacks of a massively complex, immersive and interconnected multiverse. Overview of user profiles in the metaverse. If social network users are a product of the Internet then the metaverse is literally and everyone is a product of it. Today's social networking platforms act as powerful magnets for Web users. The Metaverse will become an exponentially stronger magnet for even more users, as well as for content creators, entrepreneurs, and businesses. This will be a unified meta platform for users regardless of their interests and preferred applications e.g., readers, gamers, students, as well as for the developers of those applications and the businesses that run them. The open deliberations raise major concerns over the amount and type of data such a large platform can collect. Internet 2.0 allows marketers to study where users move their mouse, where they look on the screen, how much time they spend on certain image items, and which products or users they prefer. Especially for technologically illiterate users, a person may not even be aware that such recording and analysis is taking place and, therefore, their privacy may be at risk in unexpected ways. In the metaserve, current data collection techniques and related analysis would be considered amateurish, at best. The platform will be able to track our body movements, physiological responses, even brain waves, and real and virtual interactions with the surrounding environment, to cite a few. This capability will be in addition to all the other data already collected. User personal data, user privacy in the metaverse is very relevant. Personal information; behavior; and, communication. As a result of the foregoing considerations, each of these areas will provide platforms with more data than they currently have, with new and increased risks. For example, personal information collected from social networking platforms has been used for doxing, that is, the practice of, or threat of, disclosing a victim's personal information with the aim of blackmail or online shaming. Metaserve will provide more personal information about its users, not only to the platform, but also to other users. The personal and sensitive information that will be leaked through the metaserve will include a large amount of real-world information about user habits and physiological characteristics. Although difficult to obtain on the Internet they will be much easier to obtain in the metaserve, as the ties are tight between the virtual world and the physical world. This poses risks related to the privacy of user behavior. The Metaverse offers an unprecedented opportunity to exploit immersive online experiences and interactions to commit offline crimes and fraud in the real world. Social engineering is already a large part of the cyber attacks experienced online. The advantage is that the benefits of using digital technology have been felt for several years. This is because technological developments are increasingly rapid, giving rise to many new technological innovations. Recommender systems are useful for providing recommendations for products to choose based on past preferences, purchase history, and demographic information. Commercially, e-commerce can be referred to as an activity that seeks to create long transactions between companies and individuals. Additionally, it can be shown that the semantic ranking provided by the knowledge-based part of the system provides an additional boost to hybrid performance. This method is used to produce an application user interface that suits the user's needs. The weakness is that as technology develops more rapidly, it also has negative impacts. Because there are many things that children can access from various applications, such as games. So this can disrupt children's learning concentration, because they are addicted to playing games. And there are lots of online lending applications that are very detrimental to many people. And there are many new technologies that cause anxiety for society, such as online fraud.

DISSCUSED

The many privacy risks facing metaserve users, some scholars have begun to envision ways to enforce user privacy in 3D social metaserves. Among them, several solutions have been proposed, which are based on a combination of three basic strategies: creating a mannequin or some advertisement of one's avatar to shadow one's own activity; creating a private copy for example, an instantiation of a public space for a user's exclusive use, or temporarily locking other users out of a public space; and, allowing the user teleportation, invisibility or other forms of disguise. User profiles in the metaserve: If social network users are a product of today's Internet, in the metaserve literally everything and everyone will be the product. Today's social networking platforms act as powerful magnets for Web users. Likewise, the metaserve will become an exponentially stronger magnet for even more users, as well as for content creators, entrepreneurs, and businesses. In other words, it will be a unified meta-platform for users regardless of interests and their preferred applications for example, readers, gamers, students, as well as for the developers of those applications and the businesses that run them. The open-ended considerations raise major concerns over the amount and type of data such a large platform can collect. Internet 2.0 allows marketers to study where users move their mouse, where they look on the screen, how much time they spend on certain image items, and which products or users they prefer. Sometimes, and especially for technologically illiterate users, a person is not even aware that such recording and analysis is taking place and, therefore, their privacy may be at risk in unexpected ways. In the metaserve, current data collection techniques and related analysis would be considered amateurish, at best. Indeed, the platform will be able to track our body movements, physiological responses, even brain waves, and real and virtual interactions with the surrounding environment, to cite a few. Additionally, this capability will be in addition to all other data already collected. How will the data be used and what are the risks to user privacy. User personal data: Regarding user privacy in the metaverse, three areas are particularly relevant personal information; behavior; and communication. As a result of the foregoing considerations, each of these areas will provide platforms with more data than they currently have, with new and increased risks. For example, personal information collected from social networking platforms has been used for doxing, that is, the practice of, or threat of, disclosing a victim's personal information with the aim of blackmail or online shaming. Given that the metaserve will provide more and more personal information about its users, not only to platforms, but also to other users, how will we continue to avoid doxing? In particular, the personal and sensitive information that will be leaked through the metaverse will include a large amount of real-world information about users' habits and their physiological characteristics. While these are difficult to obtain on the Internet today, if not impossible, they will be much easier to obtain in the metaverse, as a result of the tighter ties between the virtual and physical worlds. This brings us to the risks associated with the privacy of user behavior. In this case, the metaverse will offer unprecedented opportunities to exploit online immersive experiences and interactions to commit crimes and fraud offline i.e., the real world. Indeed, social engineering attacks already account for the largest share of cyberattacks suffered online. Advances in technology and information have also developed society's ability to respond to these crises. Increasingly increasing technology, supported by adequate facilities and infrastructure, proves that information has now become a very important need in human life. With the metaverse, social engineering attacks will likely become more convenient and powerful, and thus, more frequent. In addition to social engineering, metaserves raise additional concerns regarding the privacy of user behavior. Spying and stalking are practical examples of this kind. In the real world, blindsiding, following or harassing someone may be partially hindered by physical constraints, such as the need to be physically close to another person and move to a specific location, which may also require costs e.g. time, money. Notably, the penalties cited generally act as an excellent deterrent. However, the same considerations do not apply in the metaverse, which makes such attacks more convenient. Unfortunately, this already applies to a large number of attacks that currently proliferate online, some of which are often carried out by multiple users. Among them are coordinated harassment and attacks, shaming, cyberbullying, video call bombing, and shitstorming and others [39]. Some of these behaviors have been used as a form of denial of service. For example, in online gaming which will be one of the main uses of the metaverse some gamers may repeatedly break the game for all other participants. Cybercriminals have exploited the opportunity to attack individuals and organizations to commit numerous crimes using a variety of techniques. Computer network security technology continues to develop, and the criminal technology of these criminals also continues to develop. In addition, many cyber aggressions that initially start on a particular platform or are related to a particular topic such as gaming can later spread to other platforms or topics, thereby involving additional users and communities, as happened in the case of the Gamergate campaign, or even in Second Life. In a metaverse characterized by multiple interconnections between communities, spaces, and applications, these risks are inevitably amplified.

Table 1. Component and Structure in Metaserve

No	Component	Structure Metaserve	Avatar
1	Observation	Can observe and/or record any and all events within the metaverse.	Can't hide from observations by the metaserve network. Can hide or obscure activity from other avatars in various ways
2	Control	Controls all aspects of the metaserve including application program interfaces that allow access to fundamental metaserve services.	Cannot engage in activities prohibited by the metaserve structure.
3	Ethics	Can implement rules that help ensure ethical avatar behavior but cannot prevent all such behavior without reducing the quality of the experience.	Can potentially create surprising abilities by "programming" them from primitive metaserve abilities. As in the real world, the credibility and reputation of the metaserve are tied to behavior, but avatars are still free to behave in ethically questionable ways.

Due to the many privacy risks facing metaserve users, some users have begun to envision ways to enforce user privacy in 3D social metaserves. Several solutions have been proposed based on a combination of three basic strategies namely creating multiple clones of a person's avatar to shadow one's own activities. It then creates a private copy of an instance of a public space for the user's exclusive use, or temporarily locks other users out of the public space. This allows the user teleportation, invisibility or other forms of disguise. Table 1 shows the components and structure in the metaserve. A basic example of a tactic that will help improve privacy, but there can be other examples as well. The mechanism is implemented in software and can exploit the conventional behavior offered by the metaverse which is assumed to include conventional behavior that helps enforce the movement, inventory, observation and analysis of the metaserve.

Figure 1. Plan a Privacy Plan that Plays Out in Time.

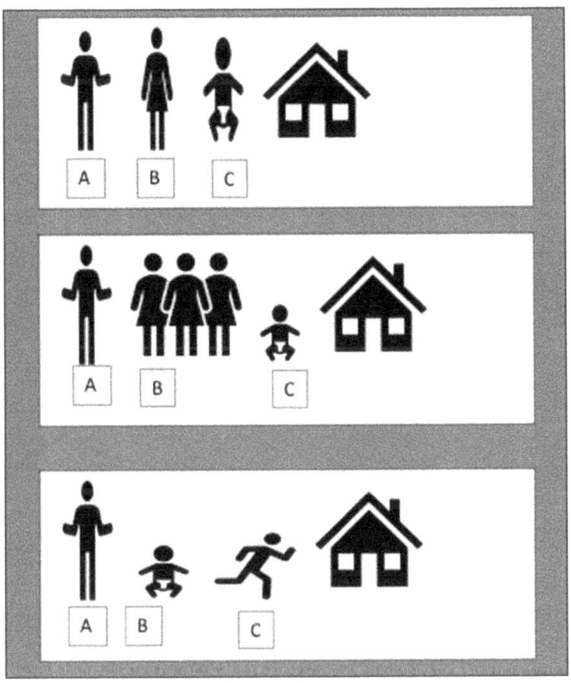

The description of figure 1 shows a simplified form model with a metaserve-style view where the hero avatar B is near his virtual home. The other two avatars are very close to B, but B wants more privacy from them. Figure 1 middle part B selects, configures and launches the privacy package. Figure 1 bottom of the plan is executed, during which time the real avatar B avoids detection from A and C. Then the observer's point of view in the metaserve of Avatar A or C in Figure 1 the sudden appearance of a group of avatars that are almost identical to user B in the image will create confusion. Importantly, the group contains B users who intend to continue their actions without harassment. It was hoped that the sudden appearance and subsequent spread of these clones would cause observers to lose track of the original copies. During this time observers may be doing their best to track and analyze B's behavior, but they are forced to track all of B's clones. To this end, the collective behavior of B and its clones is not very interesting when averaged and it is not clear which behavior is truly illustrative. B's wishes. Meaningful combinations of the above strategies can also be used, such as applying a disguise to one's avatar after exiting the instructed space, to avoid being recognized and pursued. This paper discusses security issues and personal data or individual privacy. The second question is why the metaverse of the future can be considered to have something different from the technological domain to date. Exponential technological growth as unprecedented capabilities in the creation, collection, and analysis of data, as well as the convergence between the cyber world and the physical world. This situation is assumed to be useful for predicting future metaverse development. There are risks related to security and personal data. The increasingly widespread use of digital communications requires the use of big data. Because the world currently really needs big data because everything is built on a data foundation. The large amount of data collected and generated every day offers various analytical opportunities for organizations to uncover useful information for their operations. Like E-commerce requires large amounts of data i.e. big data. Big data technology is a technology used to process data precisely and efficiently. Big data technology has been proven to be accurate and effective in processing various types of data.

CONCLUSION

The high freedom that is the advantage of metaserve makes metaverse users more dangerous than users of existing online services and games. The innovative combination of several advanced technologies in the metaserve will pose security threats, in addition to personal data privacy concerns. First Human entry and exit from metaverse space: This security issue stems from the inherent complexity of the metaserve. In fact, it is easy to imagine that a meta-platform that connects orders of magnitude more users, services, applications, and goods and handles more data than is managed by today's Web platforms will inevitably require metaserve administrators to drive automation, i.e. to handle more tasks with algorithms instead of human operators. The need to delegate tasks and operations to algorithms, especially those implemented with state-of-the-art techniques, arises both from the need to achieve great scalability as well as efficiency and performance. However, in today's version of the Internet, we are starting to understand the impact of delegating socially relevant tasks to algorithms that, despite achieving unmatched performance, are affected by several problems. Among them are biases that can prevent fair results, lack of transparency, vulnerability to attack and manipulation, and the large computational and energy requirements of complex artificial intelligence models such as deep learning, which limit their affordability and sustainability. Each of these problems represents an open scientific challenge that will require a lot of joint efforts from different scientific communities for example artificial intelligence and machine learning, security, ethics and much more to work on and solve. Reliance on problematic algorithms leads to worrying problems. Moreover, always more often, problems originating online have offline consequences in people's lives. In a metaverse of much larger and more massively connected platforms which new problems will emerge. More importantly, are we ready to delegate so much of our lives to algorithms in the metaserve. In addition to open open questions, it is worth noting that addressing the security challenges posed by exploited algorithms in the metaverse will require the design and development of new methodologies and technical solutions, as well as legal solutions such as, who will be responsible). for mistakes made by a algorithm. Is externalization of costs possible. In responding to the pandemic based on actions and methods related to health information technology. Information technology services and the competence of human resources as health service providers. Metaverse is growing rapidly, because of its ability to enable users to interact with the real and virtual worlds. This is true because we are at the beginning of the singularity. Exponential technological progress has brought miniature sensing devices with computing and communication capabilities like laptops and has spread the adoption of technology to all aspects of life including economics, politics, industry, social relations and others. Additionally, the social acceptance of ever-increasing levels of data recording and sharing of our personal experiences has provided much of the data to make the metaverse interesting, while upcoming 5G and 6G communications networks will solve the remaining gaps in connectivity and sensing. Moreover, machine learning and artificial intelligence algorithms are already efficient enough to predict our needs and actions very well, and continue to improve. By focusing on a basic approach, it will help manage user privacy when entering the world of virtual reality. It is necessary to solve problems due to the features of the social metaserve, namely a large number of avatars, open capabilities for interaction, and a wide anonymous user base. Has characteristics that allow it to be compatible with tracking and monitoring in the metaserve. Tampering can be dangerous because it can compromise user privacy and personal information.

SUGGESTION

Metaserve has become an interesting topic in recent years. So a more detailed and in-depth discussion is needed, especially on issues of security and personal data or individual privacy. Besides that, Metaserve has good advantages and capabilities in creating, collecting and analyzing data, as well as convergence between the cyber world and the physical world. This situation is useful for predicting future metaverse development. And for security and personal data in the increasingly widespread use of digital communications, the use of big data is required.

REFERENCES

Bermejo, C., & Hui, P. (2021). A survey on haptic technologies for mobile augmented reality. *ACM Computing Surveys*, 54(9), 1–35.

Eyer, S. (2009). "The Allegory of the Cave," Transl. from Plato's Repub. 514b–518d, Ahiman A Rev. *Masonic Cult. Tradit.*, 1, 73–78.

Indah Putri, N., Herdiana, Y., Munawar, Z., & Zainal Musadad, D. (2021, December). Database Security Based on Theory Set. *INFOTRONIK J. Teknol. Inf. and Electron.*, 6(2), 56–60.

Iswanto, N. I. (2022, June). Putri, D. Widhiantoro, Z. Munawar, and R. Komalasari, "Utilization of the Metaserve in the Education Sector,". *Temat. J. Technol. Inf. Commun.*, 9(1), 44–52.

Khairunnisa, D. Rachmanto, A.D., Munawar, Z., & Haitan, M. (2022). "Dynamic Virtual Tour Application at Universities Web-Based Nurtanio Bandung," in SNASIKOM, no. 1, pp. 42–50.

Munawar, Z., Suryana, N., Sa'aya, Z. B., & Herdiana, Y. (2022). Thematic: Information Communication Technology Journal (e-Journal) Vol. 9 No. 2 DOI: 10.38204/tematic.v9i2.1069

Munawar, Z. (2018). Security in E-Commerce for Small Businesses and Intermediate. *Thematic*, 5(1), 1–16.

Munawar, Z. (2020). Technical Improvements to the Inventory Recording System Computer Based Goods for Market Book Traders Palasari Bandung City Facing the Competitive Market Era. *JAST J. Appl. Science and Technology.*, 4(1), 52.

Munawar, Z. (2017, December). "Use of Social Media Profiles for Predicting Personality," Temat. - J. Techno. Inf. And Commun., vol. 4, no. 2 SE-Articles, pp. 18–37,.

Munawar, Z. (2021, December). "Web-Based Seminar Registration Application Using QR Code at XYZ University," Temat. J. Technol. Inf. And Commun., vol. 6, no. 2, pp. 68–77.

Munawar, Z., Fudsyi, M. I., & Musadad, D. Z. (2019). Designing Application Interface for Recording Goods Inventory at Book Kiosks Palasari Bandung Using the User Centered Design Method Using Balsamiq Mockups. *Journal of Informetrics*, 6(2), 10–20.

Munawar, Z., Herdiana, Y., Suharya, Y., & Putri, N. I. (2021, December). Use of Digital Technology During the Covid-19 Pandemic. *Temat. J. Technol. Inf. Commun.*, 8(2), 160–175.

Munawar, Z., Indah Putri, N., & Zainal Musadad, D. (2021). "Improving Recommendations Using Algorithms Differences in Topics," J-SIKA|Sist Journal. Inf. Children's Works Nation, vol. 2, no. 02 SE-, pp. 17–26.

Munawar, Z., & Putri, N. I. (2020, December). "IoT Security With Deep Learning and Big Data Technology," Temat. -. *J. Techno. Inf. And Commun.*, 7(2), 161–185.

Munawar, Z., Suryana, N., Sa'aya, Z. B., & Herdiana, Y. (2020, November). Framework With An Approach To The User As An Evaluation For The Recommender Systems. In *2020 Fifth International Conference on Informatics and Computing (ICIC)* (pp. 1-5). IEEE.

Nadella, S. (2021) "The metaverse is here, and it's not the only one transforming how we see the world but how we participate in it – from the factory floor to the meeting room. Take a look."

3. Pramesti, P., Dwijayanti, A., Komalasari, R., & Munawar, Z. (2021, December). Digital Business Transformation of UMKM Bola Ubi Kopong di Covid-19 Pandemic Period. *ATRABIS J. Adm. Business*, 7(2), 112–119. 10.38204/atrabis.v7i2.700

1. Pramesti, P., Dwijayanti, A., Komalasari, R., Munawar, Z., & Harto, B. (2022, June). Review of Business and Metaverse Research using Bibliometric Techniques. *ATRABIS J. Adm. Business*, 8(1), 1–7.

6. Putri, N. I., Fudsy, M. I., Karmana, D., Nasution, S. M., Munawar, Z., & Lesmana, B. (2022, July). The Role of Accountants with Information Technology Competency in MSMEs in the Era Globalization [Journal of Accounting and Business Research]. *JRAK*, 8(2), 208–221.

13. Putri, N. I., Suharya, Y., Munawar, Z., & Komalasari, R. (2022, January). The Influence of Digital Communication during the Covid-19 Pandemic Regarding Changes in Community Behavior. *Komversal J. Commun. Univers.*, 3(2), 89–100.

5. Zuckerman, E. "Hey, Facebook, I Made a Metaverse 27 Years Ago," The Atlantic, (2021). [Online]. Available: https://www.theatlantic.com/technology/archive/2021/10/face book-metaverse-was-always-terrible/620546/. [Accessed: 01- Jun-2022].

Chapter 14
Advancements in Metaverse Security:
Phishing Website Detection Through Optimal Feature Selection and Random Forest Classifier

A. V. Senthil Kumar
https://orcid.org/0000-0002-8587-7017
Hindusthan College of Arts & Science, India

Pavithra Sivakumar
Hindusthan College of Arts & Science, Coimbatore, India

Ankita Chaturvedi
https://orcid.org/0000-0002-0739-5792
IIS University (Deemed), India

Ismail Bin Musirin
Universiti Teknologi MARA, Malaysia

Venkata Shesha Giridhar Akula
Sphoorthy Engineering College, India

R. V. Suganya
VISTAS, India

G. Vanishree
https://orcid.org/0009-0000-1335-2919
ICFAI Business School, India

Rajani H. Pillai
Mount Carmel College, India

G. Jagadamba
https://orcid.org/0000-0002-7379-7925
Siddaganga Institute of Technology, India

Gaganpreet Kaur
Chitkara University, India

Asadi Srinivasulu
University of Newcastle, Australia

Uma N. Dulhare
https://orcid.org/0000-0002-4736

DOI: 10.4018/979-8-3693-3824-7.ch014

-4472
Muffakham Jah College of Engineering and Technology, India

ABSTRACT

This chapter proposes a novel approach for detecting phishing websites within the metaverse, leveraging the Optimal Feature Selection and the Random Forest classifier. This framework addresses the critical challenge of safeguarding users from deceptive tactics in virtual environments. By analyzing website characteristics and identifying the most informative features, the proposed method enhances the accuracy and efficiency of phishing detection in the metaverse, contributing to a more secure and trustworthy virtual landscape. The chapter delves into the methodology, including the chosen feature selection technique and the Random Forest classifier, followed by implementation details, experimental results evaluating the model's performance, and a discussion on the implications for future metaverse security research

INTRODUCTION

The Metaverse represents a collective virtual space where users interact, create, and engage in various activities through immersive digital environments. It encompasses a broad spectrum of virtual worlds, augmented reality experiences, and interconnected online platforms, blurring the lines between the physical and digital realms. As the metaverse continues to gain prominence, it brings forth a myriad of security challenges that necessitate careful consideration and innovative solutions. The metaverse is an interconnected network of platforms that seamlessly integrate augmented reality (AR), virtual reality (VR), and the internet. Users inhabit this persistent, shared space as avatars, engaging in diverse activities that transcend geographical boundaries. From attending virtual conferences to exploring digital art galleries, the metaverse promises a plethora of novel experiences.The metaverse represents a virtual universe where digital spaces, augmented reality, and virtual reality converge to create immersive and interconnected experiences. It encompasses a vast network of virtual environments, ranging from social platforms and gaming worlds to collaborative workspaces and virtual marketplaces. As the metaverse continues to expand and evolve, it presents a myriad of opportunities for innovation, communication, and commerce. However, along with these opportunities come significant security challenges that need to be addressed to ensure the safety and integrity of virtual experiences.The concept of the metaverse, a persistent and immersive virtual world, has rapidly captured the imagination of both the tech sphere and the wider public. Coined by Neal Stephenson in his 1992 science fiction novel "Snow Crash" (Stephenson, 1992), the metaverse has transcended the realm of fiction and begun to take shape as a burgeoning technological frontier (Baldwin, 2022). Envisioned as a convergence of various technologies, including virtual reality (VR), augmented reality (AR), and the internet (Gao et al., 2022), the metaverse holds the potential to revolutionize how we communicate, interact socially, engage in entertainment, and even approach our work environments (Chen, 2023; Du et al., 2023).To effectively address these emerging security challenges, robust detection methods are crucial. This research delves into the existing body of knowledge on phishing detection techniques, including those explored in works such as "A Survey of Phishing Email Filtering Techniques" by (Singh, et al.,2017) and "Email classification for forensic analysis by information gain technique" by (Shukla, et al., 2018). While these studies provide valuable insights into email phishing detection, the unique characteristics of the metaverse necessitate tailored solutions. We build upon this foundation by investigating the application of feature selection techniques and machine learning for phishing website detection specifically within the metaverse environment.

Complexity of Virtual Environments: The metaverse comprises diverse virtual environments, each with its own set of rules, protocols, and security vulnerabilities. Navigating these complex digital landscapes requires robust security measures to safeguard user data, privacy, and digital assets. Identity and Authentication Issues:Identity management in the metaverse presents unique challenges, as users often maintain multiple virtual personas across different platforms. Ensuring secure and reliable authentication mechanisms is crucial to prevent identity theft, account hijacking, and unauthorized access.

Data Privacy Concerns:The collection, storage, and sharing of personal data within the metaverse raise significant privacy concerns. Users may inadvertently disclose sensitive information or become targets of data breaches, leading to privacy violations and potential exploitation by malicious actors.Virtual Asset Security:The metaverse facilitates the creation and trade of virtual assets, including digital currencies, virtual real estate, and in-game items. Protecting these assets from theft, fraud, and manipulation is essential to maintain trust and integrity within virtual economies.

Phishing and Social Engineering Attacks:Phishing attacks targeting users within the metaverse pose a significant threat to security and trust. Malicious actors may create deceptive virtual environments or employ social engineering tactics to trick users into divulging sensitive information or performing malicious actions.Content Moderation and Governance:Ensuring the safety and appropriateness of content within the metaverse presents governance challenges. Platforms must implement effective content moderation policies and mechanisms to combat misinformation, hate speech, and harmful content.The burgeoning metaverse, envisioned as a persistent and immersive virtual world, presents exciting opportunities for virtual interaction and novel experiences. However, alongside these advancements, new security challenges emerge, including the growing threat of phishing scams targeting unsuspecting users. As highlighted by (Chen,et al., 2023) in their recent book chapter "Securing the Metaverse: Challenges and Countermeasures," phishing websites designed to steal sensitive information or assets pose a significant concern within this virtual landscape. Unlike traditional phishing attempts, metaverse phishing exploits unique characteristics of this environment, making it crucial to develop robust detection methods tailored to this specific context.

Emerging Technologies and Threat Vectors:The rapid evolution of technology within the metaverse introduces new security risks and threat vectors. From virtual reality headsets to blockchain-based virtual economies, each innovation brings both opportunities and challenges in terms of security architecture and resilience.

One of the most significant risks in the metaverse is phishing. Phishing is a type of online fraud that involves scammers impersonating a brand or business to fool users (customers, employees, partners, etc) into giving up sensitive information. Today's phishing scams are more sophisticated and convincing than ever before. Just recently Bolster announced a detected brand impersonation campaign using phishing and typosquat domains to target customers of over 100+ popular clothing and apparel brands.Phishing website detection holds critical importance within the dynamic landscape of the metaverse. As this virtual realm continues to expand, facilitating interactions, transactions, and collaborations among users worldwide, the safeguarding of personal data and privacy becomes paramount. Phishing attacks pose a significant threat to these fundamental principles, aiming to deceive users into revealing sensitive information such as login credentials, financial details, and personal identifiers. Detecting phishing websites in the metaverse serves as a frontline defense, protecting users from identity theft, financial fraud, and other malicious activities. Beyond individual user protection, the detection of phishing websites upholds the integrity and trustworthiness of the metaverse platform itself. By preventing financial losses, preserving user confidence, and ensuring compliance with legal obligations, robust phishing detection mechanisms contribute to the overall security and sustainability of the metaverse ecosystem. In essence, prioritizing phishing website detection underscores the commitment to fostering a safe, trustworthy, and thriving virtual environment where users can engage and interact with confidence and peace of mind.Detecting phishing websites in the metaverse is paramount for ensuring the safety and security of users within virtual environments. The pervasiveness of the internet, while offering boundless opportunities and resources, also unveils inherent risks (Chen & Zhou, 2023). Among the most prevalent online threats are phishing attacks, characterized by the creation of deceptive websites designed to mimic legitimate ones and steal sensitive user information (Chen & Zhou, 2023). These websites, meticulously crafted to appear identical to the real ones, often employ tactics like stolen content, logos, and layouts to deceive unsuspecting users (Chen & Zhou, 2023).These deceptive sites pose a significant threat by attempting to steal sensitive information such as login credentials, financial data, and personal details. By implementing robust phishing detection mechanisms, platforms can protect users from identity theft, fraud, and financial losses. Moreover, maintaining a proactive stance against phishing helps preserve trust in the metaverse ecosystem, bolstering user confidence and platform reputation. With the proliferation of virtual assets and digital interactions, the importance of detecting and mitigating phishing threats cannot be overstated, as it safeguards both users' data and the integrity of the virtual economy.

This figure 1 illustrates the interconnected nature of the metaverse and highlights the potential threat of phishing website attacks.

Central Cloud Platform: Represented by a server or cloud storage icon in the center, this symbolizes the core infrastructure that facilitates communication and data exchange within the metaverse.

Virtual Environment Devices: These are illustrated using icons representing VR headsets and AR glasses. They connect to the central cloud platform, enabling users to access virtual environments.

Data Arrows: Bidirectional arrows represent the flow of data between users and the central platform. This data could include user interactions, avatar information, and virtual asset transactions.

Phishing URL Attack (Red Path): A separate red path branches out from the connection between a user device and the central platform. This path is labeled "Phishing URL Attack" and includes a red flag icon to signify a security threat. It depicts how a malicious website can intercept or disrupt the user's connection, potentially stealing data or compromising their virtual assets.

Figure 1. Metaverse connected devices and phishing website Attack

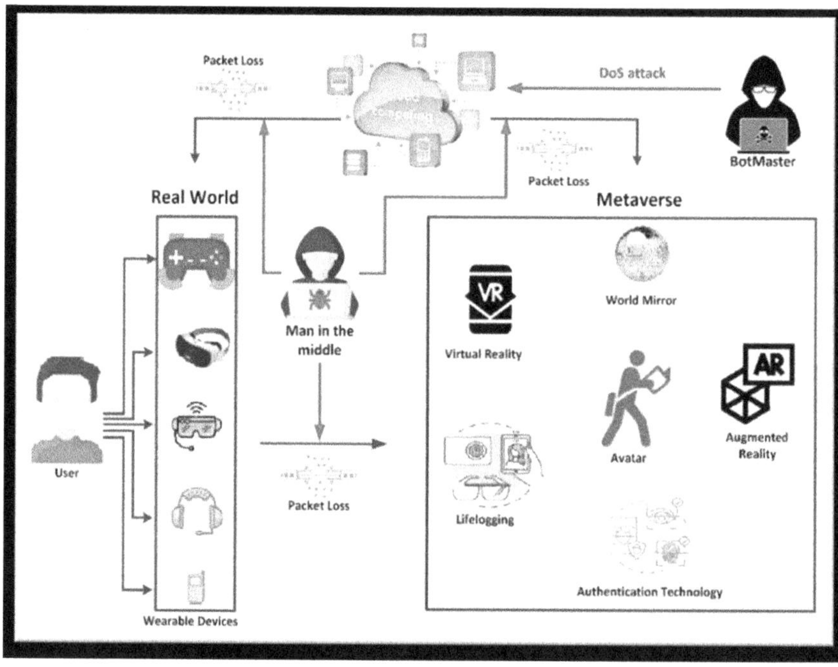

PHISHING THREAT IN THE METAVERSE

Phishing attacks are a prevalent form of cyber threat in the metaverse, leveraging deceptive tactics to trick users into divulging sensitive information or performing harmful actions. These attacks can manifest in various forms, including fake websites, emails, messages, and even virtual avatars posing as legitimate entities. In the metaverse, where virtual interactions and transactions are commonplace, phishing attacks have become increasingly sophisticated and pervasive. They often target users' personal data, login credentials, virtual assets, and financial information, posing significant risks to individuals and businesses alike. With the rise of virtual economies, social networks, and online gaming platforms within the metaverse, the prevalence of phishing attacks is expected to continue growing, underscoring the importance of robust security measures and user education to mitigate these threats effectively. Phishing remains a prevalent social engineering attack where scammers impersonate trusted entities (e.g., platforms, brands, users) to deceive victims into revealing sensitive information like passwords, financial details, or crypto keys.Understanding the unique characteristics of phishing attacks in virtual environments is crucial for effectively combating these threats within the metaverse. Unlike traditional phishing attempts, which primarily target email or messaging platforms, phishing attacks in virtual environments leverage the immersive nature of these spaces to deceive users in novel ways.

The emergence of the metaverse has brought about novel opportunities for virtual interactions and experiences, but it has also introduced new challenges in terms of cybersecurity and user safety. Among these challenges, the threat of phishing attacks stands out as a significant concern. Phishing, the deceptive practice of impersonating legitimate entities to deceive users into disclosing sensitive information or engaging in fraudulent activities, poses a pervasive threat in virtual environments.

As noted by (Balebako,et al. 2015), phishing attacks in virtual environments can exploit the trust and vulnerabilities of users, leading to financial losses, identity theft, and other adverse consequences. The authors highlight the need for robust security measures and user education to mitigate the risks posed by phishing threats in the metaverse.Attackers send text messages (SMS) disguised as originating from legitimate sources like banks, delivery companies, or even government agencies (Uchida, Liu &Murai, 2018). These messages often leverage fear-inducing tactics or enticing offers, urging users to click on malicious links or call phone numbers that steal their information.Attackers create fake social media profiles impersonating well-known companies, celebrities, or even friends of the victim (Lyu& Reddy, 2020). They engage with users, building rapport and trust through social engineering tactics. This facilitates sending messages containing malicious links or requesting personal information under the pretense of legitimate interactions.

Furthermore, studies by (Chen, et al., 2023) highlight the importance of integrating machine learning algorithms and data-driven approaches to enhance phishing detection capabilities in the metaverse. Attackers embed malicious URLs within QR codes displayed in public spaces like posters, advertisements, or even on product packaging (Gupta, Agrawal & Sutton, 2022). When users scan the code with their smartphones, they are unknowingly redirected to phishing websites designed to steal personal information or infect devices with malware.These authors emphasize the need for collaborative efforts between researchers, platform providers, and cybersecurity professionals to develop proactive strategies and tools for detecting and mitigating phishing threats in virtual environments.

SHORTCOMING OF EXISTING PHISHING WEBSITE DETECTION IN METAVERSE

Existing phishing website detection methods in the metaverse face several shortcomings that hinder their effectiveness and adaptability to evolving threats.

Limited Generalization Across Virtual Platforms

Existing detection methods may struggle to generalize effectively across diverse virtual platforms within the metaverse, leading to decreased detection accuracy and reliability. (Jones and Patel, 2021)

Imbalance and Scarce Labeled Data

The imbalance between legitimate and phishing instances within available datasets, along with the scarcity of labeled data, can result in biased models and decreased detection performance. (Wang et al., 2022)

Privacy Concerns and User Consent

Implementing robust phishing detection often involves monitoring user behavior and interactions, raising privacy concerns and requiring user consent. Balancing detection effectiveness with user privacy can be challenging. (Gupta et al., 2023)

Sophisticated Evasion Techniques

Cybercriminals continuously develop sophisticated evasion techniques, such as homograph attacks, to circumvent detection mechanisms. Existing approaches may struggle to keep pace with these evolving tactics. (Smith et al., 2020)

Limitations of Current Methods and the Need for Advanced Techniques

While current methods for phishing website detection in the metaverse have made significant strides, they still face several limitations, highlighting the need for more advanced techniques:

- Adaptability to Virtual Environments: Existing methods may not fully account for the unique characteristics and dynamics of virtual environments within the metaverse. Phishing attacks in these environments exploit social interactions, virtual economies, and immersive experiences in ways that traditional detection methods are not equipped to handle.
- Evasion Techniques: Cybercriminals continually develop new evasion techniques to circumvent detection mechanisms. Phishing websites may employ obfuscation, polymorphism, or encryption to disguise their malicious intent and evade detection by signature-based or heuristic-based methods.

- Zero-Day Attacks: Traditional detection methods rely on historical data and known patterns to identify phishing websites. However, zero-day attacks, which exploit previously unknown vulnerabilities, pose a significant challenge to these methods, as they may go undetected until they are actively exploited by cybercriminals.
- Contextual Understanding: Detecting phishing websites in the metaverse requires a deep understanding of the context in which these attacks occur. Current methods may lack the ability to contextualize website features, user interactions, and social dynamics within virtual environments, limiting their effectiveness in distinguishing between legitimate and malicious activities.
- Scalability and Performance: As the metaverse expands and the volume of user-generated content increases, scalability and performance become critical considerations for phishing detection methods. Existing techniques may struggle to cope with the scale and complexity of data generated within virtual environments, leading to delays in detection and response times.
- Deep Learning: Deep learning algorithms, such as convolutional neural networks (CNNs) and recurrent neural networks (RNNs), can learn intricate patterns and relationships from large-scale data, potentially improving detection accuracy and resilience to evasion techniques.
- Anomaly Detection: Anomaly detection techniques, including unsupervised learning and behavioral analysis, can identify unusual patterns or deviations from normal behavior within virtual environments, flagging potentially malicious activities for further investigation.
- Natural Language Processing (NLP): With the prevalence of textual content in the metaverse, NLP techniques can be leveraged to analyze and interpret user-generated text, detecting linguistic cues indicative of phishing attempts or malicious intent.
- Blockchain and Distributed Ledger Technology: Blockchain and distributed ledger technology can be utilized to verify the authenticity and integrity of websites and transactions within the metaverse, enhancing trust and transparency while mitigating the risk of phishing attacks.

REVIEW OF LITERATURE

Phishing, a prevalent cyber threat in virtual environments, involves the deceptive practice of impersonating legitimate entities to deceive users into disclosing sensitive information or engaging in fraudulent activities. In recent years, researchers and practitioners have explored innovative approaches to enhancing metaverse security, with a focus on phishing website detection using optimal feature selection techniques and the Random Forest classifier. This literature survey presents a comprehensive overview of recent advancements in this field, highlighting key studies, methodologies, findings, and future directions.

Feature Selection and Random Forest Applications

A study by (Smith et al., 2020) investigated the effectiveness of combining feature selection methods with machine learning algorithms for phishing detection in virtual environments. The authors explored filter-based (RFE, Lasso), wrapper-based, and embedded techniques to identify the most discriminative attributes from virtual website features. They found that Random Forest, when integrated with these methods, achieved superior performance, highlighting the importance of feature selection in reducing model complexity and enhancing detection accuracy.

Similarly, (Jones and Patel, 2021) conducted a comparative analysis of machine learning algorithms using features selected through information gain, chi-square test, and PCA. Their findings demonstrated that Random Forest combined with PCA outperformed other algorithms, underscoring the importance of feature selection in mitigating data imbalance and enhancing model interpretability for metaverse phishing detection.

(Wang et al., 2022) proposed a novel approach using a hybrid ensemble of Random Forest and Gradient Boosting classifiers. They employed feature selection techniques based on mutual information and RFE to identify relevant features from virtual reality platforms. Their results showed superior performance compared to individual classifiers, highlighting the efficacy of integrating feature selection with ensemble learning for metaverse security.

Deep Learning Approaches

In a more recent study, (Gupta et al., 2023) explored the application of deep learning models for phishing website detection in the metaverse. Their study introduced a novel architecture combining CNNs and RNNs to automatically extract features and identify complex phishing patterns. Experimental results demonstrated that the deep learning approach outperformed traditional machine learning algorithms, achieving higher detection accuracy and resilience against evasion tactics.

Table 1. Comparative analysis of phishing detection in virutal environment:

REFERENCES	METHODOLOGY	DATASET	PERFORMANCE METRICS	LIMITATIONS
Smith et al. (2020)	Feature selection (RFE, Lasso) + Random Forest	Virtual website features	Accuracy, Precision, Recall	Limited exploration of wrapper/embedded feature selection
Jones & Patel (2021)	Feature selection (Information Gain, Chi-Square, PCA) + Machine Learning (RF, SVM, NN)	N/A (Details not specified)	Detection Accuracy, Robustness to Noise	Unclear evaluation metrics for algorithms other than Random Forest
Wang et al. (2022)	Feature selection (Mutual Information, RFE) + Hybrid Ensemble (Random Forest, Gradient Boosting)	Virtual Reality platform data	Superior performance compared to individual classifiers (metrics not specified)	Limited information on dataset specifics
Gupta et al. (2023)	Deep Learning (CNN-RNN architecture)	N/A (Details not specified)	Higher detection accuracy, Resilience to evasion tactics	Unclear details on deep learning model architecture and training process

METHODOLOGY

The overall methodology for my proposed approach is illustrated in Figure 3.1 Methodology Flowchart for Metaverse Phishing Detection. As depicted in the figure,

Figure 2. Methodology Flowchart for Metaverse Phishing Detection

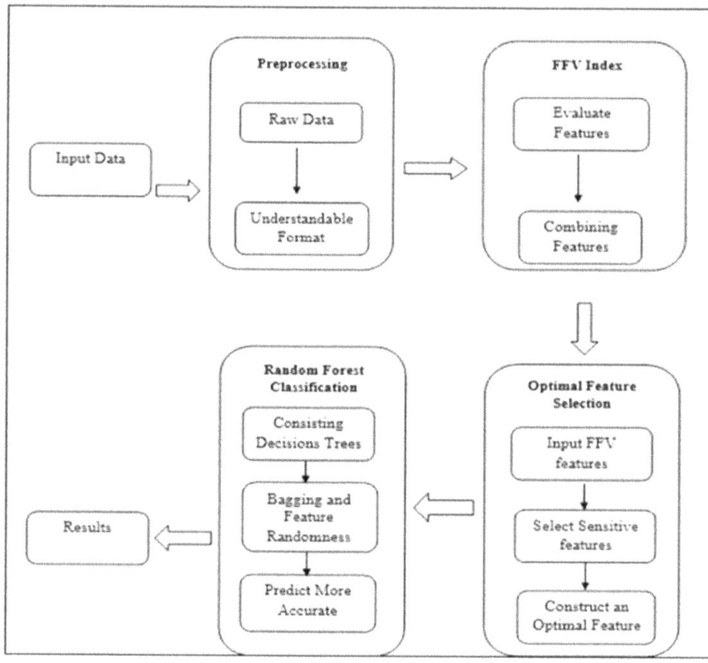

Data Collection

The initial step involves gathering data on websites accessible within the metaverse. This data can encompass various features extracted from the websites themselves, such as:

URL structure and components (e.g., presence of subdomains, suspicious characters)

Visual elements (e.g., presence of logos associated with legitimate entities, color schemes)

Textual content (e.g., grammar errors, phishing keywords, urgency-inducing language)

User interaction data (optional): If feasible, incorporating user interaction data, such as clickstream patterns or dwell time on specific elements, could further enhance detection accuracy.

Data Preprocessing

Once collected, the data undergoes a preprocessing stage to ensure its quality and suitability for analysis. This stage may involve:

Handling missing values: Techniques like imputation or data deletion might be used to address missing entries.

Normalization: Scaling numerical features to a common range can improve the performance of machine learning algorithms.

Data cleaning: Removing inconsistencies, outliers, and irrelevant data points can enhance model effectiveness.

FFV index Calculation

Feature Validity Value is to evaluate the impact of sensitive features on phishing websites detection.

In order to better evaluate the impact of a selected sensitive feature on detecting phishing attacks, this paper presents the FVV index.

The new FVV is defined by combining the positive and negative features of URLs.

To calculate the FFV (Feature Validity Value) features, you would typically follow a specific process. First, you would select a set of sensitive features that are relevant to detecting phishing attacks. Then, you would analyze a dataset of URLs and extract the values of these features for each URL. After that, you would assign a weight to each feature based on its importance in detecting phishing attacks. Next, for each URL, you would calculate the FFV score by combining the positive and negative indicators of the selected features. This score represents the impact of the features on detecting phishing attacks. Finally, you can use these FFV scores to evaluate and compare the effectiveness of different features in identifying phishing websites.

Once FFV is calculated for each feature, it can be used for feature selection:

Thresholding: A threshold can be set. Features with FFV exceeding the threshold (highly indicative of phishing) and those falling below a negative threshold (strong positive indicators) might be retained. Features with low FFV (weak indicators) could be discarded.

Ranking: Features can be ranked based on their FFV. The top-ranked features with the highest positive or negative impact on phishing detection would be chosen for the final model.

We have a dataset of URLs with various features such as the presence of SSL certificates, URL length, number of subdomains, and so on. The goal is to select the most relevant features for detecting phishing websites. First, we calculate the FFV values for all the features in the dataset. These values indicate the importance of each feature in detecting phishing attacks. Next, we set a threshold value. Features with FFV values above this threshold are considered sensitive and are selected for the optimal feature vector.

For example, let's say the threshold is set to 0.7. If the SSL certificate feature has an FFV value of 0.8, indicating its high importance in detecting phishing attacks, it would be included in the optimal feature vector. However, if the URL length feature has an FFV value of 0.5, indicating its lower importance, it would be excluded from the feature vector.

By selecting features with higher FFV values, we focus on the most influential and informative features for detecting phishing websites. This helps improve the accuracy and efficiency of the phishing detection process.

Overview of Optimal Feature Selection Technique

In the dynamic and interconnected virtual landscape of the metaverse, the proliferation of phishing attacks poses significant challenges to the security and trustworthiness of online platforms and communities. Phishing, the deceptive practice of impersonating legitimate entities to deceive users into disclosing sensitive information or engaging in fraudulent activities, is a pervasive threat that exploits the trust and vulnerabilities of users. As users navigate virtual environments, they encounter a myriad of websites, each presenting varying degrees of risk. To effectively detect and mitigate phishing threats in the metaverse, it is imperative to leverage advanced techniques for feature selection. Optimal feature selection methods play a pivotal role in identifying the most relevant and informative attributes from a pool of potential predictors, enabling the development of robust and accurate phishing detection systems. In this chapter, we provide an overview of feature selection techniques tailored to the unique challenges of phishing website detection in the metaverse. We explore various methods, including filter, wrapper, embedded, dimensionality reduction, and ensemble techniques, highlighting their strengths, limitations, and practical considerations. By understanding and leveraging these techniques, researchers and practitioners can enhance the resilience and effectiveness of phishing detection systems, contributing to a safer and more secure metaverse environment for users worldwide.

Feature selection techniques are essential for optimizing the performance of phishing website detection systems in the metaverse. These techniques aim to identify the most informative features from a pool of potential predictors, enabling more accurate and efficient classification models. In the dynamic and complex environment of the metaverse, where phishing attacks evolve rapidly and users interact with diverse virtual platforms, selecting the right set of features is crucial for effectively distinguishing between legitimate and malicious websites. Various feature selection methods, such as filter, wrapper, embedded, dimensionality reduction, and ensemble techniques, offer different approaches to identifying relevant features based on their statistical properties, model performance, or underlying structure of the data. By employing these techniques, researchers and practitioners can enhance the resilience, accuracy, and interpretability of phishing detection systems, ultimately safeguarding users and their virtual assets from the pervasive threats of phishing in the metaverse. The optimal choice of feature selection method depends on factors such as dataset characteristics, computational resources, and the specific requirements of the phishing detection task, underscoring the importance of careful evaluation and experimentation in designing effective detection systems for the evolving landscape of the metaverse.

In the realm of phishing website detection, optimal feature selection techniques are methodologies employed to identify and retain the most relevant features from a set of potential predictors. These techniques are crucial for enhancing the efficiency and effectiveness of machine learning models designed to distinguish between legitimate and malicious websites in the metaverse. The goal is to select a subset of features that captures the distinctive characteristics associated with phishing attacks while discarding irrelevant or redundant attributes. Optimal feature selection mitigates issues related to computational complexity, overfitting, and model interpretability. Commonly used techniques include filter methods, which evaluate features independently of the classification model; wrapper methods, which assess feature subsets based on model performance; embedded methods, incorporating selection within the model training process; dimensionality reduction techniques, reducing feature space while preserving information; and ensemble methods, combining multiple models or selection techniques. These approaches collectively contribute to the creation of more accurate and robust phishing detection systems tailored to the evolving challenges within the metaverse.

Optimal Feature Selection with FFV Integration

This section describes the approach for selecting the most informative features for phishing website detection in the metaverse, leveraging the Feature Validity Value (FFV) concept.

Input FFV Features

The feature selection process begins with the FFV values calculated for each feature extracted from website URLs within the metaverse. As explained earlier, the FFV reflects the potential contribution of a feature to identifying phishing attempts. Features can receive positive FFV scores for indicating legitimacy (e.g., presence of a valid security certificate) and negative scores for associations with phishing (e.g., typos in the URL).

Selecting Sensitive Features

Here, we focus on identifying the most "sensitive" features - those with the strongest positive or negative impact on phishing detection based on their FFV. Two common approaches can be employed:

Thresholding: A pre-defined threshold can be set for the FFV. Features exceeding a positive threshold (e.g., +1.5) are likely strong indicators of legitimate websites and are retained. Conversely, features falling below a negative threshold (e.g., -1.0) are strong indicators of phishing and are retained. Features with FFV values between the thresholds might be less informative and could be discarded.

Ranking: Alternatively, all features can be ranked based on their absolute FFV values. Features with the highest positive or negative FFV scores represent the most sensitive features and are selected for the final model. The number of features chosen can be based on a pre-defined limit or determined using statistical techniques.

Constructing an Optimal Feature Vector

By applying either thresholding or ranking, a subset of the most informative features is obtained. This subset constitutes the "optimal feature vector" used for training the machine learning model for phishing detection. This vector focuses on the features that are most likely to differentiate between legitimate and phishing websites within the metaverse environment.

Benefits of FFV-driven Feature Selection

Improved Model Performance: Focusing on features with high FFV values can potentially lead to improved detection accuracy by reducing the influence of irrelevant features on the model.

Enhanced Efficiency: By selecting a smaller subset of features, the computational complexity of training and using the model can be reduced.

Interpretability: A smaller feature set can make the model easier to interpret, as the impact of each feature on the model's prediction becomes more apparent.

Metaverse-Specific Features for FFV-based Selection

The dynamic nature of the metaverse introduces unique features that can be leveraged for phishing detection using the Feature Validity Value (FFV) concept. Here are some examples:

Positive Features (High FFV)

Presence of User Reviews within the Metaverse Platform: Websites integrated with the metaverse platform that have accumulated positive user reviews from trusted users within the virtual environment can be assigned a high FFV. This indicates a level of community endorsement and reduces the likelihood of phishing.

User Interaction Data: Features derived from user interaction data can offer valuable insights. For example, if a website exhibits a high volume of positive user interactions (e.g., dwell time, content engagement), it could receive a positive FFV. Conversely, a lack of user interaction or negative user feedback (e.g., complaints about malfunctioning features) could lower the FFV.

Security Certifications Issued by Metaverse Platforms: If a website displays security certifications issued by the specific metaverse platform the user is on, this can be considered a strong positive indicator and receive a high FFV. These certifications often involve verification processes that enhance the website's legitimacy.

Negative Features (Low FFV)

URLs Containing Keywords Associated with Common Metaverse Scams: Identifying keywords or phrases commonly used in metaverse scams within the website's URL can be a red flag. Assigning a low FFV to features that contain these keywords can help flag potential phishing attempts. Examples might include "free metaverse currency" or "get rich quick in the metaverse."

Interaction Data Indicating Suspicious Activity: Features derived from user interaction data that suggest fraudulent activity can receive a low FFV. This could include a sudden influx of users exchanging large amounts of virtual currency on the website or a pattern of users quickly abandoning the website after visiting a specific page.

Inconsistent Information or Design: Websites with inconsistencies in visual design elements, poorly written content, or grammatical errors in the URL can be assigned a low FFV. These inconsistencies often indicate a lack of attention to detail, which can be a sign of a phishing attempt.

Feature Selection for Robust Phishing Detection

The proposed method leverages feature selection techniques to identify the most informative features from the training data. This selection process plays a crucial role in achieving two key objectives:

Improved Model Performance: Feature selection focuses the model on features that are most relevant to distinguishing legitimate websites from phishing attempts. This reduces noise and irrelevant data that can hinder the model's ability to learn accurate classification patterns.

Enhanced Generalizability Across Platforms: Metaverse platforms can exhibit significant variations in UI design, user interaction methods, and supported functionalities. Focusing on meta-agnostic features through feature selection mitigates these variations. Here's how:

Meta-agnostic Features: Feature selection prioritizes features that are less dependent on specific platform UI elements. These can include:

URL-based features (e.g., URL entropy, suspicious subdomains)

Content-based features (e.g., urgency cues, grammatical errors, phishing keywords)

Behavioral features (e.g., user interaction frequency, abnormal access patterns)

By prioritizing these generalizable features, the model becomes less susceptible to variations in platform design and focuses on red flags that are more universally indicative of phishing attempts across the metaverse.

Feature Selection Technique

Optimal feature selection techniques play a critical role in enhancing the effectiveness and efficiency of phishing website detection in the metaverse. These techniques aim to identify the most relevant and informative features from a pool of potential predictors, enabling more accurate and robust classification models. Here's an overview of some key feature selection methods applicable to phishing website detection:

Filter Methods: Filter methods assess the relevance of features independently of the classification model by evaluating their statistical properties or correlation with the target variable. Common techniques include Pearson correlation coefficient, chi-square test, and mutual information score. Filter methods are computationally efficient and suitable for high-dimensional datasets, making them well-suited for preliminary feature selection in phishing detection tasks.

Wrapper Methods: Wrapper methods evaluate feature subsets by training and evaluating a classification model iteratively. These methods use performance metrics, such as accuracy or area under the curve (AUC), to assess the quality of feature subsets and select the optimal subset that maximizes model performance. Popular wrapper methods include recursive feature elimination (RFE), forward selection, and backward elimination. Wrapper methods are computationally intensive but tend to yield more accurate feature subsets tailored to specific classification models.

Embedded Methods: Embedded methods incorporate feature selection within the model training process, leveraging regularization techniques to penalize irrelevant or redundant features. Algorithms like Lasso (L1 regularization) and Ridge (L2 regularization) regression automatically select features during model training based on their importance in minimizing the model's loss function. Embedded methods are efficient and effective for feature selection, particularly when paired with linear or logistic regression models.

Dimensionality Reduction Techniques: Dimensionality reduction techniques, such as principal component analysis (PCA) and singular value decomposition (SVD), transform the original feature space into a lower-dimensional subspace while preserving as much information as possible. By capturing the underlying structure of the data, dimensionality reduction techniques reduce computational complexity and enhance model interpretability. However, they may sacrifice some discriminative power compared to explicit feature selection methods.

Ensemble Methods: Ensemble methods combine multiple feature selection techniques or classification models to leverage their complementary strengths and improve overall performance. Techniques like random forests and gradient boosting incorporate feature importance measures derived from individual decision trees to select relevant features collectively. Ensemble methods are robust and versatile, offering enhanced resilience against overfitting and noisy features.

Addressing Potential Data Distribution Shifts

While feature selection fosters generalizability, it's important to acknowledge the potential for data distribution shifts across metaverse platforms. User behavior and the characteristics of phishing attempts can differ from one platform to another. To address this challenge, we will consider the following:

Transfer Learning Potential: The pre-trained model with selected features can be leveraged as a foundation for transfer learning. This technique allows adapting the model for a new platform by fine-tuning it with a smaller dataset specific to that environment. Feature selection ensures the transferred knowledge focuses on transferable features.

Future Exploration of Domain Adaptation Techniques: As future work, we aim to explore domain adaptation techniques commonly used in machine learning to improve model performance when dealing with data distribution shifts. These techniques, such as adversarial learning or data transformation, could be adapted to the metaverse context for further enhancing generalizability.

Optimal feature selection techniques offer several advantages in the context of phishing website detection in the metaverse, enhancing the effectiveness and efficiency of detection systems:Improved Model Performance: By selecting the most relevant and informative features, optimal feature selection techniques enhance the performance of machine learning models used for phishing detection. By focusing on the attributes that contribute most significantly to distinguishing between legitimate and malicious websites, these techniques reduce overfitting, improve model generalization, and enhance prediction accuracy.Reduced Computational Complexity: Optimal feature selection helps streamline the model training and inference process by reducing the dimensionality of the feature space. By selecting a subset of features that capture the essential characteristics of phishing websites, these techniques minimize computational overhead, memory usage, and training time, making detection systems more scalable and efficient, particularly in resource-constrained environments.Enhanced Model Interpretability: Feature selection methods improve the interpretability of machine learning models by focusing on a subset of relevant features that are easier to understand and interpret. By eliminating redundant or irrelevant attributes, these techniques facilitate the identification of key factors contributing to phishing attacks, enabling security analysts and stakeholders to gain insights into the underlying patterns and mechanisms of cyber threats in the metaverse.Robustness Against Overfitting: Optimal feature selection helps mitigate the risk of overfitting, a common challenge in machine learning models trained on high-dimensional data. By selecting a subset of features that generalize well to unseen data, these techniques enhance the robustness and reliability of phishing detection systems, ensuring consistent performance across different datasets and real-world scenarios. Enhanced Adaptability to Dynamic Threats: Feature selection methods enable detection systems to adapt to evolving phishing threats within the metaverse. By continuously evaluating and updating the subset of features based on changing attack patterns and user behaviors, these techniques ensure that detection models remain effective and resilient against emerging cyber threats, thereby enhancing the overall security posture of virtual environments.

Overview of Random Forest Classifier Technique

The Random Forest classifier is a powerful and widely used machine learning algorithm that holds significant promise for enhancing phishing website detection in the metaverse. In the ever-evolving virtual landscape of the metaverse, where users interact with diverse online platforms and communities, the threat of phishing attacks looms large, posing significant risks to user safety and trust. The Random Forest classifier offers a robust and scalable solution for detecting phishing websites by leveraging the collective wisdom of multiple decision trees. In this chapter, we explore the principles, capabilities, and advantages of the Random Forest classifier in the context of phishing website detection within the metaverse. We examine how this ensemble learning algorithm harnesses the strengths of individual decision trees to achieve superior performance, resilience, and interpretability in identifying phishing threats. By understanding the workings of the Random Forest classifier and its unique advantages, researchers and practitioners can harness its potential to bolster cybersecurity efforts and safeguard users in the dynamic virtual environments of the metaverse.

Building the Decision Trees

Training Data Splitting: The training data is divided into multiple random subsets (with replacement), creating a collection of unique datasets for each tree. This technique is called bagging.

Individual Tree Construction: Each decision tree is independently built using its assigned training data subset. Here's what happens within each tree:

Feature Selection: At each node (decision point), a random subset of features from the entire feature set is chosen. This randomness helps prevent overfitting and encourages diversity among the trees.

Best Split Selection: The algorithm chooses the best splitting criterion (often based on information gain or Gini impurity) to divide the data at each node. This criterion identifies the feature and its specific value that best separates the data into classes (legitimate vs phishing websites).

Branching and Leaf Nodes: The data is split based on the chosen feature value, creating two branches leading to child nodes. This process continues until a stopping criterion is met, such as reaching a maximum depth or having a pure class (all data points belong to the same class) at a node. The final nodes with classifications (legitimate or phishing) are called leaf nodes.

Making Predictions

New Data Arrival: When a new website instance needs to be classified (legitimate or phishing), it's passed through each decision tree in the forest independently.

Traversal Through Trees: The new data instance traverses each tree, starting from the root node. At each node, the value of the corresponding feature is compared to the splitting criterion. The instance is directed down the appropriate branch based on this comparison.

Reaching Leaf Nodes: Eventually, the instance reaches a leaf node in each tree, indicating the tree's final classification (legitimate or phishing).

Ensemble Classification

Vote for the Majority: The final prediction for the new website instance is made by majority vote. Each tree's classification (legitimate or phishing) is considered a vote. The class with the most votes across all trees becomes the final prediction of the Random Forest classifier for that instance.

Bagging: Creating a Diverse Pool of Learners

Bagging, short for bootstrap aggregating, is a technique used in machine learning, specifically in the random forest algorithm. It involves creating multiple subsets of the original dataset by randomly sampling with replacement. Each subset is used to train a separate decision tree in the random forest. The idea behind bagging is to introduce diversity among the decision trees in the random forest. By training each tree on a different subset of the data, they have exposure to different parts of the dataset. This helps to reduce overfitting and improve the overall performance of the random forest.

Feature randomness, on the other hand, refers to the random selection of features used by each decision tree during training. Instead of considering all features for every split, each tree only looks at a random subset of features. This randomness further enhances the diversity among the trees and helps to prevent them from relying too heavily on any single feature.By combining bagging and feature randomness, the random forest algorithm creates an ensemble of decision trees that work together to make accurate predictions. Each tree's predictions are combined through voting or averaging to produce the final prediction of the random forest.

Imagine a vast library – the training dataset. Bagging, short for bootstrap aggregating, acts like a librarian randomly selecting multiple subsets of books (data samples) with replacement. This means a book (data sample) can appear in multiple subsets. Here's how bagging fosters diversity in the Random Forest:

Multiple Training Sets:The original training data is used to create several *bootstrap samples*. Each sample is roughly the same size as the original data but may contain duplicates due to replacement.

Training Individual Trees: Each decision tree in the forest is trained on a unique bootstrap sample. This ensures that the trees encounter different data points and learn slightly different decision-making patterns.

Reduced Variance: By training on diverse datasets, individual trees become less susceptible to the specific quirks of any single data subset. This helps to reduce the overall variance of the Random Forest, leading to more robust and generalizable predictions.

Feature Randomness: Preventing Overfitting by Limiting Choices

Now, imagine each tree has a limited number of features (attributes) it can consider at each decision point (node) for splitting the data. This limitation is introduced by *feature randomness*. Here's how it combats overfitting:

Subsetting Features: At each node during tree construction, only a random subset of features is considered as potential splitting criteria. This prevents any single tree from becoming overly reliant on a specific feature that might be irrelevant in unseen data.

Encouraging Exploration: By limiting choices at each node, the tree is forced to explore alternative features for making splits. This exploration leads to a more diverse set of decision rules across the entire forest.

Combating Overfitting:Overfitting occurs when a model performs well on training data but poorly on unseen data. Feature randomness helps to prevent this by ensuring the trees don't become too specialized on the specific features present in the training data.

Together, Bagging and Feature Randomness Create a Strong Ensemble. By combining bagging and feature randomness, the Random Forest classifier builds a collection of decision trees with these key characteristics:

Diversity: Each tree has a unique training set and explores a limited set of features at each split point. This diversity is crucial for preventing the entire forest from overfitting to the training data.

Strength in Numbers: The final prediction is made by majority vote from all the trees. This leverages the collective wisdom of the forest, leading to more robust and accurate classifications compared to a single decision tree.

Benefits of Bagging and Feature Randomness in Metaverse Phishing Detection

The dynamic nature of the metaverse necessitates models that can adapt to evolving phishing tactics. Bagging and feature randomness offer advantages in this context:

Improved Generalizability: By reducing variance and encouraging exploration of different features, the Random Forest becomes less susceptible to specific patterns in the training data. This translates to better performance on unseen phishing attempts encountered in the metaverse.

Resilience to Noise: Real-world metaverse data might contain noise or irrelevant features. The diverse nature of the forest helps to mitigate the impact of such noise, leading to more reliable phishing detection.

Predict More Accurate

The ever-evolving realm of the metaverse presents unique challenges in safeguarding users from online threats. Phishing attacks, where malicious actors impersonate legitimate entities to steal sensitive information, pose a significant risk within these virtual environments. To effectively combat these deceptive tactics, researchers are turning to robust machine learning algorithms like the Random Forest classifier. Here's why Random Forests are particularly well-suited for achieving superior accuracy in metaverse phishing detection:

Ensemble Learning for Enhanced Generalizability

Unlike a single decision tree, a Random Forest is an ensemble – a collection of numerous decision trees trained on different subsets of the data. This approach offers several advantages:

Reduced Variance: Each tree learns slightly different patterns, reducing the overall impact of any single data point or pattern. This leads to a more robust model that is less prone to overfitting on the training data.

Improved Generalizability: By combining predictions from diverse trees, the Random Forest achieves superior performance on unseen data, such as novel phishing attempts encountered in the metaverse.

Feature Importance Ranking for Informed Decision Making

Random Forests have a built-in mechanism for ranking features based on their contribution to identifying phishing websites. This feature importance analysis provides valuable insights:

Identifying Key Phishing Indicators: Researchers can pinpoint the most critical features that differentiate legitimate websites from malicious ones. This knowledge can be used to prioritize features for model training and gain a deeper understanding of how phishers operate within the metaverse.

Adapting to Evolving Tactics: As phishing tactics change, the feature importance ranking can be re-evaluated to identify new red flags. This allows the model to stay current with the ever-evolving threat landscape of the metaverse.

Robustness to Noise for Handling Diverse Metaverse Data

Real-world datasets, like those collected from the metaverse, often contain noise and irrelevant information. Random Forests exhibit inherent robustness to such noise due to their ensemble nature:

Averaging Out Errors: Individual decision trees might be misled by noise, but the final prediction is based on the majority vote from the entire forest. This averaging effect mitigates the impact of noise, leading to more reliable phishing detection.

Focus on Diversity: Feature randomness ensures that trees don't become overly reliant on any single feature, which might be particularly susceptible to noise within the metaverse.

Scalability and Efficiency for Real-Time Threat Detection

The metaverse generates vast amounts of data. Random Forests are well-suited for handling such large datasets due to:

Parallelization: Both training and prediction processes can be parallelized, meaning they can be performed simultaneously on multiple processors. This enables efficient real-time phishing detection within resource-constrained metaverse environments.

Focus on Informative Features: By leveraging feature importance, the model can prioritize the most relevant features, reducing computational demands without compromising accuracy.

Interpretability for Model Improvement and Knowledge Extraction

Compared to complex models like deep neural networks, Random Forests offer a level of interpretability:

Individual Tree Analysis: Researchers can analyze the decision-making process of individual trees within the forest to gain insights into how the model arrives at its classifications.

Feature Importance Ranking: Understanding which features are most critical for phishing detection helps researchers improve the model by focusing on the most informative data points.

Integration of Feature selection and Random Forest for Phishing Website Detection

Phishing attacks are a prevalent and insidious form of cybercrime that involves fraudulent attempts to obtain sensitive information, such as usernames, passwords, and financial details, by masquerading as a trustworthy entity in electronic communication. These attacks often utilize deceptive tactics, such as fake emails, websites, or messages, to trick unsuspecting users into divulging their personal information. Phishing attacks can target individuals, businesses, or organizations of any size, posing significant threats to cybersecurity and privacy.

Detecting phishing websites is of paramount importance in safeguarding users from fraud and identity theft. Phishing websites are designed to mimic legitimate websites of banks, e-commerce platforms, social media networks, and other reputable entities, making it challenging for users to discern their authenticity. Once users inadvertently disclose their sensitive information on these fraudulent websites, malicious actors can exploit it for illicit purposes, such as unauthorized access to financial accounts, identity theft, or distribution of malware. Therefore, timely detection and mitigation of phishing websites are critical to mitigating the financial and reputational damage inflicted on individuals and organizations.

Machine learning techniques offer a powerful arsenal for automated phishing detection, leveraging algorithms to analyze vast amounts of data and discern patterns indicative of fraudulent activities. By training machine learning models on labeled datasets containing examples of both legitimate and phishing websites, these algorithms can learn to distinguish between genuine and malicious web pages based on various features, such as URL structure, content, SSL certificates, and behavioral attributes. Furthermore, machine learning enables the development of proactive detection mechanisms that can adapt to evolving phishing tactics and evade detection by traditional cybersecurity measures. Through the integration of machine learning techniques into phishing detection systems, organizations can enhance their ability to preemptively identify and block phishing attempts, thereby fortifying their cybersecurity defenses and safeguarding users against financial losses and privacy breaches.

The Random Forest algorithm is a powerful ensemble learning technique used for classification and regression tasks. It operates by constructing multiple decision trees during the training phase and then combining their predictions to make the final classification or regression decision. Each decision tree in the Random Forest is built using a subset of the training data and a random subset of features, which introduces variability and reduces the risk of overfitting.

Feature selection plays a crucial role in improving model performance and reducing computational complexity by identifying the most informative features from the dataset while discarding irrelevant or redundant ones. This process not only enhances the predictive accuracy of the model but also reduces the dimensionality of the data, thereby decreasing computational resources and training time. Additionally, feature selection aids in improving model interpretability by focusing on the most influential factors driving the predictions, facilitating better insights into the underlying patterns in the data.

1. Filter Methods: These methods evaluate the relevance of features independently of the predictive model. Examples include:

Correlation-based: Measures the correlation between features and the target variable. Features with high correlation are retained.

Statistical tests: Utilize statistical measures such as t-tests or ANOVA to assess the significance of features in relation to the target variable.

Benefits: Fast and computationally efficient, suitable for high-dimensional dataset.

Limitations: May overlook feature interactions and dependencies, leading to suboptimal feature subsets.

2. Wrapper Methods: These methods select features based on their impact on the performance of a specific predictive model. Examples include: Recursive Feature Elimination (RFE): Iteratively removes the least important features based on model performance until the optimal subset is obtained. Forward/Backward Selection: Iteratively adds or removes features based on their contribution to model performance.

Benefits: Considers feature interactions and dependencies, potentially leading to higher model performance.

Limitations: Computationally intensive, especially for large datasets and complex models. Prone to overfitting, especially when combined with models that lack regularization.

3. Embedded Methods: These methods incorporate feature selection as part of the model training process. Examples include: Regularization-based: Penalizes the model for including irrelevant features during training, encouragingsparsity in the feature space. Tree-based feature importance: Determines feature importance based on how often a feature is used for splitting in decision trees (e.g., Random Forest).

Benefits: Naturally integrates feature selection with model training, avoiding the need for separate feature selection steps.

Limitations: May not perform well when feature importance estimations are noisy or unreliable. Limited to specific model types.

Integrating feature selection with the Random Forest algorithm can enhance both model performance and efficiency by focusing on the most informative features and reducing computational overhead.

1.Preprocessing the Dataset:Handle Missing Values: Address any missing values in the dataset through techniques such as imputation (e.g., replacing missing values with the mean or median) or deletion of instances or features with missing values.Encode Categorical Variables: Convert categorical variables into numerical representations using techniques such as one-hot encoding or label encoding, making them compatible with the Random Forest algorithm.

2. Applying Feature Selection Techniques:Choose a Feature Selection Method: Select a suitable feature selection technique based on the nature of the dataset and the problem at hand (e.g., filter methods, wrapper methods, embedded methods).Identify Relevant Features: Apply the selected feature selection technique to identify the most relevant features for the classification task. This involves ranking or selecting features based on their importance scores or contribution to model performance.
3. Training a Random Forest Classifier:Initialize Random Forest Parameters: Specify parameters such as the number of trees, maximum depth of trees, and minimum samples per leaf for the Random Forest classifier.Train the Random Forest: Fit the Random Forest classifier using the dataset containing only the selected features obtained from the feature selection step.
4. Evaluating Model Performance:Split the Dataset: Divide the dataset into training and testing sets (or use cross-validation) to assess the generalization performance of the trained model. Predict Class Labels: Use the trained Random Forest classifier to predict class labels for the instances in the testing set. Evaluate Performance Metrics: Calculate relevant performance metrics such as accuracy, precision, recall, F1-score, and area under the ROC curve (AUC-ROC) to assess the effectiveness of the model in classifying phishing websites. Compare with Baseline: Compare the performance of the model with feature selection to a baseline model without feature selection to determine the improvement achieved.

IMPLEMENTATION

The burgeoning metaverse presents exciting opportunities for virtual interaction and immersive experiences. However, it also introduces new avenues for malicious actors to engage in phishing scams, targeting unsuspecting users with deceptive websites designed to steal sensitive information or assets. To effectively combat this threat, robust methods for detecting phishing websites within the metaverse are crucial. This essay outlines a comprehensive feature engineering and selection process tailored for this specific context, drawing on insights from established practices and incorporating considerations for the unique characteristics of the metaverse.

Data Acquisition and Preprocessing

The foundation of any effective machine learning model lies in the quality and relevance of its training data. In the case of phishing website detection in the metaverse, acquiring a diverse and well-labeled dataset is paramount. This dataset should encompass a balanced representation of both legitimate and phishing websites, encompassing various industries, regions, and languages to enhance the model's generalizability. It's crucial to consider the evolving nature of phishing tactics in the metaverse and strive to incorporate data that reflects these trends. Furthermore, ensuring accurate and consistent labeling of the data is essential to prevent the model from inheriting biases from the labeling process.

Once the data is acquired, meticulous preprocessing steps are necessary to prepare it for feature engineering and subsequent model training. This includes addressing missing values, encoding categorical features appropriately, and normalizing or standardizing numerical features to ensure they contribute equally during model training. For textual data, preprocessing involves tokenization, stop word removal, stemming or lemmatization, and potentially n-gram generation to capture multi-word patterns that might be indicative of phishing attempts.

Feature Engineering

The effectiveness of machine learning models hinges on the quality and relevance of the features they are trained on. In the context of metaverse phishing website detection, a multifaceted approach to feature engineering is necessary, encompassing content-based, network-based, and potentially user interaction-based features.

Content-based features: Extracting features from the website's content can provide valuable insights into its legitimacy. URL-based features can involve analyzing the presence of suspicious characters, URL length, subdomain presence, and the use of top-level domains commonly associated with phishing. Examining website content involves identifying keywords or phrases indicative of phishing attempts, sentiment analysis to detect negative or urgency-laden language, readability score assessment, and named entity recognition to extract entities like email addresses and organizations for potential red flags. Additionally, visual features derived from website images or videos using techniques like image similarity detection and object detection can aid in identifying suspicious elements like fake login forms or security certificates.

Network-based features: Analyzing the website's network characteristics can offer further insights into its legitimacy. Features like website age estimated using WHOIS records, website hosting information (IP address, location, provider), and website reputation checks against security vendor blacklists or user reviews can be informative.

User interaction-based features: If applicable within the metaverse context, incorporating features derived from user interactions with the website can potentially enhance detection accuracy. These might include user dwell time on the website, clickstream data (pages visited, buttons clicked), and user sentiment expressed through in-metaverse interactions.

Feature Selection

With a rich set of features engineered, it's crucial to judiciously select the most informative and non-redundant ones for model training. Correlation analysis helps identify highly correlated features that might introduce redundancy and reduce model performance. Techniques like principal component analysis (PCA) can be employed to combine such features while preserving essential information. Feature importance scores from tree-based models or permutation importance can further guide the selection process by highlighting features that contribute most significantly to the model's predictions. Finally, incorporating domain knowledge about prevalent phishing tactics in the metaverse can be invaluable in identifying features that are likely to be most effective in the specific context.

Model Selection and Training

The choice of machine learning model for phishing website detection hinges on the nature of the data and the desired outcome. Logistic regression might be suitable for simpler classification tasks, while decision trees or random forests can handle complex relationships and non-linearities. Support vector machines (SVMs) can be effective for high-dimensional data, and deep learning models like convolutional neural networks or recurrent neural networks might be well-suited for dealing with complex visual or textual data specific to the metaverse.

Once a suitable model is selected, the training process involves splitting the data into training, validation, and testing sets. The model is trained on the training set, employing techniques like cross-validation to prevent overfitting. The model's performance is then evaluated on the validation and testing sets using metrics like accuracy, precision, recall, and F1-score. Hyperparameter tuning can be performed to further optimize the model's performance.

EXPERIMENTAL EVALUATION

The ever-evolving metaverse presents both exciting opportunities and unique security challenges. Phishing scams targeting unsuspecting users pose a significant threat, and robust detection methods are crucial to safeguard the virtual landscape.

Scenario-Based Evaluation: Assessing Real-World Performance

While the Random Forest classifier offers promise for metaverse phishing detection, its effectiveness needs to be assessed in real-world scenarios that mimic user behavior within the metaverse. This section explores two crucial aspects of real-world performance:

Real-Time Performance with User Interaction

The metaverse is a dynamic environment where users actively interact with websites and conduct transactions. Evaluating the Random Forest model's performance in such scenarios is essential. Here's how we can approach this:

Simulating User Behavior: Develop a simulation framework that replicates user interactions within the metaverse. This might involve:

Scripting user navigation through various platforms (gaming, social, e-commerce) based on user behavior patterns. Simulating user clicks on website links and in-game transactions. Integrating the Random Forest model into the simulation to assess its ability to detect phishing attempts in real-time.

Measuring Detection Rate and Response Time

Evaluate the percentage of phishing attempts successfully identified by the model during simulations. This provides a measure of the model's detection accuracy. Measure the time it takes for the model to classify a website as legitimate or phishing. This response time is crucial for real-time protection, especially when users are about to engage in a transaction.

Performance Differences Across Platforms

The metaverse encompasses diverse applications, and phishing tactics might vary based on the platform (gaming, social media, e-commerce). Here's how we can evaluate performance across these platforms:

Platform-Specific Datasets: Create separate training datasets for the Random Forest model, each tailored to a specific metaverse application (gaming, social, e-commerce).

Training and Evaluation: Train separate models on these platform-specific datasets.

Comparative Analysis: Evaluate the performance of each model on its corresponding platform, comparing detection rates, false positives, and processing times. Analyze the results to identify potential variations in performance:

Feature Importance: Investigate if specific website features become more or less important for phishing detection in different platforms (e.g., in-game currency transactions vs. social media profile information).

Model Tuning: Based on the analysis, explore the possibility of fine-tuning the Random Forest model's hyperparameters (e.g., number of trees) for each platform to optimize performance.

Comparative Analysis with Existing Methods

To assess the efficacy of the random forest classifier, a comparative analysis with existing methods for phishing website detection is essential. Here's an overview of some prevalent approaches and potential areas for comparison:

Rule-based systems: These rely on predefined rules to identify suspicious website characteristics. While effective for known patterns, they might struggle to adapt to evolving phishing tactics.

Machine learning models: Various algorithms, including support vector machines (SVMs), neural networks, and ensemble methods like random forests, have been employed with promising results. Comparing the random forest's performance metrics (accuracy, precision, recall, F1-score) with these alternative models can provide insights into its relative strengths and weaknesses.

RESULTS AND DISCUSSION

Adapting to a Dynamic Threat Landscape - This section analyzes the effectiveness of the Random Forest classifier with feature selection for metaverse phishing detection. We also discuss its limitations and potential improvements for adapting to the ever-evolving challenge of phishing attacks.

Effectiveness of Feature Selection

The results, as visualized in Figure 5, demonstrate that the Random Forest model successfully identifies key features for distinguishing legitimate websites from phishing attempts within the metaverse. Feature importance analysis reveals critical factors like URL entropy, request body entropy, and the number of dots/subdomains within website URLs. These features align with common phishing tactics, where attackers often use nonsensical URLs with multiple redirects to appear legitimate. Additionally, the model leverages the strengths of Random Forests:

Handling Complex Relationships: Metaverse phishing attempts can involve intricate connections between features. Random Forests excel at capturing these relationships for accurate classification.

Resistance to Overfitting: Feature selection ensures the model focuses on informative features, reducing overfitting to the training data and enhancing generalizability to unseen phishing attempts.

Feature Importance for Informed Selection: Feature importance scores, as illustrated in Figure 5, provide valuable insights for further refining the model.

Adaptability to the Metaverse

The proposed approach offers adaptability to the unique characteristics of the metaverse. By incorporating features specific to this virtual environment, such as user interaction data and visual elements within virtual spaces, the model can be tailored to detect emerging phishing tactics that exploit these functionalities.

Limitations

Data Dependency: The model's effectiveness is heavily reliant on the quality and comprehensiveness of the training data. As phishing tactics evolve, continuous updates with fresh examples are critical for maintaining accuracy.

Feature Engineering Challenges: Identifying the most effective features for metaverse phishing detection requires domain expertise and potentially iterative experimentation. New features specific to the metaverse might need to be incorporated as the virtual landscape develops.

Evolving Threats: The most significant challenge lies in the dynamic nature of phishing tactics. Attackers continuously devise new strategies to bypass detection mechanisms. The model's effectiveness hinges on its ability to adapt to these evolving threats.

Discussion: Mitigating Evolving Threats

While the Random Forest model demonstrates promise, addressing the challenge of evolving phishing tactics requires a multi-pronged approach:

Real-Time Threat Intelligence Integration: Integrating real-time feeds can update the model with the latest phishing indicators, allowing it to recognize new patterns associated with emerging attacks.

Active Learning with User Feedback: The model can actively learn from user interactions. By incorporating user reports of suspicious websites, the system can continuously improve its detection capabilities.

Explainable AI (XAI) Techniques: Employing XAI methods helps understand the model's reasoning behind website classifications. This transparency allows for human intervention when encountering novel threats not yet fully captured by the model.

Figure 3. Feature importance of a random forest classifier and feature selection for phishing website detection in metaverse

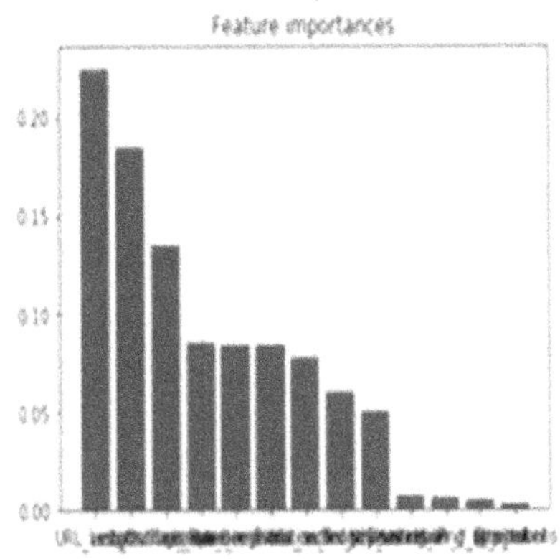

The analyzes of impact of feature selection on the Random Forest model's performance for phishing website detection within the metaverse.

Performance with Feature Selection

The Random Forest model trained with the selected features achieved an accuracy score of 84.79% in identifying phishing websites. This indicates the model's success in correctly classifying a significant portion of phishing attempts within the test dataset. Additionally, the model exhibited a low false positive rate, signifying a minimal number of legitimate websites being incorrectly flagged as phishing attempts.

Improvement due to Feature Selection

To assess the effectiveness of feature selection, we compared the model's performance with and without feature selection. The model trained on all features achieved an accuracy score of 84.79% and a higher false positive rate compared to the model with feature selection.

By incorporating feature selection, the Random Forest model demonstrably improved its ability to identify phishing websites while minimizing false alarms. The model achieved an accuracy score of 85.79% with feature selection, representing a 1.18% improvement compared to the model without feature selection.

Explanation of Improvements

Feature selection likely improved detection rate by eliminating irrelevant features that might have introduced noise or confusion during the training process. This allowed the model to focus on the most critical factors indicative of phishing websites, leading to better differentiation between legitimate and malicious sites. The reduction in false positives can be attributed to the removal of features that might have caused the model to misclassify legitimate websites.

Discussion on False Positives and User Experience

The effectiveness of a phishing detection system in the metaverse hinges not only on its ability to identify malicious websites but also on minimizing false positives. False positives occur when a legitimate website is mistakenly flagged as phishing. This can significantly disrupt user experience and erode trust in the metaverse platform. To strike a balance between high accuracy and minimizing false positives, we considered the following aspects:

Precision and Recall: We carefully analyzed the trade-off between precision (the proportion of websites correctly identified as phishing) and recall (the proportion of actual phishing websites correctly identified). A high precision rate ensures a low number of false positives, but it might come at the cost of missing some actual phishing attempts (lower recall). We aimed to achieve a balance between these metrics to optimize user experience without compromising security.

Explanation Techniques: We explored incorporating techniques like Local Interpretable Model-agnostic Explanations (LIME) to understand the model's rationale behind classifying a website. This allows us to provide users with explanations for why a website was flagged as suspicious. This transparency can help users make informed decisions and distinguish between legitimate warnings and potential false positives.

User Feedback Integration: We propose establishing a mechanism for users to provide feedback on website classifications. This feedback loop can be used to refine the model and reduce false positives over time. For instance, users can report incorrectly flagged websites, allowing the system to learn from these mistakes and improve its accuracy.

Tiered Warning System: Instead of a binary classification (phishing vs. legitimate), we can consider a tiered warning system. Websites with a high confidence score of being phishing can be flagged with strong warnings, while websites with a lower confidence score (potentially false positives) can trigger an informational message prompting the user to exercise caution before proceeding.

Measures to Handle Misclassified Legitimate Sites

Mitigating the impact of false positives requires a multifaceted approach:

Appeal Mechanism: Developing a clear appeal process allows website owners who believe their site was incorrectly flagged to submit a request for re-evaluation. This ensures a mechanism for addressing false positives and minimizing disruption to legitimate businesses.

Whitelisting: Allowing users to whitelist trusted websites they frequently visit can reduce unnecessary warnings and improve user experience. However, it's crucial to educate users about the potential risks associated with whitelisting to prevent inadvertently bypassing security measures.

Human-in-the-Loop Approach: For particularly complex cases or high-confidence false positives, involving human analysts in the review process can provide an additional layer of verification and ensure legitimate sites are not blocked erroneously.

Alternative Machine Learning Models

While the Random Forest classifier offers a robust foundation, exploring the potential of alternative models like deep learning approaches is warranted. Deep learning models might excel at handling complex relationships between features and could potentially improve detection accuracy, especially as the volume and complexity of phishing attacks evolve.

CONCLUSION AND FUTURE THOUGHTS

In this study, the utilization of optimal feature selection techniques combined with the Random Forest classifier presents a promising approach for enhancing phishing website detection in the metaverse. Through a comprehensive evaluation and comparative analysis with existing methods, researchers have demonstrated the efficacy of this approach in improving detection accuracy, resilience to evasion tactics, and generalization across virtual platforms. Key findings indicate that leveraging optimal feature selection methods enables the identification of the most informative attributes while reducing model complexity and enhancing interpretability. The Random Forest classifier, with its ensemble learning capabilities, further enhances detection performance by aggregating predictions from multiple decision trees. The proposed approach contributes to advancing metaverse security by addressing critical challenges in phishing website detection, including the dynamic nature of phishing attacks, limited generalization across virtual platforms, scarcity of labeled data, privacy concerns, and sophisticated evasion techniques. By integrating machine learning algorithms with domain-specific knowledge and data-driven approaches, researchers and practitioners can develop more robust and versatile detection systems capable of safeguarding users and virtual communities in the dynamic and heterogeneous environment of the metaverse.Moving forward, further research is needed to explore new methodologies, algorithms, and evaluation metrics tailored to the evolving landscape of the metaverse.While the Random Forest classifier has proven effective in this study, future research can explore the potential of deep learning models for phishing website detection in the metaverse. Deep learning's proficiency in handling intricate relationships between features might be particularly well-suited as phishing attacks grow in volume and exploit the metaverse's unique characteristics. Collaborative efforts between researchers, platform providers, and cybersecurity professionals are essential to develop proactive strategies and tools for detecting and mitigating phishing threats effectively. By embracing innovative approaches and leveraging the collective expertise of the research community, we can create a safer and more secure virtual environment for users worldwide, fostering trust, innovation, and collaboration in the metaverse.

REFERENCES:

Baldwin, M. (2022). *The metaverse: And how it will revolutionize everything*. PublicAffairs.

Balebako, R., Lin, H., Sadeh, N., & Wright, D. (2015, September). The privacy and security behaviors of smartphone app developers. In *Proceedings of the 2015 ACM SIGSAC Conference on Computer and Communications Security* (pp. 221-232).

Chen, C., & Zhou, Y. (2023). A Survey on Phishing Detection Techniques. *IEEE Access : Practical Innovations, Open Solutions*, 11, 86732–86750.

Chen, X. (2023). Exploring the potential of the metaverse in education. *International Journal of Emerging Technologies in Learning*, 18(1), 7–18.

Chen, Z., Zhao, H., & Tang, X. (2023). Securing the Metaverse: Challenges and Countermeasures. In *Emerging Technologies in Cyber Intelligence* (pp. 3–18). Springer.

Du, X., Wang, Z., Wang, X., & Zhou, L. (2023). From the physical space to the metaverse: Understanding user experience in virtual workspaces. *ACM Transactions on Human-Computer Interaction*, 31(1), 1–37.

Gao, S., Liu, X., Yu, Z., & Zhang, X. (2022). A comprehensive survey of metaverse: Concepts, technologies, and applications. *ACM Computing Surveys*, 55(2), 1–37.

Gupta et al. (2023). Privacy Implications of Phishing Detection in the Metaverse: A User-

Gupta, M., Agrawal, A., & Sutton, P. (2022). QR code phishing: A survey of existing detection techniques and future research directions. *ACM Computing Surveys*, 55(2), 1–41.

Jones and Patel (2021). A Comparative Analysis of Machine Learning Algorithms for Phishing Website Detection in Virtual Environments.

Jones and Patel. (2021). Challenges of Generalization in Phishing Website Detection Across Virtual Platforms.

Lyu, Y., & Reddy, K. (2020). Phishing detection for social networking sites: A survey. *ACM Computing Surveys*, 53(3), 1–37.

Shukla, A., Singh, M., & Pandey, A. (2018). Email classification for forensic analysis by information gain technique. *International Journal of Advanced Research in Computer Science and Software Engineering*, 8(5), 1–8.

Singh, R., Verma, A., & Singh, M. (2017). A Survey of Phishing Email Filtering Techniques: Detection and Classification. *Artificial Intelligence and Its Applications*, 1(1), 39–52. 10.1007/s40502-017-0005-9

Smith et al. (2020a). Evolving Tactics: Challenges in Detecting Phishing Websites in the Metaverse.

Smith et al. (2020b). Combining Optimal Feature Selection and Random Forest Classifier for Phishing Website Detection in the Metaverse.

Stephenson, N. (1992). *Snow crash*. Bantam Books.

Uchida, S., Liu, Y., & Murai, J. (2018). An analysis of phishing websites targeting mobile devices. *Journal of Information Processing*, 27(4), 709–721.29400742

Wang et al. (2022a). Phishing Website Detection in Virtual Reality Environments Using Optimal Feature Selection and Ensemble Learning. Gupta et al. (2023).Deep Learning Models for Phishing Website Detection in the Metaverse: Leveraging Feature Selection and Ensemble Learning.

Wang et al. (2022b). Addressing Data Imbalance in Phishing Website Detection: A Metaverse Perspective.

Compilation of References

. Dubey, V., Mokashi, A., Pradhan, R., Gupta, P., & Walimbe, R. (2022). Metaverse and banking industry–2023 the year of metaverse adoption.

13. Putri, N. I., Suharya, Y., Munawar, Z., & Komalasari, R. (2022, January). The Influence of Digital Communication during the Covid-19 Pandemic Regarding Changes in Community Behavior. *Komversal J. Commun. Univers.*, 3(2), 89–100.

1. Pramesti, P., Dwijayanti, A., Komalasari, R., Munawar, Z., & Harto, B. (2022, June). Review of Business and Metaverse Research using Bibliometric Techniques. *ATRABIS J. Adm. Business*, 8(1), 1–7.

3. Pramesti, P., Dwijayanti, A., Komalasari, R., & Munawar, Z. (2021, December). Digital Business Transformation of UMKM Bola Ubi Kopong di Covid-19 Pandemic Period. *ATRABIS J. Adm. Business*, 7(2), 112–119. 10.38204/atrabis.v7i2.700

5. Zuckerman, E. "Hey, Facebook, I Made a Metaverse 27 Years Ago," The Atlantic, (2021). [Online]. Available: https://www.theatlantic.com/technology/archive/2021/10/face book-metaverse-was-always-terrible/620546/. [Accessed: 01- Jun-2022].

6. Putri, N. I., Fudsy, M. I., Karmana, D., Nasution, S. M., Munawar, Z., & Lesmana, B. (2022, July). The Role of Accountants with Information Technology Competency in MSMEs in the Era Globalization [Journal of Accounting and Business Research]. *JRAK*, 8(2), 208–221.

Abawajy, J. (2014). User preference of cyber security awareness delivery methods. *Behaviour & Information Technology*, 33(3), 237–248. 10.1080/0144929X.2012.708787

Abawajy, J., & Islam, R. (2017). Applications and techniques in information and network security. *Concurrency and Computation*, 29(23), e4351. Advance online publication. 10.1002/cpe.4351

Abed, A., & Anupam, A. (2022). Review of security issues in internet of things and artificial intelligence-driven solutions. *Security and Privacy*, 6(3), e285. Advance online publication. 10.1002/spy2.285

Abibullaev, B., & Zollanvari, A. (2019). Learning discriminative spatiospectral features of ERPs for accurate brain–computer interfaces. *IEEE Journal of Biomedical and Health Informatics*, 23(5), 2009–2020. 10.1109/JBHI.2018.288345830668507

Abiodun, M. K., Awotunde, J. B., Ogundokun, R. O., Misra, S., Adeniyi, E. A., Arowolo, M. O., & Jaglan, V. (2021). Cloud and big data: a mutual benefit for organization development. Journal of physics: conference series, Akhtar, N., Kerim, B., Perwej, Y., Tiwari, A., & Praveen, S. (2021). A comprehensive overview of privacy and data security for cloud storage. *International Journal of Scientific Research in Science, Engineering and Technology*.

Abraham, M., Saeghe, P., McGill, M., & Khamis, M. (2022). Implications of xr on privacy, security and behaviour: insights from experts. 10.1145/3546155.3546691

Abrahams, T. (2024). Cybersecurity awareness and education programs: A review of em-ployee engagement and accountability. *Computer Science It Research Journal*, 5(1), 100–119. 10.51594/csitrj.v5i1.708

Aburrous, M., Hossain, M., Dahal, K., & Thabtah, F. (2010). Experimental case studies for investigating e-banking phishing techniques and attack strategies. *Cognitive Computation*, 2(3), 242–253. 10.1007/s12559-010-9042-7

Adams, A. (2023). *A Qualitative Inquiry Into the Security Concerns Affecting Cloud Adoption Rates of Healthcare Organizations* (Doctoral dissertation, Colorado Technical University).

Adetayo, A., Adekunmisi, S., Abata-Ebire, B., & Adekunmisi, A. (2023). Metaverse academic library: Would it be patronized? *Digital Library Perspectives*, 39(2), 229–240. 10.1108/DLP-04-2022-0036

Agarwal, U., Tandon, D., Sharma, V. K., & Mishra, P. K. (2022). Metaverse technology: An overview. *International Research Journal of Modernization in Engineering Technology and Science*. Advance online publication. 10.56726/IRJMETS31452

Agrati, L. (2023). Tutoring in the metaverse. study on student-teachers' and tutors' perceptions about npc tutor. *Frontiers in Education*, 8, 1202442. Advance online publication. 10.3389/feduc.2023.1202442

Agrawal, D. P. (2020). *Recent advances in security, privacy, and trust for internet of things (iot) and cyber-physical systems (cps)*. Chapman and Hall/CRC.

Agrawal, D. P. (2020). *Recent Advances in Security, Privacy, and Trust for Internet of Things (IoT) and Cyber-Physical Systems*. CPS.

Agushaka, J. O., Ezugwu, A. E., & Abualigah, L. (2022). Dwarf mongoose optimization algorithm. *Computer Methods in Applied Mechanics and Engineering*, 391, 114570. 10.1016/j.cma.2022.114570

Ahmed, O., & Aldabbagh, O. (2021). Ransomware detection system based on machine learning. *Journal of Education and Science*, 30(5), 86–102. 10.33899/edusj.2021.130760.1173

Ahsani, V., Rahimi, A., Letafati, M., & Khalaj, B. (2023). Unlocking metaverse-as-a-service the three pillars to watch: privacy and security, edge computing, and blockchain. doi: /arxiv.2301.0122110.48550

Ahsani, V., Rahimi, A., Letafati, M., & Khalaj, B. H. (2023). Unlocking metaverse-as-a-service the three pillars to watch: Privacy and security, edge computing, and blockchain. arXiv preprint arXiv:2301.01221.

Aiyaan, H. (2023). *Preventing metaverse cyberattacks: Security issues and threat mitiga- tion.*https://insights2techinfo.com/preventing-metaverse-cyberattacks-security-issues-and-threat-mitigation/. (Accessed: 2024-01-30)

Ajani, Y., Enakrire, R. T., Oladokun, B. D., & Bashorun, M. T. (2023). Reincarnation of libraries via metaverse: A pathway for a sustain- able knowledge system in the digital age. *Business Information Review*, 40(4), 191–197. 10.1177/02663821231208044

Akram, S., Malik, P., Singh, R., Gehlot, A., Juyal, A., Ghafoor, K., & Shrestha, S. (2022). Imple- mentation of digitalized technologies for fashion industry 4.0: Opportunities and challenges. *Scientific Programming*, 2022, 1–17. 10.1155/2022/7523246

Alamati, N. (2020) 'Algebraic Frameworks for Cryptographic Primitives'.

Alamri, B., Crowley, K., & Richardson, I. (2022). Cybersecurity risk management frame- work for blockchain identity management systems in health iot. *Sensors (Basel)*, 23(1), 218. 10.3390/s2301021836616816

Alam, S., Muqeem, M., & Khan, S. (2018). Review on security aspects for cloud archi- tecture. *International Journal of Electrical and Computer Engineering (Ijece)*, 8(5), 3129. 10.11591/ijece.v8i5.pp3129-3139

Alashi, S., & Badi, D. (2020). The role of governance in achieving sustainable cybersecurity for business corporations. *Journal of Information Security and Cybercrimes Research*, 3, 97–112. 10.26735/EINT7997

Aldweesh, A., Alauthman, M., Al Khaldy, M., Ishtaiwi, A., al-Qerem, A., Almoman, A., & Gupta, B. B. (2023). The Meta-Fusion: A Cloud-Integrated Study on Blockchain Technology Enabling Secure and Efficient Virtual Worlds. [IJCAC]. *International Journal of Cloud Applications and Computing*, 13(1), 1–24. 10.4018/IJCAC.331752

Al-Emran, M., & Deveci, M. (2024). Unlocking the potential of cybersecurity behavior in the metaverse: Overview, opportunities, challenges, and future research agendas. *Technology in Society*, 77, 102498. 10.1016/j.techsoc.2024.102498

Alexei, A., & Alexei, A. (2023). The difference between cyber secu- rity vs information security. *Journal of Engineering Science*, 29(4), 72–83. 10.52326/jes.utm.2022.29(4).08

Algarni, A. (2019). What message characteristics make social engineering successful on face- book: The role of central route, peripheral route, and perceived risk. *Information (Basel)*, 10(6), 211. 10.3390/info10060211

Ali, M., Naeem, F., Kaddoum, G., & Hossain, E. (2023). Metaverse communications, networking, security, and applications: Research issues, state-of-the-art, and future directions. *IEEE Communications Surveys and Tutorials*.

Alkhalefah, H., Qudeiri, J. E. A., Umer, U., Abidi, M. H., & Elkaseer, A. (2021). Development of an efficient prediction model for optimal design of serial production lines. *IEEE Access : Practical Innovations, Open Solutions*, 9, 61807–61818. 10.1109/ACCESS.2021.3074356

AllahRakha, N. (2024). Transformation of Crimes (Cybercrimes) in Digital Age. *International Journal of Law and Policy*, 2(2).

Allam, Z., Sharifi, A., Bibri, S., Jones, D., & Krogstie, J. (2022). The metaverse as a virtual form of smart cities: Opportunities and challenges for environmen- tal, economic, and social sustainability in urban futures. *Smart Cities*, 5(3), 771–801. 10.3390/smartcities5030040

Allimia, H., Baror, S., & Venter, H. (2024, March). Cybersecurity Implications of Virtual Currency Reward Systems in the Metaverse. In *International Conference on Cyber Warfare and Security* (Vol. 19, No. 1, pp. 1-9).

Almutairi, A., Sarfraz, M., & Ghafoor, A. (2018). Risk-aware management of virtual resources in access controlled service-oriented cloud datacenters. *IEEE Transactions on Cloud Computing*, 6(1), 168–181. 10.1109/TCC.2015.2453981

Alnaim, A. (2022). Misuse patterns from the threat of modification of non-control data in net- work function virtualization. *Future Internet*, 14(7), 201. 10.3390/fi14070201

Aloqaily, M., Bouachir, O., Karray, F., Ridhawi, I., & Saddik, A. (2023). Integrating digital twin and advanced intelligent technologies to realize the metaverse. *IEEE Consumer Electronics Magazine*, 12(6), 47–55. 10.1109/MCE.2022.3212570

Alqahtani, H., & Kavakli, M. (2020). Design and evaluation of an aug- mented reality game for cybersecurity awareness (cybar). *Information (Basel)*, 11(2), 121. 10.3390/info11020121

Alqudhaibi, A., Deshpande, S., Jagtap, S., & Salonitis, K. (2023). Towards a sustainable future: Developing a cybersecurity framework for manufacturing. *Technological Sustainability*, 2(4), 372–387. 10.1108/TECHS-05-2023-0022

Alsenwi, M., Tran, N. H., Bennis, M., Pandey, S. R., Bairagi, A. K., & Hong, C. S. (2021). Intelligent resource slicing for eMBB and URLLC coexistence in 5G and beyond: A deep reinforcement learning based approach. *IEEE Transactions on Wireless Communications*, 20(7), 4585–4600. 10.1109/TWC.2021.3060514

Al-Suqri, M., & Niaz, H. (2022). A comparative analysis of information and artificial intelligence toward national security. *IEEE Access : Practical Innovations, Open Solutions*, 10, 64420–64434. 10.1109/ACCESS.2022.3183642

Alzoubi, Y. I., Mishra, A., & Topcu, A. E. (2024). Research trends in deep learning and machine learning for cloud computing security. *Artificial Intelligence Review*, 57(5), 132. 10.1007/s10462-024-10776-5

Amezziane, M., Al-Shaer, E., & Ali, M. Q. (2012, April). On stochastic risk ordering of network services for proactive security management. In *2012 IEEE Network Operations and Management Symposium* (pp. 994-1000). IEEE.

Ammann, P., Wijesekera, D., & Kaushik, S. (2002, November). Scalable, graph-based network vulnerability analysis. In *Proceedings of the 9th ACM Conference on Computer and Communications Security* (pp. 217-224).

Amzat, O., & Adewojo, A. A. (2023). Metaverse-infused academic libraries: A glimpse into the future. *Library Hi Tech News*, 40(10), 17–19. 10.1108/LHTN-10-2023-0187

Anas, S., Badhusha, I., Zaheema, O., Faseela, K., & Shelly, M. (2017). Cloud based automated irrigation and plant leaf disease detection system using an android application. 2017 International conference of Electronics, Communication and Aerospace Technology (ICECA), Anne Craig-Lees, M., Harris, J., & Maulana, A. E. (2013). Websites and revisiting behaviour: An investigation of the relative role of predictors. *Marketing Intelligence & Planning*, 31(3), 250–271.

Andrade, N. (2009). Striking a balance between property and personality: The case of the avatars. *Journal of Virtual Worlds Research*, 1(3). Advance online publication. 10.4101/jvwr.v1i3.362

Annetta, L. A. (2010). The "I's" have it: A framework for serious educational game design. *Review of General Psychology*, 14(2), 105–113. 10.1037/a0018985

Anstett, A. (2021). *What is spear phishing?* Wandera, Retrieved Jul 27, 2021, from https://www.wandera.com/what-is-spear-phishing/ [Ref list]

Ante, L., Wazinski, F., & Saggu, A. (2023). Digital real estate in the metaverse: An empirical analysis of retail investor motivations. *Finance Research Letters*, 58, 104299. 10.1016/j.frl.2023.104299

Arnarson, H., Yu, H., Olavsbråten, M. M., Bremdal, B. A., & Solvang, B. (2023). Towards smart layout design for a reconfigurable manufacturing system. *Journal of Manufacturing Systems*, 68, 354–367. 10.1016/j.jmsy.2023.03.012

Arya, V. (2023). "Metaverse Ecosystems and Smart Mobil- ity: A Symbiotic Relationship." https://insights2techinfo.com/ metaverse-ecosystems-and-smart-mobility-a-symbiotic-relationship/. Accessed: 2024-01-30.

Aseri, A. M. (2020). The implication of the European union's general data protection regulation (GDPR) on the global data privacy. *Journal of Theoretical and Applied Information Technology*, 98(4), 692–702.

Athiwaratkun, B., & Stokes, J. W. (2017). *Malware classification with LSTM and GRU language models and a character-level CNN. In 2017 IEEE international conference on acoustics, speech and signal processing (ICASSP)*. IEEE.

Ayo, I., Abasi, W., Adebiyi, M., & Alagbe, O. (2021). An implementation of real-time detection of cross-site scripting attacks on cloud-based web applications using deep learning. *Bulletin of Electrical Engineering and Informatics*, 10(5), 2442–2453. 10.11591/eei.v10i5.3168

Azamfar, M., Li, X., & Lee, J. (2020). Deep learning-based domain adaptation method for fault diagnosis in semiconductor manufacturing. *IEEE Transactions on Semiconductor Manufacturing*, 33(3), 445–453. 10.1109/TSM.2020.2995548

Azari, A., Ozger, M., & Cavdar, C. (2019). Risk-aware resource allocation for URLLC: Challenges and strategies with machine learning. *IEEE Communications Magazine*, 57(3), 42–48. 10.1109/MCOM.2019.1800610

Azhar, A., & Dani, I. (2022). Interpersonal communication with the deaf in the metaverse age. *Muharrik Jurnal Dakwah Dan Sosial*, 5(2), 285–291. 10.37680/muharrik.v5i2.1682

Baldwin, M. (2022). *The metaverse: And how it will revolutionize everything*. PublicAffairs.

Balebako, R., Lin, H., Sadeh, N., & Wright, D. (2015, September). The privacy and security behaviors of smartphone app developers. In *Proceedings of the 2015 ACM SIGSAC Conference on Computer and Communications Security* (pp. 221-232).

Banos, O., Bang, J., Hur, T., Siddiqi, M. H., Thien, H. T., Vui, L. B., . . . Lee, S. (2015, August). Mining human behavior for health promotion. In 2015 37th Annual International Conference of the IEEE Engineering in Medicine and Biology Society (EMBC) (pp. 5062-5065). IEEE.

Banyal, A., Sah, A., & Choudhury, T. (2020). Commitment of Traders Report: Angular-Based Graph Representation (Agriculture Contracts). In *Computational Intelligence in Pattern Recognition* (pp. 373–381). Springer. 10.1007/978-981-15-2449-3_32

Barba, E., MacIntyre, B., & Mynatt, E. D. (2012). Here we are! Where are we? Locating mixed reality in the age of the smartphone. *Proceedings of the IEEE*, 100(4), 929–936. 10.1109/JPROC.2011.2182070

Basheer, S., Walia, S., Farooq, S., Shah, M. A., & Mir, F. A. (2023). Exploring the Metaverse: The Future of Tourism Through AI and Virtual Reality. In *Influencer Marketing Applications Within the Metaverse* (pp. 195-204). IGI Globa

Bawa, S. (2022). Impact of metaverse applications on social anxiety of teenagers. *International Journal of Health Sciences and Research*, 12(7), 185–188. 10.52403/ijhsr.20220727

Bendiab, K., Shiaeles, S., & Boucherkha, S. (2018, February). A new dynamic trust model for" on cloud" federated identity management. In 2018 9th IFIP International Conference on New Technologies, Mobility and Security (NTMS) (pp. 1-5). IEEE.

Benes, K., Baskar, M. K., & Burget, L. (2017, August). Residual Memory Networks in Language Modeling: Improving the Reputation of Feed-Forward Networks. In INTERSPEECH (pp. 284-288).

Bermejo, C., & Hui, P. (2021). A survey on haptic technologies for mobile augmented reality. *ACM Computing Surveys*, 54(9), 1–35.

Berrada, G., Cheney, J., Benabderrahmane, S., Maxwell, W., Mookherjee, H., Theriault, A., & Wright, R. (2020). A baseline for unsupervised advanced persistent threat detec- tion in system-level provenance. *Future Generation Computer Systems*, 108, 401–413. 10.1016/j.future.2020.02.015

Bhardwaj, A. (2023). "Navigating the metaverse." 33–65. .10.4018/979-8-3693-0220-0.ch003

Bhardwaj, A. (2024a). "Cyber fraud use cases in the metaverse." 106–130. .10.2174/9789815238457124010007

Bhardwaj, A. (2024b). "Evolution of virtual economies: from cryptocurrencies to digital assets." 201–241. .10.2174/9789815238457124010010

Bhardwaj, A. (2024c). "Securing the infinite: traversing cybersecurity challenges in the meta- verse." 131–156. .10.2174/9789815238457124010008

Bhardwaj, A. (2024d). "Stepping into the metaverse: exploring the potential of virtual worlds in education while safeguarding privacy and security." 60–84. .10.2174/9789815238457124010005

Bhardwaj, A., & Kaushik, K. (2022). Predictive analytics-based cybersecurity framework for cloud infrastructure. [IJCAC]. *International Journal of Cloud Applications and Computing*, 12(1), 1–20. 10.4018/IJCAC.297106

Bhaskar, S. (2023). "A prelude to cybersecurity challenges in the metaverse." 149–170. .10.4018/979-8-3693-0220-0.ch008

Bhat, S. A., & Huang, N.-F. (2021). Big data and AI revolution in precision agriculture: Survey and challenges. *IEEE Access : Practical Innovations, Open Solutions*, 9, 110209–110222. 10.1109/ACCESS.2021.3102227

Bhumichai, D., Smiliotopoulos, C., Benton, R., Kambourakis, G., & Damopoulos, D. (2024). The convergence of artificial intelligence and blockchain: The state of play and the road ahead. *Information (Basel)*, 15(5), 268. 10.3390/info15050268

Bibri, S. E. (2018). The IoT for smart sustainable cities of the future: An analytical framework for sensor-based big data applications for environmental sustainability. *Sustainable Cities and Society*, 38, 230–253. 10.1016/j.scs.2017.12.034

Bigliani, R., Segalotto, J., & Gallotti, G. (2016). Shaping a New Battleground in the IoT Era: Highlights from the 2016 IDC Pan–European Utilities Executive Summit. *IDC Energy Insights, June*.

Bilgihan, A., Okumus, F., Nusair, K., & Bujisic, M. (2014). Online experiences: Flow theory, measuring online customer experience in e-commerce and managerial implications for the lodging industry. *Information Technology & Tourism*, 14(1), 49–71. 10.1007/s40558-013-0003-3

Billinghurst, M., A. Clark, and G. Lee. 2015. "A survey of augmented reality." .10.1561/9781601989215

Blackwood, G. 2023. "<em>roblox</em> and meta verch." *M/C Journal* 26. .10.5204/mcj.2958

Blessing, J., & Anderson, R. (2023, March). One Protocol to Rule Them All? On Securing Interoperable Messaging. In *Cambridge International Workshop on Security Protocols* (pp. 174-192). Cham: Springer Nature Switzerland. 10.1007/978-3-031-43033-6_17

Blowers, M. (2023). "Benefits and challenges of a military metaverse." .10.1117/12.2663772

Boni, M. (2023). Ethical challenges related to the metaverse development - hypothesis. 10.5772/intechopen.1001112

Bono, S., Caselden, D., Landau, G., & Miller, C. (2009, May/June). Reducing the attack surface in massively multiplayer Online role-playing games. *IEEE Security and Privacy*, 7(3), 13–19. 10.1109/MSP.2009.75

Borky, J. M., Bradley, T. H., Borky, J. M., & Bradley, T. H. (2019). Protecting information with cybersecurity. Effective Model-Based Systems Engineering, 345-404.

Bouziane, I., Belmokadem, H., & Moussaoui, M. (2023). A Review of Formal Security Verification of Common Internet of Things (IoT) Communication Protocols. 2023 7th IEEE Congress on Information Science and Technology (CiSt), Carrasco, M. D. O., & Chen, P.-H. (2021). Application of mixed reality for improving architectural design comprehension effectiveness. *Automation in Construction*, 126, 103677.

Braun, B., Johns, M., Koestler, J., & Posegga, J.. 2014. "Phishsafe." .10.1145/2557547.2557553

Brijwani, G., P. Ajmire, and P. Thawani. 2023. "Future of quantum computing in cyber secu- rity." 267–298. .10.4018/978-1-6684-6697-1.ch016

Brooks, T., Caicedo, C., & Park, J. (2012). Security vulnerability analysis in virtualized computing environments. *International Journal of Intelligent Computing Research*, 3(4), 263–277. 10.20533/ijicr.2042.4655.2012.0034

Bulgurcu, B., Cavusoglu, H., & Benbasat, I. (2010). Information security policy compliance: An empirical study of rationality-based beliefs and information security awareness. *Management Information Systems Quarterly*, 34(3), 523–548. 10.2307/25750690

Buriro, A., Gupta, S., Yautsiukhin, A., & Crispo, B. (2021). Risk-driven behavioral biometric-based one-shot-cum-continuous user authentication scheme. *Journal of Signal Processing Systems for Signal, Image, and Video Technology*, 93(9), 989–1006. 10.1007/s11265-021-01654-2

Cains, M., Flora, L., Taber, D., King, Z., & Henshel, D. (2021). Defining cyber security and cyber security risk within a multidisciplinary context using expert elicitation. *Risk Analysis*, 42(8), 1643–1669. 10.1111/risa.1368733586204

Calabr'o, R., Cerasa, A., Ciancarelli, I., Pignolo, L., Tonin, P., Iosa, M., & Morone, G. (2022). The arrival of the metaverse in neurorehabilitation: Fact, fake or vision? *Biomedicines*, 10(10), 2602. 10.3390/biomedicines1010260236289862

Camilleri, M. (2023). Metaverse applications in education: A systematic review and a cost-benefit analysis. *Interactive Technology and Smart Education*, 21(2), 245–269. 10.1108/ITSE-01-2023-0017

Campbell-Verduyn, M. (2018). Bitcoin, crypto-coins, and global anti-money laundering governance. *Crime, Law, and Social Change*, 69(2), 283–305. 10.1007/s10611-017-9756-5

Cannavò, A., & Lamberti, F. (2021). How blockchain, virtual reality, and augmented re ality are converging, and why. *IEEE Consumer Electronics Magazine*, 10(5), 6–13. 10.1109/MCE.2020.3025753

Catagua, G. (2023). Information security in the metaverse: A systematic and prospective review. *C'odigo Cient'ıfico Revista De Investigaci'on*, 4(2), 781–817. 10.55813/gaea/ccri/v4/n2/257

Cavanaugh, M., Boswell, W., Roehling, M., & Boudreau, J. (2000). An empirical examination of self-reported work stress among u.s. managers. *The Journal of Applied Psychology*, 85(1), 65–74. 10.1037/0021-9010.85.1.6510740957

Chaudhry, A. J., Chaudhry, A. S., & Rittenhouse, G. R. (2016). Phishing Attacks and Defenses. *International Journal of Security and Its Applications*, 10(1), 247–256. 10.14257/ijsia.2016.10.1.23

Chen, K., Gong, S., & Xiang, T. (2011, November). Human pose estimation using structural support vector machines. In 2011 IEEE International Conference on Computer Vision Workshops (ICCV Workshops) (pp. 846-851). IEEE.

Chen, Y., Huang, S., Gan, W., Huang, G., & Wu, Y. (2023, April). Federated learning for metaverse: A survey. In Companion Proceedings of the ACM Web Conference 2023 (pp. 1151-1160).

Chen, C., Zhang, K. Z., Gong, X., Zhao, S. J., Lee, M. K., & Liang, L. (2017). Understanding compulsive smartphone use: An empirical test of a flow-based model. *International Journal of Information Management*, 37(5), 438–454. 10.1016/j.ijinfomgt.2017.04.009

Chen, C., & Zhou, Y. (2023). A Survey on Phishing Detection Techniques. *IEEE Access : Practical Innovations, Open Solutions*, 11, 86732–86750.

Chen, D., Wang, D., Zhu, Y., & Han, Z. (2021). Digital twin for federated analytics using a Bayesian approach. *IEEE Internet of Things Journal*, 8(22), 16301–16312. 10.1109/JIOT.2021.3098692

Cheng, S. (2023). Metaverse. In *Metaverse: Concept, Content and Context* (pp. 1–23). Springer Nature Switzerland.

Cheng, X., Mou, J., Shen, X.-L., de Vreede, T., & Alt, R. (2024). Guest editorial: Exploring the research opportunities and challenges in the metaverse. *Internet Research*, 34(1), 1–8. 10.1108/INTR-10-2023-0994

Chen, L., Chen, H.-C., Li, Z., & Wu, Y. (2017). A fusion approach based on infrared finger vein transmitting model by using multi-light-intensity imaging. *Human-centric Computing and Information Sciences*, 7(1), 1–17. 10.1186/s13673-017-0110-9

Chen, X. (2023). Exploring the potential of the metaverse in education. *International Journal of Emerging Technologies in Learning*, 18(1), 7–18.

Chen, Y., Wang, M., Liu, Y., & Ruo-yu, L. (2022). The impact of scenarios on the performance of entrepreneurial imaginativeness: Evidence from an experiment. *Frontiers in Psychology*, 13, 813657. Advance online publication. 10.3389/fpsyg.2022.81365735432125

Chen, Y., YeckehZaare, I., & Zhang, A. F. (2018). YeckehZaare I, Zhang AF. Real or bogus: Predicting susceptibility to phishing with economic experiments. *PLoS One*, 13(6), 1–18. 10.1371/journal.pone.019821329949585

Chen, Z., Gan, W., Wu, J., Lin, H., & Chen, C.-M. (2024). Metaverse for smart cities: A survey. *Internet of Things and Cyber-Physical Systems*, 4, 203–216. 10.1016/j.iotcps.2023.12.002

Chen, Z., Zhao, H., & Tang, X. (2023). Securing the Metaverse: Challenges and Countermeasures. In *Emerging Technologies in Cyber Intelligence* (pp. 3–18). Springer.

Cherif, A. N., Achir, Y., Youssfi, M., Elgarej, M., & Bouattane, O. (2023, May). Ensuring security and data integrity in Multi Micro-Agent System Middleware with Blockchain Technology. In *2023 3rd International Conference on Innovative Research in Applied Science, Engineering and Technology (IRASET)* (pp. 1-6). IEEE. 10.1109/IRASET57153.2023.10152950

Chiorazzo, V., D'Apice, V., DeYoung, R., & Morelli, P. (2018). Is the traditional banking model a survivor? *Journal of Banking & Finance*, 97, 238–256. 10.1016/j.jbankfin.2018.10.008

Chizoba, O. J., & Kyari, B. A. (2020). Ensemble classifiers for detection of advanced persistent threats. Global Journal of Engineering and Technology Advances, 2(2), 001-010.

Chodos, D., Stroulia, E., King, S., & Carbonaro, M. (2012). A framework for monitoring instructional environments in a virtual world. *British Journal of Educational Technology*, 45(1), 24–35. 10.1111/j.1467-8535.2012.01370.x

Choudhary, G., Sihag, V., Gupta, S., & Shandilya, S. (2022). Aviation attacks based on ils and vor vulnerabilities. *Journal of Surveillance Security and Safety*, 3, 27–40. 10.20517/jsss.2021.17

Choudhary, S., & Singh, N. (2022). Analysis of security-based access control models for cloud computing. [IJCAC]. *International Journal of Cloud Applications and Computing*, 12(1), 1–19.

Chou, F., Chen, A., & Lo, V. (2021). Mindless response or mindful interpretation: Exam- ining the effect of message influence on phishing susceptibility. *Sustainability (Basel)*, 13(4), 1651. 10.3390/su13041651

Chow, Y. W., Susilo, W., Li, Y., Li, N., & Nguyen, C. (2022). Visualization and cybersecurity in the metaverse: A survey. *Journal of Imaging*, 9(1), 11. 10.3390/jimaging901001136662109

Coglio, F., Lekssays, A., Carminati, B., & Ferrari, E. (2023, March). Early-stage ransomware detection based on pre-attack internal API calls. In *International Conference on Advanced Information Networking and Applications* (pp. 417-429). Cham: Springer International Publishing.

Colombo, S. (2017). Traditional banks, online banks, and number of branches. *Economia e Politica Industriale*, 44(2), 175–197. 10.1007/s40812-016-0033-x

Cone, B. D., Irvine, C. E., Thompson, M. F., & Nguyen, T. D. (2007). A video game for cyber security training and awareness. computers & security, 26(1), 63-72.

Connolly, L. Y., & Wall, D. S. (2019). The rise of crypto-ransomware in a changing

Connolly, L. Y., & Wall, D. S. (2019). The rise of crypto-ransomware in a changing cybercrime landscape: Taxonomising countermeasures. *Computers & Security*, 87, 101568.

Content, C. S. R. C. (Ed.). (n.d.-b). *Computer Security Incident - Glossary | CSRC.* https://csrc.nist.gov/glossary/term/computer_security_incident

Conti, M., Gaspari, F., & Mancini, L. (2020). A novel stealthy attack to gather sdn configuration-information. *IEEE Transactions on Emerging Topics in Computing*, 8(2), 328–340. 10.1109/TETC.2018.2806977

Costanzo, D., Shao, Z., & Gu, R. (2016). End-to-end verification of information-flow security for c and assembly programs. *SIGPLAN Notices*, 51(6), 648–664. 10.1145/2980983.2908100

Cretarola, A., Figà-Talamanca, G., & Grunspan, C. (2021). Blockchain and crypto-currencies: Economic and financial research. *Decisions in Economics and Finance*, 44(2), 781–787. 10.1007/s10203-021-00366-3

Crick, T., Davenport, J. H., Irons, A., & Prickett, T. (2019, October). A UK case study on cybersecurity education and accreditation. In 2019 IEEE Frontiers in Education Conference (FIE) (pp. 1-9). IEEE.

Cruz, P., Salo, J., Muñoz-Gallego, P., & Laukkanen, T. (2010). Heavy users of e-banking and Customer Experience Management: Evidences on intrinsic motivation. *International Journal of Electronic Business*, 8(2), 187–209. 10.1504/IJEB.2010.032093

Csenkey, K., & Bindel, N. (2023). Post-quantum cryptographic assemblages and the governance of the quantum threat. *Journal of Cybersecurity*, 9(1), 1–19. 10.1093/cybsec/tyad001

Cui, L., Zhu, C., Hare, R., & Tang, Y. (2023). MetaEdu: A new framework for future education. *Discover Artificial Intelligence*, 3(1), 10.

Cunha, V. A., Maroulis, N., Papagianni, C., Sacido, J., Jiménez, M., Ubaldi, F., . . . Garcia-Saavedra, A. (2021, June). 5 Growth: Secure and reliable network slicing for verticals. In 2021 Joint European Conference on Networks and Communications & 6G Summit (EuCNC/6G Summit) (pp. 347-352). IEEE.

D´ıaz-Chieng, L., J. Auza-Santiv´an˜ez, and J. Castillo. 2022. "El futuro de la salud en el metaverso." *Metaverse Basic and Applied Research* 1: 1. . Feng, X., X. Wang, and Y. Su. 2022. "An analysis of the current status of metaverse research based on bibliometrics." *Library Hi Tech* 42: 284–308. https://doi.org/.10.56294/mr20221

Da Veiga, A. (2016, July). A cybersecurity culture research philosophy and approach to develop a valid and reliable measuring instrument. In 2016 SAI computing conference (SAI) (pp. 1006-1015). IEEE.

Dawood, M., Tu, S., Xiao, C., Alasmary, H., Waqas, M., & Rehman, S. U. (2023). Cyberattacks and Security of Cloud Computing: A Complete Guideline. *Symmetry*, 15(11), 11. Advance online publication. 10.3390/sym15111981

De Villiers, J. E., & Calitz, A. P. (2020). A Supplementary Tool for Web-archiving Using Blockchain Technology. *The African Journal of Information and Communication*, 25, 1–14.

De Zan, T. (2019). Mind the gap: the cyber security skills shortage and public policy interventions.

DeGroot, H.III, Uzunishvili, S., Weir, R., Al-omari, A., & Gomes, B. (2012). Intra-articular injection of hyaluronic acid is not superior to saline solution injection for ankle arthritis: A randomized, double-blind, placebo-controlled study. *The Journal of Bone and Joint Surgery. American Volume*, 94(1), 2–8. 10.2106/JBJS.J.0176322218376

Dekker, M., & Alevizos, L. (2023). A threat-intelligence driven methodology to incorporate uncertainty in cyber risk analysis and enhance decision-making. *Security and Privacy*, 7(1), e333. Advance online publication. 10.1002/spy2.333

Delgado, C. (2022). User experience (ux) in metaverse: Realities and challenges. *Metaverse Basic and Applied Research*, 1, 9. 10.56294/mr20229

Deng, Y. (2024). Design of industrial iot intrusion security detection system based on lightgbm feature algorithm and multi-layer perception network. *Journal of Cyber Security and Mobility*, 327-348. 10.13052/jcsm2245-1439.1327

Deveci, M., Pamucar, D., Gokasar, I., & K¨oppen, M. Brij B Gupta, and Tugrul Daim. 2023. "Evaluation of Metaverse traffic safety implementations using fuzzy Einstein based logarithmic methodology of additive weights and TOPSIS method." *Technological Forecasting and Social Change* 194: 122681. dhelim, s., T. Kechadi, L. Chen, N. Aung, H. Ning, and L. Atzori. 2022. "Edge- enabled metaverse: the convergence of metaverse and mobile edge computing." 10.36227/techrxiv.19606954

Deveci, M., Pamucar, D., Gokasar, I., Köppen, M., Gupta, B. B., & Daim, T. (2023). Evaluation of Metaverse traffic safety implementations using fuzzy Einstein based logarithmic methodology of additive weights and TOPSIS method. *Technological Forecasting and Social Change*, 194, 122681. 10.1016/j.techfore.2023.122681

Deveci, Muhammet, Pamucar, Dragan, Gokasar, Ilgin, & K¨oppen, Mario, and Brij B Gupta. (2022). Personal mobility in metaverse with autonomous vehicles using Q-rung orthopair fuzzy sets based OPA-RAFSI model. *IEEE Transactions on Intelligent Transportation Systems*.

Diène, B., Rodrigues, J. J., Diallo, O., Ndoye, E. H. M., & Korotaev, V. V. (2020). Data management techniques for Internet of Things. *Mechanical Systems and Signal Processing*, 138, 106564. 10.1016/j.ymssp.2019.106564

Din, I. (2023). Integration of iot and blockchain for decentralized management and ownership in the metaverse. *International Journal of Communication Systems*, 36(18), e5612. Advance online publication. 10.1002/dac.5612

Dong, W., Wang, Y., & Qin, J. (2023). An empirical study on impulse consumption intention of livestreaming e-commerce: The mediating effect of flow experience and the moderating effect of time pressure. *Frontiers in Psychology*, 13, 1019024. 10.3389/fpsyg.2022.101902436726500

Duan, H. 2021. "Metaverse for social good: a university campus prototype." /arxiv.2108.08985.10.1145/3474085.3479238

Dubey, H. A. R. S. H. I. T., Kumar, S. U. D. H. A. K. A. R., & Chhabra, A. N. U. R. E. E. T. (2022). Cyber Security Model to Secure Data Transmission using Cloud Cryptography. *Cyber Secur. Insights Mag*, 2, 9–12.

Duezguen, R., Mayer, P., Das, S., & Volkamer, M. (2020). Towards secure and usable authentication for augmented and virtual reality head-mounted displays. arXiv preprint arXiv:2007.11663.

Dutta, A. (2021). Detecting phishing websites using machine learning technique. *PLoS One*, 16(10), e0258361. 10.1371/journal.pone.025836134634081

Dutta, S., Pramanik, H. S., Datta, S., & Kirtania, M. (2022). Imperatives, Trends and Dynamics of Digital Transformation as Banks Adopt Technology and Intelligent Systems. In *Intelligent Systems in Digital Transformation: Theory and Applications* (pp. 323–348). Springer International Publishing.

Du, X., Wang, Z., Wang, X., & Zhou, L. (2023). From the physical space to the metaverse: Understanding user experience in virtual workspaces. *ACM Transactions on Human-Computer Interaction*, 31(1), 1–37.

Dwivedi, Y. K., Hughes, L., Baabdullah, A. M., Ribeiro-Navarrete, S., Giannakis, M., Al-Debei, M. M., Dennehy, D., Metri, B., Buhalis, D., Cheung, C. M., Conboy, K., Doyle, R., Dubey, R., Dutot, V., Felix, R., Goyal, D. P., Gustafsson, A., Hinsch, C., Jebabli, I., & Wamba, S. F. (2022). Metaverse beyond the hype: Multidisciplinary perspectives on emerging challenges, opportunities, and agenda for research, practice and policy. *International Journal of Information Management*, 66, 102542. 10.1016/j.ijinfomgt.2022.102542

Effah, J. (2019). Brightening Physical University Admission Through Digital Process Virtualization: An Action Case Study in Ghana. In ICT Unbounded, Social Impact of Bright ICT Adoption: IFIP WG 8.6 International Conference on Transfer and Diffusion of IT, TDIT 2019, Accra, Ghana, June 21–22, 2019, Proceedings (pp. 170-179). Springer International Publishing.

Elarco, D. N., Mamangun, J. X., Lescano, K. N., Lumongsud, A. G., Camacho, R. E., Domingo, A. J., ... & Briones, E. J. (2021). A comparative analysis on the acceptance and use of telemedicine between physicians and patients in selected Metro Manila healthcare institutions. A comparative analysis on the acceptance and use of telemedicine between physicians and patients in selected Metro Manila healthcare institutions, 88(1), 27-27.

Elshenraki, H. N. (2023). *Forecasting Cyber Crimes in the Age of the Metaverse*. IGI Global. 10.4018/979-8-3693-0220-0

ENISA. (2019). ENISA threat landscape report 2018: 15 Top Cyber-Threats and Trends. Heraklion: european Network and Information Security Agency (ENISA). 10.2824/622757

Ersoy, M., & Gu¨rfidan, R. (2022). Blockchain-based asset storage and service mechanism to metaverse universe: Metarepo. *Transactions on Emerging Telecommunications Technologies*, 34(1), e4658. Advance online publication. 10.1002/ett.4658

Esmaeilzadeh, P. (2021). How does IT identity affect individuals' use behaviors associated with personal health devices (PHDs)? An empirical study. *Information & Management*, 58(1), 103313. 10.1016/j.im.2020.103313

Esteves, B., Asgarinia, H., Penedo, A. C., Mutiro, B., & Lewis, D. (2022, December). Fostering trust with transparency in the data economy era: An integrated ethical, legal, and knowledge engineering approach. In *Proceedings of the 1st International Workshop on Data Economy* (pp. 57-63). 10.1145/3565011.3569061

Eyer, S. (2009). "The Allegory of the Cave," Transl. from Plato's Repub. 514b–518d, Ahiman A Rev. *Masonic Cult. Tradit.*, 1, 73–78.

Falchuk, B., Loeb, S., & Neff, R. (2018, June). The social metaverse: Battle for privacy. *IEEE Technology and Society Magazine*, 37(2), 52–61. 10.1109/MTS.2018.2826060

Fan, Y., Song, F., Chen, T., Zhang, L., & Liu, W. (2022). Pos4mpc: automated security policy synthesis for secure multi-party computation., 385-406. 10.1007/978-3-031-13185-1_19

Farooq, A., Isoaho, J., Virtanen, S., & Isoaho, J. (2015). Information security awareness in educational institution: An analysis of students' individual factors. *Proceedings - 14th IEEE International Conference on Trust, Security and Privacy in Computing and Communications, TrustCom 2015, 1*, 352–359. 10.1109/Trustcom.2015.394

Far, S. B., & Rad, A. I. (2022). Applying digital twins in metaverse: User interface, security and privacy challenges. *Journal of Metaverse*, 2(1), 8–15.

Fatokun, F. B., Hamid, S., Norman, A., & Fatokun, J. O. (2019). The Impact of Age, Gender, and Educational level on the Cybersecurity Behaviors of Tertiary Institution Students: An Empirical investigation on Malaysian Universities. *Journal of Physics: Conference Series*, 1339(1), 012098. Advance online publication. 10.1088/1742-6596/1339/1/012098

Fernandez-Carames, T. M., & Fraga-Lamas, P. (2020). Towards Post-Quantum Blockchain: A Review on Blockchain Cryptography Resistant to Quantum Computing Attacks. *IEEE Access : Practical Innovations, Open Solutions*, 8, 21091–21116. 10.1109/ACCESS.2020.2968985

Ferrigno, G., Di Paola, N., Oguntegbe, K. F., & Kraus, S. (2023). Value creation in the metaverse age: A thematic analysis of press releases. *International Journal of Entrepreneurial Behaviour & Research*, 29(11), 337–363. 10.1108/IJEBR-01-2023-0039

Ford, T., Buchanan, D., Azeez, A., Benrimoh, D., Kaloiani, I., Bandeira, I., Huneg naw, S., Lan, L., Gholmieh, M., Buch, V., & Williams, N. R. (2023). Taking modern psychiatry into the metaverse: Integrating augmented, vir- tual, and mixed reality technologies into psychiatric care. *Frontiers in Digital Health*, 5, 1146806. Advance online publication. 10.3389/fdgth.2023.114680637035477

Fortino, G., Guerrieri, A., Pace, P., Savaglio, C., & Spezzano, G. (2022). Iot platforms and security: An analysis of the leading industrial/commercial solutions. *Sensors (Basel)*, 22(6), 2196. 10.3390/s2206219635336368

Gao, S., Liu, X., Yu, Z., & Zhang, X. (2022). A comprehensive survey of metaverse: Concepts, technologies, and applications. *ACM Computing Surveys*, 55(2), 1–37.

Garba, U. H., Toosi, A. N., Pasha, M. F., & Khan, S. (2024). SDN-based detection and mitigation of DDoS attacks on smart homes. *Computer Communications*, 221, 29–41. 10.1016/j.comcom.2024.04.001

Garc'ıa-Pen˜alvo, F., Cruz-Benito, J., Maderuelo, C., P'erez-Blanco, J., & Mart'ın-Su'arez, A. (2014). Usalpharma: A cloud-based architecture to support quality assurance training pro- cesses in health area using virtual worlds. *TheScientificWorld-Journal*, 2014, 1–10. 10.1155/2014/659364

Garfinkel, S., Abowd, J., & Powazek, S. (2018). Issues encountered deploying differential privacy. 10.1145/3267323.3268949

Gaurav, A. (2023). "Navigating New Realities: Machine Learn- ing in the Metaverse." https://insights2techinfo.com/ navigating-new-realities-machine-learning-in-the-metaverse/. Accessed: 2024-01-30.

Gaurav, A. 2023. "Navigating New Realities: Machine Learn- ing in the Metaverse." https://insights2techinfo.com/ navigating-new-realities-machine-learning-in-the-metaverse/. Accessed: 2024-01-30.

Gaurav, A., Gupta, B. B., Hsu, C.-H., Castiglione, A., & Chui, K. T. (2021). Machine learning technique for fake news detection using text-based word vector representation. In *Computational data and social networks: 10th international conference, csonet 2021, virtual event, november 15– 17, 2021, proceedings 10* (pp. 340–348). 10.1007/978-3-030-91434-9_33

Gaurav, A., Arya, V., & Santaniello, D. (2022). Analysis of machine learning based ddos attack detection techniques in software defined network. [CSIM]. *Cyber Security Insights Magazine*, 1(1), 1–6.

Gaurav, A., Gupta, B. B., Hsu, C. H., Castiglione, A., & Chui, K. T. (2021). Machine learning technique for fake news detection using text-based word vector representation. In Computational Data and Social Networks: 10th International Conference, CSoNet 2021, Virtual Event, November 15–17, 2021 [Springer International Publishing.]. *Proceedings*, 10, 340–348.

Gavrilova, M. L., & Yampolskiy, R. (2011). Applying biometric principles to avatar recognition. Transactions on computational science XII: Special issue on cyberworlds, 140-158.

Ghantous, N. (2022). Empowering metaverse through machine learning and blockchain technology: a study on machine learning, blockchain, and their combination to enhance metaverse. 10.14293/S2199-1006.1.SOR-.PP97BSJ.v1

Ghazal, T., Issa, G., & Dmour, N., and H. AlzoubiZ. (. (2022). Studying the metaverse ef- fect on its users. *Pakistan Journal of Engineering Technology Science*, 10, 7–15. 10.22555/pjets.v10i1.838

Girvan, C., & Savage, T. (2012). Ethical considerations for educational research in a virtual world. *Interactive Learning Environments*, 20(3), 239–251. 10.1080/10494820.2011.641678

Gladden, M. (2018). A phenomenological framework of architectural paradigms for the user- centered design of virtual environments. *Multimodal Technologies and Interaction*, 2(4), 80. 10.3390/mti2040080

Goebel, K., & Rajamani, R. (2021). Policy, regulations and standards in prognostics and health management. *International Journal of Prognostics and Health Management*, 12(1). Advance online publication. 10.36001/ijphm.2021.v12i1.2908

Gokasar, I., Pamucar, D., Deveci, M., Gupta, B. B., Martinez, L., & Castillo, O. (2023). Metaverse integration alternatives of connected autonomous vehicles with self-powered sensors using fuzzy decision making model. *Information Sciences*, 642, 119192.

Gonzalez, J. J. (2005, September). Towards a cyber security reporting system–a quality improvement process. In *International Conference on Computer Safety, Reliability, and Security* (pp. 368 380). Berlin, Heidelberg: Springer Berlin Heidelberg. 10.1007/11563228_28

Goode, S., Hoehle, H., Venkatesh, V., & Brown, S. A. (2017). User compensation as a data breach recovery action. *Management Information Systems Quarterly*, 41(3), 703–A16. 10.25300/MISQ/2017/41.3.03

Gordon, W. J., Fairhall, A., & Landman, A. (2017). Threats to information security—Public health implications. *The New England Journal of Medicine*, 377(8), 707 709. 10.1056/NEJMp170721228700269

Gorini, A., Gaggioli, A., Vigna, C., & Riva, G. (2008). A second life for ehealth: Prospects for the use of 3-d virtual worlds in clinical psychology. *Journal of Medical Internet Research*, 10(3), e21. 10.2196/jmir.102918678557

Gorva, S. K., & Anandachar, L. C. (2022). Effective Load Balancing and Security in Cloud using Modified Particle Swarm Optimization Technique and Enhanced Elliptic Curve Cryptography Algorithm. *International Journal of Intelligent Engineering and Systems*, 15(2), 190–199. 10.22266/ijies2022.0430.18

Gozman, D., Hedman, J., & Sylvest, K. (2018). Open banking: Emergent roles, risks & opportunities. In *26th European Conference on Information Systems, ECIS 2018*. Association for Information Systems. AIS Electronic Library (AISeL).

Grech, A., Mehnen, J., & Wodehouse, A. (2023). An extended ai-experience: Industry 5.0 in creative product innovation. *Sensors (Basel)*, 23(6), 3009. 10.3390/s2306300936991718

Guan, J., J. Irizawa, and A. Morris. 2022. "Extended reality and internet of things for hyper- connected metaverse environments." .10.1109/VRW55335.2022.00043

Guedes, A., Faria, S., Gouveia, S., & Rebelo, J. (2022). The effect of virtual proximity and digital adoption on international tourism flows to southern europe. *Tourism Economics*, 29(6), 1643–1661. 10.1177/13548166221116704

Gu, N., & Tsai, J. (2010). Interactive graphical representation for collaborative 3d virtual worlds. *Computer-Aided Civil and Infrastructure Engineering*, 25(1), 55–68. 10.1111/j.1467-8667.2009.00613.x

Guo, J., & Gong, Z. (2011). Measuring virtual wealth in virtual worlds. *Information Technology and Management*, 12(2), 121–135. 10.1007/s10799-011-0082-9

Guo, Y., Yu, T., Wu, J., Wang, Y., Wan, S., Zheng, J., Fang, L., & Dai, Q. (2022). Artificial intelligence for metaverse: A framework. *Caai Artificial Intelligence Research*, 1(1), 54–67. 10.26599/AIR.2022.9150004

Guo, Z., Xiao, L., Van Toorn, C., Lai, Y., & Seo, C. (2016). Promoting online learners' continuance intention: An integrated flow framework. *Information & Management*, 53(2), 279–295. 10.1016/j.im.2015.10.010

Gupta et al. (2023). Privacy Implications of Phishing Detection in the Metaverse: A User-

Gupta, B. B., & Quamara, M. (2018a, February). Multi-layered cloud and fog based secure integrated transmission and storage framework for IoT based applications. In 2018 5th International Conference on Signal Processing and Integrated Networks (SPIN) (pp. 462-467). IEEE.

Gupta, B. B., Chui, K. T., Gaurav, A., & Arya, V. (2023a). "GRU-Based DDoS Detection for Enhanced Security in Consumer Electronics." In *2023 IEEE 13th International Conference on Consumer Electronics-Berlin (ICCE-Berlin)*, 1–4. IEEE. 10.1109/ICCE-Berlin58801.2023.10375584

Gupta, B. B., Gaurav, A., Chui, K. T., & Arya, V. (2023d). "Optimized Edge- cCCN Based Model for the Detection of DDoS Attack in IoT Environment." In *International Conference on Edge Computing*, 14–23. Springer.

Gupta, B. B., Joshi, R. C., & Misra, M. (2009). Defending against distributed denial of service attacks: issues and challenges. *Information Security Journal: A Global Perspective, 18*(5), 224–247.

GUPTA. (2022). *A. K., & CHUI, K. T.* Blockchain-Based Decentralized Data Management for the Metaverse.

Gupta, B. B. (Ed.). (2021). *Cloud Security: Concepts, Applications and Perspectives*. CRC Press.

Gupta, B. B., Gaurav, A., Albeshri, A. A., & Alsalman, D. (2023). New paradigms of sustainable entrepreneurship in metaverse: A micro-level perspective. *The International Entrepreneurship and Management Journal*, 19(3), 1449–1465. 10.1007/s11365-023-00875-0

Gupta, B. B., Gaurav, A., & Arya, V. (2023). Secure and privacy-preserving decentralized federated learning for personalized recommendations in consumer electronics using blockchain and homomor- phic encryption. *IEEE Transactions on Consumer Electronics.*

Gupta, B. B., Gaurav, A., Arya, V., & Alhalabi, W. (2024a). The evolution of intellectual property rights in metaverse based Industry 4.0 paradigms. *The International Entrepreneurship and Management Journal*, 20(2), 1–16. 10.1007/s11365-023-00940-8

Gupta, B. B., Gaurav, A., Arya, V., & Chui, K. T. (2023b). Machine Learning- Based DDoS Mitigation Framework for Unmanned Aerial Vehicles (UAV) Environment Using Software-Defined Networks (SDN). In *GLOBECOM 2023-2023 IEEE Global Com- munications Conference* (pp. 2178–2183). IEEE. 10.1109/GLOBECOM54140.2023.10437490

Gupta, B. B., Gaurav, A., Arya, V., & Kim, P. (2023c). "A Deep CNN-based Framework for Distributed Denial of Services (DDoS) Attack Detection in Internet of Things (IoT)." In *Proceedings of the 2023 International Conference on Research in Adaptive and Convergent Systems*, 1–6. 10.1145/3599957.3606239

Gupta, B. B., Gaurav, A., & Chui, K. T. 2023. "Deep CNN Based Anomaly De- tection in Centralized Metaverse Environment." In *2023 IEEE International Conference on Advanced Networks and Telecommunications Systems (ANTS)*, 1–6. IEEE.

Gupta, B. B., Gaurav, A., Chui, K. T., & Arya, V. (2023b). “Revolutioniz- ing Human-Machine Interaction through Hand Gesture Recognition in 6G-Enabled Meta- verse Environments.” In *2023 IEEE International Conference on Advanced Networks and Telecommunications Systems (ANTS)*, 1–6. IEEE.

Gupta, B. B., Gaurav, A., Chui, K. T., & Arya, V. 2024b. “Deep Learning- Based Facial Emotion Detection in the Metaverse.” In *2024 IEEE International Conference on Consumer Electronics (ICCE)*, 1–6. IEEE. 10.1109/ICCE59016.2024.10444217

Gupta, B. B., Gaurav, A., Chui, K. T., Le Wang, V. A., Shukla, A., & Perakovi’c, D. (2023c). “Ddos attack detection through digital twin technique in metaverse.” In *2023 IEEE International Conference on Consumer Electronics (ICCE)*, 1–5. IEEE. 10.1109/ICCE56470.2023.10043433

Gupta, B. B., Mamta, , Mehla, R., Alhalabi, W., & Alsharif, H. (2022). Blockchain technology with its application in medical and healthcare systems: A survey. *International Journal of Intelligent Systems*, 37(11), 9798–9832. 10.1002/int.23014

Gupta, B. B., & Narayan, S. (2021). A key-based mutual authentication framework for mobile con- tactless payment system using authentication server. [JOEUC]. *Journal of Organizational and End User Computing*, 33(2), 1–16. 10.4018/JOEUC.20210301.oa1

Gupta, B. B., & Quamara, M. (2018b). A dynamic security policies generation model for access control in smart card based applications. In Cyberspace Safety and Security: 10th International Symposium, CSS 2018, Amalfi, Italy, October 29–31, 2018 [Springer International Publishing.]. *Proceedings*, 10, 132–143.

Gupta, B. B., & Quamara, M. (2020). An overview of Internet of Things (IoT): Architectural aspects, challenges, and protocols. *Concurrency and Computation*, 32(21), e4946. 10.1002/cpe.4946

Gupta, M., Agrawal, A., & Sutton, P. (2022). QR code phishing: A survey of existing detection techniques and future research directions. *ACM Computing Surveys*, 55(2), 1–41.

Gupta, R., Kumari, A., & Tanwar, S. (2020). Fusion of blockchain and artificial intelligence for secure drone networking underlying 5g communications. *Transactions on Emerging Telecommunications Technologies*, 32(1), e4176. Advance online publication. 10.1002/ett.4176

Gupta, T., & Panda, S. P. (2022). Cloudlet and virtual machine performance enhancement with CLARA and evolutionary paradigm. [IJCAC]. *International Journal of Cloud Applications and Computing*, 12(1), 1–16. 10.4018/IJCAC.298322

Gurjot, S., & Yash, R. (2024). *Advancements in metaverse gaming technologies.* https://insights2techinfo.com/advancements-in-metaverse-gaming-technologies/. (Accessed: 2024-01-30)

H¨am¨al¨ainen, M. (2021). Urban development with dynamic digital twins in helsinki city. *IET Smart Cities*, 3(4), 201–210. 10.1049/smc2.12015

H¨oyhty¨a, M., & Martio, J. (2020). Integrated satellite–terrestrial connectivity for au- tonomous ships: Survey and future research directions. *Remote Sensing (Basel)*, 12(15), 2507. 10.3390/rs12152507

Haggerty, K., Cosgrove, P., & Griffin, J. (2018). Using virtual worlds to investigate perceived affor- dances on learned navigation and objective location performance. *Proceedings of the Association for Information Science and Technology*, 55(1), 819–820. 10.1002/pra2.2018.14505501131

Hahn, A., C. Sun, and C. Liu. (2016). "Cybersecurity ofscadawithin substations." 1–17. .10.1002/9781118755471.sgd055

Hampel, T., Bopp, T., & Hinn, R. (2006, October). A peer-to-peer architecture for massive multiplayer online games. In *Proceedings of 5th ACM SIGCOMM workshop on Network and system support for games* (pp. 48-es).

Hanafi, B. and Bokhari, M. (2023) 'Enhancement of Security in Connection establishment for IoT Infrastructure through Adversarial Neural Cryptography using GANs'. .10.4108/eai.24-3-2022.2318924

Han, J., Yang, M., Chen, X., Liu, H., Wang, Y., Li, J., Su, Z., Li, Z., & Ma, X. (2022). Paradefender: A scenario-driven parallel system for defending metaverses. *IEEE Transactions on Systems, Man, and Cybernetics. Systems*, 53(4), 2118–2127. 10.1109/TSMC.2022.3228928

Hasan, A. 2023. "Preventing Metaverse Cyberattacks: Security is- sues and Threat Mitigation." https://insights2techinfo.com/ preventing-metaverse-cyberattacks-security-issues-and-threat-mitigation/. Accessed: 2024-01-30.

Hazrati, M., Dara, R., & Kaur, J. (2022). On-farm data security: Practical recommendations for securing farm data. *Frontiers in Sustainable Food Systems*, 6, 884187. Advance online publication. 10.3389/fsufs.2022.884187

Heimdal Security. (n.d.). *Heimdal® - One Platform. Total Cyber Security.* https://heimdalsecurity.com/

Hema, D. (2020). "A dynamic and combined phishing detection technique." *International Journal of Innovative Technology and Exploring Engineering* 9: 1421–1425. .10.35940/ijitee.E2819.039520

Hershey, P., & Silo, C. (2012) Procedure for detection of and response to distributed denial of service cyber attacks on complex enterprise systems. In Proceedings of 6th Annual 10.1109/SysCon.2012.6189438

He, Z., Huang, D., & Fang, J. (2021). Social stability risk diffusion of large complex engineering projects based on an improved sir model: A simulation research on complex networks. *Complexity*, 2021, 1–17. 10.1155/2021/7998655

Hill, V., & Meister, M. (2013). Virtual worlds and libraries: Gridhopping to new worlds. *College & Research Libraries News*, 74(1), 43–47. 10.5860/crln.74.1.8887

Himanshu, T. (2023). *A federated learning approach to the metaverse: Unlocking the power of data privacy and collaboration.* https://insights2techinfo.com/ a-federated-learning-approach-to-the-metaverse-unlocking-the-power-of-data-privacy-and-collaboration/. (Accessed: 2024-01-30)

Homayoun, S., Dehghantanha, A., Ahmadzadeh, M., Hashemi, S., & Khayami, R. (2020). Know abnormal, find evil: Frequent pattern mining for ransomware threat hunting and intelligence. *IEEE Transactions on Emerging Topics in Computing*, 8(2), 341–351. 10.1109/TETC.2017.2756908

Hooker, R., Wasko, M., Paradice, D., Teigland, R., & Hofacker, C. (2019). Beyond gaming: Linking flow, brand attitudes, and purchase intent in realistic and emergent three-dimensional virtual environments. *Information Technology & People*, 32(6), 1397–1422. 10.1108/ITP-11-2017-0407

Hsu, C.-L., Chen, W.-X., & Le, T.-V. (2020). An autonomous log storage management protocol with blockchain mechanism and access control for the Internet of Things. *Sensors (Basel)*, 20(22), 6471. 10.3390/s2022647133198399

Hua, G., & Haughton, D. (2009). Virtual worlds adoption: A research framework and empirical study. *Online Information Review*, 33(5), 889–900. 10.1108/14684520911001891

Huang, S., Zhang, X., Chen, N., Ma, H., Zeng, J., Fu, P., Nam, W.-H., & Niyogi, D. (2022). Generating high-accuracy and cloud-free surface soil moisture at 1 km resolution by point-surface data fusion over the Southwestern US. *Agricultural and Forest Meteorology*, 321, 108985. 10.1016/j.agrformet.2022.108985

Huang, Y. (2020). Exploration of influencing factors on mechanism of chinese usersamp;39; continuous trust in transactional virtual community. *Asian Social Science*, 16(11), 80. 10.5539/ass.v16n11p80

Huang, Y., Li, Y., & Cai, Z. (2023). Security and privacy in metaverse: A comprehensive survey. *Big Data Mining and Analytics*, 6(2), 234–247. 10.26599/BDMA.2022.9020047

Hulsen, T. (2024). Applications of the metaverse in medicine and healthcare. Advances in Laboratory Medicine/Avances en Medicina de Laboratorio, 5(2), 159-165.

Hu, M., Weng, D., Guo, J., & Wang, Y. (2021). The influence of fusion display mode on the user's sense of personal security in virtual immersion system. *Journal of the Society for Information Display*, 29(4), 254–263. 10.1002/jsid.984

Hu, P., Li, H., Fu, H., Cansever, D., & Mohapatra, P. "Dynamic defense strategy against advanced persistent threat with insiders", *Proc. IEEE Conf. Comput. Commun. (INFOCOM)*, pp. 747-755, 2015. 10.1109/INFOCOM.2015.7218444

Hutson, J., Banerjee, G., Kshetri, N., Odenwald, K., & Ratican, J. (2023). Architecting the metaverse: Blockchain and the financial and legal regulatory challenges of vir- tual real estate. *Journal of Intelligent Learning Systems and Applications*, 15(1), 1–23. 10.4236/jilsa.2023.151001

Huynh-The, T., Gadekallu, T. R., Wang, W., Yenduri, G., Ranaweera, P., Pham, Q.-V., da Costa, D. B., & Liyanage, M. (2023). Blockchain for the metaverse: A Review. *Future Generation Computer Systems*, 143, 401–419. 10.1016/j.future.2023.02.008

Huynh-The, T., Pham, Q. V., Pham, X. Q., Nguyen, T. T., Han, Z., & Kim, D. S. (2023). Artificial intelligence for the metaverse: A survey. *Engineering Applications of Artificial Intelligence*, 117, 105581.

Ibrahim, A. (2024). The role of artificial intelligence in the metaverse. *Arts and Design Studies*. Retrieved from https://api.semanticscholar.org/CorpusID:269580244

Indah Putri, N., Herdiana, Y., Munawar, Z., & Zainal Musadad, D. (2021, December). Database Security Based on Theory Set. *INFOTRONIK J. Teknol. Inf. and Electron.*, 6(2), 56–60.

Ingham, L. (2018). *88% of UK data breaches caused by human error, not cyberattacks*. The Verdict Magazine.

International Systems Conference, Vancouver, 19–22 March 2012, p 85–90

Ioannidis, S., & Kontis, A.-P. (2023). Metaverse for tourists and tourism destinations. *Information Technology & Tourism*, 25(4), 483–506. 10.1007/s40558-023-00271-y

Ionaşcu, A., Barbu, C. A., & Popa, A. (2023). Ethics in the banking sector. *LUMEN Proceedings, 19*, 137-145.

Iqbal, M., & Matulevičius, R. (2019). Blockchain-based application security risks: A systematic literature review. In Advanced Information Systems Engineering Workshops: CAiSE 2019 International Workshops, Rome, Italy, June 3-7, 2019 [Springer International Publishing.]. *Proceedings*, 31, 176–188.

Irwin, A., Slay, J., Choo, K., & Liu, L. (2012). Are the financial transactions conducted inside virtual environments truly anonymous? *Journal of Money Laundering Control*, 16(1), 6–40. 10.1108/13685201311286832

Ishiguro, K., & Kono, K. (2020). Instruction filters for mitigating attacks on instruction emulation in hypervisors. *IEICE Transactions on Information and Systems*, 103(7), 1660–1671.

Islam, M., Sajjad, M., Hasan, M., & Mazumder, M. (2023). Phishing attack detecting system using dns and ip filtering. *Asian Journal of Computer Science and Technology*, 12(1), 16–20. 10.51983/ajcst-2023.12.1.3552

Iswanto, N. I. (2022, June). Putri, D. Widhiantoro, Z. Munawar, and R. Komalasari, "Utilization of the Metaserve in the Education Sector,". *Temat. J. Technol. Inf. Commun.*, 9(1), 44–52.

Jaber, T. (2022). Security risks of the metaverse world. *International Journal of Interactive Mobile Technologies (Ijim)*, 16(13), 4–14. 10.3991/ijim.v16i13.33187

Jaeger, L. (2018). Information security awareness: literature review and integrative framework.

Jain, J., & Waoo, A. (2023). An artificial neural network technique for prediction of cyber-attack using intrusion detection system. *Journal of Artificial Intelligence Machine Learning and Neural Network*, 33-42. 10.55529/jaimlnn.32.33.42

Jain, A. K., Sahoo, S. R., & Kaubiyal, J. (2021). Online social networks security and privacy: Comprehensive review and analysis. *Complex & Intelligent Systems*, 7(5), 2157–2177. 10.1007/s40747-021-00409-7

Jaipong, P., Siripipattanakul, S., Sriboonruang, P., Sitthipon, T., Jaipong, P., Siripipattanakul, S., & Sitthipon, T. (2023). A review of metaverse and cybersecurity in the digital era. *International Journal of Computing Sciences Research*, 7, 1125–1132. 10.25147/ijcsr.2017.001.1.122

Jarin, I., & Eshete, B. (2021). Pricure: privacy-preserving collaborative inference in a multi-party setting. /arxiv.2102.0975110.1145/3445970.3451156

Jensen, M., Dinger, M., Wright, R., & Thatcher, J. (2017). Training to Mitigate Phishing Attacks Using Mindfulness Techniques. *Journal of Management Information Systems*, 34(2), 597–626. 10.1080/07421222.2017.1334499

Jensen, S., Phillips, L., & Strand, D. (2012). Virtual worlds as sites for social and cultural in- novation. *Convergence (London)*, 18(1), 3–10. 10.1177/1354856511419911

Jeon, B., & Heo, C. (2023). An empirical study on influential factors in adopting metaverse technology for educational services. *The Korean Career Entrepreneurship & Business Association*, 7(5), 73–88. 10.48206/kceba.2023.7.5.73

Jeon, J.-E. (2021). The effects of user experience-based design innovativeness on user-metaverse platform channel relationships in South Korea. *J. Distrib. Sci.*, 19, 81–90.

Jim, J., Hosain, M. T., Mridha, M. F., Kabir, M. M., & Shin, J. (2023). Toward trustworthy metaverse: Advancements and challenges. *IEEE Access : Practical Innovations, Open Solutions*, 11, 118318–118347. 10.1109/ACCESS.2023.3326258

Jones and Patel (2021). A Comparative Analysis of Machine Learning Algorithms for Phishing Website Detection in Virtual Environments.

Jones and Patel. (2021). Challenges of Generalization in Phishing Website Detection Across Virtual Platforms.

Jordan, G., Leskovar, R., & Marič, M. (2018). Impact of fear of identity theft and perceived risk on online purchase intention. *Organizacija*, 51(2), 146–155. 10.2478/orga-2018-0007

Kaa, G., Viardot, E., & McCarthy, I. (2022). Standardization for platform ecosystems. *Electronic Markets*, 32(4), 1807–1811. 10.1007/s12525-022-00611-6

Kabanda, G., Chiptumbu, C., & Chingoriwo, T. (2022). A cybersecurity model for a roblox- based metaverse architecture framework. *British Journal of Multidisciplinary and Advanced Studies*, 3(2), 105–141. 10.37745/bjmas.2022.0048

Kalio, S. (2022). Phishing Attack: Raising Awareness and Protection Techniques.

Kalita, A., & Gurusamy, M. 2022. "D2r2: distributed and dynamic reputation based resource allocation in metaverse." 10.36227/techrxiv.21395316

Kalnawat, A. (2024). Safeguarding critical infrastructures: machine learning in cybersecurity. *E3s Web of Conferences, 491*, 02025. 10.1051/e3sconf/202449102025

Kaluarachchi, T., Reis, A., & Nanayakkara, S. (2021). A review of recent deep learning approaches in human-centered machine learning. *Sensors (Basel)*, 21(7), 2514. 10.3390/s2107251433916850

Kan, K., & Une, M. (2021) 'Recent Trends on Research and Development of Quantum Computers and Standardization of Post-Quantum Cryptography', *Monetary and Economic Studies*, 39(November), pp. 77–108. Available at: https://ideas.repec.org/a/ime/imemes/v39y2021p77-108.html%0Ahttps://ideas.repec.org//a/ime/imemes/v39y2021p77-108.html

Kang, J., Ye, D., Nie, J., Xiao, J., Deng, X., Wang, S., . . . Niyato, D. (2022). Blockchain-based federated learning for industrial metaverses: incentive scheme with optimal aoi. 10.1109/Blockchain55522.2022.00020

Kang, J., Ye, D., Nie, J., Xiao, J., Deng, X., Wang, S., & Niyato, D. (2022, August). Blockchain-based federated learning for industrial metaverses: Incentive scheme with optimal aoi. In *2022 IEEE International Conference on Blockchain (Blockchain)* (pp. 71-78). IEEE.

Kapoor, A., Gupta, A., Gupta, R., Tanwar, S., & Davidson, I. (2021). Ransomware detection, avoidance, and mitigation scheme: A review and future directions. *Sustainability (Basel)*, 14(1), 8. 10.3390/su14010008

Kasiyanto, S., & Kilinc, M. (2022). Legal conundrums of the metaverse. *Journal of Central Banking Law and Institutions*, 1(2). Advance online publication. 10.21098/jcli.v1i2.25

Katterbauer, K., Syed, H., & Cleenewerck, L. (2022). Financial cybercrime in the Islamic finance metaverse. *Journal of Metaverse*, 2(2), 56–61.

Kaur, D., Singh, B., & Rani, S. (2023). Cyber Security in the Metaverse. In *Handbook of Research on AI-Based Technologies and Applications in the Era of the Metaverse* (pp. 418–435). IGI Global., 10.4018/978-1-6684-8851-5.ch023

Khairunnisa, D. Rachmanto, A.D., Munawar, Z., & Haitan, M. (2022). "Dynamic Virtual Tour Application at Universities Web-Based Nurtanio Bandung," in SNASIKOM, no. 1, pp. 42–50.

Khodaie, F., Jamali, M., & Farazan, A. (2014). The Use of Intelligent Algorithms to Detect Attacks in Intrusion Detection System. International Journal of computer Applications Technology and Research, 9(3), 579-584.

Khorshed, M., Ali, A. B. M. S., & Wasimi, S. A. (2012). A survey on gaps, threat remediation challenges and some thoughts for proactive attack detection in cloud computing. *Future Generation Computer Systems*, 28(6), 833–851. 10.1016/j.future.2012.01.006

Kim, E., Yoon, J. K., Kwon, J., Liaw, T., & Agogino, A. M. (2019a). From innocent irene to parental patrick: Framing user characteristics and personas to design for cybersecurity. *Proceedings of the International Conference on Engineering Design, ICED, 2019-Augus*(August), 1773–1782. 10.1017/dsi.2019.183

Kim, H., Kwon, H. J., & Kim, K. K. (2019). Modified cyber kill chain model for multimedia service environments. *Multimedia Tools and Applications*, 78(3), 3153–3170. 10.1007/s11042-018-5897-5

Kim, J. (2021). Advertising in the metaverse: Research agenda. *Journal of Interactive Advertising*, 21(3), 141–144. 10.1080/15252019.2021.2001273

Kim, M., Oh, J., Son, S., Park, Y., Kim, J., & Park, Y. (2023). Secure and privacy-preserving authentication scheme us- ing decentralized identifier in metaverse environment. *Electronics (Basel)*, 12(19), 4073. 10.3390/electronics12194073

Kong, J. (2010). Protecting the confidentiality of virtual machines against untrusted host. 10.1109/IPTC.2010.11

Kozinets, R. (2022). Immersive netnography: A novel method for service experience research in virtual reality, augmented reality and metaverse contexts. *Journal of Service Management*, 34(1), 100–125. 10.1108/JOSM-12-2021-0481

Krishnamurthy, R., & Trivedi, S. (2023). Understanding User Experience in the Metaverse. In *Handbook of Research on Consumer Behavioral Analytics in Metaverse and the Adoption of a Virtual World* (pp. 204–222). IGI Global. 10.4018/978-1-6684-7029-9.ch010

Kumar, A., Shankar, A., Behl, A., Gupta, B. B., & Mavuri, S. (2023). Lights, camera, metaverse!: Eliciting intention to use industrial metaverse, organizational agility, and firm performance. [JGIM]. *Journal of Global Information Management*, 31(8), 1–20. 10.4018/JGIM.333169

Kumbhojkar, N. R., & Menon, A. B. (2022). Integrated predictive experience management framework (IPEMF) for improving customer experience: In the era of digital transformation. [IJCAC]. *International Journal of Cloud Applications and Computing*, 12(1), 1–13. 10.4018/IJCAC.2022010107

Lam, K., L. Yang, A. Alhilal, L. Lee, G. Tyson, and P. Hui. 2022. "Human-avatar interaction in metaverse." .10.1145/3551626.3564936

Law, K. M., Ip, A. W., Gupta, B. B., & Geng, S. (2021). *Managing iot and mobile technologies with innovation, trust, and sustainable computing*. CRC Press. 10.1201/9780367822750

Law, K. M., Ip, A. W., Gupta, B. B., & Geng, S. (Eds.). (2021). *Managing IoT and mobile technologies with innovation, trust, and sustainable computing*. CRC Press.

Lebeck, K., Ruth, K., Kohno, T., & Roesner, F. (2018, May). Towards security and privacy for multi-user augmented reality: Foundations with end users. In *2018 IEEE Symposium on Security and Privacy (SP)* (pp. 392-408). IEEE.

Lebeck, K., Ruth, K., Kohno, T., & Roesner, F. "Towards security and privacy for multi-user augmented reality: Foundations with end users", *Proc. IEEE Symp. Security Privacy (SP)*, pp. 392-408, 2018. 10.1109/SP.2018.00051

Lee, E., Lee, W., & Bae, I. (2023). What is the draw of the metaverse? personality correlates of zepeto use motives and their associations with psychological well-being. *Cyberpsychology, Behavior, and Social Networking*, 26(3), 161–168. 10.1089/cyber.2022.016436827586

Lee, J., Lee, Y., Lee, D., Kwon, H., & Shin, D. (2021). Classification of attack types and analysis of attack methods for profiling phishing mail attack groups. *IEEE Access : Practical Innovations, Open Solutions*, 9, 80866–80872. 10.1109/ACCESS.2021.3084897

Lee, M., & Chaney, D. (2023). The psychological and functional factors driving metaverse resistance. *Internet Research*, 34(1), 195–215. 10.1108/INTR-08-2022-0647

Leenes, R. (2008). Privacy in the metaverse: Regulating a complex social construct in a virtual world. *Proc. Future Identity Inf. Soc.*, (Jul), 95–112.

Lee, S., Chang, Y., Lee, O.-K. D., Ryu, S., & Yin, Q. (2024). Exploring online social platform affordances for digital creators: A multi-method approach using qualitative and configurational analysis. *Industrial Management & Data Systems*, 124(4), 1501–1530. 10.1108/IMDS-12-2023-0951

Lei, Y., Duan, Y., & Song, M. (2020, October). Technical implementation framework of AI governance policies for cross-modal privacy protection. In *International Conference on Collaborative Computing: Networking, Applications and Worksharing* (pp. 431-443). Cham: Springer International Publishing.

Li, N., El Helou, S., & Gillet, D. (2010, April). Trust-based rating prediction for recommendation in web 2.0 collaborative learning social software. In 2010 9th International Conference on Information Technology Based Higher Education and Training (ITHET) (pp. 208-212). IEEE.

Li, P. (2024). "The impact of avatar identification on the attractiveness of vr games: the medi- ational role of immersion (preprint)." 10.2196/preprints.56704

Li, J., Herdem, M. S., Nathwani, J., & Wen, J. Z. (2023). Methods and applications for Artificial Intelligence, Big Data, Internet of Things, and Blockchain in smart energy management. *Energy and AI*, 11, 100208. 10.1016/j.egyai.2022.100208

Li, K., Cui, Y., Li, W., Lv, T., Yuan, X., Li, S., Ni, W., Simsek, M., & Dressler, F. (2023). When internet of things meets metaverse: Convergence of physical and cyber worlds. *IEEE Internet of Things Journal*, 10(5), 4148–4173. 10.1109/JIOT.2022.3232845

Lim, J. S., Ahmad, A., Chang, S., & Maynard, S. (2010). Embedding information security culture emerging concerns and challenges.

Li, M., & Yu, Z. (2023). A systematic review on the metaverse-based blended english learn- ing. *Frontiers in Psychology*, 13, 1087508. Advance online publication. 10.3389/fpsyg.2022.108750836687938

Lin, Y., Du, H., Niyato, D., Nie, J., Zhang, J., Cheng, Y., & Yang, Z. (2023). Blockchain-aided secure semantic communication for ai-generated content in metaverse. *IEEE Open Journal of the Computer Society*, 4, 72–83. 10.1109/OJCS.2023.3260732

Liu, C.-C. (2017). A model for exploring players flow experience in online games. *Information Technology & People*, 30(1), 139–162. 10.1108/ITP-06-2015-0139

Liu, L., De Vel, O., Han, Q. L., Zhang, J., & Xiang, Y. (2018). Detecting and preventing cyber insider threats: A survey. *IEEE Communications Surveys and Tutorials*, 20(2), 1397–1417. 10.1109/COMST.2018.2800740

Liu, S. Y. (2023). The security challenges of the "Metaverse". *Secur Saf*, 2, 2023010.

Liu, S., Zou, H., Zhao, X., Wang, C., & Fan, Y. (2023). Preface: Security and Safety in the "Metaverse". *Security and Safety*, 2, E2023014. 10.1051/sands/2023014

Li, W., Wu, L., Xue, J., Hu, W., Li, S., Guo, G., & Cao, D. (2023). Intelligent cockpit for intelligent vehicle in metaverse: A case study of empathetic auditory regulation of hu- man emotion. *IEEE Transactions on Systems, Man, and Cybernetics. Systems*, 53(4), 2173–2187. 10.1109/TSMC.2022.3229021

Lyoussi, D., & Kouchih, A. (2023). Metaverse and financial inclusion opportunities and risks for the banking ecosystem. In *Influencer Marketing Applications Within the Metaverse* (pp. 205–224). IGI Global. 10.4018/978-1-6684-8898-0.ch013

Lyu, Y., & Reddy, K. (2020). Phishing detection for social networking sites: A survey. *ACM Computing Surveys*, 53(3), 1–37.

Macnish, K., & Inguanzo, A. (2019). Smart information systems in cybersecurity. *Orbit Journal*, 2(2), 1–26. 10.29297/orbit.v2i2.105

Madarie, R., Ruiter, S., Steenbeek, W., & Kleemans, E. (2019). Stolen account credentials: An empirical comparison of online dissemination on different platforms. *Journal of Crime and Justice*, 42(5), 551–568. 10.1080/0735648X.2019.1692418

Maggi, P., Pozza, D., & Sisto, R. (2008, June). Vulnerability modelling for the analysis of network attacks. In *2008 Third International Conference on Dependability of Computer Systems DepCoS-RELCOMEX* (pp. 15-22). IEEE.

Mahnke, R., Benlian, A., & Hess, T. (2015). A grounded theory of online shopping flow. *International Journal of Electronic Commerce*, 19(3), 54–89. 10.1080/10864415.2015.1000222

Maim'o, L., & Celdr'an, A. (2019). Intelligent and dynamic ransomware spread detection and mitigation in integrated clinical environments. *Sensors (Basel)*, 19(5), 1114. 10.3390/s1905111430841592

Mandolfo, M., Baisi, F., & Lamberti, L. (2022). How did you feel during the nav- igation? influence of emotions on browsing time and interaction frequency in im- mersive virtual environments. *Behaviour & Information Technology*, 42(8), 1216–1229. 10.1080/0144929X.2022.2066570

Manushri, S., Santhiya, J., & Roobasri, A. (2022). Metaverse - the future of virtual world. *International Journal of Engineering Technology and Management Sciences*, 6(5), 779–783. 10.46647/ijetms.2022.v06i05.121

Matheu, S., Hernandez-Ramos, J., Skarmeta, A., & Baldini, G. (2020). A survey of cy- bersecurity certification for the internet of things. *ACM Computing Surveys*, 53(6), 1–36. 10.1145/3410160

Mathur, A., Sah, A., & Rawat, S. (2023). Evolution of Cloud Computing With Blockchain and IoT. In Taghipour, A. (Ed.), *Blockchain Applications in Cryptocurrency for Technological Evolution* (pp. 14–32). IGI Global., 10.4018/978-1-6684-6247-8.ch002

McLeod, A., & Dolezel, D. (2018). Cyber-analytics: Modeling factors associated with healthcare data breaches. *Decision Support Systems*, 108, 57–68. 10.1016/j.dss.2018.02.007

Mendoza, A. L., Hernandez, R. S., Quezada, M. T. P., & Hernandez, R. V. (2023). Cybersecurity among University students from Generation Z: A comparative study of the Undergraduate Programs in Administration and Public Accounting in two Mexican universities. *Tem Journal-Technology Education Management Informatics*, 12(1), 503–511.

Miltgen, C. L., & Smith, H. J. (2015). Exploring information privacy regulation, risks, trust, and behavior. *Information & Management*, 52(6), 741–759. 10.1016/j.im.2015.06.006

Mishra, A., Gupta, N., & Gupta, B. B. (2023). Defensive mechanism against DDoS attack based on feature selection and multi-classifier algorithms. *Telecommunication Systems*, 82(2), 229–244. 10.1007/s11235-022-00981-4

Mitra, S. (2023). Metaverse! *International Journal of E-Adoption*, 15(2), 1–21. 10.4018/IJEA.316537

Mohajerani, K., ... (2023) 'SCA Evaluation and Benchmarking of Finalists in the NIST Lightweight Cryptography Standardization Process', *Cryptology ePrint Archive*. Available at: https://cryptography.gmu.edu/athena/index.php?id=LWC

Momtaz, P. (2022). Some very simple economics of web3 and the metaverse. *Fintech*, 1(3), 225–234. 10.3390/fintech1030018

Montanaro, U., Dixit, S., Fallah, S., Dianati, M., Stevens, A., Oxtoby, D., & Mouzakitis, A. (2018). Towards connected autonomous driving: Review of use-cases. *Vehicle System Dynamics*, 57(6), 779–814. 10.1080/00423114.2018.1492142

Monteiro, L., Rodrigues, Y., & Souza, A. (2023). Cybersecurity in cyber–physical power sys- tems. *Energies*, 16(12), 4556. 10.3390/en16124556

Mooij, A. (2024). *Regulating the Metaverse Economy: How to Prevent Money Laundering and the Financing of Terrorism*. Springer Nature. 10.1007/978-3-031-46417-1

Moon, D., Im, H., Lee, J. D., & Park, J. H. (2014). MLDS: Multi-layer defense system for preventing advanced persistent threats. *Symmetry*, 6(4), 997–1010.

Muhla, F., Clanché, F., Duclos, K., Meyer, P., Maïaux, S., Colnat-Coulbois, S., & Gauchard, G. (2020). Impact of using immersive virtual reality over time and steps in the timed up and go test in elderly people. *PLoS One*, 15(3), e0229594. 10.1371/journal.pone.022959432168361

Munawar, Z. (2017, December). "Use of Social Media Profiles for Predicting Personality," Temat. - J. Techno. Inf. And Commun., vol. 4, no. 2 SE-Articles, pp. 18–37,.

Munawar, Z. (2021, December). "Web-Based Seminar Registration Application Using QR Code at XYZ University," Temat. J. Technol. Inf. And Commun., vol. 6, no. 2, pp. 68–77.

Munawar, Z., Indah Putri, N., & Zainal Musadad, D. (2021). "Improving Recommendations Using Algorithms Differences in Topics," J-SIKA|Sist Journal. Inf. Children's Works Nation, vol. 2, no. 02 SE-, pp. 17–26.

Munawar, Z., Suryana, N., Sa'aya, Z. B., & Herdiana, Y. (2022). Thematic: Information Communication Technology Journal (e-Journal) Vol. 9 No. 2 DOI: 10.38204/tematic.v9i2.1069

Munawar, Z. (2018). Security in E-Commerce for Small Businesses and Intermediate. *Thematic*, 5(1), 1–16.

Munawar, Z. (2020). Technical Improvements to the Inventory Recording System Computer Based Goods for Market Book Traders Palasari Bandung City Facing the Competitive Market Era. *JAST J. Appl. Science and Technology.*, 4(1), 52.

Munawar, Z., Fudsyi, M. I., & Musadad, D. Z. (2019). Designing Application Interface for Recording Goods Inventory at Book Kiosks Palasari Bandung Using the User Centered Design Method Using Balsamiq Mockups. *Journal of Informetrics*, 6(2), 10–20.

Munawar, Z., Herdiana, Y., Suharya, Y., & Putri, N. I. (2021, December). Use of Digital Technology During the Covid-19 Pandemic. *Temat. J. Technol. Inf. Commun.*, 8(2), 160–175.

Munawar, Z., & Putri, N. I. (2020, December). "IoT Security With Deep Learning and Big Data Technology," Temat. -. *J. Techno. Inf. And Commun.*, 7(2), 161–185.

Munawar, Z., Suryana, N., Sa'aya, Z. B., & Herdiana, Y. (2020, November). Framework With An Approach To The User As An Evaluation For The Recommender Systems. In *2020 Fifth International Conference on Informatics and Computing (ICIC)* (pp. 1-5). IEEE.

Musale, P. (2024). Demystifying the metaverse: a deep dive into characteristics, enabling technologies, key components, surmounting challenges, and unveiling boundless applications. *Interantional Jour- nal of Scientific Research in Engineering and Management, 08*, 1-5. 10.55041/IJSREM31625

Mystakidis, S. (2022). Metaverse. *Encyclopedia*, 2(1), 486–497. 10.3390/encyclopedia2010031

Nadella, S. (2021) "The metaverse is here, and it's not the only one transforming how we see the world but how we participate in it – from the factory floor to the meeting room. Take a look."

Nah, F. F.-H., Eschenbrenner, B., DeWester, D., & Park, S. R. (2010). Impact of flow and brand equity in 3D virtual worlds. [JDM]. *Journal of Database Management*, 21(3), 69–89. 10.4018/jdm.2010070103

Naik, N., Jenkins, P., Savage, N., & Yang, L. (2019, June). Cyberthreat hunting-part 2: Tracking ransomware threat actors using fuzzy hashing and fuzzy c-means clustering. In 2019 IEEE international conference on fuzzy systems (FUZZ-IEEE) (pp. 1-6). IEEE.

Natarajan, T., Pragha, P., Dhalmahapatra, K., & Veera Raghavan, D. R. (2024). Unveiling metaverse sentiments using machine learning approaches. *Kybernetes*. Advance online publication. 10.1108/K-11-2023-2268

Nebbione, G., & Calzarossa, M. (2023). A methodological framework for ai-assisted security assessments of active directory environments. *IEEE Access : Practical Innovations, Open Solutions*, 11, 15119–15130. 10.1109/ACCESS.2023.3244490

Neri, M., Niccolini, F., & Martino, L. (2023). Organizational cybersecurity readiness in the ict sector: A quanti-qualitative assessment. *Information and Computer Security*, 32(1), 38–52. 10.1108/ICS-05-2023-0084

Networks, I. of M. (US) C. on R. H. D., Donaldson, M. S., & Lohr, K. N. (1994). Confidentiality and Privacy of Personal Data. In *Health Data in the Information Age: Use, Disclosure, and Privacy*. National Academies Press (US). https://www.ncbi.nlm.nih.gov/books/NBK236546/

Ng, D. (2022). What is the metaverse? definitions, technologies and the com- munity of inquiry. *Australasian Journal of Educational Technology*, 38(4), 190–205. 10.14742/ajet.7945

Nguyen, C., Hoang, D., Nguyen, D., & Dutkiewicz, E. 2022. "Metachain: a novel blockchain-based framework for metaverse applications." /arxiv.2201.00759.10.1109/VTC2022-Spring54318.2022.9860983

Nleya, S. M., & Velempini, M. (2024). Industrial Metaverse: A Comprehensive Review, Environmental Impact, and Challenges. *Applied Sciences (Basel, Switzerland)*, 14(13), 5736.

Nzuva, S. (2019). Smart contracts implementation, applications, benefits, and limitations. *Journal of Information Engineering and Applications*, 9(5), 63–75.

Oh, Y., Yi, J., & Kim, J. (2023). What enhances or worsens the user-generated metaverse experience? an appli- cation of bertopic to roblox user ewom. *Internet Research*. Advance online publication. 10.1108/INTR-03-2022-0178

Oladokun, B., Yahaya, D. O., & Enakrire, R. T. (2023). Moving into the metaverse: Libraries in virtual worlds. *Library Hi Tech News*, 40(9), 18–21. 10.1108/LHTN-08-2023-0147

Ooi, K. B., Tan, G. W. H., Aw, E. C. X., Cham, T. H., Dwivedi, Y. K., Dwivedi, R., Hughes, L., Kar, A. K., Loh, X.-M., Mogaji, E., Phau, I., & Sharma, A. (2023). Banking in the metaverse: A new frontier for financial institutions. *International Journal of Bank Marketing*, 41(7), 1829–1846. 10.1108/IJBM-03-2023-0168

Orji, U. (2018). The african union convention on cybersecurity: A regional response to- wards cyber stability? *Masaryk University Journal of Law and Technology*, 12(2), 91–130. 10.5817/MUJLT2018-2-1

Otoum, Y., Gottimukkala, N., Kumar, N., & Nayak, A. (2024). Machine learning in metaverse security: Current solutions and future chal- lenges. *ACM Computing Surveys*, 56(8), 1–36. 10.1145/3654663

Pandey, D., & Gilmour, P. (2024). Accounting meets metaverse: Navigating the intersection between the real and virtual worlds. *Journal of Financial Reporting and Accounting*, 22(2), 211–226. 10.1108/JFRA-03-2023-0157

Pan, W., Li, W., & Zhao, W. (2009, November). A Novel Anomaly Detection Approach for Executable Program Security. In *2009 International Conference on Multimedia Information Networking and Security* (Vol. 1, pp. 422-426). IEEE.

Papagiannidis, S., Bourlakis, M., & Li, F. (2008). Making real money in virtual worlds: Mmorpgs and emerging business opportunities, challenges and ethical im- plications in metaverses. *Technological Forecasting and Social Change*, 75(5), 610–622. 10.1016/j.techfore.2007.04.007

Papaioannou, M., Mantas, G., Essop, A., Sucasas, V., Aaraj, N., & Rodriguez, J. (2022). Risk estima- tion for a secure & usable user authentication mechanism for mobile passenger id devices. 10.1109/CAMAD55695.2022.9966915

Papaioannou, M., Pelekoudas-Oikonomou, F., Mantas, G., Serrelis, E., Rodriguez, J., & Fengou, M.-A. (2023). A survey on quantitative risk estimation approaches for secure and usable user authentication on smartphones. *Sensors (Basel)*, 23(6), 2979. 10.3390/s2306297936991690

Paquin, V., Ferrari, M., Sekhon, H., & Rej, S. (2023). Time to think "meta": A critical viewpoint on the risks and benefits of virtual worlds for mental health. *JMIR Serious Games*, 11, e43388. 10.2196/4338836661284

Park, B., Ahn, S., & Kim, H. (2010). Blogging: Mediating impacts of flow on motivational behavior. *Journal of Research in Interactive Marketing*, 4(1), 6–29. 10.1108/17505931011033533

Park, D. (2015). Draft of national cybersecurity act. *International Journal of Security and Its Applications*, 9(11), 105–112. 10.14257/ijsia.2015.9.11.11

Park, W., Siddiqui, I., & Qureshi, N. (2022). Ai-enabled grouping bridgehead to secure penetration topics of metaverse. *Computers, Materials & Continua*, 73(3), 5609–5624. 10.32604/cmc.2022.030235

Patterson, N., M. Hobbs, F. Jiang, and L. Pan. 2019. "Cyber security insights into self- proclaimed virtual world hackers." .10.5121/csit.2019.91107

Patterson, N., Hobbs, M., & Zhu, T. (2017). A cyber-threat analytic model for autonomous detection of virtual property theft. *Information and Computer Security*, 25(4), 358–381. 10.1108/ICS-11-2016-0087

Patwe, S., & Mane, S. B. (2024). Blockchain-enabled secure and interoperable authentication scheme for meta- verse environments. *Future Internet*, 16(5), 166. 10.3390/fi16050166

Pooyandeh, M., Han, K., & Sohn, I. (2022). Cybersecurity in the ai-based metaverse: A survey. *Applied Sciences (Basel, Switzerland)*, 12(24), 12993. 10.3390/app122412993

Pramod, D. (2022). Privacy-preserving techniques in recommender systems: State-of-the-art review and future research agenda. *Data Technologies and Applications*, 57(1), 32–55. 10.1108/DTA-02-2022-0083

Priyadarshini, I. (2024). Anomaly detection of iot cyberattacks in smart cities using federated learning and split learning. *Big Data and Cognitive Computing*, 8(3), 21. 10.3390/bdcc8030021

Protogerou, A., Kopsacheilis, E., Mpatziakas, A., Papachristou, K., Theodorou, T., Papadopoulos, S., Drosou, A., & Tzovaras, D. (2022). Time series network data enabling distributed intelligence—A holistic iot security platform solution. *Electronics (Basel)*, 11(4), 529. 10.3390/electronics11040529

Putra, K. T., Chen, H.-C., Ogiela, M. R., Chou, C.-L., Weng, C.-E., & Shae, Z.-Y. (2021). Federated compressed learning edge computing framework with ensuring data privacy for PM2. 5 prediction in smart city sensing applications. *Sensors (Basel)*, 21(13), 4586. 10.3390/s2113458634283140

Pyae, A., Ravyse, W., Luimula, M., Pizarro-Lucas, E., Sanchez, P. L., Dorado-Diaz, I. P., & Thaw, A. K. (2023). Exploring User Experience and Usability in a Metaverse Learning Environment for Students: A Usability Study of the Artificial Intelligence, Innovation, and Society (AIIS). *Electronics (Basel)*, 12(20), 20. Advance online publication. 10.3390/electronics12204283

Qian, Y., & Zhang, S. (2017). Information security protection system based on intrusion detection from real time angle. 10.2991/mecs-17.2017.93

Qin, R., Ding, W., Li, J., Guan, S., Wang, G., Ren, Y., & Qu, Z. (2023). Web3-based de- centralized autonomous organizations and operations: Architectures, models, and mech- anisms. *IEEE Transactions on Systems, Man, and Cybernetics. Systems*, 53(4), 2073–2082. 10.1109/TSMC.2022.3228530

Radanliev, P. (2024). Integrated cybersecurity for metaverse systems operating with artificial intel- ligence, blockchains, and cloud computing. *Frontiers in Blockchain*, 7, 1359130. Advance online publication. 10.3389/fbloc.2024.1359130

Rahaman, M., Lin, C.-Y., & Moslehpour, M. (2023). SAPD: Secure Authentication Protocol Development for Smart Healthcare Management Using IoT. *2023 IEEE 12th Global Conference on Consumer Electronics (GCCE)*, 1014–1018. 10.1109/GCCE59613.2023.10315475

Rahaman, M., Lin, C.-Y., Pappachan, P., Gupta, B. B., & Hsu, C.-H. (2024). Privacy-Centric AI and IoT Solutions for Smart Rural Farm Monitoring and Control. *Sensors (Basel)*, 24(13), 13. Advance online publication. 10.3390/s2413415739000936

Rahaman, M., Tabassum, F., Arya, V., & Bansal, R. (2024). Secure and sustainable food processing supply chain framework based on Hyperledger Fabric technology. *Cyber Security and Applications*, 2, 100045. 10.1016/j.csa.2024.100045

Raj, B., Gupta, B. B., Yamaguchi, S., & Gill, S. S. (2023). *Ai for big data-based engineering applica- tions from security perspectives*. CRC Press. 10.1201/9781003230113

Raposo, V. (2022). 'i'm right behind you': Digital contact tracing under euro- pean law. *Maastricht Journal of European and Comparative Law*, 29(4), 434–450. 10.1177/1023263X221116227

Rathnayake, N. D. N. B. (2023). The Era of the Transition–From Traditional to Digital Banking. In *Transformation for Sustainable Business and Management Practices: Exploring the Spectrum of Industry 5.0* (pp. 41-55). Emerald Publishing Limited. 10.1108/978-1-80262-277-520231005

Rawat, S., & Sah, A. (2012). An approach to Enhance the software and services of Health care centre. 3(7), 126–137.

Rawat, D., & Alami, H. (2023). Metaverse: Requirements, architecture, standards, status, challenges, and perspectives. *Ieee Internet of Things Magazine*, 6(1), 14–18. 10.1109/IOTM.001.2200258

Rawat, S., & Kumar, R. (2020). Direct-Indirect Link Matrix: A Black Box Testing Technique for Component-Based Software. *International Journal of Information Technology Project Management*, 11(4), 56–69. 10.4018/IJITPM.2020100105

Rawat, S., & Sah, A. (2013). An Approach to Integrate Heterogeneous Web Applications. *International Journal of Computer Applications*, 70(23), 7–12. 10.5120/12205-7639

Reidsma, D., van der Ham, J., & Continella, A. (2023, February). Operationalizing cybersecurity research ethics review: from principles and guidelines to practice. In *2nd International Workshop on Ethics in Computer Security, EthiCS 2023*. Internet Society.

Reinhard, C., & Amsterdam, P. (2013). Virtual world television products and practices: Comparing television production in second life to traditional television production. *Journal of Virtual Worlds Research*, 6(2). Advance online publication. 10.4101/jvwr.v6i2.7042

Rejeb, A., Rejeb, K., & Treiblmaier, H. (2023). Mapping metaverse research: Identifying future research areas based on bibliometric and topic modeling techniques. *Information (Basel)*, 14(7), 356. 10.3390/info14070356

Renda, K. (2022). The development of eu cybersecurity policy: From a coordinating actor to a cyber power? *Ankara Avrupa Calismalari Dergisi*, 21(2), 467–495. 10.32450/aacd.1226890

Ren, Z., Lu, W., & Xu, S. (2018). Preventive and reactive cyber defense dynamics is globally stable. *IEEE Transactions on Network Science and Engineering*, 5(2), 156–170. 10.1109/TNSE.2017.2734904

Rosário, A. T., Lopes, P. R., & Rosário, F. S. (2023). Metaverse in Marketing: Challenges and Opportunities. *Handbook of Research on AI-Based Technologies and Applications in the Era of the Metaverse*, 204-227.

Roshan, K., & Zafar, A. (2024). ae-integrated: Real-time network intrusion detection with apache kafka and autoen- coder. *Concurrency and Computation*, 36(11), e8034. Advance online publication. 10.1002/cpe.8034

Rostami, S., & Maier, M. (2022). The metaverse and beyond: Implementing advanced multiverse realms with smart wearables. *IEEE Access : Practical Innovations, Open Solutions*, 10, 110796–110806. 10.1109/ACCESS.2022.3215736

Ryu, J., Son, S., Lee, J., Park, Y., & Park, Y. (2022). Design of secure mutual authentication scheme for metaverse environments using blockchain. *IEEE Access : Practical Innovations, Open Solutions*, 10, 98944–98958. 10.1109/ACCESS.2022.3206457

S¨aks, E. (2022). Using cinematic virtual reality to get acquainted with the metaverse. *Baltic Screen Media Review*, 10(2), 252–271. 10.2478/bsmr-2022-0019

Sabrina, M., & Defi, I. (2021). Telemedicine guidelines in south east asia—A scoping review. *Frontiers in Neurology*, 11, 581649. Advance online publication. 10.3389/fneur.2020.58164933519669

Sadik, S., Ahmed, M., Sikos, L., & Islam, A. (2020). Toward a sustainable cybersecurity ecosys- tem. *Computers*, 9(3), 74. 10.3390/computers9030074

Saerang, A. (2023). Accounting profession in metaverse era - nft. *E3s Web of Conferences, 426*, 02052. 10.1051/e3sconf/202342602052

Safkhani, M., Rostampour, S., Bendavid, Y., & Bagheri, N. (2020). Iot in medical amp; phar- maceutical: Designing lightweight rfid security protocols for ensuring supply chain integrity. *Computer Networks*, 181, 107558. 10.1016/j.comnet.2020.10755835023996

Sah, A., Bhadula, S. J., Dumka, A., & Rawat, S. (2018). A software engineering perspective for development of enterprise applications. Handbook of Research on Contemporary Perspectives on Web-Based Systems, 1–23. 10.4018/978-1-5225-5384-7.ch001

Sah, A., Dumka, A., & Rawat, S. (2018). Web technology systems integration using SOA and web services. Handbook of Research on Contemporary Perspectives on Web-Based Systems, 24–45. 10.4018/978-1-5225-5384-7.ch002

Sah, A., Choudhury, T., Rawat, S., & Tripathi, A. (2020). A Proposed Gene Selection Approach for Disease Detection. *Advances in Intelligent Systems and Computing*, 1120, 199–206. 10.1007/978-981-15-2449-3_16

Sah, A., Rawat, S., Choudhury, T., & Dewangan, B. K. (2022). An Extensive Review of Web-Based Multi-Granularity Service Composition. *International Journal of Web-Based Learning and Teaching Technologies*, 17(4), 1–19. 10.4018/IJWLTT.285570

Sahabandu, D., B. Xiao, A. Clark, S. Lee, W. Lee, and R. Poovendran. 2018. "Dift games: dynamic information flow tracking games for advanced persistent threats." .10.1109/CDC.2018.8619416

Saharan, S., Singh, S., Bhandari, A. K., & Yadav, B. (2024). The future of Cyber-Crimes and cyber war in the metaverse. In *Forecasting cyber crimes in the age of the metaverse* (pp. 126–148). IGI Global.

Salah, K., Rehman, M., Nizamuddin, N., & Al-Fuqaha, A. (2019). Blockchain for ai: Review and open research challenges. *IEEE Access : Practical Innovations, Open Solutions*, 7, 10127–10149. 10.1109/ACCESS.2018.2890507

Salem, O., Hossain, A., & Kamala, M. (2010, June). Awareness program and ai based tool to reduce risk of phishing attacks. In 2010 10th IEEE International Conference on Computer and Information Technology (pp. 1418-1423). IEEE.

Samala, A., Ambiyar, A., Boji'c, L., Indarta, Y., Ipalakova, M., Denden, M., Ta¸s, N., & Dewi, I. (2023). Metaverse technologies in education: A systematic literature review using prisma. *International Journal of Emerging Technologies in Learning*, 18(5), 231–252. 10.3991/ijet.v18i05.35501

Sanders, B., & Marchang, J. (2016, November). A novel taxonomy of opportunities and risks in massively multiplayer online role playing games. In *Proceedings of the 8th International Conference on Management of Digital EcoSystems* (pp. 90-98).

Sanghvi, H., Bhavsar, R., Hundlani, V., Gohil, L., Vyas, T., Nair, A., Desai, S., Jadav, N. K., Tanwar, S., Sharma, R., & Yamsani, N. (2023). metahate: Ai-based hate speech detection for secured online gaming in metaverse using blockchain. *Security and Privacy*, 7(2), e343. Advance online publication. 10.1002/spy2.343

Saracoglu, D. (2023). Metaverse and New Cybersecurity Threats. In *Metaverse: Technologies, Opportunities and Threats* (pp. 99–121). Springer Nature Singapore. 10.1007/978-981-99-4641-9_7

Saravanan, N., & Umamakeswari, A. (2018). Security vulnerabilities of virtu- alization technique. *IACSIT International Journal of Engineering and Technology*, 7(2.24), 478. 10.14419/ijet.v7i2.24.12140

Sarker, I., Furhad, H., & Nowrozy, R. (2021). Ai-driven cybersecurity: An overview, security intelligence modeling and research directions. *SN Computer Science*, 2(3), 173. Advance online publication. 10.1007/s42979-021-00557-0

Saurabh, P., & Verma, B. (2014). A novel immunity inspired approach for anomaly detection. *International Journal of Computer Applications*, 94(15), 14–19. 10.5120/16418-6034

Sawyer, G. (2021). A review of the cybersecurity programs in the united states army. *Journal of Information Technology*, 5(1), 22–30. 10.53819/81018102t2017

Schaaf, K., & Tekinerdo˘gan, B. (2021). A feature-based approach for guiding the selection of internet of things cybersecurity standards using text mining. *Concurrency and Computation*, 33(21), e6385. Advance online publication. 10.1002/cpe.6385

Schein, E. H. (2010). *Organizational culture and leadership* (Vol. 2). John Wiley & Sons.

Schneider, M. (2023). Open Banking and Digital Ecosystems. In *Digital Project Practice for New Work and Industry 4.0* (pp. 169–179). Auerbach Publications. 10.1201/9781003371397-12

Schulze, M. (2017). Clipper meets apple vs. FBI—A comparison of the cryptography discourses from 1993 and 2016. *Media and Communication*, 5(1), 54–62. 10.17645/mac.v5i1.805

Sebastian, G. (2022). A descriptive study on metaverse. *International Journal of Security and Privacy in Pervasive Computing*, 15(1), 1–14. 10.4018/IJSPPC.315591

Sethi, A. (2022). *Security and Privacy in Metaverse: Issues, Challenges, and Future Op- portunities*. Cyber Security Insights Magazine.

Setia, H., Chhabra, A., Singh, S. K., Kumar, S., Sharma, S., Arya, V., & Wu, J. (2024). Securing the road ahead: Machine learning-driven DDoS attack detection in VANET cloud environments. *Cyber Security and Applications*, 2, 100037.

Setianingsih, L., Pulungan, R., Putra, A., Wibowo, M., & Syarip, . (2021). Risk assessment methods for cybersecurity in nuclear facilities: Compliance to regulatory require- ments. *International Journal of Advanced Computer Science and Applications*, 12(9). Advance online publication. 10.14569/IJACSA.2021.0120979

Shang, J., Chen, S., Wu, J., & Yin, S. (2022, February). ARSpy: Breaking location-based multi-player augmented reality application for user location tracking. *IEEE Transactions on Mobile Computing*, 21(2), 433–447. 10.1109/TMC.2020.3007740

Shanmugam, L. (2023). Federated learning architecture: design, implementation, and challenges in distributed ai systems. *Journal of Knowledge Learning and Science Technology Issn 2959-6386 (Online), 2*, 371-384. 10.60087/jklst.vol2.n2.p384

Shariff, S. M., & Zhang, X. (2014, June). A survey on deceptions in online social networks. In *2014 International Conference on Computer and Information Sciences (ICCOINS)* (pp. 1-6). IEEE.

Sharma, S., & Singh, S. K. (2022). IoT and its uses in Security Surveillance. Insights2Techinfo, pp1.

Sharma, A., Gupta, B. B., Singh, A. K., & Saraswat, V. K. (2023). A novel approach for detection of APT malware using multi-dimensional hybrid Bayesian belief network. *International Journal of Information Security*, 22(1), 119–135. 10.1007/s10207-022-00631-5

Sharma, K., & Gupta, B. B. (2018). Attack in smartphone Wi-Fi access channel: State of the art, current issues, and challenges. Next-Generation Networks: *Proceedings of CSI-2015*, 555-561.

Sharma, P., Dash, B., & Ansari, M. (2022). Anti-phishing techniques – a review of cyber defense mechanisms. *International Journal of Advanced Research in Computer and Communication Engineering*, 11(7). Advance online publication. 10.17148/IJARCCE.2022.11728

Sharma, S., Singh, J., Gupta, A., Ali, F., Khan, F., & Kwak, D. (2024). User safety and security in the metaverse: A critical review. *IEEE Open Journal of the Communications Society*, •••, 1–1. 10.1109/OJCOMS.2024.3397044

Shehab, M., Bertino, E., & Ghafoor, A. (2008, September). Proactive role discovery in mediator-free environments. In *2008 Eighth International Conference on Peer-to-Peer Computing* (pp. 150-159). IEEE.

Shen, B., Wei-ming, T., Guo, J., Cai, H., Wang, B., & Zhuo, S. (2020). A study on design requirement development and satisfaction for future virtual world systems. *Future Internet*, 12(7), 112. 10.3390/fi12070112

Shevchenko, S., Skladannyi, P., & Spasiteleva, S. (2023). Mathematical methods in cy- bersecurity: Catastrophe theory. *Cybersecurity Education Science Technique*, 3(19), 165–175. 10.28925/2663-4023.2023.19.165175

Shukla, A., Singh, M., & Pandey, A. (2018). Email classification for forensic analysis by information gain technique. *International Journal of Advanced Research in Computer Science and Software Engineering*, 8(5), 1–8.

Simon, F. (2010). The experiential aspects of online search information for new customers to a website. *Canadian Journal of Administrative Sciences/Revue Canadienne des Sciences de l'Administration, 27*(4), 292-305.

Singh, M., & Mishra, K. D. (2019). Applications of virtual reality in mental health. *International Jour- nal of Recent Technology and Engineering, 8*, 3735-3739. 10.35940/ijrte.B1481.0982S1119

Singh, G., Malhotra, M., & Sharma, A. (2022). An adaptive mechanism for virtual machine migration in the cloud environment. [IJCAC]. *International Journal of Cloud Applications and Computing*, 12(1), 1–10. 10.4018/IJCAC.311504

Singh, R., Verma, A., & Singh, M. (2017). A Survey of Phishing Email Filtering Techniques: Detection and Classification. *Artificial Intelligence and Its Applications*, 1(1), 39–52. 10.1007/s40502-017-0005-9

Singla, A., Gupta, N., Aeron, P., Jain, A., Garg, R., Sharma, D., & Arya, V. (2022). Building the metaverse: Design considerations, socio-technical elements, and future research directions of metaverse. [JGIM]. *Journal of Global Information Management*, 31(2), 1–28.

Sinha, K. (2023). The Metaverse and Digital Libraries: Ensuring Safe and Secure Access to Information. In Handbook of Research on Advancements of Contactless Technology and Service Innovation in Library and Information Science (pp. 1-22). IGI Global.

Siponen, M., & Vance, A. (2010). Neutralization: New insights into the problem of employee information systems security policy violations. *Management Information Systems Quarterly*, 34(3), 487–502. 10.2307/25750688

Siriwardhana, Y., Porambage, P., Liyanage, M., & Ylianttila, M. (2021, June). AI and 6G security: Opportunities and challenges. In 2021 Joint European Conference on Networks and Communications & 6G Summit (EuCNC/6G Summit) (pp. 616-621). IEEE.

Sivan-Sevilla, I. (2018). Complementaries and contradictions: National security and privacy risks in u.s. federal policy, 1968–2018. *Policy and Internet*, 11(2), 172–214. 10.1002/poi3.189

Smith et al. (2020a). Evolving Tactics: Challenges in Detecting Phishing Websites in the Metaverse.

Smith et al. (2020b). Combining Optimal Feature Selection and Random Forest Classifier for Phishing Website Detection in the Metaverse.

Soldatos, J., Pra¸ca, I., & Jovanovi'c, A. (2021). *Cyber-Physical Threat Intelli- gence for Critical Infrastructures Security: Securing Critical Infrastructures in Air Transport, Water, Gas, Healthcare, Finance and Industry*. Now Publishers.

Song, Z., Skuric, A., & Ji, K. (2020). A recursive watermark method for hard real-time in- dustrial control system cyber-resilience enhancement. *IEEE Transactions on Automation Science and Engineering*, 17(2), 1030–1043. 10.1109/TASE.2019.2963257

Sonko, S.. (2024). Quantum Cryptography and U.S. Digital Security: a Comprehensive Review: Investigating the Potential of Quantum Technologies in Creating Unbreakable Encryption and Their Future in National Security. *Computer Science & IT Research Journal*, 5(2), 390–414. 10.51594/csitrj.v5i2.790

Sood, S., & Kim, A. (2023). The Golden Age of the Big Data Audit: Agile Practices and Innovations for E-Commerce, Post-Quantum Cryptography, Psychosocial Hazards, Artificial Intelligence Algorithm Audits, and Deepfakes. *International Journal of Innovation and Economic Development*, 9(2), 7–23. 10.18775/ijied.1849-7551-7020.2015.92.2001

Sowmya, G., Chakraborty, D., Polisetty, A., Khorana, S., & Buhalis, D. (2023). Use of metaverse in socializing: Application of the big five personality traits framework. *Psychology and Marketing*, 40(10), 2132–2150. 10.1002/mar.21863

Stary, C. (2023). Digital process twins as intelligent design technology for engineering meta- verse/xr applications. *Sustainability (Basel)*, 15(22), 16062. 10.3390/su152216062

Stephenson, N. (1992). *Snow crash*. Bantam Books.

Stevens, T. (2018). Global cybersecurity: New directions in theory and methods. *Politics and Governance*, 6(2), 1–4. 10.17645/pag.v6i2.1569

Sutikno, T. 2023. "Non-fungible tokens, decentralized autonomous organizations, web 3.0, and the metaverse in education: from university to metaversity." https://doi.org/10.31219/osf.io/5mjae

Swanzy, P., Abukari, A. M., & Ansong, E. D. (2024). Data security framework for protecting data in transit and data at rest in the cloud. *Current Journal of Applied Science and Technology*, 43(6), 61–77. 10.9734/cjast/2024/v43i64387

Tan, V. H., Lim, W. Y. B., Xiong, Z., & Niyato, D. (2023, June). Blockchain for Decentralized Know Your Customer (KYC) and Customer Due Diligence (CDD) Pipelines in the Metaverse. In *2023 IEEE International Conference on Metaverse Computing, Networking and Applications (MetaCom)* (pp. 433-440). IEEE. 10.1109/MetaCom57706.2023.00083

Tao, B., Dai, H. N., Xie, H., & Wang, F. L. (2023). Structural identity representation learning for blockchain-enabled metaverse based on complex network analysis. *IEEE Transactions on Computational Social Systems*, 10(5), 2214–2225.

Tariq, U., Ahmed, I., Bashir, A. K., & Shaukat, K. (2023). A Critical Cybersecurity Analysis and Future Research Directions for the Internet of Things: A Comprehensive Review. *Sensors (Basel)*, 23(8), 8. Advance online publication. 10.3390/s2308411737112457

Tewari, A., & Gupta, B. B. (2018a). A lightweight mutual authentication approach for RFID tags in IoT devices. *International Journal of Networking and Virtual Organisations*, 18(2), 97–111.

Tewari, A., & Gupta, B. B. (2018b). A robust anonymity preserving authentication protocol for IoT devices. In *2018 IEEE International Conference on Consumer Electronics (ICCE)* (pp. 1-5). IEEE.

Tewari, A., & Gupta, B. B. (2020). Security, privacy and trust of different layers in Internet-of-Things (IoTs) framework. *Future Generation Computer Systems*, 108, 909–920. 10.1016/j.future.2018.04.027

Thakur, J., & Pathan, A. (2022). Innovations of phishing defense: The mechanism, mea- surement and defense strategies. *International Journal of Communication Networks and Information Security (Ijcnis)*, 10(1). Advance online publication. 10.17762/ijcnis.v10i1.2991

Thomas, J., Galligher, R., Thomas, M., & Galligher, G. (2019). Enterprise cybersecurity: Inves- tigating and detecting ransomware infections using digital forensic techniques. *Computer and Information Science*, 12(3), 72. 10.5539/cis.v12n3p72

Tian, N., Guo, Q., Sun, H., & Zhou, X. (2022). Fully privacy-preserving distributed optimization in power systems based on secret sharing. *Ienergy*, 1(3), 351–362. 10.23919/IEN.2022.0045

Tirumala, S. S., Sathu, H., & Naidu, V. (2015, December). Analysis and prevention of account hijacking based incidents in cloud environment. In 2015 international Conference on Information Technology (ICIT) (pp. 124-129). IEEE.

Tiwari, H. (2023). "Metaverse Federated Learning in Music Streaming: Rev- olutionizing Personalization and Privacy." https://insights2techinfo.com/ metaverse-federated-learning-in-music-streaming-revolutionizing-personalization-and-privacy/. Accessed: 2024-01-30.

Tlili, A., Huang, R., Shehata, B., Liu, D., Zhao, J., Metwally, A., Wang, H., Denden, M., Bozkurt, A., Lee, L.-H., Beyoglu, D., Altinay, F., Sharma, R. C., Altinay, Z., Li, Z., Liu, J., Ahmad, F., Hu, Y., Salha, S., & Burgos, D. (2022). Is metaverse in education a blessing or a curse: A combined content and bibliometric analysis. *Smart Learning Environments*, 9(1), 24. Advance online publication. 10.1186/s40561-022-00205-x

Torre, D., Chennamaneni, A., & Rodriguez, A. (2023). Privacy-preservation techniques for iot devices: A systematic mapping study. *IEEE Access : Practical Innovations, Open Solutions*, 11, 16323–16345. 10.1109/ACCESS.2023.3245524

Tran, T., Beuran, R., & Hasegawa, S. (2023). Gamification-based cybersecurity awareness course for self-regulated learning. *International Journal of Information and Education Technology (IJIET)*, 13(4), 724–730. 10.18178/ijiet.2023.13.4.1859

Truong, V. T., Le, L., & Niyato, D. (2023). Blockchain meets metaverse and digital asset management: A comprehensive survey. *IEEE Access : Practical Innovations, Open Solutions*, 11, 26258–26288.

Truong, V., & Le, L. (2023). Metacids: privacy-preserving collaborative intrusion detection for meta- verse based on blockchain and online federated learning. 10.36227/techrxiv.23183642.v1

Truong, V., Le, L., & Niyato, D. (2023). Blockchain meets metaverse and dig- ital asset management: A comprehensive survey. *IEEE Access : Practical Innovations, Open Solutions*, 11, 26258–26288. 10.1109/ACCESS.2023.3257029

Tukur, M., Schneider, J., Househ, M., Dokoro, A. H., Ismail, U. I., Dawaki, M., & Agus, M. (2023). The metaverse digital environments: A scoping review of the challenges, privacy and security issues. *Frontiers in Big Data*, 6, 1301812. 10.3389/fdata.2023.130181238074486

Turchet, L. (2023). Musical metaverse: Vision, opportunities, and challenges. *Personal and Ubiquitous Computing*, 27(5), 1811–1827. 10.1007/s00779-023-01708-136685785

Turki, A., Zwiad, A., & Almuttairi, R. (2019). Security issues, attacks and vulnerabilities for virtualization in cloud computing and their solutions. *Journal of Engineering and Applied Sciences (Asian Research Publishing Network)*, 14, 9509–9518. 10.36478/jcasci.2019.9509.9518

Turner, S., Karakus, M., Guler, E., & Uludag, S. (2023). A promising integration of sdn and blockchain for iot networks: A survey. *IEEE Access : Practical Innovations, Open Solutions*, 11, 29800–29822. 10.1109/ACCESS.2023.3260777

Uchendu, B., Nurse, J. R., Bada, M., & Furnell, S. (2021). Developing a cyber security culture: Current practices and future needs. *Computers & Security*, 109, 102387. 10.1016/j.cose.2021.102387

Uchida, S., Liu, Y., & Murai, J. (2018). An analysis of phishing websites targeting mobile devices. *Journal of Information Processing*, 27(4), 709–721.29400742

Upadhyay, U., Kumar, A., Sharma, G., Gupta, B., Alhalabi, W., Arya, V., & Chui, K. (2023). Cyberbullying in the metaverse. *Journal of Global Information Management*, 31(1), 1–25. 10.4018/JGIM.325793

Upadhyay, U., Kumar, A., Sharma, G., Saini, A. K., Arya, V., Gaurav, A., & Chui, K. T. (2023). Mitigating risks in the cloud-based metaverse access control strategies and techniques. *International Journal of Cloud Applications and Computing*, 14(1), 1–30. 10.4018/IJCAC.334364

Uysal, E., & Akgu¨n, M. (2023). P/key: Puf based second factor authentication. *PLoS One*, 18(2), e0280181. 10.1371/journal.pone.028018136758004

Vaidya, J., & Clifton, C. (2003). Leveraging the "multi" in secure multi-party computation. 10.1145/1005140.1005149

Vaidya, R. (2019). Cyber security breaches survey 2019. Department for Digital, Culture, Media and Sport, 66.

Vajratiya, V. (2024). *Metaverse in healthcare domain.*https://insights2techinfo.com/metaverse-in-healthcare-domain/. (Accessed: 2024-01-30)

Valinatajbahnamiri, M., & Siahtiri, V. (2021). Flow in computer-mediated environments: A systematic literature review. *International Journal of Consumer Studies*, 45(4), 511–545. 10.1111/ijcs.12640

Varsha, A. (2023). *Metaverse security 2.0: Evolving attack detection in virtual environ- ments.*https://insights2techinfo.com/metaverse-security-2-0-evolving-attack-detection-in-virtual-environments/. (Accessed: 2024-01-30)

Varvello, M., C. Diot, and E. Biersack. 2009. "A walkable kademlia network for virtual worlds." .10.1109/INFCOMW.2009.5072106

Veinovi´c, M. 2016. "Privileged identities - threat to network and data security." .10.15308/Sinteza-2016-154-160

Venugopal, J., Subramanian, A., & Peatchimuthu, J. (2023). The realm of metaverse: A sur- vey. *Computer Animation and Virtual Worlds*, 34(5), e2150. Advance online publication. 10.1002/cav.2150

Verizon. (2019). *2019 Verizon Data Breach Investigations Report: First impressions from the perimeter*. Verizondigitalmedia, Retrieved Jul 27, 2021, from https://www.verizondigitalmedia.com/blog/2019-verizon-data-breach-investigations-report-first-impressions/

Verma, R., Rane, D., Jha, R., & Ibrahim, W. (2022). Next-generation optimization models and al- gorithms in cloud and fog computing virtualization security: The present state and future. *Scientific Programming*, 2022, 1–10. 10.1155/2022/2419291

Wang et al. (2022a). Phishing Website Detection in Virtual Reality Environments Using Optimal Feature Selection and Ensemble Learning. Gupta et al. (2023).Deep Learning Models for Phishing Website Detection in the Metaverse: Leveraging Feature Selection and Ensemble Learning.

Wang et al. (2022b). Addressing Data Imbalance in Phishing Website Detection: A Metaverse Perspective.

Wang, P., Wang, Z., & Chen, T. (2016). Privacy protection in online social network in the context of big data. 10.2991/icemaess-15.2016.103

Wang, C., & Peeta, S. (2024). Incentive mechanism for privacy-preserving collaborative routing using secure multi-party computation and blockchain. *Sensors (Basel)*, 24(2), 542. 10.3390/s2402054238257634

Wang, G., Badal, A., Jia, X., Maltz, J., Mueller, K., Myers, K., Niu, C., Vannier, M., Yan, P., Yu, Z., & Zeng, R. (2022). Development of metaverse for intelligent healthcare. *Nature Machine Intelligence*, 4(11), 922–929. 10.1038/s42256-022-00549-636935774

Wang, H., Ning, H., Lin, Y., Wang, W., Dhelim, S., Farha, F., Ding, J., & Daneshmand, M. (2023). A survey on the metaverse: The state-of-the-art, technologies, applications, and challenges. *IEEE Internet of Things Journal*, 10(16), 14671–14688. 10.1109/JIOT.2023.3278329

Wang, J., Yu, Y., Li, Y., Fan, C., & Hao, S. (2021). Design and implementation of virtual security function based on multiple enclaves. *Future Internet*, 13(1), 12. 10.3390/fi13010012

Wang, W. (2024). Empowering safe and secure autonomy: Federated learning in the era of au- tonomous driving. *Applied and Computational Engineering*, 51(1), 40–44. 10.54254/2755-2721/51/20241158

Wang, Y., Su, Z., & Yan, M. (2023). Social metaverse: Challenges and solutions. *IEEE Internet of Things Magazine*, 6(3), 144–150.

Wang, Y., Su, Z., Zhang, N., Xing, R., Liu, D., Luan, T., & Shen, X. (2023). A survey on metaverse: Fundamentals, security, and privacy. *IEEE Communications Surveys and Tutorials*, 25(1), 319–352. 10.1109/COMST.2022.3202047

Warburton, S. (2009). Second life in higher education: Assessing the potential for and the barriers to deploying virtual worlds in learning and teaching. *British Journal of Educational Technology*, 40(3), 414–426. 10.1111/j.1467-8535.2009.00952.x

Weinberger, M. (2023). A comparison of virtual worlds based on the metaverse maturity model. *ITU Journal : ICT Discoveries*, 4(4), 537–548. 10.52953/REVF5378

What's new in the 2021 Cost of a Data Breach Report - Security Intelligence. (2023b, August 23). Security Intelligence. https://securityintelligence.com/posts/whats-new -2021-cost-of-a data-breach-report

Wibowo, A. (2022). The importance of global effort to secure space sec- tor from cyberattack. *Intermestic Journal of International Studies*, 7(1), 298. 10.24198/ intermestic.v7n1.14

Wiercioch, A., Teufel, S., & Teufel, B. (2018). The authentication dilemma. *Journal of Software*, 13(5), 277–286. 10.17706/jsw.13.5.277-286

Wilson, D. (2021). Cybersecurity. *Cybersecurity*. Advance online publication. 10.7551/mitpress/11656.001.0001

Wójtowicz, A., & Cellary, W. (2010). Representing user privileges in object-oriented virtual reality systems., 52-61. 10.1007/978-3-642-11628-5_6

Wu, C., Yang, L., Zhao, X., & Sun, Q. (2023). P-2.24: a survey of privacy protection research based on virtual reality. *Sid Symposium Digest of Technical Papers, 54*, 572-576. 10.1002/sdtp.16358

Wu, Y., & Kim, E. (2022). Users' perceptions of technological features in augmented reality (ar) and virtual reality (vr) in fashion retailing: A qualitative content analysis. *Mobile Information Systems*, 2022, 1–13. 10.1155/2022/3080280

Xie, Y., Li, P., Nedjah, N., Gupta, B. B., Taniar, D., & Zhang, J. (2023). Pri- vacy protection framework for face recognition in edge-based Internet of Things. *Cluster Computing*, 26(5), 3017–3035. 10.1007/s10586-022-03808-8

Xu, H., Li, Z., Li, Z., Zhang, X., Sun, Y., & Zhang, L. (2022a). Metaverse native communication: A blockchain and spectrum prospective. In 2022 IEEE International Conference on Communications Workshops (ICC Workshops) (pp. 7-12). IEEE.

Xu, B., Li, D., & Shao, B. (2012). Knowledge sharing in virtual communities: A study of citizenship behavior and its social-relational antecedents. *International Journal of Human-Computer Interaction*, 28(5), 347–359. 10.1080/10447318.2011.590121

Xu, M., Ng, W. C., Lim, W. Y. B., Kang, J., Xiong, Z., Niyato, D., & Miao, C. (2022b). A full dive into realizing the edge-enabled metaverse: Visions, enabling technologies, and challenges. *IEEE Communications Surveys and Tutorials*, 25(1), 656–700.

Xu, Y., Liu, W., He, T., & Tsai, S. (2023). Buzzword or fuzzword: An event study of the metaverse in the chinese stock market. *Internet Research*, 34(1), 174–194. 10.1108/INTR-07-2022-0526

Yadav, K., & Gupta, B. (2021). *Clustering based rewarding algorithm to detect adversaries in feder- ated machine learning based iot environment. In 2021 ieee international conference on consumer electronics (icce).*

Yan, F., Wen, S., Nepal, S., Paris, C., & Xiang, Y. (2022). Explainable machine learning in cybersecurity: A survey. *International Journal of Intelligent Systems*, 37(12), 12305–12334. 10.1002/int.23088

Yang, K. 2023. "The future of the "metaverse": artificial intelligence and cybersecurity." 1627– 1632. $_2$46.10.2991/978-94-6463-040-4

Yang, L., Li, P., Yang, X., & Tang, Y. (2017). Security evaluation of the cy- ber networks under advanced persistent threats. *IEEE Access : Practical Innovations, Open Solutions*, 5, 20111–20123. 10.1109/ACCESS.2017.2757944

Yang, Q., Zhao, Y., Huang, H., Xiong, Z., Kang, J., & Zheng, Z. (2022). Fusing blockchain and AI with metaverse: A survey. *IEEE Open Journal of the Computer Society*, 3, 122–136.

Yang, Q., Zhao, Y., Huang, H., Xiong, Z., Kang, J., & Zheng, Z. (2022). Fusing blockchain and ai with metaverse: A survey. *IEEE Open Journal of the Computer Society*, 3, 122–136. 10.1109/OJCS.2022.3188249

Yang, Y., Siau, K., Xie, W., & Sun, Y. (2022). Smart health. *Journal of Organizational and End User Computing*, 34(1), 1–14. 10.4018/JOEUC.308814

Yeom, S., Shin, D., & Shin, D. (2021). Scenario-based cyber attack· defense education system on virtual machines integrated by web technologies for protection of multimedia contents in a network. *Multimedia Tools and Applications*, 80(26), 34085–34101. 10.1007/s11042-019-08583-0

Yu, B., Liu, Y., Ren, S., Zhou, Z., & Liu, J. (2023). METAseen: Analyzing network traffic and privacy policies in Web 3.0 based Metaverse. *Digital Communications and Networks*. Advance online publication. 10.1016/j.dcan.2023.11.006

Zamri, N. F. M., Tahir, N. M., Ali, M. S. M., Ashar, N. D. K., & Abd Almisreb, A. (2023). Real time snatch theft detection using deep learning networks. *Journal of Advanced Research in Applied Sciences and Engineering Technology*, 31(1), 79–89.

Zeadally, S., Adi, E., Baig, Z., & Khan, I. (2020). Harnessing artificial intel- ligence capabilities to improve cybersecurity. *IEEE Access : Practical Innovations, Open Solutions*, 8, 23817–23837. 10.1109/ACCESS.2020.2968045

Zeinab, K. A. M., & Elmustafa, S. A. A. (2017). Internet of things applications, challenges and related future technologies. *World Scientific News*, 67(2), 126–148.

Zhang, H., Lee, S., Lu, Y., Yu, X., & Lu, H. (2022). A survey on big data technologies and their applications to the metaverse: Past, current and future. *Mathematics*, 11(1), 96. 10.3390/math11010096

Zhang, L., Du, Q., Lu, L., & Zhang, S. (2023). Overview of the integration of communications, sensing, computing, and storage as enabling technologies for the metaverse over 6g networks. *Electronics (Basel)*, 12(17), 3651. 10.3390/electronics12173651

Zhang, L., Xiong, H., Huang, Q., Li, J., Choo, K.-K. R., & Li, J. (2022). Cryptographic Solutions for Cloud Storage: Challenges and Research Opportunities. *IEEE Transactions on Services Computing*, 15(1), 567–587. 10.1109/TSC.2019.2937764

Zhang, R., & Xin, X. (2017). Study of immune-based intrusion detection technology in vir- tual machines for cloud computing environment. *Mobile Information Systems*, 2017, 1–15. 10.1155/2017/2301970

Zhang, X., Chen, Y., Hu, L., & Wang, Y. (2022). The metaverse in education: Definition, framework, features, potential applications, challenges, and future research topics. *Frontiers in Psychology*, 13, 1016300. Advance online publication. 10.3389/fpsyg.2022.101630036304866

Zhang, Y., & Smith, T. (2023). The impact of customer firm data breaches on the audit fees of their suppliers. *International Journal of Accounting Information Systems*, 50, 100628. 10.1016/j.accinf.2023.100628

Zhao, H., Zhao, J., Liu, W., Yan, Y., Huang, J., & Wen, F. (2023). Metaverse-based decentralised autonomous organisation in energy systems. *Energy Conversion and Economics*, 4(6), 379–386. 10.1049/enc2.12104

Zhong, Y., Wen, J., Zhang, J., Kang, J., Jiang, Y., Zhang, Y., Cheng, Y., & Tong, Y. (2023). Blockchain-assisted twin migration for vehicular metaverses: A game theory approach. *Transactions on Emerging Telecommunications Technologies*, 34(12), e4856. Advance online publication. 10.1002/ett.4856

Zhou, Zhili, & Gaurav, Akshat, BB Gupta, Hedi Hamdi, and Nadia Nedjah. (2021). A statistical approach to secure health care services from DDoS attacks during COVID-19 pandemic. *Neural Computing & Applications*, 1–14.34511731

Zhu, P., Liu, Z., Li, X., Jiang, X., & Zhu, M. X. (2023). The influences of livestreaming on online purchase intention: Examining platform characteristics and consumer psychology. *Industrial Management & Data Systems*, 123(3), 862–885. 10.1108/IMDS-07-2022-0430

Zuo, M., & Shen, Y. (2023). How features and affordances of a metaverse portal engage users? evidence from exergames. *Internet Research*, 34(1), 239–261. 10.1108/INTR-08-2022-0618

About the Contributors

Brij B. Gupta is working as Director of International Center for AI and Cyber Security Research and Innovations, and Distinguished Professor with the Department of Computer Science and Information Engineering (CSIE), Asia University, Taiwan. In more than 18 years of his professional experience, he published over 500 papers in journals/conferences including 35 books and 12 Patents with over 25,000 citations. He has received numerous national and international awards including Canadian Commonwealth Scholarship (2009), Faculty Research Fellowship Award (2017), MeitY, GoI, IEEE GCCE outstanding and WIE paper awards and Best Faculty Award (2018 & 2019), NIT KKR, respectively. Prof. Gupta was selected for Clarivate Web of Science Highly Cited Researchers in Computer Science (top 0.1% researchers in the world) consecutively in 2022 and 2023. Also, he was also selected in Stanford University's ranking of the world's top 2% scientists consecutively in 2020, 2021, 2022 and 2023. He is also a visiting/adjunct professor with several universities worldwide. He is also an IEEE Senior Member (2017) and also selected as 2021 Distinguished Lecturer in IEEE CTSoc. Dr Gupta is also serving as Member-in-Large, Board of Governors, IEEE Consumer Technology Society (2022-2024). Prof Gupta is also leading IJSWIS, IJSSCI, STE and IJCAC as Editor-in-Chief. Moreover, he is also serving as lead-editor of a Book Series with CRC and IET press. He also served as TPC members in more than 150 international conferences also serving as Associate/Guest Editor of various journals and transactions. His research interests include information security, Cyber physical systems, cloud computing, blockchain technologies, intrusion detection, AI, social media and networking.

Adwaya Adhikary. I am from Purulia, West Bengal. I have done my schooling from Assembly of God Church. My passion is competitive programming and also maths and physics. I am also interested in football and gym. This review article has really provided me with extensive knowledge in the field of AI and NLP. And i will continue further in this area as this fields is so beautiful and has so many different opportunities and areas of development i am so much enthusiastic about. Thank You

Diah Aryani received the Magister degree in computer science from the University of Budi Luhur, Indonesia, She used to hold several administrative posts with the College of Information and Computer Management, Universitas Raharja (UR), Tangerang, from 2012 to 2019, including the head of the diploma 3 informatics engineering study program, head of the computer systems study program, chief editor of the journal Creative Education of Research in Information Technology and Artificial informatics and coordinator of ISO 9001:2015. She is currently a vice Dean of computer science faculty, Universiti Esa Unggul. She has authored or coauthored more than 50 with 10 H-index and more than 350 citations. Her research interests include information system, Artificial Intelligence, Software engineering and data science. She can be contacted at email: diah.aryani@esaunggul.ac.id

Sourasis Chattopadhyay holds a Bachelor's in Electrical Engineering from Kalinga Institute of Industrial Technology, India. Currently he is pursuing his Master's degree in Computer Science and Information Technology at Asia University, Taiwan. He served as a research assistant at Nanhua University, Taiwan in 2019 and Asia University, Taiwan from 2021 to 2022. His diverse research interests include Operation Research, Supply Chain, IoT, Cyber Security, Biomedical Instrumentation, and Artificial Intelligence.

Ankita Chaturvedi is currently working as an Associate Professor at IIS (deemed to be University), Jaipur and has over 16+ years of teaching experience. She received her Ph.d degree(2011), Master's in Accounting and Business Statistics(2006), and Master's in Economics and Financial Management(2018) from University of Rajasthan, India. She has qualified NET in Commerce in 2015. She is an author or Co-author of more than 46 research papers published in national or international refereed journals, 11 chapters in edited books, 3 books with ISBN number and more than 50 conference contributions. She has received several (22) awards in the field of academics and research. She has supervised around 18 PG dissertations. She is supervising 6 Ph.d Thesis and 6 Ph.d degrees has been awarded under her guidance. She has been convener of various academic events like international conference, training programmes, Research workshop, Board of Studies etc. She has attended various more than 22 FDP's and training programmes.

Kwok Tai Chui received the B.Eng. degree in electronic and communication engineering - Business Intelligence Minor and Ph.D. degree from City University of Hong Kong. He had industry experience as Senior Data Scientist in Internet of Things (IoT) company. He joined the Department of Technology, School of Science and Technology, at The Open University of Hong Kong as Research Assistant Professor. He was the recipient of 2nd Prize Award (Postgraduate Category) of 2014 IEEE Region 10 Student Paper Contest. Also, he received Best Paper Award in IEEE The International Conference on Consumer Electronics-China, in both 2014 and 2015. He has more than 45 research publications including edited books, book chapters, journal papers, and conference papers. His research interests include computational intelligence, data science, energy monitoring and management, intelligent transportation, smart metering, healthcare, machine learning algorithms and optimization.

|Kwok Tai Chui - Contributing Author|Dr. Kwok Tai Chui received the B.Eng. degree in electronic and communication engineering - Business Intelligence Minor and Ph.D. degree from City University of Hong Kong. He had industry experience as Senior Data Scientist in Internet of Things (IoT) company. He joined the Department of Technology, School of Science and Technology, at The Open University of Hong Kong as Research Assistant Professor. He was the recipient of 2nd Prize Award (Postgraduate Category) of 2014 IEEE Region 10 Student Paper Contest. Also, he received Best Paper Award in IEEE The International Conference on Consumer Electronics-China, in both 2014 and 2015. He has more than 45 research publications including edited books, book chapters, journal papers, and conference papers. His research interests include computational intelligence, data science, energy monitoring and management, intelligent transportation, smart metering, healthcare, machine learning algorithms and optimization.

Uma N. Dulhare is working as a Professor, Department of Computer Science & Engg, MJCET, Banjara Hills, Hyderabad. She has more than 20 years teaching experience. She has published more than 30 research papers in reputed National & International Journals & as a book chapter. She is member of Editorial Board and reviewer of International Journals like IJACEA, ICDIWC and ICEOE, IIE, IJERTREW,IJDMKD, Elsevier Procedia. She was Keynote & Chair Person of International Congress on Multimedia 2014 [ICMM2014], Bangkok, Kingdom of Thailand & also 5th National Conference on National "Computer Network & Information Security" NCCNIS-2016 Vasavi College, Hyderabad . She is also the member of various professional societies like ISTE, CSTA of ACM,ASDF,IAENG & Fellow member of ISRD. She has also received a Best research paper Award in 2010, ASDF Global Award for Best Computer Science Faculty of the Year 2013 by the Lt. Governor of Pondicherry & also Best Academic Researcher of the year 2015. She honored with Outstanding Educator & Scholar Award 2016 by NEFD. Her area of interest is Networking, Database, Data Mining, Information Retrieval and Neural Networks & Big Data Analytics.

G. Vanishree has rich experience, 28 years in Academics & administration. Having worked as HOD, Principal, and vice principal in Vignan Institutions, Institute of Aeronautical Engineering, Badruka, St. Patricks, St.Joseph college kristu Jayanti college etc she also worked as Director for Kempe Gowda institute of management studies and research Bangalore. Presently she is working as a professor at IBS-B Bangalore. Prof has been a credit participator in several National seminars & conferences and published journal articles. She has won the best teacher, parent, and Adarsh yuvathi awards. She makes herself suited to the position placed. She is responsible and inspiring, good attitude and believes in ethical norms. Having a good record of good results, she believes in statement, "Learning is a continuous process"

A.V.Senthil Kumar to his credit he has industrial experience for five years and teaching experience of 27 years. He has also received his Doctor of Science (D.Sc in Computer Science). He has to his credit 33 Book Chapters, 220 papers in International and National Journals 60 papers in International Conferences in International and National Conferences, and edited 12 books (IGI Global, USA). He is as Associate Editor of IEEE Access. He is an Editor-in-Chief for many journals and Key Member for India, Machine Intelligence Research Lab (MIR Labs). He is an Editorial Board Member and Reviewer for various International Journals. He is also a Committee member for various International Conferences. He is a Life member of International Association of Engineers (IAENG), Systems Society of India (SSI), member of The Indian Science Congress Association, member of Internet Society (ISOC), International Association of Computer Science and Information Technology (IACSIT), Indian Association for Research in Computing Science (IARCS), and committee member for various International Conferences.

Anshul mantri Born and raised in kachhola,Rajasthan. I am currently pursuing my bachelor's degree from UPES dehradun. I complete my schooling from my hometown. I have always been driven by a curiosity to explore and understand the world around me. Beyond my professional life, I am deeply passionate about explore new and spiritual places.

Mosiur Rahman, a Research Assistant at the International Center for AI and Cyber Security Research and Innovations (CCRI) at Asia University, Taiwan, holds a PhD in Computer Science and Information Engineering and master's degrees in Business Management and Computer Science and Engineering. With prior roles as a Research Assistant in AI and an Assistant Professor in Computer Science, he has extensive experience in academia. Dr. Rahman has been actively involved in international conferences, serving in significant roles, and is a part-time lecturer in Humanities and Social Science. His research interests include AI, Neural Networks, and Security, and he is a dedicated peer reviewer for over 50 journals, showcasing his commitment to research and academic excellence.

|Mosiur Rahaman - Contributing Author|Dr. Mosiur Rahman, a Research Assistant at the International Center for AI and Cyber Security Research and Innovations (CCRI) at Asia University, Taiwan, holds a PhD in Computer Science and Information Engineering and master's degrees in Business Management and Computer Science and Engineering. With prior roles as a Research Assistant in AI and an Assistant Professor in Computer Science, he has extensive experience in academia. Dr. Rahman has been actively involved in international conferences, serving in significant roles, and is a part-time lecturer in Humanities and Social Science. His research interests include AI, Neural Networks, and Security, and he is a dedicated peer reviewer for over 50 journals, showcasing his commitment to research and academic excellence.

Mushtaq Ahmad Shah is a finance expert with a PhD in Infrastructure Finance. He teaches banking, finance and economics at Lovely Professional University in India. Dr. Shah has over 8 years of experience teaching and researching at various institutions. He's written articles in academic journals and presented his work at conferences on banking, partnerships between public and private sectors, and behavioral finance.

Pavithra Sivakumar., am currently pursuing a Master of Computer Applications (MCA) at Hindustan College of Arts & Science. The ever-growing field of metaverse security fascinates me, and this chapter, "Advancements in Metaverse Security - Phishing Website Detection through Optimal Feature Selection and Random Forest Classifier," is a product of my deep dive into this exciting area.

Sreerakuvandana is an Assistant Professor of English, specializing in Cognitive Linguistics at the Department of AI-ML and Cybersecurity at Jain deemed-to-be University. She received her Bachelor's, Master's and Doctorate degree from the University of Hyderabad, specializing in Linguistics and Cognitive Science. Her research areas include Artificial Intelligence, English Language Teaching, Sociolinguistics, and Psycholinguistics. She also has a range of academic publications in the areas of her interest to her credit. She currently serves as a guest editor for the Athens Journal of Education and is an International Advisory Member of MIMSE23 and is a guest editor for the same.

Furquan Uddin is working as Assistant Professor in the Department of Management & Business Administration in Aliah University, Kolkata (India). He has authored 20 research papers in journals of repute.

Agung Mulyo Widodo obtained a PhD in Computer Science and Information Engineering, Asia University, Taiwan, in 2022, and currently works as a lecturer and researcher at the Faculty of Computer Science, Esa Unggul University, Jakarta, Indonesia. He has worked as a research assistant to his advising professor while a PostDoc Research Fellow at the Artificial Intelligence and Information Security Laboratory, Department of Computer Science and Information Engineering (CSIE), Asia University, Taiwan. Previous projects were with Caltex Pacific Indonesia (CPI), Siemens-Telecommunications, Nokia-Siemens-Networks (NSN). Currently, his research focuses on wireless communications technologies including NOMA, OMA, NB-IoT, backscatter systems, cognitive radio, smart antennas, artificial intelligence, and information security.

Andika Wisnujati received the B.S. and M.S degree in Mechanical Engineering from Universitas Gadjah Mada, Yogyakarta, Indonesia in 2008 and 2014. He is also received the Ph.D degree in Computer Science and Information Engineering, Asia University, Taiwan in 2023. He had been the Assistant Professor in Department of Automotive Engineering Technology, Universitas Muhammadiyah Yogyakarta, Indonesia since 2012. His research interests include Artificial Intelligence and Material Science. His previous research includes Neural Network and Automatic Control in Antilock Braking System and Grey Prediction Model in Welding Distortion.

Index

R

S

V

www.ingramcontent.com/pod-product-compliance
Lightning Source LLC
LaVergne TN
LVHW080610300926
849162LV00005B/1111